Painting the Forth Bridge

A Search For Scottish Identity

Painting
the Forth Bridge

A SEARCH FOR SCOTTISH IDENTITY

CARL MACDOUGALL

AURUM PRESS

First published in Great Britain
2001 by Aurum Press Ltd
25 Bedford Avenue, London WC1B 3AT

Copyright © by Carl MacDougall 2001

The right of Carl MacDougall to be identified as the author of this
work has been asserted by him in accordance with the Copyright,
Designs and Patents Act 1988.

A catalogue record for this book is available from the British Library.

ISBN 1 85410 640 6

1 3 5 7 9 10 8 6 4 2
2001 2003 2005 2004 2002

Design by Roger Lightfoot
Printed in Great Britain by
MPG Books Ltd, Bodmin

Contents

Acknowledgements

While I was writing this book (some of 1997, all of 1998 and 1999 and a bit of 2000) my son, Euan, was a bookseller and kept me abreast of what was contemporary, republished or currently in print. And though he will deny it, this book could not have been written without my friend Dr Kenneth Simpson of Strathclyde University and his continual encouragement, advice and generous knowledge. Every suggestion he made was valuable.

Charles McKean, Gerry Carruthers and Hamish and Maggie Moore also deserve a mention, as do Dr Duncan Forbes, Assistant Curator of Photography at the National Galleries of Scotland, Joan McGirk, Education Officer at the Scottish National Portrait Gallery, Jane Petrie of Inverness Museum and Art Gallery, and many others who assisted directly or indirectly, often unknowingly. Most obvious are those who have tackled the subject before me, especially in specialist disciplines, and the compilers of our many reference books. Time and again I found myself returning to their works and am happy to acknowledge my debt and gratitude.

Mike Moir and the staff at the A. K. Bell Library, Perth, especially the reference and local studies sections, were consistently helpful, especially when I wasn't sure of the inquiry. And finally, I want to thank Bill McCreadie, Piers Burnett and Karen Ings at Aurum Press (not forgetting Anica Alvarez, whose idea this was in the first place). They have been continually patient with a book that took longer than it should have done, or was supposed to do, and somehow remained friendly and helpful throughout.

Picture Credits

For Euan and Kirsty

'Even God cannot change the past.'
          – Agathon (447–401 BC)

Andrea: 'Unhappy the land that has no heroes! …'
Galileo: 'No. Unhappy the land that needs heroes.'
          – Bertolt Brecht, *The Life of Galileo*

1

Brown Heath and
Shaggy Wood

'Stands Scotland where it did?'
WILLIAM SHAKESPEARE, *Macbeth*, III.164

I was tired. I'd driven to Glasgow and eaten too much. Driving back to Perth, passing Bishopbriggs, I switched on Radio Scotland without thinking.

This was in the early morning of 2 May 1997, and by the time I approached Bannockburn the Tory Party's position in Scotland and elsewhere was obvious. In an almost surreal coincidence, as I passed Stirling Castle, I witnessed what maybe five or six other folk in Scotland saw. Michael Forsyth's defeat was being broadcast from the Albert Hall in Stirling, and from the moment the cheers hit the airwaves, all along the M9 and up the A9, to beyond Dunblane, almost as far as Auchterarder, passing cars flashed their lights and sounded their horns. I did the same myself, not because of any personal animosity towards Mr Forsyth – I had long since ceased to care anything for what he said or did – but because his presence seemed to symbolise the frustration that had gripped Scotland.

His tenure as Secretary of State had to do with getting himself on to the teatime television news or having his photograph in the newspapers, dressed in a kilt to return the Stone of Destiny or in a baseball cap to launch an anti-drugs campaign. The fact that Forsyth was seen as an unreconstructed Thatcherite, the man who said there would be dancing in the streets because of the poll tax, gave his defeat an added piquancy. He was Scotland's Portillo.

But it also had something to do with Stirling's position. Robert the Bruce is supposed to have said that whoever holds Stirling holds Scotland; it is the traditional Highland gateway, which is how Scott perceived it in *Rob Roy*: 'Forth bridles the wild Highlandman,' said Bailie Nicol Jarvie, quoting a proverb to Frank Osbaldistone.

'Stirling, like a huge brooch, clasps Highlands and Lowlands together,' said Alexander Smith, and the town retains something of the ambience he perceived when he called Edinburgh and Stirling '. . . spinster sisters, who were both in their youth beloved by Scottish kings'.[1]

I worked in Stirling, briefly, as writer in residence, based in the library, up the hill from the Albert Hall. I had been in the Stirling job maybe two or three months when the boss, with whom I had worked well, left. After a week or two in which things carried on pretty much as usual, I was summoned to council headquarters and asked to explain myself to a man I'd never seen, but who was, apparently, my ex-boss's ex-boss.

I told him what was going on: writers' workshops, readings in the library and so on. 'That's all very well,' he said, 'but what you should be doing is writing a thriller set in Stirling District, something which could be turned into a television series or even a film, which would obviously be shot in Stirling and would attract tourists to the area.'

'I don't think I'm that sort of writer,' I said.

'Then you should bloody well find someone who can write it, a pal of yours; you must know someone.'

'Writers tend to work on their own books rather than dishing out ideas, even to friends.'

'We're not getting anywhere, are we?' he said. 'You don't seem to understand what we need. We have to think of tourism. How about a high-profile event? Could you organise that?'

At this point, I should let you understand, I was skint and in debt. I needed the job.

'Tell me what you have in mind?' I said.

'I'm not a literary man myself, but we want something no one else has got, so how about bringing a writer to Stirling, someone who wouldn't go anywhere else; say, Catherine Cookson or Jeffrey Archer.'

'I'm not trying to be unhelpful, but Catherine Cookson is bedridden; and the problem with Jeffrey Archer is that if we asked him, I think he'd probably come.'

'Okay then. I'll leave that with you.'

'What sort of notice do you want me to give?'

'I beg your pardon?'

'I'm leaving.'

In the month before I left I was asked to write a pageant to be performed when the Christmas lights were switched on. I had a word with someone, emptied my desk and never went back.

---

1. Alexander Smith, *A Summer in Skye*.

He is Scotland

'The story of Wallace poured a Scottish prejudice into my veins which will boil along there until the floodgates of life shut in eternal rest,' wrote Robert Burns.[2] Cunningham Graham, a descendant of Robert Bruce, first president of the Scottish Labour Party and later president of both the National Party and the Scottish National Party, wrote, 'Wallace made Scotland. He is Scotland; he is the symbol of all that is best and purest and truest and most heroic in our national life. You cannot figure . . . Scotland without Wallace.'[3]

According to James Moir of the Scottish Text Society, writing in 1899, 'the *Wallace* was, next to the Bible, the book most frequently found in Scottish households'. The blurb on the back of a recent edition calls it 'the book which has done more than any other to frame the notion of Scotland's national identity'.

Wallace was 'a single-minded patriot untainted by ambition, and the very rarity of that quality makes him seem legendary to us today,' wrote Moray McLaren, remarking that both Wallace and 'the movement he inspired and led, emerged mysteriously and from obscurity' at 'the most hopeless period of Scotland's prostration'.[4]

But how reliable a source is Blind Harry, who composed his poem, we are told, 170 years after the Liberator's death, bringing together the existing pieces to preserve Wallace's memory, which had fallen into decline? Wallace is cast in heroic scale, evidenced by his height and girth as well as the length of his sword, and an attempt has been made to clearly identify him with the country, from his birth in Elderslie, schooling in Dundee and so on. But the intention is clearly to inspire; and no matter how sympathetic we may be to the legend, no matter the place it has in Scottish history and romance, the fact that we are essentially dealing with a myth seems to have been lost in the search for a patriotic symbol and perpetual inspiration.

The myth has become fact. And the film *Braveheart* is an obvious example of how the myth continues. It reintroduced Scotland to the Wallace myth, a legend which has penetrated our national psyche to the extent that it now may be impossible to free ourselves from the notion that his life represents something to which we should aspire, be that love of our land or appreciation of ourselves.

It is a testament to the continual power of mythology, which Ted Hughes called the most potent and powerful force we know. Wallace's

2. Robert Burns, letter to Dr John Moore, 1787, in J. De Lancey Ferguson and G. Ross Roy (eds), *The Letters of Robert Burns* (2 volumes).
3. Quoted by Elspeth King in her Introduction to *Blind Harry's Wallace*.
4. Moray McLaren, *The Scots*.

name has been absorbed into the natural features of the Scottish land-scape, along with the innumerable wells, stones, roads, cairns and supposed sheltering places. One of many publications to arrive in the wake of the film is a guide to places mentioned in the Wallace legend, offering 'Not a lesson from history but where Wallace can be found today'.

Most obvious is the Wallace Monument. Two hundred and twenty feet high and mounted on the Abbey Craig, from where the Liberator is said to have viewed the Battle of Stirling Bridge, the monument was designed by the Glasgow architect J. T. Rochead with money raised by public sub-scription. It was completed in 1860, having taken more than eight years to build. According to Fiona Sinclair, author of *Scotstyle*, 'This building is exciting to behold and a delight to experience at close hand, whether it is through the long haul up the sides of the basaltic Abbey Craig from where only glimpses can be had until the summit is reached, or through the dizzying climb up the tight spiral staircase to the platform beneath the crown tower from where expansive panoramas unfold of the Scottish Lowlands.'

The Wallace Monument marked the shift in public buildings to the Scotch Baronial style of architecture, a term invented by the English anti-quarian William Billings to describe a distinctly national Scottish architecture.

Gyff Fredome Failyhe

As well as Wallace, Stirling has become a playground for Scotland's other hero from the Wars of Independence, Robert Bruce. And though the circumstances of Bruce's victory at Bannockburn have been disputed, its impact has never been in doubt. He not only gained Scottish independence, but successively defended it, and in the words of his sterling legacy, the Declaration of Arbroath, 'brought salvation to his people through the safeguarding of our liberties'. The House of Stewart is descended from Robert Bruce, through his daughter, Marjorie.

Of the many testimonies to Bruce's courage and humanity, none is more inspiring than his final wish that his heart be taken on a crusade to the Holy Land. Legend has it that James Douglas carried Bruce's heart into his final battle against the Moors in Spain, crying at the end, as he flung the casket towards the foe: 'Lead on brave heart, Douglas will follow you or die.' Bruce's heart is buried in Melrose Abbey, his body in Dunfermline Abbey, below the altar, wrapped in a cloth of gold.

His life and his struggle for Scottish independence were eulogised by John Barbour, a member of the royal household and 'father of Scottish vernacular poetry'.[5] *The Bruce* predates Blind Harry's *Wallace* by about a hundred years and his work is generally recognised as the first product of a national consciousness. *The Bruce* ends at Bannockburn, where Barbour describes the two-day battle, the tactical manoeuvres of the troops and the leaders' speeches in almost cinematic detail. He also gives voice to the thoughts and aspirations of the common people, giving Bruce's chivalric idealism what Rory Watson calls 'a sturdily domestic and practical sense of foundation'.[6] His best-known lines come from the opening:

A! fredome is a noble thing!	
Fredome mayss man to haiff liking,	*makes; pleasure*
Fredome all solace to man giffis:	*gives*
He levys at ess that frely levys.	*lives at ease*
A noble hart may haiff nane ess,	
All ellys nocht that may him pless,	
Gyff fredome failyhe; for fre liking	*if freedom fail; love of liberty*
Is yharnyt our all othir thing.	*yearned for over all*

But it appears we have not been party to the whole story. *The Triumph Tree* (1998) recognises the linguistic complexity of early Scotland. Gaelic and Old English, Welsh, Norse and Latin texts have survived, causing scholars to adjust the induction of Scottish poetry by eight hundred years. 'The first eight centuries of the poetry of Scotland is not so much forgotten as unrecorded and uncollected,' the editor, Thomas Owen Clancy, says in a preface. 'What is contained in this anthology is the first collection of the poetry composed by poets working in Scotland or working for Scottish patrons, or composed by poets of Scottish origin working for patrons elsewhere, in the period before 1350.' Anthologists, it seems, started in the middle of the story, and in the last hundred years 'only Hugh MacDiarmid's remarkable *Golden Treasury of Scottish Poetry* acknowledges the rich early medieval body of Gaelic verse, though it does not include translations of it'.

'It is not difficult to single out particularly striking poems from each of the five traditions,' says Edwin Morgan,

> poems which really ought to be familiar to anyone interested in Scottish literary history. Even in translation, but with the notes and explanations here offered, they open the eyes and the ears, and will not be readily forgotten. In Welsh, there is *The Gododdin of Aneirin*; in Latin, the *Altus Prosator*, attributed to St Columba; in Gaelic, Dallan Forgaill's *Elegy for Colum Cille*; in Old

5. See entry for John Barbour (c. 1320–95) in *Collins Encyclopaedia of Scotland*.
6. See 'The Beginnings of Scotland' in Roderick Watson's *The Literature of Scotland*.

English, the anonymous *Dream of the Rood*; and in Norse, Earl Rognvald
Kali's *Verses*. Can we be patient with a country which throws such sustenance
out of its knapsack?[7]

And then complains about its diet.

An Older, Purer and Uncorrupted Scotland

The end of the eighteenth century and the first thirty years or so of the
nineteenth century saw a rapid period of industrialisation and urbanisation in Scotland. This, according to the critic and historian Richard J.
Finlay, was when we began to reinvent ourselves. It was the era of

> Highlandism and tartanry, the romanticisation of the Scottish past, the
> sentimentalisation of rural life and the contribution of imperial Scotland to
> the British Empire. Much of this reinvention was manufactured by the new
> commercial middle classes who had been excluded from the traditional
> Scottish institutions through the power of aristocratic patronage. Not sur-
> prisingly, a key element in the reinvention of Scotland was that it was
> formed around a core of *laissez-faire* ideology in which characteristics such
> as thrift, self-help, temperance and hard work were presented as quintes-
> sential Scottish values.[8]

Just as the cult of Sir William Wallace was used to propagate anti-
aristocratic sentiment, so too was the cult of Robert Burns.

> Burns was a commoner, he had been let down by the aristocracy, and he
> showed that genius and talent were not the sole prerogatives of the aris-
> tocracy. Just as Highlandism was promoted because it was believed to be a
> purer and more traditional form of Scottishness, Burns was emblematic of
> an older, purer and uncorrupted Scotland, as yet untouched by industrial-
> ism and mammon . . . . The period witnessed a fad for collecting the relics
> of 'auld Scotia' before it passed into oblivion. Scott's gathering of the
> border ballads and the creation of numerous societies devoted to the
> preservation of historical manuscripts were evidence of a concern that
> Scottish identity was losing its distinctive national characteristics.[9]

The canonisation of Burns, Wallace, David Livingstone and others into

---

7. Edwin Morgan, 'Bring Back the Dragons of Gold', *Times Literary Supplement*,
   March 1999.
8. Richard J. Finlay, 'The Burns Cult and Scottish Identity' in *Love and Liberty:
   Robert Burns, A Bicentenary Celebration*, ed. Kenneth Simpson.
9. *Ibid.*

the broader lad o' pairts mythology underlined a wider myth, 'that Scottish society was inherently democratic and meritocratic'. Freedom in this sense had more to do with middle-class individualism and anti-aristocratic sentiment than with latent Jacobinism or even nationalism.

Nor was this the only myth so constructed. In the period between 1785 and 1850 a social and demographic upheaval took place in the Highlands and Islands involving the removal of tens of thousands of clansmen from their homes to make way for large-scale sheep farming. According to the *Collins Encyclopaedia of Scotland,* the Clearances 'were conducted in an autocratic and often brutal manner, and because they dissipated and impoverished a population which was also a distinct cultural entity with its own concepts of land tenure and a particularly tenacious attachment to its ancient habitat, the whole subject is fraught with emotive undertones and remains both sensitive and contentious'.

Horatio McCulloch painted *Loch Maree* in 1866, the year before his death. It is a landscape without people. McCulloch's work is part of Scottish art's transition into a native landscape. Like the simultaneous rediscovery and reinvention of a native Scottish architecture, this movement was in many ways an extension of and a response to the novels of Sir Walter Scott.

Scott had promoted Scotland as an international tourist attraction, to the extent that his house, Abbotsford, itself became an important part of the tourist circuit. Over a period of twelve years, the period of Scott's greatest literary output, he manufactured a house reminiscent of his novels in its mixture of history and romance. He oversaw every aspect of the construction and decoration of Abbotsford, referring to the place as a 'conundrum castle'. Invented aspects were incorporated into the fabric along with details borrowed from existing buildings. The main entrance is based on the porch at Linlithgow Palace, birthplace of Mary, Queen of Scots; the library ceiling is copied from Rosslyn Chapel; and arches, doors and panels from buildings such as Melrose Abbey and the Edinburgh Tollbooth are built into the fabric along with stones salvaged from historical Border sites. The architectural influence of Abbotsford was enormous. First Abbotsford and then Balmoral were the springboards into the rediscovery and reinvention of the Scotch Baronial style.

And Scott's influence on painting was no less immediate or dramatic. John Knox's painting *Landscape with Tourists at Loch Katrine* was a response to *The Lady of the Lake.* Painted in the 1820s, the key elements of Highland tourism are in place, including scenic grandeur, rural pastimes such as fishing, and a piper. More importantly, the view is tranquil. Every hint of warlike restlessness has been purged from the landscape. This is a pliant, agreeable people, a peaceful place where tourists are welcome.

McCulloch's paintings are something of a bridge between the essentially Classical approach of painters such as Alexander Nasmyth

(1758–1840), and what must have seemed like the blunt modernism of William McTaggart (1835–1910) and the Glasgow Boys. McCulloch's landscapes seem exaggerated. *Glencoe*, painted in 1864, is dominated by a slightly misted mountain, with rocks and a clutch of stags in the foreground. Rocks and hills, the sky and water dominate *Loch Maree*. Of living creatures there are only cattle, four in the stream and two on the ridge above the stream. Neither sheep nor people can be seen; and the only evidence of humanity is the scattering of cottages by the lochside and what could be the laird's house or a church tucked away to the left. There is a road to the right, on the hill above the hamlet, discernible by the bridge, but the road goes nowhere and has no one on it.

McCulloch's use of stags and cattle is interesting. Sheep had previously represented an Arcadian landscape, reminiscent of Marie Antoinette's *bergeresse* frolics. Reality had altered that perception.

So had Landseer's *The Monarch of the Glen*, painted in 1851. By the mid-1860s the stereotypes of Scottish identity – heather, landscape, tartan – were in placc. The railways had opened the country to a more adventurous breed of tourist, anxious to visit a place that provided the thrill of discovery in a romantic wilderness. And painters underlined that perception, providing a romantic fiction to fit the landscape.

The overt social commentary of David Wilkie (1785–1841), evidenced in pictures such as *Distraining For Rent* and *The Penny Wedding*, were lost in sentiment, just as the sentimentality of the Kailyard school[10] in the late nineteenth century emulsified the directness and energy of Burns and Scott. Gone too were Wilkie's direct references to literature and all that implies in paintings such as *The Rent Day*, inspired by Burns's poem 'Twa Dogs', and *The Blind Fiddler*, which has echoes of 'The Jolly Beggars'.

As it was then, so is it now. The quest to make ourselves acceptable, to appear as urbane and refined as our neighbours, has been a perpetual feature of Scottish life since the Union of 1707. It is paralleled only by our search for a hero, the man with the big idea who could show us the way forward, someone who could do for us what we seem to be incapable of doing for ourselves.

And lest we think romantic sentimentalism is a thing of the past – that

10. The term Kailyard (literally, cabbage patch) is used to describe a group of Scottish writers working at the end of the nineteenth century, led by J. M. Barrie, Ian Maclaren and S. R. Crockett, who presented a sentimental, romanticised image of small-town Scottish life. The term has expanded from its literary setting to include any aspect of Scottish life and letters that can be seen in a relentless monotone of good and better, where sentiment rules, changes of heart are common and where balancing virtues of almost any description are similarly absent. The name was given to the style of writing by J. H. Millar.

since we are aware of the disease, we can recognise the symptoms – consider the death of Donald Dewar. Those who clearly hated him while he was alive christened him 'Father of the Nation', and one could be forgiven for thinking that Scottish Presbyterianism had revived canonisation; while Gordon Brown made a speech so good it was almost believable.

Sophistication and Taste

This apparent dichotomy is at the heart of Scottish identity. The so-called Caledonian Antisyzygy, literally a yoking of opposites, is a symptom rather than a cause. A phenomenon originally recognised by G. Gregory Smith in his book *Scottish Literature* and relentlessly explored since, it is a combination of opposites, reflecting 'the contrasts which the Scot shows at every turn, in his political and ecclesiastical history, in his polemical restlessness, in his adaptability . . . . We need not be surprised to find that in his literature the Scot presents two aspects which appear contradictory. Oxymoron was ever the bravest figure and we must not forget that disorderly order is order after all.'[11] Which presupposes the phenomenon can be extended into every area of artistic endeavour, though up till now the main source of investigations and applications has been confined to literature. It also sees the yoking of opposites as an end rather than a means, a cause rather than a symptom. If we look on the phenomenon as a symptom, it immediately becomes much more interesting, for such oppositions then become evidence rather than results.

That the Caledonian Antisyzygy, in whatever form, evidences a lack of national identity, or, at least, a confused national identity, cannot be fallacious in a country where those aspects of national identity which serve other nations – our language and traditional arts – have been undervalued and ignored, considered unsophisticated, thus causing us to distort their basis and impact in an attempt to make them acceptable to people other than ourselves. The desire to appear sophisticated has distorted our entire culture, altering our native, traditional arts, especially music and song – where the desire to sound American dominates – not only into caricatures of themselves, pale imitations of what they could be, but also often embarrassingly imitative of the conditions to which they aspire.

Or, as in the case of exponents as varied as Sir Walter Scott and Sir Harry Lauder, Sir J. M. Barrie and the like, they are statements of national identity that are aimed at an audience beyond ourselves. Just as

11. G. Gregory Smith, *Scottish Literature.*

Sir Edward Landseer's *Monarch of the Glen* was aimed towards London, so his other paintings with Scottish themes were intended for a market out-with Scotland. Landseer was, of course, Queen Victoria's favourite artist, whom Scott's works inspired to venture north. His popularity was dependent on an uncanny ability to present animals that appear to have been endowed with human characteristics and emotions, a skill which can appear misplaced in works featuring humans as themselves.

It is possible to see Landseer paintings such as *Flood in the Highlands* as allegorical. The flood could be figurative rather than literal. The people, landscape and animals could be threatened by the floodtide of com-merce. The explicit advance of progress and the desire for wealth that is seen as the imperative behind the Highland Clearances could have ruined the young mother and her children, perched as they are with their beasts, including sheep, and belongings on the roof of their home while disaster roars around them, the symbols of national identity such as pipes and a targe discarded near the feet of a shivering patriarch. The family are fearful, the old man resigned; they see nothing but disaster approaching.

No matter the allegory, no matter the message of faded glory, lost causes and an appalling future; the important voice is Landseer's. His subjects are viewed sentimentally, with a professional detachment, which draws attention to the artist and his abilities rather than sympathising with the plight of his subjects. Proficient, skilled and shining, the techni-cal brilliance not only divorces the painting from its subjects, but also places them beyond compassion, giving the work a questionable hold on reality. But Landseer obviously had his eye on a ready market; this paint-ing was done with prospective clients in mind, as surely as the Kailyard novelists transcribed rurality for urban consumption.

Tom Faed's influence on the succeeding generation of Scottish artists was in many ways as significant as Landseer's, and while he was more than capable of producing works of depth and sensitivity, he shared Landseer's preference for depicting the material world over the plight of his sub-jects, irrespective of their circumstances. Like most of Faed's work, *The Last of the Clan* was painted from London and makes a lachrymose com-panion to the Landseer flood.

Again, we see the Clearances as spectacle. An old and disconsolate Highlander sits astride a tired pony on the quayside, surrounded by a group of mostly young women and a very young child, with another old man at the centre of their group. The other men have gone. All the women are fearful, some in tears.

Faed's genre paintings show little of Wilkie's influence in anything other than his choice of subject. The wider social issues which Wilkie evoked have been reduced to sentimental stereotypes. In *Tussle for the Keg* the background is unstated, similar to the mists of *The Last of the Clan*.

Two men on stony ground are locked in combat. The Highlander, scrawny, kilted and red-haired, has a dirk in his right hand and is clearly intent on using it. A beefy Lowlander stands his ground, a pistol protruding from his left pocket. His face shows a look of determination which, together with the fact that he appears to be slightly elevated, suggests he will win. An abandoned whisky keg is in the foreground. Again, the allegorical implications are obvious.

Though this may not have been the artists' intention, the works of painters such as Faed and McCulloch were instrumental in making the distancing of the Highland people from their land acceptable, in spite of the realities that were soon to be exposed by the burgeoning photographic movement, which bypassed McCulloch and Faed and their contemporaries and successors. The photographs that Thomas Annan took between 1868 and 1877 of the *Old Closes and Streets of Glasgow* are a world away from *Loch Maree*. Annan's photographs are crowded with people, or there is ample evidence of their existence, again underlining the implicit message of a land without people twinned with an overcrowded urbanity.

Yet to be Done

The Highland landscape has come to represent Scotland. It has become an important part of a symbolic structure which in itself is so powerful and pernicious that the very suggestion of it conjures up the people and the place.

Symbols have a high redundancy level, and therefore these symbols have to be repeated, their image stated and restated, their message reinforced for their impact to be made, let alone understood. And they have to be varied, ranging across an assortment of artistic and social disciplines. Most obvious is the landscape itself, proud and majestic with high hills, ruined castles and no people. Then there is a panoply of lesser images which conjure up the landscape and underline the impact, while often making a simultaneous impact of their own: tartan, bagpipes, dogs, kilts, thistles, heather and cattle have come to represent the people and the place, to the extent that we often identify with the symbols rather than the place, feel sentimental about the heather and the tartan rather than the place they represent.

We are not alone in this; our neighbours suffer similar reflections, often, as in Ireland, with bewildering results. Yet it is true to say that, here at least, things are changing. There is every indication that the power of our symbols is diminishing, that a new sense of national pride is emerging, with the scattering, if not the actual abolition, of the disparaging Scottish cringe factor. This is the sense of shame, maybe even humiliation, that comes from the more obviously mawkish representations of the

Scot and Scottishness, be they from sub-Lauderish entertainers or our national football team.

There are now no regular radio or television programmes devoted to the type of Scotch entertainment that was popular a generation ago, where the obvious symbolic components of our national identity were continually on display. And while there is a market for these sorts of amusements, the fact that the expressions of nationhood and national identity they represent are no longer generally accepted as representing the Scots of today and their culture has given their appearances a lost quality, as if we are seeing something whose time has passed and whose force has been forgotten. Events have moved on.

Today, despite the fact that the new Parliament has undoubtedly brought a renewed sense of nationhood, there is a relentless stream of negative statistics. Time and again they reinforce a series of images that were familiar a generation ago; they present a picture reminiscent of neglect and waste, something which speaks of an underclass.

In late 1997 'statistics that add up to a Dickensian image of Scotland'[12] were revealed by the children's charity Barnardo's. Thirty-eight per cent of Scotland's population live in poverty (defined as receiving 50 per cent or less of the national average income), a figure which has trebled since 1979. One house in twenty is 'below tolerable standard'[13] and more than a quarter are affected by damp. Twenty-eight per cent of Scottish households have children who are less than four years old, but fewer than one in five of three- to four-year-olds have a full-time place in nursery. Approximately 33,000 children are members of homeless households and an estimated 5000 young people sleep rough every year. Scotland has the third-highest rate of teenage conception in the western world; youth crime costs £730 million a year; and children either witness 90 per cent of incidents of domestic violence or are in an adjacent room when they occur.

'A quarter of Scottish children grow up in homes where no one works, and thousands more raised in low-income families would go as hungry and poorly dressed as any child of the thirties without free school meals and clothing grants,' according to an article in the *Herald*.

> Figures show that incidence of depression among children living in areas of deprivation is double that of children living in more affluent areas . . . children as young as 10 living out their lives against a background of poverty attempt suicide . . . . Children living in poor housing conditions suffer from asthma and severe respiratory problems. There are more accidents in

12. *Herald*, 14 October 1997, describing the Barnardo's report *Today and Tomorrow*.
13. *Ibid.*

the home ... as many as 14% of babies born in areas of deprivation in Scotland have low birth weights, a statistic which equates with countries such as Tanzania. Low birth weight babies are shown to have lower IQs than healthy children.[14]

As we know, the perpetual repetition of images and statistics, no matter how telling, can emulsify their effect. It is often difficult to extract relevance from a mass of data. Even when it is something familiar, we tend to think of causes rather than effect, especially when politicians blame the individuals for their condition. But spiritual poverty knows no boundaries. It is not confined to housing schemes and community centres.

'Doctors say alcohol is Scotland's biggest drug problem and it is thought to be linked to the rise in teenage pregnancies. It is responsible for one in four male acute hospital admissions, more than half of assault victims' injuries and around half of serious road accidents,' runs a report in the *Sunday Herald*. 'In France, where wine drinking in a family setting has always been the norm, young people indulge at roughly similar rates to Scots. But while 53% of 15-year-old Scottish boys report having been drunk up to ten times, only 24% of French lads regularly get sozzled – and the difference is even more marked for younger children. Drunkenness among 13-year-old Scottish girls is seven times higher than in France.'[15] Children say drink gives them confidence.

But a survey of 850 youngsters and the subsequent report from the Joseph Rowntree Foundation concluded that 'children from stable families are just as likely to take drugs as those from disadvantaged backgrounds.' Drug-takers apparently 'come from settled families, have few problems with self-esteem and see drug-taking as a normal part of some social events'. They trust and respect their families as much as any other teenager, tend to be more independent and less introverted than those who did not use drugs, lead active lives and have no less self-esteem than others of their age.[16]

All this comes when the population is falling. Scotland's low birth rate was used to support the argument that Scotland's Westminster representation should be reduced from seventy-two to fifty-eight Members of Parliament. A professor of history at Bristol University, John Vincent, claimed we were 'a dying breed', quoting government fertility rates which showed Scots women were conceiving fewer children than women south of the border. 'The birthrate in Scotland was 1.55 children per woman in

14. *Herald*, 3 February 1998.
15. *Sunday Herald*, 18 April 1999.
16. Quoted in the *Scotsman*, 5 November 1997.

1995 compared to 1.72 for England and Wales.'[17] Vincent's argument led him to conclude that at a finite point in the future, no one will be born in Scotland and therefore the nation will disappear. He cited drink, drugs, diet, poverty or drolly – a preference for cars over children. 'Everyone recognises that if you don't have kids the family name will die out,' he is reported as saying. 'And therefore if you only have 1.5 kids, the family will certainly die out. Not immediately, but each successive generation will get smaller. There is no room for argument. It is purely a question of maths.'

Edinburgh alone continues to increase its population. The capital is said to be experiencing 'an economic renaissance'.[18] The populations of Glasgow, Aberdeen and Dundee are falling, and 8600 people left the country in 1996, while Edinburgh gained 1300 inhabitants.

And it seems that now we are three nations – excluded, insecure and settled people. A report from the Scottish Council Federation concludes that what it calls Excluded Scotland is an expensive place to live, where household basics take up most of the family budget. 'Residents are most at risk of long-term unemployment, most exposed to market failure and monopoly service provision and have least choice in their lives.' But most Scots live in Insecure Scotland. It is 'an anxious place' to live, where many have recent experience of low pay or unemployment. 'Families are often fearful about the future, the education of their children, and the care of their parents, and many are "only a pay-check away from slipping into poverty."' Settled Scotland is virtually everyone else: 'Residents do not all have the highest incomes but they are secure incomes and they are best equipped to cope with change and best prepared for retirement.'[19]

Violent death is twice as common here as in England and Wales. In January 1998 the *Independent* carried out a detailed analysis of the 918 recorded homicides in police regions in Scotland, England and Wales and found Central Scotland came top of the league, followed by Tayside, Northern Scotland and Strathclyde. The Central Region figure did not take the killing of seventeen people at Dunblane primary school into account since that 'was hopefully a unique event'.

Central Scotland has a population of 274,000 and recorded crime has dropped by a third since 1991. It 'is a relatively affluent picture postcard region, where the lowlands meets the highlands, being marketed as "Braveheart country" . . . . Detective Chief Superintendent John Ogg, head of CID, said: "The typical case is a husband turning violent after drinking, but that's a problem throughout the country."'[20]

17. *Scotsman*, 6 February 1998.
18. *Herald*, 9 April 1999.
19. Quoted in the *Herald*, 26 January 1998.
20. *Independent*, 12 January 1998.

It would be interesting to discover how many of the people referred to in these reports see themselves as Scots, or even question what the definition means. Perhaps they see themselves as part of a wider community with a stable, more clearly defined identity, such as that which comes from a football team with a particular sectarian history. Fully recognising that there are historical libraries devoted to the subject of national identity, a working definition for the purposes of this project is: the means whereby those of common descent, language, culture and historical tradition, usually a state or a set of people, come to distinguish and recognise themselves.

And the questions to be explored are:

1. What are our symbols of national identity?
2. Why are there so many and what is their effect?
3. How has what would appear to be a continuing search for national identity been expressed in our major arts, literature, painting, architecture and music?
4. Are there recognisable symbols or aspects of national identity which are uniquely Scots?
5. How have these recognisable symbols evolved and changed and what outside influences have they absorbed? Which aspects have been preserved and can they be cultivated?
6. Whose interests do these changes serve?

It was Only the Scots who Objected?

Despite the haste with which the Yes-Yes campaign was organised, even the most casual summary of events must concede that there was a lack of opposition to the establishment of the Scottish Parliament. This includes areas such as Orkney and Shetland, who have not only always considered themselves to be slightly separate from Scotland, but who, when they did bother to vote, previously voted to be part of the United Kingdom, it is thought because of the farming subsidies and oil revenues.

Four days before the referendum, David Walker wrote in the *Independent*:

> The residents of England are happy to let the Scots get on with it. You can read the whole of Scottish history, at least since the first Stuarts in the Middle Ages, as the history of difference. To be Scots has meant, crucially once England's political and economic power was established, defining yourself one way or another as not English. Being not-English has involved varieties of whingeing, the construction of an ersatz Highland identity (why do Scots keep singing about buts and bens and glens when the vast majority live in cities?) and beating the English at their own games, rarely

football. Being good in Scotland is rarely good enough. Why else have the brightest and best of Scots, from David Hume to wee Jimmy Naughtie, Robert Louis Stevenson to Iain Banks, David Boswell to John Lloyd (or Gordon Brown for that matter) just had to make it in London? Subconsciously there will be many Scots this week asking whether they or their children really want Edinburgh or Glasgow to be the summit of their ambitions.[21]

Of course, it's dross. No one can argue with Walker's assertion of ersatz identity, but the matrimony of David Hume and James Naughtie beggars belief, as does his later assertion that, 'In popular song from Harry Lauder to Del Amitri and in Scottish fiction from Lewis Grassic Gibbon to *Trainspotting* blaming and bemoaning the English is an old and much-loved ritual.' Examples, please; especially of an anti-English Lauder song.

It would be easy to dismiss such pieces for what they are, were it not for the fact that a trend appears to have emerged. Even before the referendum, *Private Eye's* Bookworm noticed an upsurge in publications questioning English identity, asking where it all went wrong.[22] In a piece summarised in *The Week*, Peregrine Worsthorne confessed, 'England at present is my least favourite part of the United Kingdom.' He goes on to predict: 'Scottish independence would constitute a humiliating rejection and a failure of statesmanship equalled only by the loss of the American colonies in 1776.' Rather than breed a healthy patriotism, it would breed the ugliest sort of tabloid-led nationalism. Mass democracy has merged the lower and middle classes of all Western countries, he says, but in England, 'the latter has been submerged by the former . . . the English *haute bourgeoisie* in speech, clothing and manners has been proletarianised'.[23]

The magazine's introduction to Worsthorne's piece rewrites history in a way guaranteed to provoke Scottish indignation, and almost certainly to get up Welsh and Irish danders as well, by equating British history with English history: 'There are some who feel that the break-up of the UK will herald an English renaissance comparable to that in 1940, when England "stood alone" after the fall of France.'

George Rosie in *Scotland on Sunday* quoted a question posed by the *Sunday Telegraph*: how long will London, 'which is subsidising the rest of the country (and the national pretensions of the Welsh and Scots) as never before continue to fulfil this role?'. Correspondence columns in the 'house organs of Middle England', *The Times*, the *Spectator* and the

21. *Independent*, 8 September 1997.
22. *Private Eye*, 22 August 1997.
23. *The Week*, 26 September 1998. The piece was originally published in the *Spectator*.

Daily Telegraph, echoed the dispute, which appeared to form the basis of the claims for economic redistribution by both Tory and Labour contestants for the job of London's mayor. The 'economics are easily rubbished,' says Rosie. 'But the political realities that underpin them are not. There seems little doubt that much of England – and in particular London – feels aggrieved by the home rule enthusiasms of the Scots.' While researching for a television programme on the subject he found that 'disloyal and ungrateful were two of the words that English folk were reluctant to use but obviously felt'. And they appeared to suggest: '. . . if the Scots can have their own directly elected assembly, why shouldn't we?'[24]

Three months later, Donald Macintyre wrote in the *Independent*, 'Does anybody seriously doubt that the whole of the UK is greater than the sum of its parts?' For too long, says Macintyre, English politicians have pretended that Scotland was not another country, adding that a paper by defence minister and Scottish MP (and soon to be Secretary of State for Scotland) John Reid suggests 'that Scottish nationalism fed between 1979 and 1997 on popular frustration not at being governed from Westminster, but at being governed by *Tory* governments at Westminster.'[25]

The subtext to the Reid assertion was picked up and directly stated by Harry Ritchie less than a week later: '. . . if you are English, then it is odds on that when you say "Britain", you are really thinking of England, and that the adjective 'British' evokes images that are distinctly (and anachronistically) English – stiff upper lip, Cotswoldian landscape, cricket, warm beer, village greens, and all that'. Despite what 'those charmers in their orange sashes and bowler hats like to think, there is really no such thing as "Britishness",' he concludes, 'and no point in continuing the pretence'.[26]

Along the way, he concludes that 'Culturally, England could dispense with its England/Britain confusion and update its crazy self-image, and Scotland could at least afford to phase out the Anglophobia that reached its nadir in the ludicrous *Braveheart*, a film that confidently portrayed the English as a race of sadistic, arrogant, posh poofs.'

The Ritchie images are certainly among the stock English symbols, but this is not how they see themselves at all, according to Isobel Lindsay, a sociologist in the Department of Government at the University of Strathclyde. The picture that emerges from this study is different from warm beer and village greens. 'The most striking outcome was the very negative view that English respondents also had of Englishness,' says

24. *Scotland on Sunday*, 19 April 1998.
25. *Independent*, 17 July 1998.
26. *Independent*, 22 July 1998.

Lindsay. They saw little positive in their national characteristics and Lindsay suggests English identity has suffered because they have been fed a very narrow version of their past which no longer works for them.[27]

Irvine Welsh agrees. In a piece for the *Big Issue* he argued that the English working class, 'continually vilified and abused by the nation's liberal and conservative establishment, have been left to carry the can for the country's failure to establish an inclusive post-imperial identity'. Writing in the *Independent*, Richard Hoggart confessed, 'I am usually not quite sure what I am and, in particular, whether I wish to be "British" or "English" or both.' He concludes he is primarily a Yorkshireman and rather than being British is European. The Welsh and Scots know who they are, he says, listing qualities which he sees as essentially English, concluding, 'If there is one thing I have learnt over all these years, from living on the Continent, from reading and from talk, it is that we are not only English (or Scottish or Welsh), but also and always and ineradicably European.'

For almost three hundred years Scotland has known the consequence of living beside a bigger, economically more powerful neighbour; a neighbour upon whom you are dependent, and whose economic, social and political decisions affect you directly, but over which you feel you have little control, nor even a say, since your voice is continually drowned out in the clamour of other louder, contrasting voices, in an environment where decisions will always be made for the greater good rather than being based on any regional considerations, however justly or reasonably presented. England's problem, as Hoggart correctly if indirectly defined, is not just the break-up of its corporate dual identity with the United Kingdom, but the hot breath of Brussels panting in its ear.

An Upturned Boat

Thomas Hamilton designed the Royal High School on the flanks of Calton Hill, described as 'perhaps the single most significant single monument of Edinburgh classical Romanticism, and one of the set pieces of archaeological Hellenism in Europe'.[28] Since 1979 the abandoned Royal High School has stood in splendid isolation, awaiting occupancy. A Conservative proposal to turn it into a hotel caused a public outcry, and with Parliament assembling at the top of the Mound while their new building is being debated, the Royal High School has no role, other than symbolic.

27. *Scotland on Sunday*, 16 August 1998.
28. Miles Glendinning, Ranald MacInnes and Aonghus MacKechnie, *A History of Scottish Architecture*.

Most new parliament buildings are at the top of a hill. Ours will be at the foot of one of the most famous hills in the world.

The Scottish Parliament began its life in temporary accommodation, not actually homeless, but making do with what was available. Enric Miralles's new building – inspired, it is said, by an upturned boat – was troubled from the start, with his designs being subjected to as much scrutiny as the rising cost of the project. And even after the imposition of a price ceiling and delivery date, as well as a public rebuke for the civil servant who allowed costs to rise, with a final price tag of nearer £200 million than the original estimate of £40 million, the building has already joined the Millennium Dome and the Houses of Parliament as prestigious projects that have cost the public dear. Now that the building's architect and its champion, Miralles and First Secretary Donald Dewar, have died, the project has lost momentum and increasingly looks as though it will become another government public-works fiasco, another overpriced white elephant on the wrong site.

The new building will rise beside Holyrood House at the foot of the Royal Mile, to be built on a site owned by Scottish and Newcastle Breweries, a company which 'had been prominent among those Scottish businesses which argued vociferously against the whole idea of devolution'.[29]

At the end of 1997, on a train journey from Glasgow to Edinburgh, John Clement of D. M. Hall bumped into Scottish Office officials who were advising Donald Dewar on the best site for the new Parliament. Though Clement was not initially involved, his 'solution was to act as dance-master while the Scottish Office and Scottish and Newcastle Breweries performed a stately minuet . . . . Gently, but insistently, Clement nudged the two sides together. Meanwhile the rest of Scotland was jigging towards Calton Hill, measuring up various listed buildings as press centres, members' office space, libraries, etc.'[30]

Among the site's disadvantages were that it was on the fringe of a historic centre, that the surrounding area was becoming run-down and already suffered from traffic congestion. Among the site's advantages was the fact that it wasn't Calton Hill.

> Many observers believe that Calton Hill had become too powerful an icon
> of national aspirations for New Labour to stomach. Throughout the long
> dark days of Thatcherite anti-devolutionary intransigence, Calton Hill had
> become the keeper of the flame. It is now widely believed north of the
> Border that Labour's leadership jumped at the chance of building the
> Parliament anywhere that was not associated with Calton Hill.[31]

29. *Herald*, 23 April 1998.
30. *Ibid.*
31. *Ibid.*

The Glasgow–Edinburgh rivalry, which appeared to have been temporarily resolved through a mutual interest in tourism, was revived with an acrimonious wrangle over the temporary siting of the Parliament while MSPs waited for their new building to be built. With a rare flash of the entrepreneurial spirit that was said to define the city, Glasgow offered new parliamentarians Charles Wilson's old High School building in Elmbank Street, with the redundant Strathclyde Region offices nearby. It seemed the perfect solution: Wilson is unquestionably one of Glasgow's greatest architects. More importantly, this was precisely the kind of fillip Glasgow needed, having been forced to reinvent itself over and again, while Edinburgh remained what it always had been. It was reckoned, in Glasgow at any rate, that Edinburgh had done rather well out of public buildings. Not only was the *Britannia* permanently moored at Leith, though she was built in Glasgow, but government-sponsored projects such as the Museum of Scotland and the new parliament building were being housed in Edinburgh, simply because it is the capital.

This city rivalry is often seen as further evidence of the Caledonian Antisyzygy, the split which is said to be manifest in every form of Scottish life, even in the country itself: Glasgow and Edinburgh, Highlands and Lowlands, Gaelic and English, and so on; a Caledonian Ying and Yang. However, the Chinese version reveals why one thing is like another, while we retain their essential opposition and chart their effects; the Chinese ideal does not allow for conflict, whereas conflict is often at the heart of our divisions.

Scottish Journey

In the summer of 1934 Edwin Muir set out to find the Scots in a 1921 Standard car, borrowed from his friend Stanley Cursiter, a painter and the director of the National Gallery of Scotland. He was indulging in a familiar genre, regarding Scotland as a place whose geography and culture needed explanation, a place as remote and interesting as Araby was to eighteenth- and some nineteenth-century travellers.

Until the twentieth century, the main market for such publications was undoubtedly England. Scots had mostly travelled by sea and made cultural connections with places like Ireland, the Low Countries and Scandinavia. It was easier to travel by boat than to travel overland; this simple geographic fact made England culturally and socially remote until relatively recent times.

Muir's intention was clear from the beginning. 'This book is the record of a journey,' he wrote, 'and my intention in beginning it was to give my impression of contemporary Scotland; not the romantic Scotland of the past nor the Scotland of the tourist, but the Scotland which presents itself to one who is not looking for anything in particular, and is willing to believe what his eyes and ears tell him.'[32]

Muir's book was not particularly well received, nor did Muir himself appear to think highly of it, yet *Scottish Journey* has established itself as a model of its kind. The Edinburgh chapter alone, describing tea shops 'more strange than a dream', is one of the finest pieces of Scottish descriptive writing.

Until recently, it was, as Christopher Smout has suggested, frightening to see how many recognisable features had lingered in the mirror Muir held up to the face of his country. He seems to have found on his travels a deeply disunited people; folk who were depressed rather than oppressed; a people who were quick to resent a national insult, but were at the same time incapable of taking any action which might halt the country's decline. This led him to conclude that our ills were economic rather than national and that contemporary economic systems fashioned national characteristics.

For all his sharp observation and political awareness, Muir's principal concern was with the chimera of Scottish identity. He divided the country into sections not simply to give himself convenient chapters, but, as becomes increasingly obvious, because his search uncovered a series of smaller, local identities from which a national identity is constructed. Time and again he puts his finger on the problem, approaching the subject from a variety of angles, teasing it from the darkest corners, stating why our identity is confused and ironing out the creases, defining the false hopes and starts we have encountered, identifying where it exists and often suggesting areas of encouragement. He can appear as amazed as anyone that it is still a recognisable entity after having endured such a continuous series of assaults and often acknowledges its presence without actually defining it or giving it a name. This could have been because the intellectual climate of the times made such an overt gesture redundant, but is more likely to be because Muir assumed his readership would know what he was discussing.

The fact that he continually falls into the trap of defining us in terms of what we are not, rather than what we are, and of comparing our history and literature with English history and literature is entirely concordant with the mood of the times. It would be wrong to define such a mood as anti-English, then or now, nor is it necessarily pro-Scottish. The approach is clear evidence of the cultural malaise that had gripped the country: that the simplest way of defining our culture and recognising our literature and identity was to establish the differences between ourselves and the English. English identity was taken as the

32. Edwin Muir, *Scottish Journey.*

norm, was often what was popularly meant by the term British, and differences between ourselves and the norm had firstly to be established. Scottish identity had to be defined before it could be seen to exist. That we now take such things for granted is a measure of the success of this movement and the shifts in social and cultural identity that have taken place.

Many of the institutions generally regarded as sources of national identity were put in place during two significant periods. First, in the late nineteenth century, when, with Home Rule firmly on the agenda, the office of the Secretary of State for Scotland was created, the National Portrait Gallery of Scotland was founded, and the Scottish History and Scottish Text Societies were established. This was accompanied by an intellectually challenging reassessment of painting and architecture, largely centred in Glasgow.

Second, in the 1930s the Saltire Society was founded 'to foster and enrich' Scottish culture, at around the same time as organisations as diverse as the National Trust for Scotland, the Scottish National Dictionary and the Scottish Country Dance Society. The Saltire Society's common purpose brought together such unlikely bedfellows as Tom Johnston, Walter Elliott, D. Y. Cameron, Hugh MacDiarmid, Kurt Hahn, Stanley Cursiter and Compton Mackenzie. This was also a period when Scottish artists were rediscovering the landscape, when Scottish architecture found a renewed, modernist confidence, and when a diverse group of writers used indigenous speech in much the same way that Robert Burns had pioneered something like 150 years previously.

A Twinning of Opposites

For Muir, Gregory Smith's Caledonian Antisyzygy was an overstatement, which had been accorded exaggerated importance. His analysis of how 'a nation deeply committed to greedy practicality pretends to worldly disinterest', and the results of this pretension, are clear. 'A hundred years ago Heine saw that sentimentality was the other face of materialism,' he writes,

> but materialism has many faces. Scottish fantastic poetry is the natural recoil from a 'maudlin affection for the commonplace', but it has no particular virtue beyond its naturalness . . . . To romanticize this reaction, to picture the Scotsman as making merry in a clash of strange worlds and moods (but contriving presumably to earn a living meantime) is mere sentimentality, and perpetuates an ancestral weakness of Scotland, the weakness which turned all its history into legend, mainly tawdry, and created such ludicrous misunderstandings as the myth of Bonnie Prince Charlie. The response of the Makars and Balladists to experience was a

whole response; the response of fantastic poetry is a joke followed by an explanation.[33]

This twinning of opposites is not solely a literary phenomenon; it is an equally important feature of our other major art forms. Nor is it especially Scottish. It is regarded as literary because that is where we find the best and perhaps the most obvious examples, and maybe this is where it has been most obviously developed and used most effectively. Its appearance in other art forms, especially painting and architecture, is clear enough for it to be considered as a national rather than a literary phenomenon, and to justify ferreting around for reasons as to why this should be so.

When I edited *The Devil and the Giro*, published in 1989, I had no idea it would be the first in a series of books that looked at the arts through Scottish eyes and from a Scottish perspective. Duncan Macmillan's *Scottish Art 1460–1990*, John Purser's *Scotland's Music*, and *A History of Scottish Architecture* by Miles Glendinning, Ranald MacInnes and Aonghus MacKechnie, as well as other works covering literature, art, music and theatre, all argue that we are more than a scion, that Scotland's contributions to these forms are where our independence is revealed — an independence of the mind.

Consciously or not, Scottish artists in all these disciplines demonstrate a twinning of opposites for perfectly valid reasons. To say that, for example, painters twin opposites, is to suggest nothing more than the obvious, with nothing at all evident to distinguish a Glasgow artist from someone living and working in Ulan Bator. But Scottish painters twin opposites in a particularly Scottish way, as do Scottish writers, musicians and architects.

It is in literature, because of its potential for conflict, that it makes a better story. Scottish fiction has its roots in a tradition where stories were told to entertain. This imaginative pact between speaker and audience goes back to the oral traditions of the Highlands and Islands and to the ballads. Scottish culture played an important part in the emergence of books and the rise of a reading public, not just here but throughout Europe. Publications such as the *Edinburgh Review, Blackwood's Magazine* and *Fraser's Magazine* were early and important influences, and some of the writers of this period, such as Hogg, Scott and Galt, played important roles in establishing the mood and tone of written literature. Imaginative prose was well established in Scotland when Balzac was writing in France and Edgar Allan Poe and Washington Irving were laying the foundations for American prose literature. Hogg, for example, can certainly be said to have anticipated Dostoevsky in the study of psychological division, and

33. Edwin Muir, *Scott and Scotland*.

Galt's interest in the family and social history pointed the way to the novels of Balzac and Zola. Most importantly of all, Scott was internationally famous and widely acknowledged by many European and American writers as a major influence on their work.

Imaginative prose could be said to be one of the few constants both fed and nourished by a general dissemination of ideas; certainly more so than poetry, which we tend to see in terms of individuals. Scottish writers were among the first to develop and extend the short story, I believe, for no reason other than that markets existed. In doing so they were developing and extending an oral tradition that exists to the present day, which surely makes the short story worthy of being considered as our primary literary medium.

That the main tradition of English literature is poetic is beyond question, and perhaps we assume the same to be the case in Scotland. However, despite the fact that a reassessment in the light of *The Triumph Tree* may prove we have been right in our assumptions all along, our poets scarcely sprang from a tradition as continuous and diverse as our short-story writers, unless it is the Scottish folk-song tradition, which Burns embraced and enlivened and MacDiarmid denigrated and sought to undermine.

The short story is a very subversive form, wherein images have to be sharp and characters must arrive fully formed rather than be given time to develop. This precision, which is often obvious in poetry, can be overlooked in short-story writing because we tend to be blinded by narrative; but it is a precision imposed by the form. Most of the craft of short-story writing is hidden; if you see it, it hasn't worked. But, as with any literary form, the craft and mechanics are on display if one is willing to look.

It is difficult to read a collection of Scottish stories without becoming aware of the spoken voice and the power of first-person narration, something which to me was so obvious that I was surprised to find that prior to the publication of *The Devil and the Giro* its importance had seldom, if ever, been considered. It is absolutely crucial. It establishes the tone and direction of the story by forming an immediate and firm pact with the reader, appearing in every instance to take him or her into the writer's confidence. Not surprisingly, it is the first decision a writer takes and one he is often not aware of making, since its influence is often instinctive.

It establishes the mood and, more importantly, the tone of the story, and narrows the focus by trapping the reader into seeing the action through the eyes of the character. It is also a wonderful way of insinuating detail. It is the one device a writer can use that does more than one thing simultaneously: it establishes character, background, place, nationality and class. Because the writer has established the reader's confidence, he has established an identity and trust to which the reader responds by accepting what we have to tell, usually without question.

More importantly, the voice and the role of the first-person narrator form a direct link with the oral tradition, offering more than just a method of deepening a story's range and power. It is difficult, not to say boring, within the scope and demands of a short story, to make a character narrated in the third person say more than the scope of his action permits, and to do so without implying the discreet intervention of the author. On the other hand, it is entirely legitimate for a first-person character to give himself over to reflection, reasoning, philosophical meanderings and so on.

Craftiest of all are those who employ the intimacy of first-person narration within a third-person narrative, marrying insight and detachment. Scottish writers have become especially adept in the ways in which they use this device. Stream of consciousness is common, especially when dealing with the young mind or in establishing the problems of identity, as in Iain Crichton Smith's wonderful *Murdo*. In *Celia*, George Mackay Brown interrupts a third-person narrative by inserting the principal character's own voice, and Alasdair Gray frequently employs the intimacy of correspondence. The first-person narrative is the dominant feature of Scottish writing, an essential part of what I would argue is Scotland's most important literary form. Scottish poetry can be seen in terms of individuals, but the Scottish story-telling tradition, and the role of the voice within that tradition, is a seamless, uninterrupted source of excellence from James Hogg to Irvine Welsh.

That further study is needed is obvious, especially of the ways in which this device has been used by women writers, whose approach is often entirely different. Writers as diverse as Margaret Oliphant and Muriel Spark use details to build an atmosphere, which they just as tellingly deconstruct, or allow to crumble.

In architecture, since the Renaissance, public buildings throughout Scotland, from church to city chambers, have symbolised public probity and private vice: stern exteriors with highly decorated, sensual interiors, which doubtless can be dismissed in terms of climate, but which are nowhere more obvious than in the work of Charles Rennie Mackintosh or Alexander Thomson, who believed their interiors should create an environment which ignored the world outside. Not that this opposition is particularly Scottish, but again, the suggestion is that architects have approached the matter in a particularly Scottish way. The feature is as obvious in the decorated walls of Innerpeffray Collegiate Church in Perthshire, which dates from the early sixteenth century, as in fortified tower houses, or, most obviously, in the rebuilding of the royal palaces at Falkland and Stirling, where the Franco-Scottish alliance brought an influx of French craftsman.

The Baronial tower house reached its apogee when church wealth was secularised during and after the Reformation, which in turn gave an increased emphasis to internal comfort and decoration. 'Painted ceilings were slowly replaced through the increased use of ornamental plaster-work,' says the *Collins Encyclopaedia of Scotland*, noting the Dutch influence, which arose through Scotland's trade with the Low Countries, and the increase in both town and domestic architecture as well as the changes that occurred in building use following the Reformation, when the existing churches were adapted to new forms of worship.

It has been engagingly argued that there is an enduring and continual formality in Scottish architecture, inherited from Scotland's stone-building tradition and manifest in a commitment to monuments of sufficient height and gravity to convey appropriate signals, as well as a liking for symbolic structures of an impressive height. This, it is suggested, stems from the fact that Scottish architecture is a variant of northern European, rather than English, architecture.

There has also been a traditional predisposition for Scotland to rein-vent itself through its architecture, a commitment that has been perpetually balanced by a passion for new technologies and building materials ranging from iron and steel to grid plans, concrete and pre-fabrication – anything which can readily transform itself into a monument. While this is an obvious feature of nineteenth- and twentieth-century Scottish architecture, earlier experiments were underlined by the exchanges Scottish architects made with Europe and latterly America, as well as a desire to be at the cutting edge of cultural modernity. Robert Adam's visit to Italy and the ideas it gave him is one example of many. There has been a continual exodus of Scottish architects – Alexander Kirkland to Chicago, William Stark to Russia and so on – which persisted up to the First World War. The continual movement between Scotland and the Low Countries can still be seen in the little pantiled houses in Fife, and French-influenced châteaux (some, like Chatelherault, appro-priately named) are dotted across the country.

Convincing details have emerged to show how Renaissance Scotland reflected a desire to rewrite its own history through architecture, though from the mid-seventeenth century onwards the expression of a national identity became what Charles McKean has called 'an engaging subplot', the main storyline being the fact that Scotland's place in the vanguard of British imperialism resulted in the greatest architecture. The authors of *A History of Scottish Architecture* suggest the wealth that flowed into Scotland from the empire resulted in its greatest buildings, those erected in the nineteenth century. The inference is obvious: Scotland could afford its bouts of architectural nostalgia because of the income gener-ated by Scottish investments or people abroad.

These details show that Scotland's architects were doing no more than what its writers and artists were achieving at more or less analagous peri-ods: that while Maclellan in Fortingall and Mackintosh in Glasgow sought inspiration from Scotch Baronial style, the artists known as the Glasgow Boys redefined the way we saw our landscape and our people, embracing all the country's landscape and its rural inhabitants at a time when the poor were seen as little more than set dressing for moralistic romps viewed from manse windows, or as objects of fun. The eagerness of the Glasgow Boys to embrace the new social realism they found in Paris, while at the same time trying to recreate Whistler's tonal harmonies and decorative effects, made them forsake the scenic grandeur of the Highlands for Lowland fields. The change in atmosphere, the shift towards a more realistic landscape, something more recognisable, less remote, and, more importantly, a landscape containing people, must have been felt across the artistic community as a whole.

Scottish artists have continually sought to pair opposing factions. From the early ceiling paintings in buildings such as Culross Palace, Provost Skene's House in Aberdeen or Pinkie House in Musselburgh we can see two opposing factors being conjoined: the realistic world with the fantastic, the rational and irrational, the seen and unseen. This thread runs through Scottish art. And as Duncan Macmillan has suggested, Peter Howson and Ken Currie have the same difficulties in reconciling their visions of individuality with the ideal as experienced by David Octavius Hill and David Wilkie.

And there is an interesting conjunction between art and literature, insofar as writers and artists seem to experience similar shifts in identity and perspective, apparent as a series of shared preoccupations and conjunctions, as in David Allan's and David Wilkie's visualisations of the sort of world Robert Burns depicted. Perhaps this notion meets, rather than collides, in the works of painters who also write, such as Alasdair Gray, or in the meeting of the urban social realism of John Byrne's plays in his paintings, or the way they all meet in Ian Hamilton Finlay's garden at Little Sparta.

Painters were and obviously still are aware of what was happening in literature; but I am suggesting something more than inspiration. I am suggesting a shared vision. For example, James Kelman and Ken Currie obviously share the same political and social concerns, and the ways in which these are depicted are not so different from the ways in which Henry Raeburn and John Galt, Horatio McCulloch and Sir Walter Scott, David Wilkie and Robert Burns, and William Johnstone and Hugh MacDiarmid occupied similar territories and expressed common concerns.

The Importance of Scott

Because his importance has been so continually and perniciously disregarded or underestimated, it is necessary to remind ourselves of Walter

Scott's literary standing, away from the perspective of the so-called Scottish Literary Renaissance of the 1930s, for whom he was little more than a convenient target.

This is from an ordinary and, for its time, perfectly decent literature primer, *English Literature from AD670 to 1832* by Stopford A. Brooke, written for university students and published in 1909:

> It was Walter Scott who raised the whole of the literature of the novel into one of the great influences that bear on human life. Men are still alive who remember the wonder and delight with which *Waverley* (1814) was welcomed. The swiftness of work combined with vast diligence which belongs to very great genius belonged to him. *Guy Mannering* was written in six weeks, and the *Bride of Lammermuir*, as great in fateful pathos as *Romeo and Juliet*, but more solemn, was done in a fortnight . . . . His national tales – and his own country was his best inspiration – are written with such love for the characters and the scenes, that we feel his living joy and love underneath each of the stories as a completing charm, as a spirit that enchants the whole . . . . In the vivid portraiture and dramatic reality of such tales as *Old Mortality* and *Quentin Durward* he created the historical novel. 'All is great,' said Goethe, speaking of one of these historical tales, 'in the Waverley Novels; material, effect, characterisation, execution.'

Of course, Scott's work is so varied that different aspects were reflected by separate painters, who may not necessarily be contemporary with Scott but who would certainly have been aware of his influence. McCulloch's paintings of Glencoe or Loch Lomond could fall into Scott's national and romantic aspect, and Scott's friendship with the Rev. John Thomson of Duddingston clearly influenced the latter's paintings. Duncan Macmillan sees Thomson's paintings as 'closest to a pictorial expression of Scott's own interpretation of landscape'.[34] Like Turner and Nasmyth, Thomson illustrated Scott's work.

That Scott's work influenced contemporary Scottish painters is obvious, not only from the way they approached their subjects, but perhaps from the fact that they approached these subjects at all. And it is not just the inventor of 'Caledonia stern and wild' who appealed to painters. The historical Scott can be found in John Pettie's work, in paintings such as *The Drumhead Courtmartial* and *The Disgrace of Cardinal Wolseley*, whereas the social aspects of Scott can be found in the paintings of Pettie's friend, Sir William Quiller Orchardson, from *Her First Dance* to *Marriage de Convenience*.

34. Duncan Macmillan, *Scottish Art 1460–1990*.

Kailyard and after

George Douglas Brown's *The House with the Green Shutters*, published in 1901, is often seen simply as a riposte to the Kailyard school. But this is to ignore the importance of other discoveries that were taking place in the arts throughout Scotland. This was a time when major components in the establishment of the twentieth century's idea of Scottish identity were being assembled. In 1901, for example, Gavin Greig and the Rev. James Duncan began collecting folk songs in Aberdeenshire. In architecture the search for a Scottish vernacular form of expression, begun by Rowand Anderson, reached what many consider to be its apogee with the building of Charles Rennie Mackintosh's Glasgow School of Art, the first stage of which began in 1901. And it was at the Glasgow International Exhibition of 1901 that the extraordinary collective known as the Glasgow Boys first exhibited as a group. The Glasgow Boys established the direction and in many ways the subject matter of Scottish painting for the rest of the century, taking painting out of the studio and democratising art by having as much of a love affair with Scottish landscape and the rural population as any writer.

Nonetheless, Brown's novel was certainly an attack on the Kailyard, using the fictional small-town location of Barbie as a reflection of Ayrshire and, by association, of rural Scotland as a whole. Its impact was so plain that by the time the leading exponent of the genre, J. M. Barrie, died in 1937, he was an isolated figure in Scottish literature. The novel has a cast list of worthy Kailyard-type characters, from the lad o' pairts to the returning prodigal, but Brown's treatment is entirely different. He turns their familiarity on its head by placing corruption at the heart of his story. Not only is each character corrupt at heart, but each is a mass of resentment and self-pity, spite and envy. Running alongside them are the 'bodies', the plain people of Barbie, whose gossip and innuendo resounds through the tale like a Greek chorus. Above and through them all strides John Gourlay, a man who is as sure of his own destiny as he is of his Calvinistic paternal authority, a feature Brown used to its full symbolic and psychological potential. Stevenson had used the same device in *Weir of Hermiston* and Lewis Grassic Gibbon would repeat it, this time with a daughter at the centre, in *Sunset Song*.

Brown's attack on Kailyard values is relentless, marred perhaps for contemporary readers by the voice of an omnipotent author, who not only comments on his characters, but on Scottish failings generally. The novel's importance stems from the fact that Brown used the trappings of the Kailyard novelists to damn them, not only to expose their relentless escapism but to offer an alternative that used the same devices in what Ian Campbell calls 'triumphant imitation'.[35]

35. Quoted in David Daiches (ed.), *The New Companion to Scottish Culture*.

However, the term Kailyard means more than the collective works of
J. M. Barrie, S. R. Crockett and Ian Maclaren. Nor did the genre wither
with Brown's publication. Rather, the phrase has come to imply a certain
conjunction of opposites; for as well as describing a sentimentalised view
of rural Scotland, often in favour of the harsher realities of urban experience, the term now embraces those of other disciplines who perpetuate
the relentlessly placid view from a manse window. Men have a dominant
role in the Kailyard; women are, at best, supportive. There are few
extremes, except of sickness and sentiment. The characters are perpetually self-reliant and their virtues are those which underline or enhance
the common good. There is a narrow range of plots and emotion. The
central point, in fact probably the only point, of connection between the
Kailyard novelists is the fact that they fulfilled a market need. They spot-
ted a niche and supplied the demand they created. Others, such as Harry
Lauder, have subsequently sought to do the same.

That Sir Harry Lauder was a successful entertainer is beyond doubt.
He not only earned a lot of money but also left a legacy of songs that are
sung and enjoyed to the present day. Yet his stage props and costume
fostered the notion that Scotland is a country of tartan-swathed, verti-
cally challenged, bandy-legged men, continually needing the support of
a walking stick. He left behind an image that has come to represent
Scotland across the world. Purists are appalled; and though there have
always been those who have defended Lauder, or at least tried to put him
into the context he created, usually in terms of his popularity and
wealth, the question remains: why did we accept Lauder's stage costume
as our own?

Lauder came in a package he carefully fostered: the kilt and walking
stick as indistinguishable from the songs he sang as the words or tune. It's
understandable that we should be seen in the way he presented himself,
especially since he consciously adopted an ambassadorial role. But the
mystery of why we should accept it can, to my mind, only be explained in
terms of the Kailyard and our lack of identity, terms in which Lauder
explained himself. 'I stand for nationality and the simple human things
which are its roots,' he said.

'Millions of people who have never seen, and never will see, Scotland
have experienced affection for the country whose homelier characteristics are so deliciously exaggerated in this man,' wrote H. V. Morton after
encountering Lauder in Aberdeen in the late 1920s, arrayed in Glengarry
bonnet, MacLeod tartan kilt and Inverness cape. 'Lauder's genius is a
thing apart,' he said; the 'grotesque little "Highlander" with a deformed
yellow walking-stick' rarely says anything witty, but

> his personal magnetism is irresistible. How masterly is his trick suddenly
> of breaking off in the middle of a song to treat his audience to a brief

confidential talk. The Scots expression and the Doric are the ideal medium for quiet little heart-to-heart chats; and when Harry Lauder talks between songs it is never possible to believe that he thought it all out deliberately beforehand.

He will sing a rollicking song like 'Roamin' in the Gloamin'' or 'Stop yer Ticklin', Jock', and when he has carried his audience with him, and they are ready to go on in that mood indefinitely, he will switch over to pathos. He is too clever to do it abruptly; but watch how he will concentrate his effect on one good laugh quickly followed with another, funny but with a serious side to it; and then, suddenly, startlingly, and with a simplicity and a sincerity impossible to question, he is telling some story of the war. There is not a sound in the theatre. The little Scotsman stands in the full flare of the footlights speaking words which come straight from his heart. Every word rings true. In two minutes he has carried hundreds of men and women of different types and mentalities to the opposite poles of emotion. There is real feeling in the theatre now; an emotion which few great actors can command. Something essentially honest, good, pure, and simple in the little Scotsman is speaking to those same qualities in his fellow-men. Then he switches back to laughter! All he has to do is to – smile! Smiles answer him everywhere! The band strikes up, and once more he is roamin' in the gloamin' – amazing little man! The greatest compliment the world pays him is the fact that he is the only comedian who is permitted to be serious whenever he feels like it.[36]

Lauder was the Kailyard made flesh. His technique and intentions were essentially those of a Kailyard novelist. Morton describes him as a comedian, though it is as a singer and songwriter, if not as an icon, that his reputation has survived.

Others have followed where Lauder led, but there are also those whose life, works, or both were caught in his slipstream. Scott Skinner is one, Marjory Kennedy-Fraser another, together with a host of music-hall artists who deliberately courted Lauder's clients. Others who may not have had the same intentions nevertheless found their works used and exploited. It's a practice that Scotland has almost raised to an art form: converting works for purposes for which they were never intended. It's a practice in which Robert Burns is the flesh made word.

Scott Skinner followed Lauder's lead. Tartaned and whiskered, he also exported a brand of Scotland and Scottish music that is still played today. Though his best-known tune is *The Bonny Lass o' Bon Accord*, 'as a composer Skinner is at his best in the old traditional forms of reel and strathspey, which require that special fire and energy in bowing so peculiar to

36. H. V. Morton, *In Search of Scotland*.

Scotland, but which depends, not upon the bow to rise from the string as in classical music, but on maintaining close contact with it'.[37]

The role played by the current folk revival in preserving and fostering the Scots language, and providing a focus for our national identity, has yet to be properly assessed. The breakthrough in terms of popularity came in the 1960s, but its origins are seen in terms of individuals rather than dates. Novelty tunes, pieces like *The Four-Poster Bed* or *The Hen's March To The Midden* were popular, but today these tunes are rarely heard, and unaccompanied singers are the exception.

Many younger singers present Scots songs in a strange and difficult way, adapting them into an uncomfortable rhythm to fit the accompaniment, which often means the songs are sung in reel or jig time; this presents folk song with a similar problem to art song – the words are unintelligible, rendered into sound, emasculated to fit the music.

But the most obvious difference that anyone absent from the folk scene for, say, ten years, would find today is the great difference in instrumentalists, both in terms of the range of instruments available and in the skill of the players, especially younger players, many of whom have virtuosic qualities and are capable of expanding and inventing, of working within the tradition and of using their art as a springboard. It is this rise in instrumentalism that has given Scott Skinner's music something of a revival.

Not so Marjory Kennedy-Fraser. According to Hamish Henderson,

> When Mrs Kennedy-Fraser arrived on the folk scene, in the early years of [the twentieth] century, she found that the Irish had got in ahead of her with a really profitable Celtic Twilight racket, which was fast ripening into a boom. It says much for her artistic virtuosity as well as her business acumen that by the time she rested from her labours, for every person in Muswell Hill or South Kensington who associated fairy-knolls and lovelorn cattle-croons with Killarney, Donegal or Ballybunion, there were at least ten who associated these same phenomena with the misty islands of the Highlands. However, the cultural price was heavy – nothing less than the distortion of an entire folk-tradition.[38]

In *A Short History of Scotland* (1929), George Malcolm Thomson refers to Mrs Kennedy-Fraser's discovery 'of an exquisite folk-poetry and folk-music among the Gaelic-speaking fisherfolk of Eriskay and other Hebridean islands: it is one of the most romantic and fortunate accidents in modern history that this small and lively world yielded up its treasure before it passed away'. Rait and Pryde in *Scotland* (1934) wrote of

37. John Purser, *Scotland's Music*.
38. Hamish Henderson, *Alias MacAlias*.

the Kennedy-Fraser collection: 'Not only is it clear that the essentials of the originals are generally preserved and that the alterations and additions are improvements; it is even doubtful if in many cases, anything would have survived without the interested labours of these collectors.'

These are contemporary accounts, the sort of patronage that presupposes working people are incapable of producing anything which can be appreciated, learned from, or even found interesting by those with more money, and therefore what exists must be on its last legs and needs to be rescued in the nick of time. Folk song and folk poetry, indeed the folk arts in general, are well used to such insubstantiated malarkey, which is almost invariably proven wrong by time; there are other versions from other singers, separate pieces which occur as far away as Cape Breton or Australia and have been preserved because people found them beautiful.

Morag MacLeod, writing in 1983, points out that 'there is not one of the songs in her [Marjory Kennedy-Fraser's] collection which cannot be recorded in its original form to this day, from people who may or may not have heard her. Not only the tunes – especially the rhythms, tempi and placings of stress – were changed but the words were "improved" by her collaborator, the Rev. Kenneth Macleod.'[39]

The improvements seem to rest upon gentility. Texts were changed, says Morag MacLeod, 'merely to corroborate the "noble savage" idea that was so trendy at that time'. But they brought other alterations in their wake. The piano was used as an accompanying instrument, choirs used vocal harmonies which were completely new to Gaelic song, singers had their voices trained, and the annual National Mod encouraged competition: 'Since few or no Gaels were musically literate, the music for these competitions was written by outsiders, and the performances were judged by outsiders . . . . Scales and rhythms were adapted to the well-tempered, easily assimilated Western European norm. They probably decided that deviations from these were just native errors,' MacLeod suggests. Which puts a new perspective on what was rescued and what was nearly lost, or irremediably altered through bowdlerisation.

Perhaps because he is motivated by less of a direct cultural imperative, John Purser calls for reasoned argument: 'To consider her contribution fairly, it has to be understood in the cultural climate of the day and given the same courtesy that is finally being shown to MacPherson (whose handling of his raw material is not dissimilar) of acknowledging that a new interest in Gaelic material was fostered by her efforts.' While asserting that she 'is certainly not blameless on the musical front,' he nevertheless concludes, 'Taking her songs as art songs, without any pretensions to

---

39. Morag MacLeod, 'The Folk Revival in Gaelic Song,' in Ailie Munro, *The Folk Music Revival in Scotland.*

authenticity, then she can be claimed to have produced some very fine work'.[40]

The one thing made obvious by John Purser's book is that the study of Scottish music is as specialised as with any other country; and even though ours has received unjustly scant attention, it is an area where even well-intentioned enthusiasts tread at their peril. Since the publication of *Scotland's Music*, and the broadcasting of the radio series that accompanied the book, a wonderfully diverse and exciting range of composers, whose voices were mysteriously but collectively silenced, have found new and receptive audiences through concerts, broadcasts and recordings. Not so long ago, one could have been forgiven for assuming that Scotland had produced no composers of worth. Our architecture, art and literature have been recognised, though not without some difficulties along the way. They have perhaps received more attention recently, but no discipline, or its study, has been so comprehensively marginalised as the work of Scotland's composers and musicologists, perhaps through ignorance, perhaps by deliberate neglect. What is now needed is what will surely happen; others will follow where Purser has led.

Scottish composers were not immune from the changes that affected the other arts, nor were they immunised against the movements that were sweeping Europe. Since there was no music academy in Scotland, musicians had to go to London or the Continent for their higher musical education. Yet in the early twentieth century, a group of Scottish composers succeeded in mastering the expanding harmonic landscape which was developing across Europe. Sir Alexander Mackenzie and Sir John Blackwood McEwen, along with other Scottish composers such as William Wallace, 'first British exponent of the symphonic poem', and Hamish MacCunn, lived and worked in London; indeed, Mackenzie and McEwen were successive principals of the Royal Academy of Music, where MacCunn and Wallace also taught.

Music in Scotland was a part-time activity and Scottish professional musicians were forced to work away from home. But the composers seemed to catch the feeling of expansion, of using nationalism as a springboard, that was abroad at the time. Their titles alone indicate a nationalist commitment which is entirely in keeping with the mood of the times, not only in Scotland but across Europe.

Mackenzie dedicated his second *Scotch Rhapsody* to one of Wagner's patrons, Madam Jessie Hildebrand, in 1881; and after hearing the same piece Edvard Grieg not only reasserted his Scottish ancestry, of which he was extremely proud, but was anxious to 'assert an affinity between Norwegian and Scottish traditional music which Mackenzie was not willing

40. Purser, *op. cit.*

to share'. Mackenzie followed his violin concerto with *Pibroch*, a suite for violin and orchestra, written for and frequently performed by Sarasate; his piano concerto, entitled *The Scottish Concerto*, was premiered by Paderewski in 1897. And among the titles of works by his near contemporary, Sir John Blackwood McEwen, are *Under Northern Skies*, *A Solway Symphony* and *Hills o' Heather*. These works are more than lonely evocations of a faraway home; though *Pibroch* is something of a misnomer, since it bears little resemblance to the *ceol mor*, the 'big music' often considered to be the classical music of the bagpipes, as opposed to *ceol beag*, dance music such as jigs, strathspeys and reels.

Scots still sing in all three of our languages, Scots, Gaelic and English; the latter, though regarded as the dominant spoken language, is least favoured in song, with the obvious exception of art song. 'From an early date music from Scotland seems to have had a clear identity,' says John Purser, quoting a predilection for melodic and harmonic patterns based on chords a tone apart, known as a double tonic, and the Scottish Snap, which uses dotted rhythms. And traditional Scottish music has different regional styles of playing, which are as identifiable as regional accents. Just as we can easily identify someone from Glasgow or Aberdeenshire by their accents, so a piper's or a fiddler's style will invariably express their origins, at least indicating where they were taught and often by whom.

In his follow-up to *Scottish Journey*, *Scott and Scotland*, published in 1936, Muir reckoned Scots were doomed to feel in Scots and think in English. 'The Curse of Scotland,' he said, 'is the lack of a whole language, which finally means the lack of a whole mind.' The great Scots literary tradition, he asserted, had sunk to the status of dialect, irresponsible and irremediably immature, for 'dialect is to a homogenous language what the babbling of children is to the speech of grown men and women'.

Wholeness, singleness and maturity were, in Muir's eyes, superior and desirable indicators of national and cultural status. But language does not work this way, nor do people think in this way. As Roderick Watson has noted,[41] Muir's desire for homogenous language takes us straight to the Victorian Empire builders and the cultural oppression that we have recently tried to unyoke. It also flies in the face of the cultural resurgence that was sweeping Scotland at the time, a movement which refused to look back to a romanticised past.

41. Roderick Watson, *The Literature of Scotland*.

2

A Mad God's Dream

'The night tinkles like ice in glasses.
Leaves are glued to the pavement with frost.
The brown air fumes at the shop windows,
Tries the doors, and sidles past.'

NORMAN MACCAIG, 'November Night, Edinburgh'

That First Half-Blind Glimpse

Karel Čapek, who came to Edinburgh to visit his friend Edwin Muir,
thought it

the finest city in the world . . . stonily grey and strange of aspect . . . . Where
in other cities a river flows, there a railway runs; on one side is the old town,
on the other side the new one; with streets wider than anywhere else, every
vista showing a statue or a church; and in the old town the houses are
appallingly high . . . and the washing is flaunted upon clothes-lines above
the street like the flags of all nations . . . and there are dirty red-headed children in the streets . . . and strange little streets, wynds or closes . . . and fat
dishevelled old women . . . . What a funny thing it is to see old houses here
with chimneys on the gable, apparently instead of towers . . . . Such a thing
exists nowhere in the world except at Edinburgh. And the city is situated on
hills; you are hurrying along somewhere or another, and all at once
beneath your feet you have a deep green chasm with a fine river below; you
are taking a walk and all of a sudden there is another street located on a
bridge above your head, as at Genoa; you are taking a walk, and you reach
a perfectly circular space, as at Paris. The whole time there is something for
you to be surprised at.[1]

1. Karel Čapek, *Letters From England.*

Muir would have agreed. 'That first half-blind glimpse of Edinburgh happened by chance to catch one thing about it which anyone accustomed to cities would probably not have seen: that it is a city of extraordinary and sordid contrasts,' he wrote in *Scottish Journey*, describing the Canongate as 'a mouldering and obnoxious ruin' where people stand or sit on the pavement in groups, with their feet out in the causeway. The Princes Street crowd are never found in the Canongate, nor are the Canongate crowd ever on Princes Street. 'The entire existence of Edinburgh as a respectable bourgeois city depends on that fact.'[2]

The idea of Edinburgh as a single entity that comprises two separately defined entities, which are also Edinburgh, haunted Muir, as it haunted Stevenson, and it has affected all its writers from Robert Ferguson to Muriel Spark. For Muir the duality is not only physical, social, political and economic. It is also emotional and, especially, sexual. Muir's earliest specific memory is of coming from Orkney at fourteen years of age and seeing a statue of a naked woman inside a building. 'Two dirty boys of about my own age were standing sniggering in front of it and glancing every now and then at a particular point on it.' They left 'a great black thumb-mark on one of the breasts of the statue'. His other memories are 'plunged in complete oblivion'.[3]

Princes Street was a dividing line, a place where one Edinburgh could view the other. It was also a place where the separate Edinburghs could be entered, though 'the wholesale invasion of Princes Street by the poor would be felt not only as an offence against good taste, but a blasphemy'.[4] Unemployed hunger marchers who slept in Princes Street Gardens caused great indignation.

Edinburgh's divisions are so explicit that people from one class do not invade another's territory. There is nothing discreet about this division. There is a discernible difference between Princes Street and Leith Street and its continuation into Leith Walk, where one finds ice-cream parlours and fish-and-chip bars and pubs instead of cosy tea-rooms and hotel lounges. Muir observes that

> At one point the two different streams of promenaders are brought within a few yards of each other; yet they scarcely ever mingle, so strong is the sense of social distinction bred by city life. They turn back when they reach this invisible barrier, apparently without thought or desire, as if they were stalking in a dream; and if, through necessity or whim, an

2. Edwin Muir, *Scottish Journey*.
3. *Ibid.*
4. *Ibid.*

occasional pedestrian should trespass for a little on enemy ground, he is soon frightened and scurries back as fast as he can.[5]

Prostitutes alone can cross this division. They live in the poorer districts, but their beat is Princes Street. Muir talks of prostitutes getting up from a fight in Leith Street and dusting themselves down before walking into Princes Street: 'they might almost have been going to an important conference or to church'.[6]

Scottish Journey was written at a time when our continuing identity crisis was being addressed and when, simultaneously, a number of national and maybe even international preconceptions, especially about Glasgow and Edinburgh, were being fostered. And Muir seems almost to be aware of this, saving the best descriptive writing for the feeling of louche abandon he finds in Scottish streets. The main difference between Scottish streets and those of any other country appears to be the number of drunks. 'During a fortnight's stay in Edinburgh I did not get through a single evening without seeing at least one example of outrageous or helpless drunkenness, and I had spent more than two years in London without coming across more than four or five.' Drunks give Scottish streets an atmosphere of their own, he says. The Scots give the impression of drinking more than others because of 'the abundant signs of public drunkenness that one finds in such towns as Edinburgh and Glasgow and even in small country towns on a Saturday night'. The explanation, Muir reckoned, lay in the way they drank, that Scots drink spasmodically and intensely, whereas the English do not: 'The drinking habits of the Scots, like their dances, are far wilder than those of the English.'

What is much more interesting is the way one conducts oneself when drunk, the distinctions class produces. There are as many drunks on Princes Street as Leith Walk, but drunkenness on Princes Street is quiet and genteel,

> shown in a trifling unsteadiness of gait or a surprising affability of aspect by which the middle-class Edinburgh man manages to suggest that he is somehow upholding something or other which distinguishes him from the working classes. He is helped in this purpose by certain benevolent external circumstances, however, such as that the whisky sold in Princes Street is better than the whisky one buys in Leith Walk, and that it is always easy to get a taxi in Princes Street after ten o'clock. By means of these discreet ambulances the unconscious and semi-conscious are inconspicuously removed. In Leith Walk they lie about the pavement until their friends or the police laboriously lead them away.[7]

5. *Ibid.*
6. *Ibid.*
7. *Ibid.*

Muir was a perpetual outsider. It was a position he maintained both intellectually and physically, living as he did for long periods away from Scotland, in Prague and Dresden, London and Rome. It is something continually found in his work, a position which he articulated in *Scott and Scotland*, when he raised personal concerns to a national level with his aforementioned statement that Scots were doomed to feel in Scots and think in English. Muir wrote verses in English while the literary movement in Scotland was writing in Scots; he translated Kafka and other European writers at a time when intellectual opinion found American literature exciting. Every page of *Scottish Journey* lays testament to Muir's need to discover himself, to belong, to find himself part of something larger than himself. Nowhere is he more an outsider than in the Edinburgh streets and tea-rooms, a city whose divisions were so obvious he felt he need do little more than name them for the implications to be digested.

The street life Muir imagined is now more obvious in Glasgow than Edinburgh. Princes Street is like any high street. National and multinational stores occupy prime positions. The Canongate is perpetually filled with tourists. Backpackers roam around mesmerised, guidebooks in hand, staring upward. Edinburgh's prostitutes are in the massage and sauna parlours, which have spread across the town and advertise openly in the newspapers. Glasgow's prostitutes are on the streets.

According to a Lonely Planet guide – a publication which is said to 'bestow a kind of backpackers' nationhood on countries around the globe' – Edinburgh is recognised as one of the world's most beautiful cities, with a world-class city centre. 'The flip-side to the gloss, however, is the grim reality of life in the bleak council housing estates surrounding the city, the thriving drug scene and a distressing Aids problem.'[8]

> Embro my ain, ye are aye meant
> tae be a city o middle-class douceness
>   mediocrity
>   bourgeois obtuseness
> but
>   (listen tae what I'm tellin ye!)
>   The ithir nicht
> in the Morninside chippie
> I was confrontit by nae fewer than ten
>   o the reuchest and the teuchest
>   o yer haurdest haurd haurd men
>   – *and (O Gode) hou I wished I was in Glasgow!*[9]

8. *Herald*, 9 April 1999.
9. Donald Campbell, 'Betrayal in Morninside', in *Murals*, 1975.

Long-winded and Sanguine Arguments

Muir saw Edinburgh as a place history had abandoned.

> In Edinburgh, where the past is so strong, and the memory of Scottish his-
> tory is perpetually reminding you, if you are a Scotsman, that this was once
> a capital, the half-meaninglessness of Scottish life overwhelms you more
> strongly than anywhere else. The Scots have always been an unhappy
> people; their history is a varying record of heroism, treachery, persistent
> bloodshed, perpetual feuds and long-winded and sanguine arguments . . .
> they were once discontentedly unhappy, and they are now, at least the
> better off of them, almost contentedly so. And this acceptance of the sordid
> third or fourth best, imported from every side, is what oppresses one so
> much as one walks down their streets.[10]

The originality of Muir's approach can be realised by comparing his
observations with other contemporary accounts. In his introduction to *In
Search of Scotland*, first published in 1929, H. V. Morton claims one can
'look in vain for intimate, personal records of journeys round Scotland'.
Muir's stated intention, copied by those who followed his lead, was to
present a picture of Scotland that Morton reckoned had not been
painted since the eighteenth century: largely anecdotal, aimed at the
new car-owning traveller and packed with descriptive passages which owe
much to the burgeoning cinema industry and radio journalism.

But to understand the Scottish identity crisis as it appears today, with its
conglomerate of symbols and surfeit of symbolism, it is necessary to
understand how our most positive characteristics have been repressed
and subsumed into a larger identity within which they were often barely
accorded any status at all. So-called expressions of Scottish identity are
often cruel misrepresentations of actual Scottish life, so that authentic
expression has been absent from the cultural life of the nation.

Figures such as Robert Burns and Sir Walter Scott presented us with
what is immediately recognisable as an authentic view of ourselves, not
only because of the quality of their work, but also because of the ways in
which their works have been interpreted and reinterpreted. In Scott's
case, of course, the issue is confused by the fact that, as well as presenting
an authentic view of Scotland, he also did the opposite. But one need not
necessarily obliterate the other, since most of us simultaneously hold
contradictory opinions.

The main point is authenticity. The works of Burns and Scott stem from
and are often part of an indigenous, native tradition. The painters and

10. Edwin Muir, *op. cit.*

musicians who were influenced by Burns and Scott, and the architects who were influenced by the climate these works created, often encountered authentic expressions of Scottish national and cultural life, expressions which have not been filtered through the mists of a Celtic twilight.

Some other Scottish arts and art forms are rootless, or have absorbed influences other than our own, and while this can be perfectly acceptable, such a trend can also present a diversion. This does not necessarily imply a lack of confidence in the native culture, for often these works are recognisably Scottish. It is simply artists doing what they have always done – absorbing influences that appeal to them. But whereas artists from other countries could approach these movements with the weight of a tradition behind them, Scots could not; especially in the so-called Scottish Renaissance of the 1930s, when writers, painters and architects sought to give their works a modernist as well as a Scottish dimension, removed from the sentimentality and parochialism of popular culture.

MacDiarmid continually asserted the need to determine the activities that define Scottish character and to place them at the centre of a reinvigorated Scottish cultural life. Moreover, he argued that these practical things at which the Scots excelled – mostly manufacturing bases, which now are missing or have been greatly reduced – should provide the springboard into an authentic, native Scottish art. Muir is firmly in this tradition. He took MacDiarmid's advice and was prepared to look at Edinburgh and the rest of the country as it was, rather than at the image; and he encouraged others to do the same.

In his Introduction to *The Scottish Thirties*, written in January 1987, Charles McKean remarks on the similarities between the 1930s and the 1980s, an implication which is repeated, however tacitly, throughout the text. The 1930s, he says, was a time when Scotland moved visibly from the old to the new:

> New materials and structures led to new architectures appropriate for the programmes of social welfare, of housing, and of state intervention in the economy, with which the country intended to tackle possibly the worst economic, overcrowding, and health record in Europe . . . . Books, journals and interviews conveyed belief in an ever-improving future, and a determination to achieve it in Scotland. They had a fervour that nowadays is only found in Japan. The Scots of the Thirties – even in the heat of the 'renaissance' – did not reject the past; neither were they going to use it as a convenient retreat from the present. They used that cultural legacy to create a future that was as modern and as adventurous as could be found in Europe – but nonetheless Scottish.[11]

11. Charles McKean, *The Scottish Thirties*.

Through it all Edinburgh appears as itself and, then as now, such improvements or changes to the fabric were largely cosmetic. There were obviously new structures for new activities such as cinemas and dance halls, which many found vulgar and unwelcome, even though these changes altered the basic fabric of the city only slightly, since, in the main, the new bungalows and factories, hotels, schools and offices were confined to the burgeoning suburbs. The major change to the city centre was the introduction of night architecture, when buildings such as cinemas were transformed into palaces of light in the evening, with neon signs and electric illumination on the posters, hoardings and the buildings themselves.

Her Face to the Wall

Edinburgh Old Town is unique, a city virtually without streets – two great spaces and a hundred wynds and closes. Muir saw the city as 'a very big and inefficiently yet strictly run house', and this is the flavour which most accurately seems to match Edinburgh today, where even the New Town is now divided. Georgian houses have been turned into flats or hotels. Yet Moray McLaren recalls a time when doors were opened by a maid, when the family had domestic prayers and the servants entered in reverse order of seniority, with the butler at the rear.

My mother began her working life as a domestic servant. In January 1926 she went into service with Mr Francis R. Sim, a banker, and his wife Katherine at 1 Randolph Place, Edinburgh. She was contracted until Christmas. On her first day the housekeeper told her to turn her face to the wall if she passed a member of the family in any part of the house. There were household prayers every morning and she was expected to attend the Sunday-morning church service. When the housekeeper found an edition of Robert Burns's poems in my mother's room, she confiscated and then burned it, telling my mother she was lucky not to be reported. Mr Sim would immediately dismiss anyone found with such a book in their possession.

Edinburgh grew down the High Street from the Castle, bursting out of its medieval boundaries as far as Holyrood House in the eighteenth century. Then they drained the Nor' Loch, which covered what is now Waverley Station, Princes Street Gardens and the Mound, whose trout had been prized and where, according to the *Collins Encyclopaedia of Scotland*, women whose behaviour offended public morality were 'dookit twa times frae the pillar and stule be the lochside'. Witches were also dookit before being strangled and burned on Castlehill.

The Mound was built from the earth dug from the New Town foundations; and the North Bridge crossed the eastern edge of the Nor' Loch into what became the 'New Streets and Squares extended for His ancient

Capital of North Britain' in James Craig's first New Town plan of 1767, dedicated 'To His Sacred Majesty George III, the Munificent Patron of Every Polite and Liberal Art'. Edinburgh New Town is one of the finest planned urban quarters in Europe and the largest Georgian city development in the world, covering an area of about 1 square mile with over 11,000 listed properties. It is an exemplification of Classicism, a deliberately constructed grid of carefully planned, elegant streets and houses whose very spirit rises in direct opposition to the Old Town, an area described by the antiquarian Robert Chambers in *Traditions of Edinburgh* as 'a picturesque, odorous, inconvenient, old-fashioned town of about 70,000 inhabitants', a place which for more than 250 years had been confined by the Flodden Wall.

The New Town was built in two stages. The first followed Craig's prize-winning plan, consisting of three streets – George Street, Queen Street and Princes Street – running east to west, with the lesser Rose and Thistle Streets, little more than lanes, in between. St Andrew and Charlotte Squares balanced the design at either end. Charlotte Square is called St George's Square on Craig's plan. The second phase was a staggered development to the north of the first, running downhill towards the Water of Leith. The scheme, designed by Robert Reid and William Sibald, focuses on Great King Street, terminating in Drummond Place and William Playfair's Royal Circus. There were later extensions into the twelve-sided Moray Place by James Gillespie Graham at one end and around Calton Hill at the other.

Simultaneously they form not two, but three separate Edinburghs, the Old Town, the New Town and the Capital, the place where public buildings of national importance are sited.

The Royal Institution Under Construction

Edinburgh's most obvious building of national importance, apart of course from the Castle, is William Henry Playfair's Royal Scottish Academy (1834) at the foot of the Mound, a capital project and therefore sited in Edinburgh.

Playfair is Edinburgh's pre-eminent designer of public buildings. His work covers the Mound. As well as the Royal Scottish Academy, he also designed the neighbouring National Galleries of Scotland, both at the foot of the brae, as well as the Free Kirk's dour and Gothic New College and Assembly Hall at the head.

The building of the RSA was painted by Alexander Nasmyth. *Edinburgh From Princes Street with the Royal Institution under Construction* shows the view along Princes Street looking east, with what was then called the Royal Institution being built upon the New Town excavations. In common with building sites everywhere, a small crowd has gathered to the left of the picture to admire the work. A small boy points towards the building where William Playfair, in black hat and coat, is directing operations. Around them, Edinburgh goes about its business, generally unconcerned, though the mood of the picture is far from apathetic; rather the inhabitants appear to be accepting the city's rightful place in the world. The construction is in the foreground, in a complex corner to the right beside the drained Nor' Loch. One of the great Classical pillars is being lowered into place, while another is being shaped on the ground. And in the background is the city itself, the Old Town harmoniously merging with the New, existing together in a communally supportive union which embraces society's other oppositions – wealth and poverty, work and leisure.

The Enlightenment proposed that man's place within the order of nature was secured through the exercise of his proper gifts, and the Edinburgh New Town was the embodiment of this ideal. As Duncan Macmillan has pointed out,[12] the layout of human order had been the subject of other works, but here Nasmyth not only shows harmony with progress, but does so away from an idealised setting, rather showing man himself as part of his own creation, marvelling at and participating in Edinburgh's first specially constructed building devoted to art, and the most important building of its kind in Scotland – a capital project where national treasures will be displayed.

Completed in 1834, the Royal Scottish Academy has the National Gallery, designed in 1845, tucked behind it. The pair form Princes Street's most impressive structures, bringing stability and formality to the foot of the Mound. These buildings were the start of Edinburgh's love affair with public structures, an attitude that combines grandeur with generous statement.

The Scottish National Portrait Gallery opened in 1882 at 1 Queen Street, a red-sandstone, Venetian Gothic building, designed by Rowand Anderson. In its architecture and immediate interior it not only shows a concern for history, identity and improvement, but also declares its main commitment to the Victorian passion for displaying images of edifying and inspiring individuals. The new gallery was founded using a donation of £50,000 from John Richard Findlay, proprietor of the *Scotsman*. The portrait collection was originally transferred from the National Gallery of Scotland and included paintings such as Alexander Nasmyth's portrait of Robert Burns and Allan Ramsay's of David Hume. Others, such as Raeburn's portrait of Scott, have been bought and many more have been commissioned.

Rowand Anderson, who also designed Mount Stuart for the third

12. Duncan Macmillan, *Scottish Art 1460–1990*.

Marquis of Bute, was the central force in a revival which 'differed from the earlier in that it was based not upon pictures, but upon an accurate recording and measuring of Scots buildings; and leavened with medieval, French, Arts and Crafts and not a little baroque . . . . The focus was now upon the middle-ranking houses – neither baronial nor vernacular.'[13]

In the late nineteenth century the visionary town planner Patrick Geddes sought to reintegrate art and craft in his short-lived magazine *Evergreen*, a title borrowed from the Edinburgh publication by Allan Ramsay which aimed to preserve our linguistic identity after the Union of 1707. Geddes took his inspiration from Enlightenment Edinburgh. He believed cities could be studied in a way which was comparable to animal or insect communities and that, like them, human populations would change according to their density, and their access to air and light. He celebrated the workers and their dwellings, basing his new town-planning concept on what he found in Edinburgh, and his ideas radically altered much of the city-centre housing.

In 1886 Geddes founded the Edinburgh Social Union and began an ambitious renewal programme of housing redevelopment. The ESU took over and restored buildings, especially in Edinburgh's Old Town, which had fallen into a near disastrous state of decay since the New Town's arrival. Geddes pioneered the reoccupation of the Royal Mile by Edinburgh University's intelligentsia and promoted art as a necessary tool in the regeneration of society. This was art with a public dimension that could be harnessed to the service of the whole community. Murals were therefore especially important, and Geddes's ideas found a wonderful interpreter in Phoebe Traquair, the first woman member of the Royal Scottish Academy and an artist with an extraordinary range of skills. Her finest work can be seen in the Song School of St Mary's Cathedral Choir School and the Edinburgh Catholic Apostolic Church.

Writing of the architectural developments, Charles McKean cites Geddes and Anderson as

> the context within which Robert Lorimer, Charles Rennie Mackintosh and their followers flourished. They were probably influenced by the pioneering work of James Maclaren's 1879 Kirkton Cottages and farmhouses in Glenlyon, amongst the first buildings of the new generation of Anderson-inspired Scottishness to deploy the rational planning and simple massing from seventeenth-century Scotland.[14]

Mackintosh and Lorimer eventually went their separate ways. Mackintosh used seventeenth-century architecture as a springboard into

13. Charles McKean, The Scottishness of Scottish Architecture' in Paul H. Scott (ed.), *Scotland: A Concise Cultural History.*.
14. *Ibid.*

modernism. Lorimer continued to develop the ideals of the Arts and Crafts movement, being especially gifted in adapting them to the needs and necessities of the Scottish vernacular revival, and though his preoccupation went into decline, the vision never left him. Most of Lorimer's work was domestic and included restorations and alterations, often on national monuments such as Paisley Abbey and Dunblane Cathedral, work undertaken with Sir Rowand Anderson, or the replenishment of Dunrobin and Balmanno Castles. His standing can be gauged from the fact that he was awarded two of the most prestigious public commissions of his time: the Knights of the Thistle Chapel in St Giles's Cathedral and, more importantly, the Scottish National War Memorial Chapel in Edinburgh Castle, 'the fullest expression of the social and collaborative ideal of art'.[15]

The memorial sits on the north side of the Crown Square, on the site of the twelfth-century St Mary's Kirk. Figurative sculptures representing Valour, Justice, Peace, Mercy, Knowledge, Freedom, Truth and the Survival of the Spirit surround a subdued exterior. Inside, the names of about 100,000 dead are inscribed in Rolls of Honour and placed in a steel casket, which rests on a granite altar guarded by bronze angels.

We Have Asked the People of Scotland to Decide

The Royal Scottish Museum in Chambers Street was completed in 1861. The charming, almost passive exterior gives little indication of what lies within, a brilliant use of cast-iron pillars, timber balconies, arches and copious glazed roofs. By then a national style of public building had been established, but the interesting concordance of public exterior and inner statement maintained an aspect of Scottish architecture which was to achieve brilliant heights on the other side of the country at the turn of the century, a second architectural revival which turned away from urbanism.

The new Museum of Scotland is the latest capital project built to house exhibits. The purpose of such buildings creates a curious brief for any architect, insofar as the structure is clearly meant to be subservient to what it contains, but architects have willingly risen to the challenge. The competition to build the new museum was won in 1991 by Gordon Benson and Alan Forsyth.

'By the mid-1980s,' writes Alexander Linklater,

the idea of a new museum for Scotland had become something with almost no contemporary equivalent in the world. The basic notion of a national

15. Duncan Macmillan, 'Scottish Art' in Paul H. Scott (ed.), *Scotland: A Concise Cultural History*.

museum – something a small country holds up to the world as evidence of
historical prowess – essentially belongs to the nineteenth century. Yet here,
at the end of the twentieth, is an idea of a building which will . . . 'tell the
story of this nation'. It is a museum which must theorise a Scottish identity
. . . . It may well be that certain infamous Scottish shibboleths – romantic
disappointment, glorious defeatism, anti-English resentments – are actually
being resolved into something level-headed and open-hearted. The purpose of the museum may truly be to psychoanalyse pale Scotia's way out of
historical neurosis.[16]

What has been created is a building for artefacts whose purpose is to
establish and define our identity. Almost as a by-product, it tells us who we
are, informs us of our past, bringing together the multi-faceted aspects of
ourselves, our country and the places we inhabit. It would have been
impossible even to conceive of a structure such as the Museum of
Scotland without addressing the question of Scottish identity, and though
the building has obvious influences and internal references, these are
mostly achieved within a Scottish context.

Exhibits range from a fossil estimated to be 3300 million years old to
something that could have been manufactured yesterday. There is no
consecutive story, nor even an implicit message. Yet most of the museum
gives an impression of identity, or at least provides a communal sense of
identification. The items are not arranged chronologically, but grouped
in themes, which gives little sense of continuity, the visitors progressing
through a series of cycles where the themes of human activity are delin-
eated and explained.

Nothing is displayed in isolation; the burgeoning Industrial Revolution is
shown in conjunction with agrarian subsistence; the Reformation is paired
with church carvings; we hear as well as see the clarsach; and Jacobite
memorials are twinned with Georgian Edinburgh. But the museum's most
significant display of matching conflicts is on the fifth floor, which is
devoted to the twentieth century. Here none of the earlier thought, care
and concern is evident. The guidebook simply announces that 'we have
asked the people of Scotland to decide what should be displayed'.

So if a contributor does not suggest an object, that aspect of the twentieth century is not covered. How a museum can justify the abdication of
responsibility for the artefacts it displays is never explained – although
the resulting lack of cohesion may well come to represent Scotland in the
twentieth century. There is no attempt to include significant objects of
the last century and, because the slant is personal, the overall effect is a
lack of purpose or even reason. The objects have little or no significance

16. *Herald*, 28 November 1998.

to anyone but the giver, with the possible exception of Eric Linklater's tin hat – since were it not for the tin hat Eric Linklater would have written no novels, nor, presumably, would his grandson Alexander have written about the museum.

The floor has all the identity and cohesion of a bazaar, where individuals have been asked to set out their stalls. There is an inbuilt lack of permanence. Exhibits will, presumably, have to change as exhibitors die or fall out of fashion. Even the guidebook is embarrassed: 'Washing machines and Biro pens have affected the lives of most of us, but many of the objects have a very personal meaning, for example, the organ donor card and a grandmother's perfume. The material is divided into areas covering aspects of life at home and at work, at war and at leisure. You will find not only the objects themselves, but also the contributors' reasons for suggesting them.'

It could be argued there is a greater need for Scotland in the twentieth century to be explained than at any other time. It has been better and more diversely documented; there were two World Wars in which Scots played a prominent part, especially the First, when 3.1 per cent of our population was lost, and we have witnessed massive and continuing deindustrialisation of an area whose identity was defined by what was produced. But the Museum of Scotland has been defeated by the task. No village in Scotland is without its war memorial, but in the Museum of Scotland the twentieth century is represented with no mention of either of the World Wars. This is a single example of an obvious missed opportunity which insults those it supposedly serves.

Romantic Extremities

'With the rise of Glasgow in the West and the increasing power of London in the South it seemed to many that Edinburgh's position as a Capital had now at last inevitably declined beyond redemption,' Moray McLaren wrote in 1951, describing Edinburgh's 'nineteenth century decline into complacent near provinciality'.[17]

To those who can remember such a time, 'Edinburgh's present vitality in Scotland is yet another and happy instance of her incalculability'. The new vitality came not only from the success of her international Festival (one of the boldest and most remarkable civic ventures in Britain since the war), three consecutive outstanding Lord Provosts, or the plans for growth and internal rehabilitation. These, McLaren says, were merely manifestations. The fact was that Edinburgh

> has now begun to think of herself as a Capital, and not only in name. For
> the first time since the sunset glories of the Walter Scott Romantic period

17. Moray McLaren, *The Scots*.

> Edinburgh is more actively aware of herself as something more than a
> museum of Scottish antiquities, a pleasant gentlemanly backwater in a
> northern province preserving within its ancient walls the customs, habits,
> and few remaining privileges mostly connected with the Law and the
> Church from the time when that province was a country.[18]

Half a century after Moray McLaren's endorsement of the 'Walter
Scott Romantic period', Scott has become a convenient hate figure, condemned as much for his politics as for his inventions. Sides and
entrenched positions have made it difficult to distinguish truth from
opinion. But there is no doubt that he gave us the vision of ourselves we
simultaneously accept and reject, the romantic tartan kitsch and the
sense of nationhood.

Walter Scott was born in the College Wynd, at the heart of Old
Edinburgh, in 1771. At least six of his parents' children died in infancy,
though six survived. Scott was eighteen months old when a bout of polio
left his right leg permanently lame, forcing him to spend the next eight
years at his grandfather's farm at Sandyknowe, near Kelso. This, it is said,
was where he absorbed the tales and ballads of the Borders which
inspired his love of romance and adventure, living as a boy almost in the
shadow of Smailholm Tower, to which he returned with Turner in the last
year of his life.

Scott joined his father's law firm in 1786 and was admitted to the
Faculty of Advocates six years later. And he never gave up his day job, for
all that he was Sheriff-Depute of Selkirkshire from 1799 until the year of
his death, and Principal Clerk to the Court of Session from 1806 to 1830.
It seems remarkable that all of his passion, energy and enthusiasms –
especially during the crisis of 1826, when, instead of declaring himself
bankrupt, he pledged his future literary earnings to a trust and gradually
repaid his creditors something like £120,000 – were conducted behind a
legal edifice.

A patriotic fervour fuelled most of his fiction and led him to adopt
ridiculous positions of romantic extremities. The unpliant truth is that
Scott was a patriot who saw no contradiction in being both a Scot and a
Briton, even accepting himself as a North Briton. Often criticised for an
overwhelming interest in history when his life spanned the American,
French, Industrial and Agrarian Revolutions, as well as the Napoleonic
Wars, he was perfectly capable of using the past to inform the present.

His reputation as a writer seems to have settled, though historians still
debate his importance. It is now generally accepted that by concentrating
on Scottish history, by using our landscape, language and institutions, he

18. *Ibid.*

created a Scottish consciousness that sustained a sense of nationhood; though this has also brought his reputation into decline.

In *Scottish Journey* Muir shudders at the very mention of the name. E. M. Forster had attacked Scott for being a bad artist in *Aspects of the Novel*, and Muir would certainly have been aware of Forster's opinion. More importantly, he would also have been aware of the blanket rejection of the kind of Scotland Scott represented.

But when Muir compares Scott's death mask with the Raeburn portrait – 'passion in every line: offended pride, hurt vanity, defeated ambition, frustrated hope' – he says as much about himself as about Scott. It is perfectly possible to look at the death mask and the Raeburn portrait and see certainty, especially in the jaw line, a gentle dignity in the set of the mouth and, though there is an air of resignation, there is an attraction in the eyes. Rather than being aloof and distant, Scott looks interested in others and in what is going on around him. But Muir clearly brought another agenda to the portrait: his dislike of Scott as pageant master and inventor of traditions for the visit of King George IV in August 1822.

Angus Calder has noted that, in this instance, tradition *had* to be invented: 'There were no precedents at all for the entry into his Northern capital of the monarch of a Union constituting the most thriving commercial nation in the world.'[19] But Scott's son-in-law and biographer, John Gibson Lockhart, grumbled that Scott 'has ridiculously made us appear to be a nation of Highlanders, and the bagpipe and the tartan are the order of the day'.[20] As well as formalising rituals such as Highland Games, the city was laid out as a theatrical arena of living history.

In stage-managing such an auspicious occasion, Scott emulated the panoply that accompanied Charles I's entry into Scotland two hundred years earlier, where the event and the iconography were stage-managed by the painter George Jameson and the poet William Drummond of Hawthornden. These events had been imported from Germany and the Low Countries, where they provided confirmation of the town's privileges. Rubens and Dürer had participated in similar events, something which, Duncan Macmillan suggests, underlined their importance. The Scottish pageants contrived what he called 'public statements in which imagery had a central role'.[21]

Turner came north for the occasion, as did Sir David Wilkie, whose recent work *Chelsea Pensioners reading the Waterloo Dispatch*, painted for the Duke of Wellington and displayed at Apsley House, had to be protected with crush barriers to keep the crowds from damaging it. The success of *Chelsea Pensioners* appears to have led him towards modern historical

19. Angus Calder, *Revolving Culture: Notes From the Scottish Republic.*
20. John Gibson Lockhart, *Life of Sir Walter Scott.*
21. Duncan Macmillan, *Scottish Art 1460–1990.*

representations, and the visit provided the perfect opportunity for overt symbolism: *George IV Receiving the Keys of Holyrood*, where a kneeling, bearded figure presents the king with what could well be the keys of the kingdom.

Wilkie's portrait of Scott was painted two years after the royal visit, by which time he had been appointed the first King's Limner in Scotland, following the death of Raeburn in 1823. It is reminiscent of Raeburn's first painting of Scott insofar as both affirm his poetic credentials, the earlier by setting the bard in a pleasing rural background as inspiration descends, while Wilkie painted Scott in Homeric pose, robed and sagacious as both bard and historian.

So the image of the man and the country that was being exported and simultaneously adapted for national consumption was of a land of heroes, a land where the likes of Ossian could live and roam.

> Land of brown heath and shaggy wood
> Land of the mountain and the flood.

This was the land of Wallace, Bruce and Burns. And its onlie begetter continued to undergo apotheosis at the hands of the image-makers and publicists. 'Scotland is Scott-land,' wrote Alexander Smith, in a style and fervour Cunningham Graham would later recall in praise of Wallace. 'He is the light in which it is seen.'[22]

'The post-1815 years of British triumph, paradoxically, were combined with a new and confident assertion of *Scottish* nationality, replacing the uncertainties of "North Britain" by a new, proudly "national" Imperial Scotland,' says *A History of Scottish Architecture*.

> Because of its unique position as a culturally autonomous nation within the world's most powerful state, [Scotland] was able to project on a global scale a new and highly specific set of images of itself. These were founded on the existing prestige of Ossian and further accentuated by the achievements of Sir Walter Scott . . . one of the leaders of the international trend to heighten Romanticism and modify the early Scottish Enlightenment's ideas of simple, linear intellectual and material Progress. Architecture played a key part in Scott's efforts – as we can see, for example, in his organisation of the visit of King George IV to Edinburgh in 1822 . . . and in his building, or rather rebuilding of his own Borders house, Abbotsford.

Tourists came to see the sites celebrated by Burns and Ossian, but Scott gave the burgeoning industry a momentum so that not just Abbotsford

---

22. Alexander Smith, *A Summer in Skye*.

but Scott himself became an attraction. His works were central to the National Drama, defined as 'a nineteenth century dramatic genre, peculiar to Scotland and dealing with Scottish subjects'.[23]

The National Drama is said to have brought many Scots into the theatre for the first time, 'eager to see plays featuring Scots as major characters in familiar settings, speaking in Scots dialect and singing Scots songs'. The best were representations of national history and character, the worst were tartan melodramas; though initially certain of commercial success, productions diminished to coincide with the local trades and religious-fair holidays, with revivals continuing into the early part of the twentieth century.

Scott still overwhelms us, diminishing those who came later as well as his contemporaries, in many ways defining their efforts by setting a standard no one could achieve. And as we have come to expect, Iain Crichton Smith provides a reasoned judgement in the second stanza of 'At The Scott Exhibition, Edinburgh Festival':

> It was all in his life, not in his books
> 'Oh I am dying, take me home to Scotland
> where I can breathe though that breath were my last.'
> He limped through an Edinburgh being made anew.
> He worked his way through debts, past a dead wife.
> My dear, we love each other in our weakness
> as he with white grave face diminishing through
> stroke after stroke down to the unpaid room.
> We know what we are but know not what we will be.
> I tremble in this factory of books.
> What love he must have lost to write so much.

Burns and Scott

William Borthwick Johnstone, an Edinburgh lawyer who gave it all up to study painting in Rome, became the first principal curator and keeper of the Scottish National Gallery, and the first curator of the National Gallery of Scotland. He was also the creator of one of Scotland's best-known pictures, a work of such power that its image is embossed on the Scottish psyche. *Robert Burns in James Sibbald's Circulating Library in Parliament Square, Edinburgh* was painted in 1856, when Horatio McCulloch was recreating Highland landscapes and the *Whistle-Binkie* anthologies were modifying the couthy myth of the ploughman bard as hero – works by butcher poets, lawyer poets and the like are crammed into its pages.

23. *Collins Encyclopaedia of Scotland.*

Johnstone's painting shows Robert Burns at the library door, third in a group to the left of the picture. He could be listening to one of the two Edinburgh intellectuals on his right; his poetic gaze is turned towards the middle distance. Seven people are in the library background, between Burns and the boy seated on a stool in the corner, book in hand, terrier dog at his feet. The boy may have glanced up from reading at the sound of Burns's voice, or maybe the very sight of the phenomenon startled the lad. His hair is slightly on end, his jaw has dropped, but the eyes are transfixed. The young Walter Scott sees Robert Burns. The light from the door Burns has opened floods over the boy.

That this man by the door could end his life in illness and poverty is nowhere evident, nor is there anything to distinguish Burns from those around him, other than the fact that he is the object of the picture, robed in flame. A riding crop in his left hand, his right inside his waistcoat, Robert Burns is taller than the others and is recognisable from the standing portrait Alexander Nasmyth painted in 1828 – with Burns more than thirty years dead – which was engraved for the frontispiece of Lockhart's *Life of Burns* and shows the poet as a gentleman farmer. Johnstone unfolded Burns's arms and put a riding crop in his left hand, giving him the air of a visitor farmer whose riding boots were enough to distinguish him as a countryman. But the lasting impression is with the boy among the books.

There are continuing efforts to place Burns and Scott in perpetual opposition, citing one's dislike for the other. But what is beyond doubt is Scott's admiration for Burns's work, something which has become all the more obvious since the publication of Scott's *Journals*, where there are many references to Burns, especially during Scott's financial troubles. As well as comparing their financial difficulties, he parallels their melancholic bouts and disposition. He frequently pairs Burns and Byron: 'the most genuine poetical geniuses of my time and a half a century before me,' he wrote on 9 February 1826. And on 11 December of the same year he quotes a couplet from Burns's 'Epistle to James Smith', ending, 'Long life to thy fame and peace to thy soul, Rob Burns. When I want to express a sentiment which I feel strongly, I find the phrase in Shakespeare or thee.'[24]

These are scarcely the words of a man who actively dislikes his subject. And almost eighteen months later, on 29 May 1828, he notes that his son-in-law John Lockhart, in the *Life of Burns*, 'judicious[ly] slurd over his [Burns's] vices and follies for although Currie, I myself, and others, have not said a word more on that subject than is true yet as the Dead corpse is straightend, swathd and made decent so ought the character of such an inimitable genius as Burns to be tenderly handled after the death. The

24. W. E. K. Anderson (ed.), *The Journal of Sir Walter Scott*.

knowledge of his various weaknesses or vices are only subjects of sorrow to
the well disposed and triumph to the profligate.' Concern for another
writer's reputation scarcely denotes personal dislike, especially when coupled with regret for the ways in which one's work could be used to demean
that reputation. If Scott did demean Burns, he not only regrets it, but goes
further, suggesting Burns's genius outweighed his 'vices and follies'.

The spring 1996 issue of the *Scott Newsletter* contains a previously
unpublished, autographed letter, with notes by Gerard and Martin
Carruthers. The original in the Mitchell Library, Glasgow, dated 8
January 1800, is one of a sequence of letters Scott wrote to Burns's first
editor Dr James Currie 'on the possibility of the large collection of Burns
manuscripts then in Currie's possession yielding material for Scott's projected *Minstrelsy of the Scottish Border*'.

Scott later collaborated with Currie in correcting the collected works of
Burns for the second edition. Writing about the first edition, he says, 'The
success of Burns Works while it does honor to the taste of the public must
afford the highest satisfaction to all who reflect on the benevolent purpose to which the profits have been dedicated.' The profits of the first
and subsequent editions of *Burns Works* were used for the relief of Burns's
immediate family, and a few lines later Scott refers to Burns as 'my
favourite author'.

A Dialect Of Voice and Place

Presenting Burns as hero and Scott as villain, one an honest son of toil,
the other a rapacious aristocrat jealous of his predecessor's success,
diminishes its subjects, reduces them to ciphers, almost obliterates the
impact of their work and, worse still, stands between their work and any
critical judgement or even understanding.

Scott began his career where Burns left off, collecting folk songs; this
and an interest in medieval adventure poems led him to prose fiction,
resulting in the virtual invention of the historical novel. He established a
dialect of voice and place which has run through Scottish literature ever
since, from John Galt to Allan Massie, and though little or no use is made
of the Scots vernacular, the associated instabilities of identity and a certainty of place are bound up with character.

Scott continues to exert an influence; most obviously in the works of
Alasdair Gray, who shares with both Scott and Burns a longing to return
to the political and moral values of a previous age. And Scott's instabilities are evident in the explorations of self and delusion developed by Iain
Banks, and the continual search for self undertaken by Edinburgh's other
internationally successful authors, Robert Louis Stevenson, Muriel Spark
and Irvine Welsh.

Nevertheless, Scott remained what he had always been: a convenient target. His politics marginalised him. Worse still, he can be seen as the forebear of the Kailyard school, whose effusions blinded Scotland not only to its identity, but also to the possibility that it could even have such a thing. Muir was aware that Burns and Scott were not only the sources of our national identity and pride, but also the makers of the perennials of Scottish literature to which we return like water to the shore: voice and place. What Muir was attacking was the stony embodiment of romance.

Scotland has been deeved by a search for heroes. Few figures fit the bill completely, so we elevate minor celebrities to a status they do not deserve or we mythologise the few genuine heroes who do exist. In this we are not alone; it's a recognisable part of the process and as necessary as the demythologising procedure which often follows. That Scotland has a tendency to skip the demythologising, and to classify our candidates as either heroes or villains, is evidence of our lack of faith in ourselves and, essentially, in our national identity. We seek the character Brian McNeill calls the Tartan Messiah:

> He'll lead us to the promised land with laughter in his eye;
> We'll aa live off the oil and the whisky bye and bye;
> Free heavy beer, pie suppers in the sky,
> Will we never have the sense to learn.[25]

MacDiarmid attacked Burns because he is the nearest thing we have to a hero, to someone who can easily be groomed to fit all sides of a very twisted anti-Establishment coin. In many ways, by attacking Burns, MacDiarmid was laying out his own credentials, campaigning for the job himself. As well as attacking the Establishment, it is always good policy to approach its lackeys, the running dogs and apologists, those whom we believe have deluded the masses into accepting the unpalatable, those who ought to know better, have a hidden agenda, or, worse still, are deluded by wealth and a 'ribband star', those who accept the bauble and the shilling.

Andrew Marr explains the dichotomy rather well.

> By the 1920s radical politicians and poets who thought of themselves as sternly historical, progressive nationalists were prepared to wear tartan again – though it was discouraged by the early leaders of the Nationalist party. The poet MacDiarmid adopted a cod-Gaelic name and a kilt for his national-revivalist persona. Yet he came from the Borders and did not speak Gaelic. He was tricking himself out in trumpery associated originally with Sir Walter Scott, who was among the Scotsmen MacDiarmid most hated and railed against.[26]

25. Brian McNeill, *No Gods and Precious Few Heroes.*
26. Andrew Marr, *The Battle For Scotland.*

He Made Us All

It is neither Scott, nor his work, but a symbol of their impact which dominates Edinburgh. In a capital which 'has no shortage of fantastic monuments . . . the Scott Monument in Princes Street soars up and out of its surround of lush foliage to challenge the very best'.[27] A Gothic steeple, it is, according to the *Collins Encyclopaedia of Scotland*, 'probably the largest memorial raised to a writer anywhere'. The story goes that Georges Simenon was surprised to find they had built a monument to a writer. Then he thought for a little. 'Why not?' he said. 'He made us all.'

George Meikle Kemp, who designed the Scott Monument, had worked on a book of drawings (completed by William Billings) intended to introduce ancient Scottish architecture to a wider public. *The Baronial and Ecclesiastical Antiquities of Scotland* provided an architectural language that could respond to the romantic surge Scott's work had generated. The Scott Monument marks Edinburgh's shift towards tourism, which Charles McKean defined as the movement from Enlightenment Edinburgh, inquiry and rationale, to a city of romanticism and the picturesque.[28]

Edinburgh has scarcely featured as subject for Scottish artists. And though any survey of Scottish art must include Edinburgh's portrait painters like Ramsay and Raeburn, it would appear that the energy and most of the subjects in Scottish painting came from outside the capital. Notable exceptions are Alexander Nasmyth's paintings *Edinburgh from Princes Street* and *Edinburgh from the Calton Hill*. Painted in 1825, they record the partnership of the Old and New Town and were, according to Duncan Macmillan, 'perhaps the crowning achievement of Nasmyth's career'.[29]

Nasmyth ignores the theatrical trappings of the royal visit and plays down the smoky majesty of the city and the crowded, awed spectators that captivated J. W. Eubank in *The Entry of George IV Into Edinburgh From the Calton Hill*. Instead,

> he captures the feeling of the people's city. In both paintings the openness of the sky and the landscape beyond the immediate context of the architecture together give to the scene a grandeur worthy of the ideals enshrined in the building of the New Town. Through the interpretation of nature with the city, the city itself is seen as a natural organism.[30]

And though the city has been the home of artists and artistic movements such as the Edinburgh Social Union, whose activities dovetailed

27. Fiona Sinclair, *Scotstyle*.
28. Charles McKean, *Edinburgh: Portrait of a City*.
29. Duncan Macmillan, *op. cit.*
30. *Ibid.*

with the Glasgow Boys, or the Edinburgh Group, which formed after the First World War, their work scarcely featured the city, either in any straightforward material representation, or as a springboard into another investigation. Edinburgh awaits the artist who will raise its oppositions above the physical.

However, its place in literature is secure. Not simply in the fact that, as Stevenson noted, from South Street one could look down upon another class in the Cowgate, but in the duality that engendered, which is 'endemic in the city, as it was throughout Scotland'.[31] Creeping in his velvet jacket away from the essence of bourgeois respectability in Heriot Row to enjoy the underworld on Calton Hill, Leith Walk or at Tollcross, Stevenson would certainly have been alive to the contrasts of a city founded upon public probity and private vice. Stevenson, as Burns, Ferguson and Ramsay before him, celebrated this submerged Edinburgh:

> I love night in the city,
> The lighted streets and the swinging gait of harlots.
> I love cool pale morning,
> In the empty bye-streets,
> With only here and there a female figure,
> A slavey with lifted dress and the key in her hand,
> A girl or two at play in a corner of waste-land
> Tumbling and showing their legs and crying out to me
> Loosely.[32]

Must Be History

If Edinburgh physically represents a theory that has permeated Scottish artistic endeavour, then it was also the birthplace and engine room of the Scottish Enlightenment, that extraordinary period when anything seemed possible, which seemed to cover every aspect of Scottish life.

It is no accident that in the generation which followed the Act of Union, Scottish artists and writers were trying to define and preserve the society they knew, a society and way of life they clearly felt was under threat. Later, in the case of Scott and Galt and also in the paintings of Raeburn, the attempt was to preserve the Scottish character and, by implication, Scottish characteristics, those things they considered native to Scots.

Interestingly enough, this was proceeding in tandem with what could be considered other expressions of national identity, which manifest themselves in and through the Scottish Enlightenment, a movement, if such it be, as difficult to date as it is to define. Some say it stretches from

31. Charles McKean, *op. cit.*
32. Robert Louis Stevenson, 'My brain swims empty and light'.

the Glorious Revolution of 1688 to the death of Sir Walter Scott in 1832. More usually, it is defined by its greatest period of activity, from the 1750s to around 1780, which means that when Robert Burns arrived in Edinburgh on November 28 in his *annus mirabilis* of 1786, the Enlightenment was effectively over. However one dates it, the diversity of activity makes it impossible to locate a single cultural movement, and while it is important to recognise the climate and intellectual environment that created the Enlightenment, it is also important to recognise it as principally an urban phenomenon. Some historians have claimed that it is a term which essentially denotes an area of scholarly interest, rather than a clearly defined period.

Charles Rennie Mackintosh's assertion that architecture 'must be history – the world's history written in stone'[33] becomes especially relevant when one considers Enlightenment Edinburgh. The builders of Edinburgh's Old Town may have constructed a city without streets, but the New Town architects had no such intentions. The broad street and the central square, nineteenth-century Europe's appurtenances of urbanity, were at the keystone of their plans. James Craig's extraordinary grid-iron scheme, which won him the 1767 competition to plan the New Town of Edinburgh, was concordant with other new town developments springing up across the land.

The Scots economy had stagnated between the Union and the 1745 rebellion, and, then as now, investment in new construction was seen as a way of generating prosperity; so the New Town was conceived as an aristocratic housing estate, modelled on a London square of terraced houses. The lairds who provided the land and financed the schemes had become quite familiar with London terraces, and set about establishing an enclave in the north. Rather like the councillors who later built the likes of Craigmillar, Lochee and Drumchapel, Edinburgh's New Town developers provided few shops and no places of entertainment. Such amenities were left with the poor, across the divide in the Old Town.

Credit for the rise of the New Town to its status as an icon of Enlightenment planning must go to Robert Adam, whose sojourn in Rome had given him an understanding of the grandeur to which his native capital should aspire. To Adam Scotland owes the architectural conceit that dominated the next seventy years, that of an entire street block of terraced houses being marshalled within a unifying noble design, best illustrated by Charlotte Square (1792). To Adam Edinburgh owes the notion of the stately public building closing a vista, as does Register House (1774), or punctuating the skyline, as did his plan for Edinburgh University. A capital required suitably impressive, noble entrances, and Adam responded with

33. Charles Rennie Mackintosh, *The Architectural Papers*, ed. Pamela Robertson.

grandiose proposals for the southern and northern ones (both executed
by lesser hands) and that to the east at Calton Hill.

The Union took the gentry south to the new places of power and privi-
lege, while minor nobility stayed in Scotland; many of them still regarded
Edinburgh as the centre of their social and political society. This aristocracy
dominated the country's professional life and turned Edinburgh into an
aristocratic city. Yet the Edinburgh of Sir Walter Scott was a place which had
undergone a profound social revolution, as well as the intellectual and
physical changes which had been effected since the Jacobite rebellion.

The Act of Union gave Scotland responsibility for its legal, educational
and religious affairs. These and the burgeoning Edinburgh University
were to provide the springboard for the astonishing number of clubs
and societies that sprang up in the city. These societies attracted those of
a literary and philosophical disposition, from all walks of life. They were,
in Nicholas Phillipson's phrase, 'institutions which were designed to
make learning and letters useful to society generally, and particularly
useful to Scotland'.[34]

Intellectual life enjoyed a remarkably high status. This seems to have
been connected with the changes that accompanied the Union, leading
some to the conclusion that the Enlightenment was essentially a response
to the Union and effectively an assertion of Scottish national identity,
however one describes the fusion that brought together a company as
diverse and entertaining as the scientists William Cullen and Joseph Black,
Adam Ferguson, founder of social science, the father of geological science
James Hutton, and their friends David Hume and Adam Smith.

The Eclectic Habits of the Scottish Intellect

Robert Adam's father, William, collaborated with Scotland's prototype gentleman o'pairts, Sir John Clerk of Penicuik in constructing Mavisbank
House, 'arguably the most important single example of early eighteenth
century Scottish architecture'.[35] Author of *The History of the Union of
Scotland and England*, written in Latin and published in 1720, Sir John studied law at the University of Leyden, where he struck up a lifelong
friendship with Hermann Boerhaave, founder of the best medical school in
Europe. Clerk was one of the sixty commoners who, with sixteen peers, represented Scotland in the new Parliament. His personal interests extended
across astronomy, chemistry, geology and medicine, as well as archaeology
and antiquarianism, the classics, and Scots poetry, history and music.

34. N. T. Phillipson, 'Scottish Enlightenment' in David Daiches (ed.), *The New
    Companion to Scottish Culture*.
35. Miles Glendinning, Ranald MacInnes and Aonghus MacKechnie, *A History of
    Scottish Architecture*.

A staunch Unionist, Clerk represents the other side of Scottish intellectual radicalism. He was a Jekyll and Hyde figure who both embraced
vernacular Scots and produced a Latin history of Scotland, which places
him in the dying humanist tradition. His agricultural improvements, as
well as his industrial and musical interests, earn him membership of the
emerging hotbed of genius society. Besides collaborating with William
Adam, Clerk studied composition in Rome with Corelli, who led the
ensemble for the first performance of one of Clerk's cantatas in Frascati.

The portrait of Sir John Clerk and Lady Clerk of Penicuik, which
Raeburn painted in 1792, shows Clerk's great-nephew as a man of
Enlightenment refinement, taste and accomplishment in the midst of the
source of his wealth, rather than displaying its products or consequences.
For another dichotomy present in the Clerk dynasty is a less closely
observed aspect of Enlightenment Scotland: the fact that learning, invention, improvement, refinement and culture continued alongside
appalling social conditions for the majority of Scotland's population.

In a letter to Boerhaave, written in Latin, Clerk describes his house and
garden:

> On the west stretches a plain for some miles, varied with hills, valleys,
> streams, springs and shrubberies. Parts are uncultivated and marshy, but
> this gives work for my tenants and servants, who are daily improving it.
> Meanwhile there is no part, however swampy, which has not its use, for the
> moors are suited for sport. There is an abundance of hares. The birds
> thrive in the heather, wild geese, partridge, quails, etc. abundantly provide
> for the conviviality of guests . . . . This country domain of mine is distin-
> guished by many enclosures and preserves, and is everywhere fed with
> springs and rivulets . . . . Part is destined for pasturage, part for hay, and
> part for grain. Here, too, the variety greatly pleases the eye – plantation of
> timber, forest trees, hills and rocks interspersed, covered with shrubs and
> thickets. Nor are there wanting rugged and contorted boulders, those
> relics of an ancient world which, if not terrible of aspect, adorn the face of
> nature.

And the house, he says, is ample rather than magnificent. 'Throughout
the hall, supper-room, dining-room, etc., are seen certain pictures, most
elegant of their kind . . . such as Raphael of Urbino, the Rhenish Guido,
Rubens, Vandyck, Paul Veronese and Francis Imperialis.'[36]

Mavisbank is in poor condition, having been damaged by fire in
1973. Now in the care of Historic Scotland, it has been neither demolished nor restored, and the public are discouraged from going near the

36. Sir John Clerk, *Memoirs 1676–1755*, ed. John M. Gray.

ruin. The place Clerk called his 'summer pavilion' stayed in the family till 1815, changed hands several times, and eventually became an asylum towards the end of the nineteenth century.

It May be Nae Surprise

Between 1752, when James Craig drew up the plans for Edinburgh New Town, and 1800, with the posthumous completion of William Adam's masterpiece in Charlotte Square, Scotland's first window-glass manufactory had been formed and Henry Bell had (unsuccessfully) launched his first steamship. The Carron furnaces were fired in 1759, the year Robert Burns was born. By the mid-1780s the site was 'a vast and busy place, its fortunes founded on weaponry',[37] which also produced boilers, stoves, grates, kettles, cylinders and anchors – in effect providing the springboard for the Victorian love of iron. Carron was first in a string of similar ventures, and by the end of the century there were eighteen blast furnaces in Scotland, including the charcoal furnaces at Furnace and Bonawe.

Kirk elders and ministers may have seen Robert Burns as the devil's creation, but Burns himself gave this distinction to Scotland's biggest iron foundry, which he claimed offered a preview of hell:

> We cam na here to view your warks
> In hope to be mair wise,
> But only, lest we gang to Hell,
> It may be nae surprise.

The arrival of the 35-mile stretch of the Forth and Clyde Canal, which followed the route of the Antonine Wall across the waist of Scotland (a route the railway engineers would later repeat), gave the Carron works access to ports on both sides of the country. The canal was first surveyed in 1768 and opened in 1790 when a ceremonial hogshead of Forth water was poured into the Clyde at Bowling.

And the social upheaval brought concomitant unrest. Merchants and their men imported more than goods from France; French ideas were beginning to impinge upon the Scottish psyche. The works of Voltaire, Rousseau and Diderot were eagerly received in Scotland, as the shock waves from the Bastille rattled across Europe. In 1792, the year after Sir John Sinclair began his compilation of the *Statistical Account of Scotland (1791–1798)*, corn was selling at 43 shillings a quarter, when available, and the average wage for a worker in the cotton mills was a shilling a day. Early copies of *The Rights of Man* sold out and the book was banned by the

37. Neil McCallum, *A Small Country*.

government. The Society of the Friends of the People held their first convention in Edinburgh, drawing delegates from more than eighty branches across the country.

Considerable attention has been given to Scotland's place in the Agricultural and Industrial Revolutions, to the Enlightenment and the general intellectual ferment that enveloped the country during the last fifty years of the eighteenth and well into the nineteenth century, but the story of the Scottish radicals has been inadequately addressed. It is as though their existence was insignificant in comparison to what was going on around them, and yet they scarcely existed in a vacuum. It is impossible not to detect a whiff of political censorship, especially when most of the popular histories of Scotland deal with the period prior to 1707.

The story of Thomas Muir of Huntershill reads like a Hollywood script, and were it not for the circumstances in which he flourished – the appalling flood of persecutions and repressions that swept Scotland in the 1790s – it could seem fanciful. His life seems to have been a continuous battle against authority. After graduating Master of Arts from Glasgow University, he studied law, but had to transfer to Edinburgh because of his part in a student protest. He entered the Faculty of Advocates in 1787 and soon gained a reputation as a man of principle, not only for giving his services free to poor clients, but for winning cases of patronage against landowners.

With William Skirving he played an active role in founding the Scottish Friends of the People in July 1792. His conspicuousness in addressing working people in Glasgow and the surrounding villages made him a prime target for the authorities, who got their chance in December 1792, when he read out the potentially seditious Address from the United Irishmen to the Convention of the Friends of the People at their first National Convention. He was arrested in January 1793 and charged with sedition.

Following an interrogation, Muir was released on bail and, fearful that the London Whigs would abandon their support for even the limited reforms which had been suggested, he went to France to plead with the revolutionaries to abandon their plans to execute the king, since this seemed to have been the aspect which panicked English Whiggery. Britain declared war on France while Muir was there, causing him to miss his trial. In June 1793 he sailed from France to Ireland, and then, apparently determined to stand trial and prove his innocence, he returned to Scotland, where he was immediately arrested.

He was tried before Lord Braxfield, who, as Robert Macqueen, had acted for the Crown in cases concerning the forfeiture of Jacobite estates following the 1745 rebellion, and had also been presiding judge over the trial of Deacon Brodie, Edinburgh's prototype master of dual identity – town councillor by day and burglar by night. Braxfield was said to make the accused tremble in the dock, and was contemporaneously described as 'a man without heart or pity'.[38] He is said to be Stevenson's model for *Weir of Hermiston*, as Brodie is said to have been his model for *Dr Jekyll and Mr Hyde*.

The verdict at Muir's trial was a foregone conclusion. Muir was sentenced to fourteen years' transportation, and no time was lost in despatching him along with Thomas Palmer, William Skirving, Joseph Gerrald and Maurice Margerot to New South Wales. Braxfield had handpicked the jurors, but even they were shocked by the severity of the sentences. The issue was raised in Parliament, but the verdicts stood. Muir's speech from the dock is considered a classic, and is still studied by American law students. His ideas seem as relevant and fresh today as they did then, and surprisingly moderate considering the panic they created.

Palmer became a businessman in Australia and left for England when his sentence was finished. He died in Guam in 1802. Skirving and Gerrald died within weeks of each other in 1796. Margerot returned to Scotland in 1810, the only one to do so. Muir escaped from Australia on an American ship which took him to Mexico. From Cuba he sailed to Spain and arrived back in France in 1797, where he was greeted as a hero by the Directory. He died in France in 1799, the year serfdom was abolished in the Scottish mines.

Adam McNaughtan, one of today's finest songwriters, wrote *The Ballad of Thomas Muir of Huntershill*[39] for an exhibition to commemorate the bicentenary of Muir's trial. He had been asked if he knew of any contemporary broadside ballads about Muir, but found none existed. Accordingly, he provided one himself:

> Skirving, Palmer, Gerrald, Thomas Muir and Margerot;
> Remember Thomas Muir of Huntershill:
> These are names that every Scottish man and woman ought to know;
> Remember Thomas Muir of Huntershill.
> When you're called for jury service and your name is drawn by lot,
> When you vote in an election, when you freely speak your thought,
> Don't take those rights for granted, for dearly they were bought;
> Remember Thomas Muir of Huntershill.

A Misty Region of Crime and Desperation

'They approached the Old Town which none of the girls had properly seen before, because none of their parents was so historically minded as to be moving to conduct their young into the reeking network of slums of which the Old Town consisted in these years. The Canongate, the

38. *Collins Encyclopaedia of Scotland.*
39. The song is given a bravura performance by its author in *Last Stand at Mount Florida.*

Grassmarket, the Lawnmarket were names which betokened a misty region of crime and desperation,' recalls Sandy in *The Prime of Miss Jean Brodie*, Muriel Spark's defining view of Edinburgh in the 1930s and, until the arrival of *Trainspotting*, the decisive fictional statement on Edinburgh. Sandy concludes that there are other Edinburghs quite different to hers, a place where only the streets and monuments and the public buildings are shared.

John Herdman was also aware of another Edinburgh, which made a seasonal encroachment on 'the *haut-bourgeois* enclaves of Murrayfield and Wester Coates, where I was brought up'. From the Victorian working-class cottages south of the main road west, 'keelies' invaded the private gardens of Wester Coates in search of conkers.

> My father waged a running war against these 'Balbirnies', as we called them from the name of one of the streets where they lived (now transformed into a chic residential area). Generally he succeeded in driving them off, but I was made aware of a vague threat emanating from a powerful, continuous but alien world which became imbued for me with its own special aura of dingy romance . . . . I remained aware of another Edinburgh, another Scotland quite different from the one with which I was principally familiar.[40]

According to a report in the *Herald* from September 1997, Edinburgh is 'the murder capital of mainland Britain, with more murders per head of population than London'; half its residents are afraid to go out after dark. A Conservative councillor said people were using Edinburgh as a haven for preying on the better off. 'There are rich pickings to be had here,' he said. The council had agreed 'to promote improvements in street lighting' in areas such as bus stops where women feel vulnerable, and after examining night staffing levels in council car parks, they had decided to install twelve close circuit television cameras to operate twenty-four hours a day on Princes Street and Lothian Road, at Haymarket, Tollcross and the Grassmarket.

Almost exactly a year later, the number of homeless families in Scotland was the highest on record and statistics were 'expected to show that the rate of home repossessions has doubled over the last five years'.[41] The Chartered Institute of Housing estimated that more than 5000 families would lose their homes by the end of 1998, a figure which had doubled in four years, and in their annual Homelessness Survey, the charity Shelter found the number of homeless applications to Scottish

40. John Herdman, *Poets, Pubs, Polls and Pillar Boxes: Memoirs of an Era in Scottish Politics and Letters.*
41. *Daily Express*, 26 November 1998.

councils had risen by almost 75 per cent in nine years. And while Edinburgh asked for an additional £1 million from the government's Rough Sleeping Initiative, 'Councillor Lindsay Walls who represents the city's Morningside area, hopes to see a blanket ban on begging in Edinburgh and has called for a begging by-law'.[42]

Six months previously, in the Platform column of the *Independent*'s Media section, Edinburgh freelance journalist Patrick Small wrote about 'an active member of the homeless campaign group Speak Out', Murray Combe, who had died of a suspected drug overdose. In an obituary, the co-directors of the *Big Issue* in Scotland had written, 'At the end he had become depressed. He couldn't understand the *Evening News* and *Scotsman* campaigns against the homeless. "Why do they blame us all the time?" he used to ask.'

Patrick Small addressed the question to Andrew Neil, editor-in-chief of The Scotsman Publications Ltd, quoting what he called a reworking of his *Scotsman* columns for the *Spectator* in which Neil addressed the issue of the decline of Edinburgh's city centre. He found it 'to be soiled by "human refuse", overrun by "aggressive beggars", "vagrants" and "vagabonds". He contrasts this with a vision of Edinburgh from his childhood – "a magical place" which included the Castle, the Scott Monument and the zoo.'

The *Scottish Daily Express* had also condemned 'Neil's hounding of the homeless'. The *Evening News* campaign, writes Small, 'descended into hubristic farce in August when it instructed its lawyers to draft a by-law banning all begging in Edinburgh. Reporters then passed this to the council.'

When the council set up a working party to look at social exclusion in Edinburgh, including homelessness, poverty and unemployment, the *Scotsman* published the names, addresses and home telephone numbers of the councillors who had supported the social exclusion move, inviting readers to contact the councillors and let them know their feelings. 'Edinburgh's shame,' Small concludes, 'is not the anti-social behaviour of some of its beggars, but that some of its inhabitants have to beg at all.'[43]

Divisions within divisions

It seems that there have always been divisions within the Edinburgh divisions. In 1935 John 'No Pope' Cormack, a former corporal with the Argyll and Sutherland Highlanders who had served in Ireland with the Black and Tans, rallied an estimated 10,000 people against a civic reception for the Catholic Young Men's Society, whose congress was being held in the Usher Hall. Roman Catholics made up 9 per cent of the city's population at that time. On 27 April local newspapers carried advertise-

42. *Herald*, 20 May 1998.
43. *Independent*, 17 November 1997.

ments calling on Protestants to gather outside the City Chambers at 7 p.m., 'ready for action if need be'. All police leave had been cancelled, the special constabulary were mobilised and 'a detachment of the Gordon Highlanders, stationed at Edinburgh Castle, was placed in readiness and the mobile section of the Royal Army Service Corps at Leith Fort was also mobilised'.[44] The evening ended with the reception being cancelled and Cormack being carried shoulder-high across the North Bridge, while Catholics mounted guards on their city-centre churches.

Something of Cormack's sectarian divisions lingers, especially, as with most cities, on the outskirts, in places like Craigmillar where the Orange Order and a pro-IRA band both marched recently, resulting in several arrests.

Craigmillar Castle is 4 miles from the Edinburgh city centre and 'one of Scotland's most impressive medieval remains'. This was where Mary, Queen of Scots came 'wishing herself dead' after the murder of David Rizzio at Holyrood. Uninhabited since the middle of the eighteenth century, the castle became increasingly ruinous and in 1946 was placed in state care.

In the 1930s Craigmillar was chosen as a site for new housing. One of the city's first council-housing schemes was built here, aimed at diminishing the Old Town overspill. The local primary school was built in the fashion of the times, an 'open air' school whose brick design and construction had been imported from England; and though the houses were better than those in the centre of Edinburgh, the scheme had neither pubs nor cinemas, only one or two shops, and it was necessary to take expensive bus trips to find work or entertainment – a mistake Glasgow, Dundee and other local authorities were to repeat thirty years later. Before long, Craigmillar became a depressed area with consequential problems of poverty and lack of opportunity.

Helen Crummy moved to Craigmillar not long after the scheme was built. After her marriage, raising her three sons and taking an interest in their education 'she realised the difficulties that people from similar communities faced in aspiring to anything beyond a basic education', according to her entry as a community activist in the Edinburgh Women's Achievement Trail Guide. She galvanised some other mothers into forming the Craigmillar Festival Society, which, like the Edinburgh People's Festival of the early 1950s, offered an alternative to the official Festival and Fringe and aimed to develop the local people's latent creativity. To this end they initiated a variety of home-grown projects, ranging from an annual pageant at Craigmillar Castle to a community newspaper and a network of neighbourhood support schemes. Helen

44. *Protestant Times* of 5 May 1935, quoted by Tom Gallagher in *Edinburgh Divided: John Cormack and No Popery in the 1930s*.

Crummy maintains she was simply a catalyst, that the development of Craigmillar's community was achieved by the people themselves, who proved that despite the many personal and social difficulties they and others in communities like Craigmillar faced, the desire for betterment and general improvement would surface if given the opportunity.

A recent report from the Accounts Commission shows that more than 14 per cent of Edinburgh's council tenants are in arrears and that Edinburgh City Council are the slowest at reletting houses – 21 per cent within six weeks.[45] This was three months after an independent inquiry into health inequalities highlighted a growing health gap between rich and poor and urged the Government to increase benefits for women and children as 'the only way of breaking the cycle of deprivation in which ill-health and disadvantage is passed down from generation to generation'.[46]

More Than Two Hours a Week

Edinburgh, like most Scottish cities, is surrounded by small, car-owning housing estates, which are in direct contrast to the tightly developed Scottish city centres, of which Edinburgh is the perfect example. This new type of mainly brick, kit-based units means the Scottish tradition of tenement building is in danger of being lost.

Edinburgh is a city of tenements. Often built to plans prepared by some of Scotland's greatest architects, their profile defines the city's skyline just as their social context gives the capital its character. Moreover, apart from the central New Town area, much of Edinburgh can boast the sort of decay which thirty years ago made its Georgian terraces unmortgageable. Multiple ownership makes conservation programmes difficult to co-ordinate, and in 1997 the total cost of restoration was estimated at £100 million.

Scotland lags behind the rest of the UK in terms of home ownership, and in both the private and public sectors many homes badly need repair or modernisation. Legislation could ensure adequate and regular maintenance; and government could assist urban regeneration in such areas as improvement grants, more shared-ownership properties, and an increase in the percentage of private ownership.

Meanwhile, a huge rise in commuter traffic is predicted: an additional 17,000 commuters in Edinburgh by 2007. Researchers from Edinburgh's Napier University found that 'poor people are far more likely to be knocked over on the roads than better-off citizens'. After studying 'thousands of accidents involving pedestrians in Edinburgh and Lothian [the

45. Quoted in the *Herald*, 5 February 1999.
46. *Independent*, 27 November 1998.

researchers] found that Craigmillar and Wester Hailes, among the least affluent areas of the city, had the worst accident rates'.[47] According to David Begg, Edinburgh's 'transport guru', 'Edinburgh had the fastest-growing rate of car ownership in the United Kingdom and Princes Street was recovering from one of the highest accident rates in Scotland'.

Traffic-induced levels of air pollution are rising. The number of vehicles using the Forth Road Bridge has risen by 60 per cent in ten years, which has increased pressure to construct another bridge to cross the Forth, upriver, nearer Kincardine, and the A80 has been officially designated as one of the UK's top five most congested routes. This follows the news that Scots motorists waste more than two hours a week in traffic jams, that traffic congestion costs the UK economy £10 billion a year, a figure that is likely to rise.[48]

The number of cars on the road has increased by 5 million to 26 million in the last ten years and will rise to an estimated 30 million by 2005: 'Some 76% of Scots drivers say they never use a bus – the highest figure for any region, with 73% saying they never use a train. And 86% of Scots drivers said that traffic congestion in towns and cities was a major problem.' But many prefer to sit in traffic jams than use public transport.

Edinburgh needs more bus drivers. Shifts operate between 4 a.m. and 1 a.m. and the job pays between £9000 and £12,000 a year. 'Edinburgh bus drivers not only have to cope with maniac motorists, a kaleidoscope of lights, awkward junctions, narrow streets and constant stop-start jolting. They also have to work in a surprisingly noisy environment.'[49] In Glasgow the stress is forcing bus drivers to quit.

A Concrete Cornucopia

Meanwhile, the issues continue to jockey for position. 'Any list of promises of objectives from any progressive party would surely include a commitment to tackle the appalling levels of dampness in Scottish housing,' says James Mitchell in a *Scotland on Sunday* article published on the first St Andrew's Day since the referendum. A quarter of Scottish homes are affected by dampness and condensation, which in turn affects the lives of about 30 per cent of Scottish children. Anyone wanting to improve the educational opportunities of these kids should, quite literally, start at home.

  Similarly, any attempt to tackle Scotland's appalling records of ill-health could start at home. With more than 40,000 Scots homeless and almost

47. *Scotsman*, 6 November 1997.
48. *Herald*, 21 January 1998.
49. *Herald*, 12 October 1998.

200,000 households on waiting lists, there are huge problems that need to be addressed. These are Scotland's excluded citizens: they need a Scottish parliament. What must they make of the column-inches of newspaper coverage devoted to where the parliament will sit – a matter which excites so much interest amongst the Edinburgh bourgeoisie? The members of Scotland's parliament will be housed – the issue is where not whether, which is more than can be said for many thousands of their constituents.

Land reform, education and transport are not mentioned in an article that questions party radicalism:

Despite the complete collapse of the Conservatives, conservatism has rarely been healthier. Indeed, we might well ask whether there is any need for a Conservative party when the interests it traditionally represented are being articulated so well by the other parties. Labour, SNP and Liberal Democrats have all been making a pitch for the business vote. But where is the natural party of the poor, the homeless, those without a voice?[50]

The number 32 bus links council schemes and suburbs. It does not penetrate Edinburgh city centre but moves around the fringe from Wester Hailes – 'a concrete cornucopia of grey harled blocks joined by shabby sci-fi bridges', according to a *Herald* reporter – stopping first at Colinton village, a 'move from an area with a two-hour police response time to an area with a five-minute police response time. In Colinton you have houses that cost more than anyone in Wester Hailes would earn in a lifetime.'[51]

A film tracing the bus route to Colinton and onwards, and the route of the number 52 bus, which makes the same journey in the opposite direction, an exhibition of photographs by the Wester Hailes group Snapcorp and a number of associated events were part of a project called *Divided City*. A tourist on a 32 would be presumed not only to be lost, but to be 'a very lost tourist indeed'.

This is the real Edinburgh, said one of the event's co-ordinators. 'It is their city. There is a rich–poor divide, but with this project people can come into the city centre united and not feel intimidated.'

50. *Scotland on Sunday*, 30 November 1997.
51. *Herald*, 12 March 1998.

3

Toy Scenery

'. . . And marvell'd as the aged hind
With some strange tale bewitch'd my mind,
Or forayers, who, with headlong force,
Down from that strength had spurr'd their horse,
Their southern rapine to renew,
Far in the distant Cheviots blue,
And, home returning, fill'd the hall
With revel, wassel rout, and brawl.'

SIR WALTER SCOTT, *The Lady of the Lake*

A Steady Thirty

Leaving Edinburgh by what he calls 'the South Road', the A7, Muir had 'an easy run' to Jedburgh. He stopped at Galashiels, had an excellent stew and milk pudding, then drove on to Melrose and Dryburgh. After an hour the car grew so hot he drove in shirt and trousers, past 'field after field of young green corn, amid which multitudes of poppies flaunted with an Arabian brilliance in the bright weather'. The car was restless doing more than 35 miles an hour, but 'at a steady thirty it produced a calm, loud snore, which had a pleasantly lulling effect in the windless bright weather'.[1]

He must have passed the Lady Victoria Colliery by Newtongrange, where 40 million tons of coal were mined in ninety years. It is now the Scottish Mining Museum, with two permanent exhibitions, a hands-on activity zone, an audio-visual presentation, and 'The Wullie Drysdale Story', where one can 'experience a wealth of sights, sounds and even

1. Edwin Muir, *Scottish Journey*.

smells, as you follow Wullie Drysdale, a nineteenth-century miner, through a typical day in his life. Wullie's home, the colliery, and the village of Newtongrange are vividly portrayed in a series of award-winning scenes, featuring life-sized speaking characters.' Former miners show visitors the coalface and Scotland's largest steam engine, 'the giant winding engine', which is still in working order.[2]

For two centuries steam drove the Industrial Revolution. For many, including John Ruskin, the steam engine is the most beautiful of man's inventions. 'I cannot express the amazed awe, the crushed humility, with which I sometimes watch a locomotive take its breath at a railway station, and think what work there is in its bars and wheels, and what matter of men they must be who dig brown iron-stone out of the ground, and forge it into THAT!' he wrote.[3]

In less than a generation, industrial sites have become museums, preservers of the working life, its skills and traditions. The desire to provide a working wage is coupled with a mime of preservation, for every new scheme comes with the promise of jobs. For a generation of men whose identity was found in their work, in a country where a person's surname often derives from a trade, there is no clearer evidence of a need to identify.

Industry and Identity

Though it was Sunday, Galashiels 'was swarming with tourists and holiday-makers'. Muir arrived the day after the Common Riding, 'when the young people had ridden the marches and crossed the Tweed, returning again in the evening'. It's an annual high point of Border life, an event that has recently allowed women to join the procession.

> These little Border towns, such as Galashiels, Kelso, Selkirk and Hawick, have all this curiously wakeful and vivid air. I say 'curiously,' for most of the other small towns I have seen in Scotland are contentedly or morosely lethargic, sunk in a fatalistic dullness broken only by scandal-mongering and such alarums as drinking produces; a dead silence punctuated by malicious whispers and hiccups. But the Border towns have kept their old traditions more or less intact, and wherever that happens it is a sign that the common life is still vigorous.

The antithesis of Border life is to be found in places like Montrose or Kirriemuir, where the source of local identity rests with the football team. 'The sole claim to eminence of the old resident there is that he knows

---

2. Promotional leaflet for Lady Victoria Colliery produced by the Scottish Mining Museum.
3. John Ruskin, *The Cestus of Aglaia*.

everything about the private lives of his townsmen; and so devoid are such places of any other interest that this claim is publicly acknowledged to be a justified source of pride.'[4]

A thinly disguised Kirriemuir acts as the setting of *A Window in Thrums* by J. M. Barrie, the second volume in a series of semi-fictional sketches of Scottish small-town life. The stories originally appeared in the *St James's Gazette* and *Cornhill Magazine* and were later published in book form, the first volume, *Auld Licht Idylls*, in 1888, with *A Window in Thrums* appearing the following year, establishing Barrie as a leading figure of the Kailyard school.

To Muir, the Thrums window is a horrific symbol of the Scottish small-town existence.

> The life of these towns, from top to bottom, is merely an aggregate of private lives under a microscope: private lives carried on with the greatest difficulty, forced indeed to become fantastically private beneath a reciprocal and insatiable scrutiny. This window with which the houses in the small towns of Scotland are fitted has the power both to enlarge and diminish everything that is seen through it; bad deeds swell and good deeds shrink; for its peculiar power is that of reducing everything to the same common measure.

Muir goes on to suggest that the constrictions brought by 'this uniform chronicle of smallness' are not felt in the Borders, because these towns have retained their pasts and have an active life, their own distinctive local industries which have 'survived the intensifying onset of Industrialism that has eaten into the core of other communities'.[5] It was clear to Muir that the retention and development of local industry played an essential part in preserving local identity. Tourism was too menial to be considered an option. If his assertion is correct, the Borders are in trouble. Those small industries Muir admired, such as knitwear and woollens, have been threatened almost to the point of extinction.

For most of the past century, we have lost, or, more specifically, sold, control of the Scottish economy. For almost a generation before the First World War, the city of Glasgow was the Second City of the Empire and one of the world's main manufacturing centres. The city and its industries never recovered from the First World War; the loss of life alone ensured the manufacturing base was irreparably weakened. Government intervention and the munitions industry brought a brief respite in the 1930s, but since the Second World War the process of dispersement has accelerated to a point where no sector seems secure.

4. Edwin Muir, *op. cit.*
5. *Ibid.*

What was Scotland's largest publisher, William Collins, is now owned by News International, and the William Low supermarkets have been absorbed into the Tesco chain. Arthur Bell and the Distillers Company are owned by Guinness, their takeover masterminded by a man who later made a miraculous recovery from senile dementia. Some takeovers, such as Kwik-Fit and William Low, were said to be friendly; others, such as the takeover of the House of Fraser stores and Distillers, were not.

Inward investment by foreign companies has placed the Scottish economy in a vulnerable position. Caterpillar tractors, Hoover washing machines and Timex watches have been and gone, leaving a bewildered, powerless and resentful workforce, and Europe's biggest building site outside Dunfermline was abandoned because of the threatened collapse of the Asian economy. Decisions made outwith Scotland and their effect on the country have been the cause of continual complaint for almost three hundred years.

And though English is the standard language in which newspapers and businesses communicate, advertisers make occasional forays into Scots, usually to sell recognisably Scots products such as whisky, often in a way which revives the Scottish cringe factor; even though the language and accents are recognisably Scots, in common with most advertising they inspire condescension.

In Times Remote

Had Muir followed the signs he saw for Dunbar and Haddington, he would have passed Athelstaneford, the place where, it is said, Andrew was chosen as the patron saint of Scotland. It was here, in 832, that an army of Picts led by King Angus, and aided by a Scots contingent, invaded the Lothians, only to find themselves surrounded by a larger force led by the Anglo-Saxon King Athelstane. As Angus led prayers for deliverance he saw a cloud formation of a white saltire – the cross upon which St Andrew was martyred – against a blue sky. 'The king vowed that if, with the saint's help, he gained victory, then Andrew would thereafter be the patron saint of Scotland. The Scots did win and the Saltire became the flag of Scotland,' says the *Athelstaneford, Birthplace of Scotland's Flag* appeal leaflet, launched on 30 November 1995 to establish a flag heritage centre in Athelstaneford. Here a memorial is located in the churchyard where a saltire flies permanently, and a plaque proclaims:

> Tradition says that near this place in times remote Pictish and Scottish
> warriors about to defeat an army of Northumbrians saw against a blue sky
> a great white cross like St Andrew's and in its image made a banner which
> became the flag of Scotland.

And on the road south, Muir would have passed Newbattle Abbey, founded by David I and colonised by monks from Melrose. Newbattle monks are credited with founding the salt-panning industry at Prestonpans and operating Scotland's first coal mine. The abbey was given in trust to the nation in the 1930s for use as an adult-education college. Muir became its warden in 1950 and stayed till 1954. It was at Newbattle that he taught a rising generation of writers such as George Mackay Brown, Tom Scott and Archie Hind.

Between Penicuik and Lasswade on the banks of the River Esk lies the mining village of Rosslyn. The ruined castle here was built by Henry Sinclair, Earl of Orkney, in the fifteenth century and later extended by his son William, who also established the remarkable Rosslyn Chapel, distinguished by its elaborately eccentric architecture and carved internal decoration. The chapel is overrun with symbolism, references to the Knights Templar and Freemasonry, depictions such as the Dance of Death, the Seven Cardinal Virtues and the Seven Deadly Sins, and a proliferation of pagan symbols. According to the promotional leaflet, *The Historical Enigma, Rosslyn Chapel*, 'Rosslyn Chapel has the largest number of "Green Men" found in any Medieval building. There are also carvings of plants from the New World which predate the discovery of that land by Columbus by one hundred years.'

Penetrating the Rosslyn mysteries is a continuously incomplete achievement, for it barely seems possible to understand the layers and subtexts of the building, far less penetrate the carvings and symbolic representations, given the building's overt and implicit associations with the Knights Templar, Freemasonry and the Rosicrucians. The place abounds with symbolism, which often makes it difficult to appreciate even an internationally recognised carving like the Apprentice Pillar.

Yet through it all a clue emerges. This is a search for something which may or may not exist and may not even be recognisable when it is found. For it is not even possible to decide whether the layers of mystery exist to defy understanding or to offer enlightenment to the initiated. 'Having spent many years in the study of the old Artisan Guilds, Fraternities and Mystical Associations of Europe, it has always appeared to me that at the heart of these institutions there lay a ritual symbolism involving a search for something remote, hidden or lost,' writes Robert Brydon in *Rosslyn – a History of the Guilds, the Masons and the Rosy Cross*. More than this he does not tell, but continues:

> The legends of Chivalry are the veiled allegories of the eternal search for spiritual truth in a world of natural realities. Bards, Troubadours, Meistersingers and strolling gypsy players, by way of song, sonnet and pageant, carried onwards such an esoteric doctrine. The wide network of Knightly Orders, Companies and Guilds, acting as the human vehicle,

transmuted the secret symbolism into the greater permanence of metal, wood and stone. Such carvers were known as 'Meassons'. Of these, the most important were the stonemasons; for what better place to plant the seed of an old democratic dream than in the design geometry and carvings of a permanent temple?

From small self-governing guilds and companies flowed the philosophic inspiration that aimed always towards a coming age of reason. An age founded on the rights of man; a spiritual and temporal world-wide common-wealth of mankind.

By explaining their importance and mystical significance we avoid their meaning. By stating their history, however incompletely, we can suggest their function. But the significant key, that of representation, is missing. By admiring the work, we lose its identity. In appreciating Rosslyn Chapel's craftsmanship, we avoid its human face; for without further knowledge we have no means of interpreting what we see. Which leaves the lonely symbols etched in stone.

Numerous Holy Days

Scotland's extremities have never had a problem of identity: the Highlands largely because of language, and the Borders because of their past. The problem of identity is national rather than local, a problem of imagination rather than substance. Few Scots doubt their nationality. The problem lies in the manifestations of that nationality.

Across the country a string of festivals take place throughout the year. Some are regional, others local. Some are particular, most are general. Edinburgh hosts the biggest arts festival in the world, with events beginning in July and staggering through to September. The Traditional Music and Song Association of Scotland publishes a yearly Festival Calendar which runs from January to November, listing between fifty and sixty separate events, all distinctive, all building on the place and its sense of identity. Some last a day, most begin on the Friday night and are finished by Sunday, offering song and music workshops, children's events, arts, craft and street fairs, dances and concerts. But the range of their activities and variety of their locations suggests a deeper significance.

Festivals occupy a traditional role in the Scottish collective consciousness. *The Silver Bough*, a four-volume study of the national and local festivals of Scotland by F. Marian McNeill, is the standard, exhaustive, brilliant study. Published between 1956 and 1968, the intention is clearly to inform and preserve and to offer a sense of local and national identity by showing a continuing strain of activities.

According to Alan Bruford,

The efforts of the Scottish Reformers and their successors the Covenanters to suppress the numerous holy days of the medieval Church were so successful that only two major festivals have retained their importance throughout the country: Hallowe'en and Christmas or Yule, the latter generally shifted to the secular holiday of New Year. Though in recent years both have been celebrated in all parts of Scotland, they are really equivalents and either may be accompanied, for instance, by guising. Hallowe'en derives from the great winter feast of the pagan Celts, marking the beginning of the winter half of the year, and Yule from the pagan Nordic or Anglian feast of the winter solstice. Both were times when spirits walked abroad while mortals celebrated at home.[6]

Quarter days came midway between the major Celtic festivals, Lammas on 1 August and Candlemas on 2 February, and they survive as seasonal markers, when fairs are held and ball games played. The other quarter days, Martinmas on 11 November and Whitsun on 15 May, are the term days, when rents were due and farm and domestic servants could seek new employment at the hiring fairs.

Alan Bruford reckons it is impossible to enumerate the many fairs, often with seasonal names like Lammas or Marymass, still kept up or remembered in Scottish towns or open-air sites. And though many of the newer events have now combined with the older fairs and festivals, others are establishing an identity of their own; and just as the older fairs played an important part in the life of their communities, so these newer events are coming to adopt a similar role. It may be fanciful to suggest that arts and music festivals are taking the place of the older events; but it is not in the least fanciful to say that despite the fact that the symbolism associated with the older occasions has been lost or misplaced, their spirit is intact and their place in the community is being re-established.

Traditional music and song, especially that branch mistakenly known as the Border Ballads, traditional dance and folk tales were an integral part of these events. They are Scotland's unique gift to the world. They have had a tenuous existence, being fostered and maintained by the very poorest, the most dispossessed outcasts of our society; or in order to fit into our society the works have been stripped of their integrity, dressed in tartan or moulded into English. And now the Scottish Parliament has established an all-party committee on the traditional arts. The aim is to make the Scots aware of their heritage, and by taking practitioners into schools to educate a new generation.

6. Alan Bruford, 'Festivities and Customs, Seasonal' in David Daiches (ed.), *The New Companion to Scottish Culture*.

Toy Scenery

Border identity, it is said, comes from the Border Reivers, figures whom George MacDonald Fraser asserts are unique in British and probably world history: cattle thieves who left to posterity a legacy of great poetry, merciless racketeers who plundered, yet formed the country's vanguard in time of war, murderous pursuers of a feud for whom little was sacred except their pledged word.[7] They vanished four centuries ago, leaving the word blackmail to the English language. According to *In Search of the Border Reivers,* a pamphlet that lists Border sites, families and incidents connected with the reivers, their bloodline included American Presidents Nixon and Johnson, Sir Walter Scott, Billy Graham, Robert Burns, Deborah Kerr, Thomas Carlyle, T. S. Eliot and Neil Armstrong.

The reivers rode the Debatable Lands, the wild tracts that now form Northumberland, Cumbria, the Scottish Borders, Dumfries and Galloway, an area still liberally dotted with castles, stately homes, towers, ruined abbeys, fortified farmhouses, and abandoned hamlets or howffs hidden up remote side valleys – places where the reivers found sanctuary. Their architecture, like the domestic architecture of the Highlands, is functional: fortified turrets built on hillsides to repel strangers; abbeys built on the lush lands by the river, where fat cattle grazed and fruit and vegetables grew. The Border forts and abbeys are among the best examples of early medieval and castellated buildings in Scotland.

Townships grew around the abbeys, castles and reiver settlements: Peebles, Selkirk, Galashiels, Melrose, Kelso, Hawick, Jedburgh. Sir Walter Scott sat as Sheriff of Selkirk for more than thirty years and he is buried at Dryburgh Abbey, his biographer Lockhart – appropriately enough, says Muir – at his feet, their bodies yards away from Field Marshal Earl Haig. It is the most romantic setting of all abbeys, in a horseshoe bend on the River Tweed, surrounded by cedars from Lebanon, brought back by crusaders to the Holy Land. It would be hard to think of two men who have had a bigger effect on Scotland than Scott and Earl Haig.

Not far away, Bruce's heart lies at Melrose, supposedly returned by a Saracen chief and buried in a leaden casket in Melrose Abbey. Excavations of the Chapel House area in 1996 uncovered such a casket, which was examined and reburied by the then Scottish Secretary of State, the late Donald Dewar.

Melrose Abbey was founded by St Aidan with Iona monks some time before AD 650, and built by Cistercian monks with funds from David I, beginning in 1136. David also founded Kelso and brought monks from Chartres to construct the buildings. It was badly damaged in the Border

7. George MacDonald Fraser, *The Steel Bonnets.*

wars, sacked by Edward II and again by Richard II in 1385, and was rebuilt by Robert Bruce, eventually being reduced to a ruin during the Reformation. A sculptor showed what he thought of his new surroundings by including a cook with his ladle and a pig playing the bagpipes in his carvings around the building.

The area is dominated by the Eildon Hills, where Thomas the Rhymer is supposed to have spent three years with the Queen of the Fairies. Muir makes a telling point: 'This landscape which Scott loved so much is not grand or savage like some of the Highlands,' he says, 'but has a curious enchantment, the intimate magic of toy scenery invented by a child.' It is, he later remarks, not quite a human landscape, 'yet it is not in the least frightening: its strangeness is like the strangeness of a magical charm which is also harmless'.

Between Melrose and Dryburgh is Scott's View, where he is said always to have stopped and where, during his funeral procession, the horses drawing his coffin to Dryburgh stopped out of habit. A mile further on, the first statue of William Wallace to be raised in Scotland (in 1814) faces Selkirk, where he was proclaimed Lord Protector. The hero appears suddenly, down a muddy, wooded track: a massive kilted figure in red sandstone, towering over the road from Dryburgh Abbey. The hollow eyes give him a strangely manic appearance; but the broadsword is shoulder-high and held in his right hand, while a shield with a saltire decoration rests against his left leg. The inscription reads:

> Great Patriot Hero!
> Ill Requited Chief!

From Scott's View, Abbotsford can be seen curled in the corner, 'lying in a green valley beside the Tweed', writes Muir, no lover of Scott.

> The ubiquity of Scott's presence in the Borders a hundred years after his death, the persistence with which he has set his mark on the landscape, as if he were resolved to be a Border laird and extort the homage of one in perpetuity, is exasperating . . . if one stayed [at Abbotsford] long enough one would at last understand the mania which drove him to create this pompous, crude, fantastic, unmanageable, heartless, insatiable, comfortless brute of a house, and sacrifice to it in turn his genius, his peace of mind, his health and his life. Everything in it, except the study with its secret stair, where Scott slipped down in the early morning to write his romances unknown to his guests, is designed for ostentation; it is a huge showroom of vulgar romantic properties.[8]

8. Edwin Muir, *op. cit.*

Scott transformed the original Clarty Hole farmhouse into Scotland's most influential contribution to the movement of Romantic troubadour houses that swept Europe in the late eighteenth and early nineteenth centuries. Its influence was enormous, far more than such nearby palaces as William and Robert Adam's Mellerstane House or Adam and Playfair's Floors Castle. In 1844 Fox Talbot photographed the house for Sun Pictures of Scotland, the second photographic book to be published that was devoted to subjects associated with Scott and his novels.

A Denial of Reason

Scott's first ballad informant was the mother of James Hogg, when Scott was compiling his collection of ballads, *Minstrelsy of the Scottish Border* (1802–03). Born in Ettrick in 1770, Hogg was an illiterate shepherd who had taught himself to read and write and play the fiddle. He declared himself 'ravished' by 'Tam O'Shanter' and resolved to be a poet like Burns, adopting Burns's birthday as his own and manipulating his background to present himself as Burns's natural successor, calling himself the Ettrick Shepherd, a role he was to regret.

Hogg met Scott, the newly appointed sheriff in Selkirk, while working as a shepherd on a farm in the Yarrow valley, and supplied him with material for *The Minstrelsy of the Scottish Border*. Six years later Hogg published a collection of his own ballads, though it wasn't until *The Queen's Wake* was published in 1813 that he achieved critical recognition, consolidating his reputation among the urban Edinburgh elite.

He became a writer by mimicking Scott, and could easily turn out verses in the style of Coleridge and Byron, which he submitted with his stories, poems and essays to the likes of *Blackwood's Magazine*. Like Burns, he played the part of the untutored rustic and was accepted into literary society with a good deal of condescension, though his work is neither as simple, nor as simplistic, as it might appear; it consistently shows an understanding of contemporary literature and literary forms.

His explorations of character and place through folklore and legend are unequalled, especially in their range, covering both poetry and prose, and though some of his novels are poorly constructed and could appear to overstretch his abilities, they share an obvious feature with his stories insofar as they have the authority of the oral tradition in both register and construction. Events occur naturally, with what would appear to be little artifice. Incidents are rarely signalled; and details of background and setting are given as they occur. He adds items of character and local colour to enhance the tale or divert the reader, often deliberately adopting the disingenuous stance of a narrator who is as bemused by the events, especially where a supernatural element is involved, as he expects the reader to be, or offering a personal assurance that the narrative is

true: '. . . for I lived twelve months in the family, and the girl was then
only about seven years of age,' he tells us in 'Seeking the Houdy'. He
often halts the narrative to explain events or determine their relevance
and explains his devices in a perfectly natural way, breaking into Scots or
altering dialect midway through a story or even changing direction altogether in the light of an unforeseen and generally unwelcome arrival or
event. Which can give his novels a ramshackle appearance. But Hogg is as
concerned with the experience as with the narrative, and, as often occurs
in folk tales, his position makes clear that the range and diversity of experience, especially when this range and diversity cannot be explained
rationally, have a place not only in our lives, but in society as a whole.

There is a constant tension between the explicable and the inexplicable which not only defies the Enlightenment stance of reason but is its
very antithesis, and offers an indication as to why reason was so important
to the Enlightened society. It was as much a means of control as of explanation. Hogg is perfectly willing to adopt a more natural approach, which
is especially effective in diminishing the prestige of editorial or authorial
control. Time and again he asserts that such a disposition scarcely exists,
suggesting that where it does exist it is an unnecessary, even a false imposition which obscures the totality of the person or the experience,
offering, at best, a single dimension. This continual denial of reason generates an outlandish range of psychological and social tensions, giving his
work an unexpectedly contemporary spirit.

It is generally accepted that a writer need not be studied, nor even
read, for their influence to be felt or exerted. One need not know the origins of the interior monologue or stream of consciousness to use the
devices; and so Hogg's persistent denial of reasoned explanation, his
concentration on character and experience, coupled with a continual
assertion of voice and place, allow him to break free of Scott and his contemporaries and to leap into contemporary Scottish fiction, where his
devices have peculiar echoes and resonances.

The Private Memoirs and Confessions of a Justified Sinner was published
anonymously by Longman in London and attracted little attention. Hogg
created a world some thought too subtle to have been devised by a shepherd. He twins opposites in marriage and families and individuals,
exploring from a variety of perspectives the ways in which contrasts can
swell in a single person, confusing the issue with discrepancies which
not only discredit his protagonists, but make the reader incapable of
exerting a judgement over either character or events. It is a remarkable
tour de force whose power is still exerted today.

When André Gide declared *The Private Memoirs and Confessions of a
Justified Sinner* 'astounding' and 'enlightening', the rehabilitation of the
novel and its author could begin. The tendency had been to see Hogg in
the same light as his contemporaries had viewed him, an accolade

awarded to few writers except when, as in Hogg's case, it was less than flattering. Like Robert Burns before him, James Hogg needed to be freed from the image he gave himself.

His plot is woven around the Presbyterian abstract of predestination, arguing that good works alone are not enough to ensure salvation, or indeed that good works and piety may not even be necessary, that God has ordained who will be with Him in paradise, and that, according to Matthew XXII:14, 'many are called, but few are chosen'. Having the Almighty's favour not only secures a special status; it renders spiritual growth unnecessary, allowing a transgressor to savour restoration to the fold, no matter the infraction, for repentance is at the heart of forgiveness: 'Joy shall be in heaven over one sinner that repenteth, more than over ninety and nine just persons, which need no repentance' (Luke XV:7). One may therefore, like Burns's Holy Willie, do what one likes with impunity, harbour all manner of negative thoughts and emotions, knowing that the cloak of repentance brings a favoured status. The lack of a balancing emotion has made it a popular doctrine in Scotland.

The central story is that Robert Colwan is disowned by his father, who believes him to be the son of the Rev. Robert Wringhim, a Calvinist minister who has a considerable influence over Colwan's wife. Robert is raised as Wringhim's son, is taught to hate his father and brother and becomes filled with a religious zeal. He stalks his brother and, following a confusing incident on Arthur's Seat, prosecutes George for trying to kill him. When Robert loses the case, George goes off to celebrate, quarrels with a Highlander and is found stabbed. The news kills Old Colwan, though eyewitnesses tell how Robert stabbed his brother while he was quarrelling.

The first part is the editor's narrative, the second the sinner's confession, which shows Robert as a noble and God-fearing, conscientious Christian who is ethically carrying out what he sees as his duty. He too is being followed, by a man he sees as his religious mentor, Gil-Martin, who continually reassures him of the righteousness of his duty, that he should seek the Lord's vengeance upon sinners in general and on George in particular. In a fit of delirium, brought on by a mysterious illness, Robert feels himself to be two people: his brother and Gil-Martin, whom the reader realises is the devil. Robert's fear of Gil-Martin forces him to find refuge in drink and, raving in the belief that he has been chosen, he publishes his confession as a pamphlet and promises to take his own life. The final section relates how the editor's quest began with an article about an unknown suicide, written by James Hogg and published in *Blackwood's Magazine*. Hogg was too busy to help the editor further, though he and his friends recovered the second part from the sinner's grave. It is the editor's opinion that Wringhim was confused, deluded in his belief that he was his own fictional creation.

Thus separate narrators contrive disparate explanations for the same events; though the novel's strength lies in its ability to set a series of tales within tales and in the way truth shifts to the point where it is anything but absolute. 'Hogg's discovery of the mirror mazes of subjectivity takes him beyond these merely relative differences,' says Rory Watson, 'and his use of "the double" anticipated Dostoevsky's Golyadkin by more than twenty years to give dramatic and psychological depth to a study of obsession and madness.'[9] He adds that the novel 'can be called a moral and cultural allegory as well as a supernatural tale or a study of psychotic delusion, for it offers a searching analysis of the nature of the Scottish psyche as it engages with its own religious history, divided loyalties and lost inheritance'.

As far as literary Edinburgh was concerned, the novel was a failure and, as Roderick Watson says, Hogg 'returned to his role as "Maga's favourite Shepherd"'. It was easier that way. *The Confessions* was published in 1824, two years after George IV's visit, which resulted in so many of today's traditions – it was a time when Scotland was on the verge of reinventing itself, when the concept of the clan and clan tartans were accepted and adapted to modern fashions. The re-creation of the Highlands, as well as the Clearances, was well underway. Clan chiefs like Macdonell of Glengarry had their portraits painted by Raeburn dressed in their newly fashioned Highland regalia. Others with the same name had no idea what their clan tartan might be. It was scarcely a time to be investigating Scottish character or identity, especially for a man who had compiled a selection of Jacobite songs, which present Highland characteristics and identity more in keeping with the times:

> Follow thee! Follow thee! Wha wadna follow thee?
> Lang hast thou loved us and trusted us fairly:
> Charlie, Charlie, wha wadna follow thee,
> King o' the Highland hearts, Bonnie Prince Charlie?

Hogg could scarcely have been unaware of what was going on, though it seems unlikely that his work was affected by contemporary events. They were the result of his subject rather than its cause. The underlying dilemma and lack of identity at the root of these events was Hogg's concern, and it says a lot about the fragility of the Scottish sense of identity of the time that a work like *The Confessions* which raises such fundamental questions was not only underplayed but effectively ignored, its writer presented as a rustic buffoon. The spirit of inquiry and the search for a national understanding that had enlivened the Enlightenment had truly vanished, and Hogg knew it; the enlightened, reasonable editor who opens graves in the spirit of inquiry is sent up from his own lips.

9. Roderick Watson, *The Literature of Scotland.*

Hogg took the core of Burns's satire and not only investigated it, but carried his investigations to their logical conclusion, showing Holy Willie's thinking with the satire removed. Hogg not only darkens Burns's wonderfully accurate portrait of unctuous hypocrisy, but provides the springboard for Scottish fiction's next major development. Robert Louis Stevenson's religious quarrels with his father may have defied the conventions of Edinburgh respectability, but in the light of Hogg's achievement they gave the young Lewis his strongest subject. Stevenson's work brims with oppositions and is filled with the sense, atmosphere and exploration of place.

The Strange Case of Dr Jekyll and Mr Hyde mirrors *Justified Sinner* insofar as Jekyll's education and position give him a superior social standing; in other words, he can be seen as a member of the elect, and the psychological conflicts that comprise the opposing sides of his character and threaten to ruin an upright and outwardly respectable nature are neither imposed nor random but come from within and are an integral part of the individual. Stevenson was concerned to root the story in a reality which adds a shocking and original dimension to the tale. Jekyll recognises the duality in his own nature, and his original experiments were meant to remove rather than release his other self. When he experiences pleasure by slipping the barriers of respectability, he believes he has found something that is a release rather than a burden, a help rather than a hindrance, far less an incubus which could lead to a darker, uncontrollable obsession, though he soon finds his only release from this freer, darker self is death.

This experience precisely mirrors that of many alcoholics, an experience which has been reflected in the accounts of addicts and obsessives everywhere, and though Hyde's final solution may appear overblown or melodramatic, it is nevertheless a central part of alcoholic thinking. Having tried what they see as every possible solution, from control to enforced abstinence, the constant fear that the demon will return and take control is forever present.

Other aspects of *Justified Sinner* appear in Stevenson's later work. In *Weir of Hermiston*, his final, unfinished work, he again gives the oppositions a psychological focus, with the added themes of family history and inheritance, as well as the continual battle against Calvinist authority. Adam Weir's distrust of his own feelings for his son Archie, and his fear that the lad will inherit his mother's character, again places duality at the heart of the narrative, coupling it with a sense of place and history, for the Borders landscape and legend would appear to be about to play a customary role.

Stevenson's range is a continual surprise. It seems scarcely credible that *Treasure Island, Kidnapped* and *The Strange Tale of Dr Jekyll and Mr Hyde* could come from the same pen. Though he appeared not to take fiction seriously, the denial of his cavalier attitude is found in the depth, range and intensity of his finest work, especially in the ways in which he continues to flesh out his themes, returning again to find something new, another aspect, even when Scotland was far behind him.

Hogg was far from popular when Stevenson was writing *Jekyll and Hyde* in the mid-1880s. At best, the Ettrick Shepherd was considered a kindly buffoon, a feature that is obvious from some of the portraits of him, though Sir John Watson Gordon painted Hogg in 1830 showing a strong, kindly face with a shepherd's plaid around his neck. This painting was intended to be hung in Blackwood's salon.

Professor John Wilson, the pseudonymous Christopher North, a continuing editor to *Blackwood's Magazine* and main producer of the *Noctes Ambrosianae*, a series of essays and conversations supposedly overheard by the diarist, portrayed Hogg as an ignorant, vain simpleton, given to meaningless discourse, which the more learned occasionally indulged, but generally ignored. Hogg was apparently amused by this, though many of his friends, especially his wife, were not so sanguine.

Sir William Allan's painting, *The Celebration of the Birthday of James Hogg*, shows a number of people who were prominent in the Edinburgh cultural world, including Scott and Allan, as well as Scott's publisher, James Ballantyne. Alexander Nasmyth and William Nicholson, who painted Hogg in 1815, are also in the picture. Hogg, in a rather antic pose, is at the edge of a table and is being toasted by John Wilson.

Allan shows the mythic Hogg, a man overawed in such company, a simple man out of place in literary society, heir of the mythic Burns. The painting demonstrates the extraordinary situation in early-nineteenth-century Edinburgh, when writers and painters met on something more than a friendly basis, but worked together, directly inspiring and encouraging each other's work.

From Rydal Mount, Wordsworth was stirred by Hogg's death in 1835. In 'An Extempore Effusion', Wordsworth places him alongside Scott, Coleridge, Charles Lamb and George Crabbe. By this time, Shelley, Keats and Byron had died young men's deaths, and the poignancy of age is evident from the opening stanza, which sets Hogg in his location. By doing so, Wordsworth sees himself as companion and follower in more than a geographic sense.

> When first, descending from the moorlands,
> I saw the stream of Yarrow glide
> Along a bare and open valley,
> The Ettrick Shepherd was my guide.
> When last along its banks I wandered,
> Through groves that had begun to shed
> Their golden leaves upon the pathways,
> My steps the Border-minstrel led.

When it has no tune

'It is a thing worth noting that the one or two great poets whom Scotland has produced have been men in the ordinary sense uncultivated,' wrote Edwin Muir in 1923.

> Excepting Scott, those of whom we know anything have sprung from peasant or humble stock; and there was even before Burns, who set a fashion, a tradition of peasant poetry and a belief that an artificer of Scottish song might most congruously be a plowman or a weaver. In poets of this degree, so scarce in English literature, Scottish poetry has almost always been prolific.[10]

Muir asserted that the distinguishing feature of Scottish peasantry was their ability to absorb a whole view of life, a view intensely simple on certain great, human things, but naturalistic and even, in a certain sense, materialistic.

> This simple vision of life, of life as a thing of sin and pleasure, passing, but passing with an intense vividness as of a flame, before something eternal, is the greatest thing which Scotland has given to the literature of the world. Everything which obscures the clearness of this vision, making it less simple than itself when it is most simple, is antagonistic to the Scottish genius; and here only, in defence of their naturalism, of this terrific, sad and simple vision of life, the Scots are iconoclasts, and contemptuous of the thing called culture or humanism which in other lands has had such glorious fruits . . . This sense of life and death, of pleasure and sin, of joy and loss, not thrown out lavishly into all the manifestations of life as Shakespeare threw them out, but intensified to one point, to the breaking point where a flame springs forth: that is the sense which inspired the greatest Scottish poetry: the poetry of Burns, the poetry of the ballads.[11]

The ballads go immediately to that point beyond which it is impossible to go, and touch the very bounds of passion and of life. They achieve this, says Muir, 'by an unconditionality which rejects, where other literature uses, the image. In no poetry, probably, in the world is there less imagery than in the ballads.'[12]

Muir's continual references to the poetry of the ballads presupposes he had never heard them sung, or that he considered the tunes unimportant. And indeed ballad study, until relatively recently, had a heavy literary

---

10. 'A Note on the Scottish Ballads' in *Freeman VI*, reproduced in Andrew Noble (ed.), *Edwin Muir: Uncollected Scottish Criticism.*
11. *Ibid.*
12. *Ibid.*

bias. Many collectors were also poets who were more interested in texts than tunes, as their collections demonstrate. Ballads which appear in collections by William Motherwell, George Kinloch and David Herd often have no tunes, or the tune is, at best, only named.

Yet Professor Bertrand Bronson, in his introduction to *The Traditional Tunes of the Child Ballads*, asserts that a ballad is not a ballad when it has no tune, even though ballads are frequently recited rather than sung, or sung in art-song arrangements which are not always suited to the text.

'We should never forget that the ballad is a sung genre,' writes Emily Lyle, 'with a whole musical dimension that is not caught by the printed text; to gain a full appreciation, every opportunity should be taken of listening to live or recorded performances.'[13] And in such performances one will almost certainly be exposed to the full range of the ballads' power, to incomplete versions that leave one bewildered at their dignity and directness, as well as a comic range and ability that defies logic and an absolute refusal to bow the knee or appear subservient.

Imagery in songs is not unknown, but it is rare, not only in the ballads, but also in folk song generally; this may be because the songs we have are versions rather than complete, finished products and are obviously the work of more than one individual. We now know that it is possible for a variety of versions of the same song, or songs from the same source, to exist simultaneously and for there to be considerable differences between the versions.

The great American ballad scholar Francis James Child, who numbered and classified ballad themes and motifs in five volumes of *The English and Scottish Popular Ballads*, first published between 1882 and 1898, may have found some Scottish ballads too coarse for his collection. Though he included songs about rape, murder, incest, fratricide and a variety of other unsavoury subjects, as well as songs such as *Captain Wedderburn's Courtship* (Child 46) where sexual desire is explicitly expressed:

> The Laird o' Roslin's daughter walked through the wood her lane,
> When by cam Captain Wedderburn, a servant to the king.
> He said unto his servant man, Were it no against the law,
> I wad tak her to my ain bed, and lay her neist the wa'.
> I'm walking here alane, she said, among my father's trees;
> And you must let me walk alane, kind sir, now if you please.
> The supper-bells they will be rung and I'll be missed awa;
> Sae I canna lie in your bed, either at stock nor wa.

Why it was against the law for Captain Wedderburn to lay the Laird o'

13. Emily Lyle, Introduction, *Scottish Ballads*.

Roslin's daughter neist the wa' is never explained, but it is generally assumed to refer to the girl's age.

Nor did Child care for *The Widow of Westmorland*, whose daughter tells her mother of a pastime she has learned from 'a nice wee man in the King's Life Guard'. When the mother curses the girl for losing her maidenhead, the girl goes to the King's Life Guard asking for it back:

> So, he kissed her and undressed her
> And he laid her on the bed;
> Then he put her heid whaur her feet were afore
> To gie back her maidenhead.

That the greatest ballad editor of the English- and Scots-speaking world should feel compelled to omit certain texts doubtless says much for the attitude of his times. We are not so easily offended. Perhaps he considered the subjects or their treatment trivial, not suitable to be ranked with the greater themes of love and death. And while there is no doubt that many bawdy ballads are textually inferior to what may be considered as the standard tales, especially in the way a ballad highlights the emotional intensity of a story and has an unerring ability to penetrate the heart of the matter, yet in almost every instance the melodic jauntiness and rhythmical directness of the tune more than compensates for, indeed enlivens, an inferior text.

'Nowhere are the characteristic attitudes of our folk culture more obvious than in the sphere of sex,' writes the scholar Hamish Henderson. 'Folk-song has no use for the conventional hypocrisies and taboos of respectable society. It handles the joys, miseries and above all the comedy of sex with medieval directness. Needless to say, this has never endeared it to the Holy Willies of Scottish life.'[14]

Child could well have thought, and others may agree with him, that the texts he omitted were not ballads at all, not because of their subject matter, nor indeed of the way it is expressed, but because of some detail in their textual arrangement. Which raises another spectre altogether. According to Margaret Drabble, a ballad 'is taken to be a single, spirited poem in short stanzas, in which some popular story is graphically narrated (e.g. *Sir Patrick Spens*) and in this sense of the word the oral tradition is an essential element . . . ballads more traditionally deal with the pagan supernatural (e.g. *Tam Lin*), with tragic love (e.g. *Barbara Allan*) or with historical or semi-historical events, e.g. the Border Ballads or the Robin Hood ballads'.[15] And though Margaret Drabble's definition omits the musical component and suggests some subjects are more suited to

14. Hamish Henderson, *Alias MacAlias*.
15. Margaret Drabble, *The Oxford Companion to English Literature*.

the form than others, her definition also suggests that ballads are inde-
finable, or that any definition will be, by the very nature of the subject,
uncomfortably narrow. M. J. C. Hodgart may well be correct when he says
that ballads in general, and the Child ballads in particular, 'are as hard to
define as they are easy to recognise'.[16]

The expulsion of tunes and certain subjects surely contributed to a literary view of ballads which still persists. It has also restructured their
identity by removing the songs from their origins. An implicit feature of
censorship, either of music or of theme, is to obliterate the role of the tradition bearer, reducing the song's survival to the condition of mystery. In
keeping with the attitude that untrained voices were unsuited for such
high art, the fact that ballads had to be purged of features that were considered impertinent to Victorian society, also removes their other implicit
feature – that they were and continue to be a viable source of national
identity, and that identity is found as much in the language of the ballads
as in any other component.

Hamish Henderson has written how Aberdeenshire folk singers could
effortlessly move from undiluted Buchan Scots

> to the unambiguous English of the broadside ballads without seeming to
> notice the difference – or else paying it scant attention if they did. Here the
> role played by broadsides from the South, and by wholesale borrowings
> from them by printers in Scotland, cannot be overestimated. In the nine-
> teenth century, broadsides and chapbooks flooded Scotland in their
> hundreds of thousands, and in many of these printed sheets songs in one
> or another form of Scots lay cheek by jowl with songs in English.[17]

Within Professor Child's canon we find the ballad of *Gud Wallace*
(Child 157), which would appear to be based on a story in the fifth book
of Blind Harry's *Wallace*, as well as *Lang Johnny More* (Child 251) a comic
reworking of the Wallace story in a manner Hollywood might have enter-
tained in the pre-*Braveheart* days. This is from a fine fifty-verse version in
Scottish Ballads called *Lang Johnny Moir*:

> Young Johnny was an airy blade,
> Fu sturdy, stout and strang;
> The sword that hang by Johnny's side
> Was just fully ten feet lang.
>
> Young Johnny was a clever youth,
> Fu sturdy, stout and wight,

16. M. J. C. Hodgart, *The Faber Book of Ballads*.
17. Hamish Henderson, *op. cit.*

> Just full three yards around the waist,
> And fourteen feet in hight.

Johnny leaves Rhynie's lands and goes to London, where he falls in love with the king's daughter, is overcome by 'draps o lodomy' and incarcerated. He finds a little, wee boy who runs to Benachie to get his uncle Auld Johnny More and Jock o Noth, who reach London in three days and kick in three yards of wall. They release Johnny and appear before a trembling king who will do anything to be rid of them, even release his daughter in marriage. If we'd known, says Jock o Noth, we'd have brought folk three times bigger than us. Johnny refuses the offer of a royal dowry and with drums beating and fifes playing:

> . . . auld Johnny Moir and young Johnny Moir,
> And Jock o Noth, a' three,
> The English lady, and the little wee boy
> Went a to Benachie.

'The early Scottish collectors were driven by a conscious desire to preserve an element of their national heritage,' says Emily Lyle, 'and their publications proudly presented their discoveries. The ballads had been Scottish in the sense that they had been collected in Scotland, but they soon became something that provided extra nourishment for Scottish identity . . . . The magic that enters the ballads on Scottish soil, however, is not purely a matter of the supernatural, as everyone who feels this magic knows. It is the language itself that has an inimitable magic, which I think may lie in the balance between what is said and what is not said – what is not said may be claimed to be part of the language.'[18]

And this was surely part of the consideration of James Hogg's mother, Margaret Laidlaw, when she rebuked Sir Walter Scott: 'There was never ane o my songs prentit till ye prentit them yoursel, and ye hae spoilt them awthegither. They were made for singing an no for readin: but ye hae broken the charm noo, and they'll never be sung mair.' That her final judgement was thankfully wrong, as was the assertion that ballads had never been printed, does not alter the substance of her complaint. The ballads are essentially folk songs which are meant to be sung, and without the role of the carrier they would not only have been lost entirely, but would not possess their characteristic identity and qualities, qualities that distinguish them from all other types of poetry and song in their unique and effective narrative drive and delivery, embracing stories of violent history, tragic romance and the supernatural incidents where

18. Emily Lyle, *op. cit.*

sexual guilt and jealousy are mingled with innocence and devotion. Their uniqueness owes much to their method of transmission, where a singer may very well juxtapose or even omit sections for all sorts of personal reasons, including loss of memory. But more important is the fact that these songs were retained because the singers liked them and enjoyed singing them, which is why they are still being sung today. The fact that they are great art and popular is no coincidence, and their effect is immediate whenever they are sung.

The way ballads are fashioned, concentrating on structure and a rhythmic imperative, has dominated poetry wherever English has been written; coincidentally, they also give a lie to the statement that Scots is unintelligible to the English ear. Yet they have remained unique, especially in the way in which they distance themselves from the action, a method both impersonal and familiar. Within their scope falls the range of Scottish literature.

Allan Ramsay was as valuable an editor as he was a poet, and he is a vital link in the preservation and promotion of the works of earlier poets in Scots. In 1724 he published *The Ever Green*, an anthology of middle-Scots verse, the work of the makars such as Dunbar and Henryson. In the same year Ramsay brought out the first of his *Tea-Table Miscellany*, where, in the five volumes published over the next thirteen years, he not only gathered together and popularised many traditional songs and ballads, but also included many of his own works, written in the ballad style.

It is impossible not to see *The Ever Green* as an early assertion of national identity, an assertion Robert Burns was to emulate more than sixty years later by using Ramsay's language and sentiments in his own work as a poet and folk-song collector. When the Parliament went south in 1707, many Scots, especially in Edinburgh, felt betrayed. Most feared our native culture would also go south, or at least become diluted by outside influences, and Ramsay's collection of songs and poems written with 'that natural Strength of Thought and Simplicity of Style our Forefathers practised' reflected this fear.

When these good old *Bards* wrote, we had not yet made Use of imported Trimming upon our Cloaths, nor of Foreign Embroidery in our Writings. Their *Poetry* is the Product of their own Country, not pilfered and spoiled in the Transportation from abroad: Their images are native, and their *Landskips* domestick; copied from those Fields and Meadows we every Day behold. The Morning rises (in the Poets Description) as she does in the Scottish Horizon. We are not carried to *Greece* or *Italy* for a Shade, a Stream or a Breeze. The *Groves* rise in our Valleys; the *Rivers* flow from our own fountains, and the *Winds* blow upon our own Hills. I find not Fault with those Things, as they are in *Greece* or *Italy*: But with a *Northern Poet* for fetching his Materials from these Places, in a Poem, of which his own Country is the Scene; as our *Hymners* to the *Spring* and *Makers* of *Pastorals* frequently do.[19]

Robert Fergusson, the man who inherited the mantle of Ramsay's poetic successor, flirted with the fashion of the times, producing pastorals and mock-heroics. In January 1772, the year after the publication of Henry Mackenzie's *The Man of Feeling* and of the first edition of *Encyclopaedia Britannica* in Edinburgh, Alexander Runciman published Fergusson's 'The Daft Days' in his *Weekly Magazine*:

> Fiddlers, your pins in temper fix,
> And rosset weel your fiddle-sticks,
> But banish vile Italian tricks
>   From out your quorum
> Nor fortes wi' pianos mix,
>   Gie's Tullochgorum.
>
> For naught can cheer the heart sae weel
> As can a canty Highland reel,
> It even vivifies the heel
>   To skip and dance:
> Lifeless is he wha canna feel
>   Its influence.

This energetic commemoration of Edinburgh's New Year celebrations heralded an extraordinary couple of years when Fergusson produced an abundance of poetry for Runciman. His life ended in tragedy. After suffering from continuous bouts of ill health and what may well have been manic depression, he was incarcerated in the local mental asylum, fornenst the Edinburgh poor house, where he died at the age of twenty-four. His grave was unmarked until Robert Burns erected a headstone.

Though his output was relatively small, Fergusson's influence was considerable, especially affecting Burns, who not only found inspiration in Fergusson's language but also in his comic spirit and style, especially his observations on gentility, which are always coupled with an unerring eye for detail and an ironic manipulation of pretension.

For a while Fergusson was a member of the Cape Club, one of Edinburgh's drinking and debating societies, where a fellow member was the folk-song collector David Herd. Here Fergusson must have absorbed a variety of songs and ballads – he is, incidentally, said to have had a fine singing voice – whose spirit, language and directness inhabit his work,

19. Allan Ramsay, *The Ever Green*.

especially in the choice and treatment of his subjects. His fears for the music's future and a desire to preserve the integrity he saw in it is evident in the 'Elegy on the Death of Scots Music', written at a time when, as John Purser has commented, 'Scots turned their backs on the new musical architecture of Haydn, Mozart and Beethoven and on anything that seemed to be leading towards it, in order to defend a musical environment which they believed was too beautiful and too vulnerable to risk'.[20]

Though Robert Burns owned two copies of *The Man of Feeling*, referred to it as 'the book I prize next to the Bible', and joined the fashionable salons where passages were read aloud and their contents wept over, he also collected, rewrote and reconstructed many traditional songs and ballads, from the little-known *Hynd Horn* to *MacPherson's Farewell*, both of which still exist in oral versions across Scotland. Burns's work as a folk-song collector is often lost in the distinction he gave them. His central role in providing material for James Johnson and George Thomson's collections occupied the last years of his life, and though he was far from the only writer working in the genre, he used his collections to create more than two hundred songs of his own. In this, as has been pointed out, he was doing little more than folk singers do, almost as a matter of course; it is rare to find a singer who will reproduce a song exactly in the manner of another singer, as it has been written or recorded. Singers will add to or amend a song as they see fit, according to their response to the material and how they feel it should be recreated. This is the process that has kept folk songs and ballads alive.

For the ballads to be experienced in their natural state, they need to be heard sung in the language in which they were written, and by the sort of singer who would have been familiar with the material, someone whose voice is natural, uninfluenced by American pop songs or classical training. The ballads are at the heart of Scottish identity and hold all its essential elements. Their language and music are a rich and clear expression of national character and conceit. They are something of which we can be inordinately proud. Preserved in their natural state by the poor and nomadic of society, our tinkers and travellers, those it was considered useless either educating or gentrifying, they existed elsewhere on paper, in a half-form, shaped and moulded into something they were not; yet they survived and were easily identifiable as themselves, even when they had been truncated or reworked. Their existence is one of our many contradictions.

The presiding spirit of the ballads is neither their tunes nor their stories, but their language. It is the engine that maintains and defines them, and often to render a single verse into any other language is to diminish it entirely:

20. John Purser, *Scotland's Music*.

First whan we cam tae Edinburgh toon
We were a comely sicht tae see;
My luv was cled in the black velvet
And I masel in crammasie.

A Whole Language

Writing in 1757, David Hume observed how remarkable it was that
Scotland should at present have produced so many men of genius: 'Is it
not strange that, at a time when we have lost our Princes, our
Parliaments, our independent Government, even the Presence of our
chief Nobility, are unhappy, in our Accent & Pronounciation, speak a very
corrupt Dialect of the Tongue which we make use of; is it not strange, I
say, that, in these Circumstances, we shou'd really be the people most distinguish'd for Literature in Europe?' Hume's own texts were sent south
to be weeded of Scotticisms.

Muir felt we produced few genteel writers before Scott, who 'lived in a
community which was not a community, and set himself to carry on a tradition which was not a tradition; and the result was that his work was an
exact reflection of his predicament'.[21] This consideration led Muir to
expand Hume's contention that a Scottish writer must absorb the English
tradition, and in doing so his work belongs to both English and Scottish
literature; that a writer wishing to add to the indigenous literature will
find little to support him. His contention was that the same language
should support both criticism and poetry. Scots has survived as a language for simple poetry and a simpler short story, he says, but its other
uses have lapsed. Were Henryson or Dunbar to write prose they would
have used the same language they used for their poetry, and Burns's and
MacDiarmid's work notwithstanding, Scots poetry can only be revived
when Scotsmen and women begin to think naturally in Scots. 'The curse
of Scottish literature is the lack of a whole language, which finally means
the lack of a whole mind.'

Notwithstanding that this argument lies at the heart of the Caledonian
Antisyzygy, Muir is surely misplaced in the assertion that we feel in one
language and think in another. How can this possibly be the case? A cur-
sory glance at recent literary developments, many of which were around
when Muir was writing, suggest the opposite.

Scottish short-story writers use the stream-of-consciousness technique
either directly or, more generally, to weave in and out of character. For a
Scottish writer, in Muir's context, this can be revealing. The reader gets to
know what the character or characters are thinking, and the ways in

21. Edwin Muir, *Scott and Scotland.*

which their minds work. The technique can provide a variety of voices. In every instance we can both see and, more importantly, hear language being used in an entirely natural and practical way, with neither division from nor barely even amendment to the spoken word. There is scarcely any division between the ways in which the characters think and speak. Short stories provide the best examples, but there are also novels that use this technique effectively.

And dramatists deliberately use a spoken Scots and craft it to shape their characters. This must call for the same standards of linguistic excellence, characterisation and control, vocabulary and range that any dramatist in any language would use. In the works written in the last fifty years by writers such as Robert MacLennan, Robert Kemp, Alexander Reid and Liz Lochhead, the Scots is not only expressive, but can become a vehicle for adaptations of other writers' works.

And what of the newer voices? Edinburgh housing schemes may well be the locations of further divisions, made explicit through the works of writers such as Duncan McLean, Laura Hird and Irvine Welsh, a movement whose significance has yet to be established, though there is no doubting the power and energy of the best of this work. This new range of voices includes a number of women, whom fiction has previously rendered invisible, other than in the works of Naomi Mitchison, Helen Cruickshank, Marion Angus and Violet Jacob.

There would appear to be no discernible difference between the ways in which Scots works and the ways in which any other language works. How then could Muir have reached his conclusion? I believe one reason was that he saw Scots as a standard, single entity, rather than accepting it as a language with the same function and variations as any other.

More importantly, Muir ignored the ballads he greatly admired. Like MacDiarmid, he saw them as poetry, which, he seemed to be suggesting, was a matter of individual creation. He saw them as single entities, fixed and static, forever existing in a single version. But if our ballad, song and story-telling traditions have shown anything, it is that great art can be created anonymously, and by more than one hand. By taking poetry as a matrix, there were indeed 'a few disconnected figures at abrupt intervals' to call on. Had he used ballad, song or story-telling as a matrix, he would have reached different conclusions. Perhaps he did not use them because he was unaware of their range and importance, or he thought they were the last leaves of a defunct tradition.

The so-called Folk-song Revival, which started in the 1950s and achieved general popularity in the mid-1960s, gave a springboard to the analysis, investigation and republication of our great song collections. The fact that a folk-song revival was necessary suggests Muir was unaware of the tradition in anything other than a literary sense, and it also raises the question: why were the songs not better known, why did generations of Scottish children not grow up singing the songs which have since been revived?

Adam McNaughtan considers the Industrial Revolution is to blame, when 'the young music industry, with an eye on the newly literate market, catered for urban tastes with music-hall songs and refined drawing-room ballads, which found their way into rural repertoires and often caused the old songs to be hidden away.'[22] 'And the hour brought forth the man!' he continues.

> Hamish Henderson. He worked with Alan Lomax on collecting tours when so many of the traditional singers who were to become household names were discovered. With the late Calum Maclean he was one of the first apostles of the School of Scottish Studies. He wrote the revival's finest songs. And in 1951 and the following years, he arranged the seminal People's Festival Ceilidhs, in which the best of our native traditions, Lowland and Gaelic, were revealed to young city-dwellers .... The People's Festivals were conceived as a counterweight to the Edinburgh International Festival with its influx of tourists and culture-vultures .... Like the Romantic antiquarians, the collectors this time saw themselves as rescuers, but they did not see the songs as museum pieces ... far from being mere stepping-stones to an appreciation of classical music, the songs were seen as an important part of our culture, as great art.[23]

That these songs existed, were kept and sung by generations, handed down like heirlooms, is the most hopeful sign that our identity has been preserved, that these things which define us as Scots and which are recognisable symbols of national identity have survived as themselves. They may have absorbed or discarded any outside influences they gathered in the process, and are therefore among the few symbols of national identity which serve Scottish interests. They exist in a form that can be built upon, and this is already happening.

Nowadays folk music exists at more than one level. There is a popular level where groups and individuals sing accompanied or in harmony, often mixing styles as freely as they select their material. Other singers follow the more traditional, unaccompanied route, or vary their accompaniment to suit the mood and tone, often the lyricism of the song.

Ewan MacColl believed it was possible to develop individual singing styles in a traditional way, that there were certain features, breathing techniques and decorative styles used by traditional singers that not only occupied the whole range of the voice, but were especially suited to their natural expression.

22. Adam McNaughtan, 'The Folksong Revival in Scotland' in Edward J. Cowan (ed.), *The People's Past.*
23. *Ibid.*

Many of today's singers who sing in a traditional style use similar techniques and, like traditional singers, are eager to expand their repertoire
as well as their range. Like any other singer, they are predisposed to
material to which they feel their voice is suited and are unlikely even to
try to sing songs with which they have little or no sympathy or that are
outwith their vocal or linguistic range. A Scots folk singer may admire the
songs, singing style and techniques of a Bulgarian shepherd, but is
unlikely to try to replicate them; whereas it would not be unknown for
the same singer to have a range of songs in all of Scotland's languages.

In an essay in the same collection as Adam McNaughtan's piece,
Duncan Macmillan points out: 'The period of most striking originality in
Scottish art coincides with that of the most widespread interest in Scottish
traditions in music and poetry.' This was a period when popular music
was missing from the European art imagery, but it was central to that of
art in Scotland. 'David Allan, Alexander Carse, William Lizars, David
Wilkie, Walter Geikie and several others all produced pictures of popular
music and dance. Raeburn made his masterpiece the portrait of Niel
Gow playing his fiddle.'[24]

Above The Crimson Burn

Like many Scottish artists, the Border artist Tom Scott had an interesting
relationship with landscape and mythology. He found his main inspiration in the tales, legends and history of the Scottish Borders, not only
depicting the landscape, but also using it as a backdrop for reproducing
local historical and mythical events, such as *The Return To Selkirk From
Flodden 1513*.

There is no Scottish account of the battle where the army was routed
and King James IV killed. But Flodden is seen as the beginning of the
end, the start of a process which made Union inevitable, especially after
the crowns had been united in 1606. *The Flowers of the Forest*, the song that
recalls the disaster, is said to have been written by Jean Elliot, daughter of
the Governor-General of India and a friend of David Hume, after a bet
with her brother:

> The Flowers of the Forest, that foucht aye the foremost,
> The prime o our land, are cauld in the clay.

The Forest is said to be the district of Ettrick and the flowers are the dead
young men, though they have come to represent all of Scotland's lost
manhood. Tom Scott clearly has the song in mind. A group of women are

24. Duncan Macmillan, 'Old and Plain: Music and Song in Scottish Art' in
    Edward J. Cowan (ed.), *The People's Past*.

gathered on a hill above the town, with a copse of trees to their right. There are four men in the picture: two on horseback, one on foot and another coming over the hill. A boy in the middle foreground looks past a patch of drooping thistles into the future, while, behind him, a woman holds her husband, a man tells two women of the loss and the third carries a battered Lion Rampant, standard of the Scottish monarchy.

A meeting with Tom Scott in 1912 gave the young William Johnstone an introduction to painting. His cousin Francis George Scott later introduced him to Hugh MacDiarmid, and a close friendship developed. Johnstone's work embodies metaphysical notions of time set in a landscape that is essentially an extension of time. Initially inspired, he said, by the Eildon Hills, Johnstone spent a period studying in France, where he came into contact with Cubism, abstract art and Surrealism. The best of his work fuses disparate ideas and tenses, building them into a statement of enormous power and intensity, often using similar shapes and the kind of sequence and logic one finds in a dream. MacDiarmid wrote a series of poems based on Johnstone's paintings, and, though the poems lay unpublished for thirty years, they show a similar preoccupation with metaphysical ideas.

In the 1930s, during a period of severe personal hardship, MacDiarmid's poetry shifted to a darker, more intellectually demanding, almost heroic search for fact and reason, which accorded with Johnstone's search to evoke what he saw as the primeval spirit of his surroundings.

As with Robert Burns, the extremes of the life of Christopher Murray Grieve, the poet, publicist and politician who adopted the pseudonym Hugh MacDiarmid, are bounded by a small area of south-west Scotland. MacDiarmid was born in Langholm in 1892, where the River Esk meets the Wauchope and Ewes Waters, not far from the border with England, and from 1951 until his death in 1978 he lived in a farm cottage at Brownsbank, near Biggar, about 40 miles north-east of Langholm.

Living in Montrose in the 1920s, MacDiarmid saw a tremendous creative potential in the Scots language and, using Jamieson's *Scots Dictionary* as his principal source, produced in rapid succession two volumes of poetry, *Sangschaw* and *Penny Wheep*, in which lyrics that initially seem to be pure poetry make cosmological statements of great intensity.

> I met ayont the cairney
> A lass wi' toosie hair
> Singin' till a bairnie
> That was nae langer there.
> Wunds wi warlds to swing
> Dinna sing sae sweet,

The light that bends owre a'thing
Is less ta'en up wi't.

George Bruce has traced *Empty Vessel*'s origins to *Jenny Nettles*, a song in
David Herd's *Ancient and Modern Scottish Songs*. The second verse, which
is still sung, reads:

> I met ayont the cairnie
> Jenny Nettles. Jenny Nettles.
> Singin til her bairnie,
> Robin Rattle's bastard.
> To flee the dool upon the stool
> And ilka ane that mocks her,
> She round about seeks Robin out
> To stap it in his oxter.

MacDiarmid's image of an indifferent earth, even for a woman mad with
grief over her dead child, follows Burns's precedent in using folk song as a
springboard to an entirely new creation. This poem also shows how
MacDiarmid revitalised the language. Bruce argues that the penultimate
line alludes to Einstein's theory of relativity, and MacDiarmid's biographer
further suggests it is a pun that links the biblical myth of creation with
Einsteinian astrophysics. This, says Alan Bold, is 'one of MacDiarmid's
most intricate lyrics, a poem that spans the centuries by interpreting a
Scottish folk-song in the light of modern scientific supposition'.[25]

MacDiarmid used facts and scientific data, often in more than one
language, beside the writings of others in an attempt to break down the
barriers between poetry and the world in which it exists. Though he
instigated and led the movement to write in Scots, using its vocabulary
and rhythms to find his own distinctive voice, he later virtually abandoned Scots, saying it could not meet his intellectual demands, and it is
argued by Tom Crawford and others that the poems in the four collections he published in the 1930s, where Scots and English poems sit
alongside private meditations, compressed lyrics and contemplative dis-
courses, form the best political poetry of the decade.

The 2600-line poem *A Drunk Man Looks at the Thistle* was suggested by
Francis George Scott, who is also credited with shaping its final draft.
Published in 1926, it has been compared to Joyce and is now seen as a significant part of the experimental phase of early modernism. It is a verse
anatomy of Scotland, expanding the internal monologue into a series of
interwoven themes. Its great achievement, according to Tom Crawford, is

---

25. Alan Bold, *MacDiarmid*.

to present concepts as they first appear in the mind, making poetry from a random kind of thinking. It is, says Rory Watson, 'one of the great poems of modernist literature – a testament to creative energy and optimism at a time when Yeats, Pound and Eliot could see only cultural decline and spiritual failure all around them'.[26]

Even in old age, MacDiarmid was a challenging and dominant, at times domineering, figure, though John Herdman's memoir of their first meeting presents an entirely typical example of his personality:

> If I had been expecting to be intimidated by the combative and excoriating poet I was in for a pleasant surprise. Grieve was all welcome and geniality, and if when he was expatiating on some of his *bêtes noires* in politics or literature his eye took on a vatic gleam and the edge of his voice hardened into Stalinist steel, these were quickly dispelled when he reached you a plate of home-made scones with a persuasive smile of unfeigned, innocent sweetness. I don't recall a great deal of what we talked about, but I do remember vividly the odd consciousness that the man surreptitiously sneaking corners of sandwiches to his Border terrier Clootie when he thought Valda wasn't looking, was the same who had penned those transcendently great early lyrics so many of which I knew by heart and recited over and over to myself as I walked the Pentland Hills.[27]

Today, his creative stature is intact, though it has necessarily been separated from his personal reputation. His poetic achievement is undiminished and seems likely to expand, though it is commonly accepted that he never managed to overcome the national inferiority complex within himself, using what Tom Crawford called 'self-advertisement as part of a literary and political strategy which became increasingly tedious from the 1950s onwards'.[28]

'In many ways, and not least in its conjunction of the national and the international in its concerns, the self-styled "Scottish Renaissance" of the 1920s stood firmly with the Scottish cultural tradition,' says Michael Lynch.[29] It was a movement within which MacDiarmid not only saw himself as the leader, but as such the arbiter of what was acceptable. Writing of the mid-1920s, Alan Bold says,

> Grieve promoted the Scottish Renaissance Movement as an antidote to the poison that had weakened the Scottish nation. He conducted his campaign

26. Roderick Watson, *op. cit.*
27. John Herdman, *Poets, Pubs, Polls and Pillar Boxes.*
28. Tom Crawford, 'Hugh MacDiarmid' in David Daiches (ed.), *The New Companion to Scottish Culture.*
29. Michael Lynch, 'Scottish Culture in its Historical Perspective' in Paul H. Scott (ed.), *Scotland: A Concise Cultural History.*

of re-education by urging the Scottish public to study the fiction of Norman Douglas and Neil Gunn; the music of Francis George Scott; the painting of William McCance (art critic of the *Spectator*); the criticism of Edwin Muir; the educational theories of A. S. Neill; the plays of George Reston Malloch; the verse of nationalist poets such as Lewis Spence and Hugh MacDiarmid. Older Scots were judged by the quality of their nationalism – R. B. Cunninghame Graham was projected as a heroic figure, Pittendrigh Macgillivray as a stalwart, R. E. Muirhead as a dedicated, if cautious, patriot.[30]

Between 1880 and 1920 Scotland had produced writers such as Robert Louis Stevenson, George MacDonald, George Douglas Brown, Neil Munro, J. M. Barrie, S. R. Crockett, the Findlater sisters, Catherine Carswell and J. MacDougall Hay; and to this list can be added poets such as James Thomson, James Young Geddes – arguably the greatest radical poet between Burns and MacDiarmid – John Davidson, Marion Angus and Violet Jacob. Add to this the achievements of artists such as William McTaggart, Phoebe Traquair and the group known, in death if not in life, as the Glasgow Boys; the development and range of the Glasgow Style by designers whose work incorporated everything from illuminated manuscripts and enamelling to furniture, entire house interiors, tea-rooms, table napkins, cushions and cutlery; the range and diversity of the works of Charles Rennie Mackintosh; the development of the Scotch Baronial style of architecture, led by Sir Rowand Anderson and continued by his disciple Robert Lorimer; the music of Sir Alexander Mackenzie and Sir John Blackwood McEwen, Hamish MacCunn and William Wallace; the folk-song collections of Gavin Greig and James Duncan; and there comes a realisation that MacDiarmid's claim that Scottish culture lay in the doldrums needs reassessment.

The main vehicle of MacDiarmid's Renaissance was his Contemporary Scottish Studies column in the *Scottish Educational Journal*, which followed *Northern Numbers* and *Scottish Chapbook* – in effect the beginnings of the Scottish Renaissance as a literary movement. This prodigious burst of energy is all the more remarkable when placed alongside MacDiarmid's other commitments; for as well as working as a full-time journalist on the *Montrose Review*, he was also publishing and editing the *Scottish Nation*, a weekly dedicated to Scottish nationalism, and the *Northern Review*, whose life was as short as its predecessors' but whose influence is as significant. C. M. Grieve was also a town councillor, a parish councillor and a justice of the peace. Over the next twenty years, often using a variety of pseudonyms, he produced a continuous flow of newspaper articles, essays, books,

30. Alan Bold, *op. cit.*

reviews, letters and speeches, as well as poems, stories, at least one playscript and a lost, unfinished novel. They made him one of the best-known cultural figures in Scotland, as well as the most contentious.

From his Contemporary Scottish Studies column onwards he urged Scots to look outwards, to seek precedents rather than models or traditions, intellectual trailblazers rather than heroes. For this reason he hated the Burns cult, whose existence he felt demeaned Burns and his achievement, and he therefore urged Scots to reach beyond Burns, back to William Dunbar, whose work provided an antidote to the sentimental mire into which Scots and Scottish poetry had descended in the post-Burnsian age. Scots, he claimed, could provide the modernist poet not only with a natural linguistic richness, but also with a series of images and a directness no longer available in English.

He deliberately used the word 'renaissance' to create a climate of creative activity which he believed would restore our national sense of self-worth. He was a founder member of the National Party of Scotland in 1928, and later became a Communist, rejoining the party in 1957 after the Hungarian Uprising. This and similar acts and statements were part of a deliberate strategy to shock, to stir Scots into eschewing the twin bedevilments of mediocrity and provincialism.

In many ways MacDiarmid set the cultural agenda, an itinerary which is to a large degree followed to this day. The fact that he was tone-deaf – an assertion made by Maurice Lindsay in his account of *Francis George Scott and the Scottish Renaissance* – did not prevent him espousing his views on music, any more than an inability to speak Gaelic debilitated his opinions on Gaelic poetry. He was especially vehement in his criticism of others, attacking friends and former allies alike; his biographer speaks of a 'desire to wound opponents in literary warfare'.[31] Nor were his methods always direct, nor even directly literary.

Writing of *Scott and Scotland*, Andrew Noble noted that, 'With the exception of MacDiarmid, Muir's major contemporaries saw the book as of seminal importance. Catherine Carswell and William Soutar were as enthusiastic as Janet Adam Smith and [Neil] Gunn.' He later summarises the essay as 'a concise and honest attempt to evaluate Scottish achievements in the light of comparable English ones and on the basis of this evaluation see how Scottish literature might develop'.

But MacDiarmid considered Muir's suggestion that Scottish literature should wholly adopt the English language, since its inheritance was strongly derived from the English tradition, to be an act of unpardonable treachery. He not only attacked Muir but continued the dispute indefinitely; for once a colleague strayed, there was no road back.

31. *Ibid.*

As well as perpetuating the dispute in the preface of his *Golden Treasury of Scottish Poetry*, in which Muir was not only omitted but also castigated, and in his autobiography *Lucky Poet*, the September–November 1938 issue of the *Voice of Scotland* carried a caricature captioned 'Willa and Edwin', drawn by Barbara Niven to the instructions of Valda, MacDiarmid's wife. Muir's wife, Willa, is shown as a prodigious, overwhelming figure stroking the ear of a lamb, which bears more than a passing resemblance to her husband. Valda and MacDiarmid were unrepentant, even when he was chided by the Scottish District Committee of the Communist Party. Muir, by contrast, never entered into debate with MacDiarmid.

Our search for a hero, and MacDiarmid's cyclical itch to satiate himself in the role, means we have always needed an ever-ready supply of villains, and what villains could be more appropriate than those the hero chooses? That MacDiarmid should turn on Muir over such an issue was, in retrospect, entirely predictable; though perhaps MacDiarmid also missed the point, as well as muddying the argument by personalising the attack.

Some of MacDiarmid's judgements could leave him uniquely stranded, for example his *Burns Today and Tomorrow*, a distillation of his persistent attacks upon a recurring subject, in which he views Burns as a great songwriter but an inferior poet. Many other pronouncements would seem to be based as much upon external factors such as political allegiances as upon his literary judgement, or, as in this case, a detestation of Burns Clubs rather than a regard for the songs. And no matter the cause or its origins, MacDiarmid's disputes almost always became personal.

MacDiarmid decried Burns in much the same way that George Bernard Shaw before him had denigrated Shakespeare, and for much the same reasons. Shaw's principal attack was on Shakespeare as an icon. In focusing his attack on the Burns Clubs, MacDiarmid had an easier target. He could criticise Burns's work as pernicious because of what it had spawned, and this placed him in a perfect position to attack other writers. It was a battleground where he chose the enemy, the battlefield and the weapons.

Muir is by no means the only writer to have suffered the long scourge of MacDiarmid's excoriations. MacDiarmid's opinions were rarely difficult to understand, nor were they in the least ambiguous; his roles as a poet and a propagandiser have mingled. The writer with whom he can most easily be contrasted is not Burns but Scott. In fact, he now occupies a position which is not dissimilar to that of Sir Walter Scott. His work is in danger of being drowned in the swell of his political opinions and he is instantly recognised for his activities in establishing or shaping Scottish identity as much as for, and in some cases rather than for, his work as a writer.

The Most Varied and Discordant Emotions

Muir shared MacDiarmid's contempt for the fact 'that Burns has been unostentatiously but securely swallowed and digested by Holy Willie during the century and a bit since his death'. Burns's fate is the fate of all writers, he says: that even though they may not reflect the economic ideology of the society in which they live, 'their writings are finally and in the long run made to reflect that ideology, by a process of elimination and transformation, until the most influential classes in society can finally put their seal on the result'.[32]

One of the things MacDiarmid achieved by demanding we return to Dunbar in order to create a climate where Scottish poetry could be properly discussed was to instigate a reassessment of Robert Burns and his extraordinary achievements, to draw attention to the fact that Burns's work had been distorted to suit a succession of agendas that were never his own, and therefore the only way we could begin a reassessment was to see the work in the light of its creation, as the poet saw it.

Burns was a superlative figure, whom one feels would have been notable no matter what he did. Scotland has no public holiday on either St Andrew's Day, 30 November, or on Burns's birthday, 25 January, but Burns is the only poet in the world whose birthday is celebrated in the same style as a national holiday. His achievement was to produce a poetry that has remained immediately accessible. Like Shakespeare, he not only seems to know more than we do, but also to understand more and to present these understandings to us in an immediately accessible and memorable form. We feel he knows us and can present complicated ideas simply; consequently he makes poetry look easy, which has led to him becoming one of the world's most imitated poets.

Muir states the point precisely:

> For a Scotsman to see Burns simply as a poet is almost impossible. Burns is
> so deeply imbedded in Scottish life that he cannot be detached from it . . .
> and regarded as we regard Dunbar or James Hogg or Walter Scott. He is
> more a personage to us than a poet, more a figurehead than a personage,
> and more a myth than a figurehead. To those who have heard of Dunbar
> he is a figure, of course, comparable to Dunbar; but he is also a figure
> comparable to Prince Charlie, about whom everyone has heard. He is a
> myth evolved by the popular imagination, a communal poetic creation, a
> Protean figure; we can all shape him to our own likeness, for a myth is end-
> lessly adaptable; so that to the respectable this secondary Burns is a decent
> man; to the Rabelaisian, bawdy; to the sentimentalist, sentimental; to the

---

32. See Andrew Noble (ed.), *Edwin Muir: Uncollected Scottish Criticism.*

Socialist, a revolutionary; to the Nationalist, a patriot; to the religious, pious; to the self-made man, self-made; to the drinker, a drinker. He has the power of making any Scotsman, whether generous or canny, sentimental or prosaic, religious or profane, more whole-heartedly himself than he could have been without assistance; and in that way perhaps more human. He greases our wheels; we could not roll on our way so comfortably but for him; and it is impossible to judge impartially a convenient appliance to which we have grown accustomed. . . . No other writer has said so fully and expressly what every man of his race wanted him to say; no other writer, consequently, has been taken so completely into the life of a people.[33]

For more than two hundred years the people of Scotland have indeed taken Burns to themselves, identifying especially with his ability to straddle contradictory aspects of our national character. Recognising his struggle to educate himself and maintain his family bolsters our myth of self-reliance; his tortured love life gave rise to the best love songs ever written; his attacks on religious and political humbug and hypocrisy are still apposite; and his political thinking, especially the social and egalitarian principles found in songs such as 'A Man's a Man', have endeared him to successive generations of Scots. They love his contradictions, they savour and relish them and use him as an adaptable national icon, often to espouse causes of which Burns would heartily disapprove.

Burns's work has been used as a source of national identity and pride, distinguishing a revival of the Scots vernacular tradition which began with Ramsay and Ferguson and which has since then remained alive in one form or another. 'Although not one person in a hundred may ever read the verses of Scottish poets, the fact that they exist has helped to maintain a sense of national identity,' says the historian Gordon Donaldson.[34]

Of course, the obverse can also be true. It is not so much that Burns has shaped our national identity; rather that our national identity, or lack of it, has shaped our view of Burns, just as it has shaped our view of other writers, painters and musicians, to say nothing of historical figures such as William Wallace and contemporary public cultural icons such as Sean Connery, Billy Connolly or Ewan McGregor.

Burns's fame is as personal as it is literary, and the affection in which he is held is as much as a person as a poet, evidenced by the way in which his name is used in a familiar, almost familial way. He is saluted both as a creative genius, as someone who not only came from common stock, but understood and championed the common man and, in a number of memorable songs and poems, placed the dignity and worth of mankind

33. Edwin Muir, 'Burns and Popular Poetry' in Andrew Noble (ed.), *op. cit.*
34. Gordon Donaldson, *Scotland: The Shaping of a Nation.*

alongside simple and memorable expressions of universal feelings and beliefs.

Scott stated what for many is the essence of his genius: 'No poet, with the exception of Shakespeare,' he wrote in the *Quarterly Review* in 1809, 'ever possessed the power of exciting the most varied and discordant emotions with such rapid transition.' In his journal in 1813 Byron wrote of Burns, 'What an antithetical mind! – tenderness, roughness – delicacy, coarseness – sentiment, sensuality – soaring and grovelling, dirt and deity – all mixed up in that one compound of "inspired clay".'

Born in 1759 in Alloway, Ayrshire, in a house his father had built, Burns was buried in Dumfries, where he died of rheumatic fever in 1796. As a young man he found work as an exciseman, being recommended to the service by Adam Smith. His early combination of love poems and satires, together with a series of romantic adventures, made life in Ayrshire so difficult that he considered emigration. When the Kilmarnock edition of his poems was published on 31 July 1786, he was projected into national fame; four months later he was Enlightenment Edinburgh's sensation of the year.

In the Kilmarnock edition Burns cast himself in the role of 'heaven-taught ploughman' and he has been consistently seen in that role, to the extent that the centenary edition of his poems presented him as someone prevented from writing the highest form of poetry because of his linguistic and intellectual contradictions and deficiencies.

Today we see him differently. His reputation has never been greater, simply because we have looked at the whole poet, seen his work in its own light, free from the bigotry of class or linguistic prejudice, heard his songs as he intended, found his political views concordant with our own, and given our own attitude to such matters, so that the twin barriers of his social and sexual escapades hardly seem to matter. We no longer see him through Victorian eyes, nor are we distorted by their vision.

For all this familiarity, his image remains tantalisingly out of reach. Though the Nasmyth head-and-shoulders portrait has been reproduced on a succession of commercial products, no two portraits of Burns painted from life resemble the same person. Which places him with the other activists in an age of social and political change and underlines his right to occupy a seat with the other contributors to our national mythology who, with the possible exception of Charles Edward Stewart, either have no portrait or the portraits that do exist appear to be of different people. Reliable images seem to elude our heroes.

Burns's body was transplanted by improving Victorians to lie beneath what must be one of the ugliest pieces of official sculpture outside the Soviet Union. The Muse is shown visiting Rabbie at the plough, thereby ensuring the image is seen as more important than Burns's poetry or what it contained.

Robert Burns was a friend of Allan Cunningham's father. Cunningham followed Burns's funeral procession and in his *Life of Burns*, written in 1834, he records the question being asked on the streets of Dumfries as Burns's cortege passed: 'Who will be our poet now?' The question suggests that Robert Burns in his lifetime had come to compensate for the loss of nation-hood, which is extremely poignant, even tragic. It not only puts Burns in an impossible position; it is also clear evidence of our second-hand attitude towards ourselves. We need a writer, not a body of literature or a group of writers, but a single writer in whom to invest our national identity. And the only difference in two hundred years is that the position has, if anything, intensified. Burns is still seen as a national icon and we trawl our literature for suitable candidates to take his place, however temporarily.

Carol McGuirk has remarked that Scott, Stevenson and MacDiarmid had to repudiate Burns to replace his mythic Scotland with their own ver-sions.[35] And Ken Simpson takes the idea further, commenting that the Scotlands these and other writers have imagined are not without their own mythic qualities.[36]

In an age when we are often unable to distinguish between notoriety and fame, MacDiarmid's work can seem truly heroic, though if ever a man campaigned for the job of Scotland's national bard-hero-icon it was Christopher Murray Grieve. Similar Herculean claims can be made for the poetry of Sorley Maclean, or for the novels and stories of Robert Louis Stevenson. And, more recently, Iain Crichton Smith and Edwin Morgan have produced bodies of work of similar formidable dimension and intensity, the one by diving down, going inwards, shining a torch into his darkest corners, the other by extending outwards, even into space.

Black, Dark Blue, Payne's Grey, Yellow

Muir thought Kirkcudbrightshire one of Scotland's most beautiful coun-ties, and the town itself 'has a great number of handsome houses, which I believe have been looked after and preserved by the colony of painters who are settled in the town. Most of the houses round the harbour square and in the streets leading off it are painted in various colours, black, dark blue, Payne's grey, yellow – a pleasant surprise in a Scottish street.'[37]

This is where Scotland's first Christian Church was founded at Whithorn by St Ninian in the fourth century, an area where ancient remnants of cairns and burial mounds, standing stones and circles can be found. This is the part of Scotland closest to Ireland, the start of the Southern Upland

35. Carol McGuirk, 'Burns and Nostalgia' in Kenneth Simpson (ed.), *Burns Now*.
36. Kenneth Simpson, 'Robert Burns: "Heaven-taught Ploughman"?' in *Burns Now*.
37. Edwin Muir, *Scottish Journey*.

Way, a walk that crosses the Borders to Cockburnspath in Berwickshire and at the end of the glorious Glen Trool stretch by Clatteringshaws Loch passes the Raiders' Road, a 10-mile forest drive by the Black Water of Dee, a route taken by armed thieves and raiders in S. R. Crockett's 1894 novel *The Raiders*, at around the time that the Glasgow Boys E. A. Hornel and George Henry were collaborating in Kirkcudbright.

Hornel had spent his childhood in Kirkcudbright. After studying in Antwerp, he met George Henry in the autumn of 1885. Henry had attended the informal life-painting classes at William Macgregor's studio in Bath Street, Glasgow, and in 1881 joined Macgregor, James Guthrie, Edward Walton and Joseph Crawhall to paint at Brig o' Turk in the Trossachs, a trip which is now seen as seminal in the development of the Glasgow Boys as a group. It was the first of many trips they made, working in small, rural communities, using natural light in landscapes that were far less dramatic than conventional notions had previously allowed, following William McTaggart's refusal to reproduce Scott's 'land of the mountain and the flood' on canvas.

Paintings such as Guthrie's *A Hind's Daughter*, Henry's *Playmates* and Macgregor's *The Vegetable Stall* came from these trips, works where the communities are accepted on their own terms and portrayed in their natural surroundings, rather than as stage dressing or subjects to be viewed from a distance, part of the landscape they inhabit, or missing altogether. In their paintings from this period the Glasgow Boys (so named mostly for exhibition purposes) painted Scotland's rural inhabitants, recording their landscape and character as faithfully as folk-song collectors had recorded their ancestors' songs. Inspired by the works of James McNeill Whistler, Jean-François Millet and Jules Bastien-Lepage, the group set out to bring what they called 'naturalism' to Scottish art, painting from nature in natural light, away from studio settings, following Bastien-Lepage by recording rural subjects and, like him, using tonal effects to create a vision that appealed more to realism than the simplified, cosmeticised views of humanity that were in vogue at the time.

This also ran counter to the conventional literary voices of the time, for although the *Whistle-Binkie* anthologies ran from 1832 to 1890 and reached their apogee around the 1860s, their influence was far more pervasive. The pages were stuffed with sentimental, complacent vernacular verse which undoubtedly softened public taste for the cosiness of the Kailyard, so that when the Glasgow Boys began painting in the early 1880s, at the same time as James Thomson published *The City of Dreadful Night*, their depictions of rural life not only ran counter to the nightmarish vision of urban realism which Thomson depicted, but followed Bastien-Lepage in ignoring industrialisation and the emerging working class to identify with a far older tradition of the landscape, the peasant and the soil, a feature they shared with Robert Louis Stevenson.

Their time was relatively brief, and although almost two dozen painters were involved, according to Roger Billcliffe, 'only about nine or ten made any real contribution to its development'.[38] Some trained with John Lavery in France while others followed James Guthrie to Cockburnspath in Berwickshire, though the list of locations where the Glasgow Boys worked ranges from Galloway, Rosneath and Brig o' Turk to Lincolnshire, eventually extending through France, Spain and Italy and into North Africa, as well as Japan.

Hornel invited Henry to join him in Kirkcudbright, and of all the associations that developed between the Glasgow Boys, theirs was to prove the most artistically innovative. Rather than follow the realistic path of their contemporaries, Hornel and Henry developed a decorative, symbolistic approach to their subject matter. The Hornel–Henry collaboration *The Druids: Bringing in the Mistletoe*, painted in 1890, is seen as being strongly influenced by Patrick Geddes's theories of decorative art, though it also recalls the more nationalist symbolism of the Ossian mythologies. The previous year, Henry had painted *A Galloway Landscape*, which Duncan Macmillan describes as 'one of the most beautiful Scottish landscapes of its time'.[39] It also combines realism and fantasy, the cattle merging with a landscape which is dappled with patches of sunlight, here and there shaded from an almost clear blue sky, in much the same way as Hornel's figures are partially obscured by foliage. The movement between light and shade brings a symbolic unity to the whole, and though there is an absence of people, this does not have the detracting effect of the earlier pictures, where the grandeur of the landscape dominates the view. This is a far more ordinary, domestic scene, whose implications are implicit in the title.

This desire to root their work in the everyday, moving away both from figurative representations of an anecdotal kind and also from Romantic Highland landscapes, while also avoiding industrial landscapes, brought painting nearer to the heart of Scottish identity. This was endorsed by other members of the Glasgow set, and was central to the architecture of James Maclaren and Charles Rennie Mackintosh, and it is also seen in the nationalistic topics and treatments of composers such as Sir Alexander Mackenzie and Sir John McEwen. It is apparent, too, in the realism that pervades the post-Kailyard domesticity of *The House with the Green Shutters* and, later, *Gillespie*.

A Galloway Landscape and many other paintings of the period not only set out to democratise art and its subject matter, but to approach the subjects in an essentially Scottish way, which, as in the contemporary fiction of Robert Louis Stevenson, not only twins opposites but has a fantastic

38. Roger Billcliffe, 'The Glasgow Boys' in Carl MacDougall (ed.), *Glasgow's Glasgow: People Within a City*.
39. Duncan Macmillan, *Scottish Art 1460–1990*.

dimension as well. This imaginative dimension, a desire for the exotic or simply a wish to extend their range of decorative possibilities with figurative composition, led some Glasgow Boys to seek inspiration elsewhere. In 1893 Henry and Hornel went to Japan, staying for nineteen months, the trip financed by the Glasgow art dealer Alexander Reid. Hornel's Japanese work is as dense as his Scots work, but Henry seems to have absorbed something of his surroundings in the simplicity of line and tone, and in the ways in which his decorative effects are muted.

Hornel later converted Broughton House in Kirkcudbright into a combined home and studio with a Japanese garden beyond. He had bought the building with the proceeds from the sale of one painting, and used it to house his extensive library, which was mostly concerned with folklore, mythology and local history.

The Glasgow Boys soon began to assert their individuality, but their influence endured long after many of them had left the city, indeed long after Alexander Reid's successors had shut up shop and moved to London in 1914. Their most immediate influence was on the established art world. They arrested the decline in Scottish painting and broke the Edinburgh establishment clique's position of abandoning their Edinburgh residence requirement for membership of the Royal Scottish Academy.

'The Glasgow Boys' adoption of French manners and style was partly a rejection of the kind of painting which then dominated Scotland through the Academy and other Establishment bodies,' writes Roger Billcliffe.

> This particular angst was unrepeated elsewhere and gave their rebellion, such as it was, a particular edge and vibrancy lacking in other similar movements in Britain. Nationalism, in its broader sense, was the second, perhaps more important element in Glasgow's artistic vitality at the turn of the century. The Boys may have looked to France for inspiration to break the stranglehold of mediocrity on most Scottish painting of the 1870s and 1880s, but they translated the new French ideas into paintings which were recognizably Scottish. Their awareness of the identifiable qualities of Scottish painting gave a new life and integrity to naturalism, which in Newlyn, for instance, was used to dress up old ideas in new clothes.[40]

An important element in the Glasgow School's quest for identity through art and landscape was their need to involve the rural working class in their search, making them part of it, as well as a means or subject. In this quest they never quite managed to avoid sentimentality, which one feels is on the edge of many pictures, but they did avoid exploitation,

40. Roger Billcliffe, 'How Many Swallows Make a Summer? Art and Design in Glasgow in 1900' in Wendy Kaplan (ed.), *Scotland Creates: 5000 Years of Art and Design.*

especially in the ways they represented work as well as the workers. To look at Guthrie's *A Hind's Daughter* is to encounter not only a robustly painted subject, but also to see the detachment with which the artist and therefore the viewer is regarded by the subject. She looks as if she has been interrupted, has just stood up from back-breaking work, her name having been called, and is anxious to get on with it, to be in from the cold. Similarly, she would recognise the contents of Macgregor's *The Vegetable Stall* in the forms in which they are painted – leeks, rhubarb, turnips, carrots covered in earth, and two colours of cabbage. It is a celebration of the means whereby the poor survive, a painting which tries to reach those who identify with the subject rather than simply recognise its components. Just as surely as James Paterson's *Autumn, Glencairn* and George Henry's *A Galloway Landscape* gives them a land-scape to inhabit, a landscape the subjects would recognise as surely as their masters, here Macgregor offers something the peasantry would recognise and appreciate much more readily than their masters, simply because it is the result of their labours.

The Glasgow Boys sought to democratise art not only by placing people in the landscape, but by placing working people in their natural envir-onment. This surely helped shift the focus of Scottish painting away from the class-based romanticism which had previously pervaded art, though there is more than a touch of romance in some of the Boys' works, Stuart Park and Hornel for instance. The influence of the Glasgow Boys at a time when Europe was awash with romantic nationalism cleared a path for later painters, such as the four individuals now known as the Scottish Colourists: Leslie Hunter, Samuel Peploe, Francis Cadell and J. D. Fergusson. The climate they created may also have influenced Muirhead Bone's turn-of-the-century depictions of Glasgow working life, which represented to Glaswegians subjects they would recognise, and enabled Joan Eardley to depict the people in the dilapidated shops and closes around her Townhead studio.

Not that this development occurred in isolation. Throughout the nine-teenth century there was extensive research into colour and optics. This was initiated by the textile companies, who were anxious to provide the tartan movement – burgeoning in the wake of the royal visit of 1822 – with newly bright, fresh colours. There was also a photographic compon-ent: knowledge we take for granted today was discovered back then. It was found that if you twist two strands of different-coloured threads together, from a distance the eye sees only one colour. Blending primary colours together results in a muddy brown, but when complementary colours are placed beside each other it makes them stand out. It was also discovered that blending primary colours of light together makes white, and that refracting a beam of light through a prism produces a rainbow, which if refracted through a second prism becomes white again.

Then, in the 1840s, tubes of paint became available for the first time. Without this invention, Impressionism would not have occurred when it did. Tubes made painting out of doors possible. Artists such as Alexander Nasmyth and Horatio McCulloch previously sketched outdoors and then painted in their studios.

With the coming of the railways in the 1860s, the middle classes from the towns enjoyed days out in the parks, the countryside and at the seaside, and, as the *Steamboat Travellers Remembrancer* reminds us, folk started sailing doon the watter. People were able to leave the city for the first time, and so naturalistic country subjects had a wider appeal.

The Mingling of Reality and Fantasy

The Galloway landscape and the effect of light on the land, facing south, producing soft colours through many tones and ranges, attracted a succession of artists. When Jessie Marion King settled in Kirkcudbright at the outbreak of the First World War, the colony that became known as the Kirkcudbright School and her own remarkable career were well established. She and her husband, Ernest Taylor, had left their own art school and studio, the Sheiling Atelier, in Paris to settle in Green Gate Close, and there they stayed for the rest of their lives.

Jessie King's father was a Bearsden minister, and she joined the staff of the Glasgow School of Art when the city's artistic influence was at its highest. By 1902 the Glasgow Boys had spread the city's reputation across Europe, and Charles Rennie Mackintosh's stature was expanding. King had won a gold medal for book design at the Turin International Exhibition of the Decorative Arts, where she exhibited with Charles Rennie Mackintosh. Her designs often have a mystical appearance, incorporating fairies and supernatural beings, and her work covered a wide range and scale, including book illustrations, ceramics, textile designs, murals, and jewellery for Liberty, as well as drawings and painting.

Ernest Taylor's work is equally diverse. The Taylors were in Paris at the same time as J. D. Fergusson, and Peploe was a frequent visitor to Green Gate Close. Here, again, the mingling of reality and fantasy not only places their work in a recognisable imaginative tradition, but also extends the sense of the fantastic that the Glasgow artists shared, especially Mackintosh and the Macdonald sisters, who produced illusory, often whimsical, designs for practical objects, or decorated their surroundings with notional panels.

Identifiably Scottish

Galloway inspired the composer Sir John Blackwood McEwen into expressing the moods of Scottish landscape, as a painter or writer may do, rather than what John Purser calls 'colouring it', as Sir Alexander Mackenzie and Hamish MacCunn had done. His chamber works are especially suited for the medium, but the *Solway Symphony* (one of five) and *Grey Galloway*, one of three 'border ballads' for full orchestra, are his best large-scale works, in which, more than any previous Scottish composer, McEwen realises a synthesis between native and contemporary classical idioms, then being repeated throughout Galloway in the medium of painting.

MacEwen followed Mackenzie and MacCunn as Scottish composers who used national themes in accordance with the style that was sweeping Europe, the spirit of romantic nationalism that had initially been inspired by Scott and given a fresh impetus by Wagner. Mackenzie's *Second Scottish Rhapsody* is an obviously nationalistic work, while Hamish MacCunn seemed to find his strongest inspiration from Scott, his opera *Jeanie Deans* (based on Scott's *Heart of Midlothian*), and a dramatic cantata, *The Lay of the Last Minstrel*, being the more obvious examples. But his commitment to the poetic and descriptive, rather than following the road of abstraction which was fashionable at the time, is found in *The Dowie Dens o' Yarrow*, a brilliantly scored and often darkly sweeping statement, based on the murder ballad. These and other Scottish composers have been unjustly neglected, a fate they share with many British composers of the period excepting, strangely enough, that most nationalistic and romantic of composers, Edward Elgar. By using such obviously Scottish themes, and especially in naming their works in such an obviously and identifiably nationalist way, they were making a series of statements that were concordant with the mood of the times, revealing themselves as intentionally and identifiably Scottish in their sources of inspiration, be they Burns, Scott or the landscape itself.

No Third Alternative

Scottish identity has long been associated with the practical things we made – in shipbuilding and heavy engineering. Lanarkshire's fate was sealed when David Napier invented the hot blast process to turn iron into steel with plenty of coal on hand to heat the furnaces.

When Muir travelled through the county, after his brakes had gone on fire outside Girvan, he missed the Lanarkshire steel mills and coal mines; he even missed the lead mines at Wanlockhead and Robert Owen's model village on New Lanark, saving his 'dark picture of industrialism' for Glasgow. This is arguably the feature of the Scottish landscape he would have difficulty with, since the city and, more especially, the impact of the city, spilled into the surrounding countryside. Even ten years ago he would have seen remnants at Ravenscraig, but the decimation of the steel and coal industries has left a landscape and a people struggling to come to terms with their industrialised past.

In Maybole Muir inquired after a friend, whom he found had emigrated, along with other acquaintances. The village hall where he had
learned to dance was filled, he said, with ghosts, the place crushed by
unemployment and emigration.

When Muir finds a crowd, he becomes disdainful. Burns's cottage was
packed: '. . . in the blazing sun hordes of people were wandering about the
courtyard behind the bars like tame animals'. And, of course, he hated it,
wondering how they would deal with their enormous traffic in fifty years'
time. 'The cottage will certainly have to be enlarged, or else the price of
admission raised until only the well-to-do can get in. There seems no
third alternative except demolition.'[41]

It's the cult that both feeds and fosters mythology and the cult that
brings the hordes. Muir claims he is concerned not with Burns, but with
the legend, and avoids the superficiality he revealed at Abbotsford. He
seems instinctively warmer to Burns than to Scott, though he was later to
pair them together as 'sham bards of a sham nation'. His purpose, of
course, was to attack those he saw as the forebears of the Kailyard. 'Of all
the identities the inhabitants of Scotland might assume, the falsest of all,
implies Muir, is the mask of couthy sentimentality and religiosity.'[42]

But the myth of Burns – and, by implication, the mythology fostered by
Scott – would not have risen at all if Scots had not an exceptionally
powerful myth-making faculty.

> The history of Scotland is filled with legendary figures, actual characters on
> which the popular imagination has worked, making them its own and by
> doing so transfiguring them. Wallace and Bruce, Mary Stuart and Prince
> Charlie, are not so much historical characters as figures in an unwritten
> ballad: they have taken on an almost purely poetical reality, and are semi-
> inventions like Mary Hamilton and the Bonny Earl of Moray, the originals of
> whom we know to have existed historically, but who are now part of a song.[43]

Even within this overt context, Muir does not refer to the quest for a
cultural identity that typified the 1930s. This may have been because he
was part of that quest; and when seen in that light his remarks on historical identity take on a new perspective. He maintained that we live in a
country whose past has been moulded by poetry, such as the ballads, but
which has produced few poets, and that the poetry which pervades our
history is purely romantic. The Industrial Revolution destroyed not only
the poetry but also the faculty for communal myth-making that was its
source, a point underlined almost fifty years later by Adam McNaughtan.

41. Edwin Muir, *op. cit.*
42. Christopher Smout, Introduction, *Scottish Journey*, 1979 edition.
43. Edwin Muir, *op. cit.*

Songs and ballads, stories and myths about mill work, coal mining, the coming of the railways and the horrors of industrialisation have been collected throughout the British Isles. But the Industrial Revolution was largely ignored by writers other than the folk poets. Especially prevalent are songs about strikes and lock-outs, working disasters and the need for workers to take collective industrial action. The folklorist A. L. Lloyd collected and studied industrial folk songs, especially in the mining communities, and his findings form the basis for a chapter of his classic study *Folksong in England*. The number of love songs and comic songs suggest that Scots industrial songs are a natural extension of work songs in general, such as the cornkisters, though a songwriter like Matt McGinn owes at least as much to the music hall:

> I had a gaffer, his name was O'Rourke,
> He had a terrible passion for work.
> In yards and in tons he took aa he could see,
> But he never was greedy – he gied it tae me.

The signs of industrialisation that accompanied Muir from Ayr to Kilmarnock have gone, as have Kilmarnock's distinctive tenements, 'of such an extraordinary variety of shapes and sizes, some tall, some squat, some straight, some crooked – they gave the impression of being more endurable, more comfortable than the vertical, high, gaunt tenement slum of Glasgow'.

Kilmarnock was thriving when John Wilson brought out the first edition of Robert Burns's poems, after Burns had raised the requisite number of subscriptions. The railway line from Kilmarnock to Troon was the first established by a parliamentary act, and was evidence of the way Kilmarnock businessmen were thinking. BMK carpets, Johnnie Walker whisky, Saxone shoes and Barclay locomotives lasted until the general decline and predatory policies of the 1980s left Kilmarnock stranded, an outpost in an arc extending from Glasgow – much of Lanarkshire finds itself in a similar position. Having lost their indigenous heavy industries, the people are trying to find replacements for the work as well as the sense of community and identity that went with it.

Lanarkshire boasts parks, a cinema and shopping complexes designed to attract the Glasgow tourist. The model village David Dale and Robert Owen built around their mill at New Lanark boasts its success in winning a tourism 'Oscar'. In Bellshill a factory unit has been taken over by a firm who call themselves 'Scotland's chocolate makers'. Duncan's most recent brand is called Independence Chocolate. And Hamilton – a 'rare example of an attractive industrial town' – boasts a curfew, Scotland's first street curfew for under-sixteen-year-olds.

The curfew was the idea of local residents. It operates in the Whitehill,

Hillhouse and Fairhill housing schemes, which are virtually intercon-
nected. One of the most common complaints made by residents
concerned what was described as 'the cult of drinking Buckfast Tonic
Wine by under-aged youngsters on Hamilton street'. According to a
Herald report in October 1997, 'A six-year-old child was among 13 children rounded up at the weekend on the third night of [the curfew]'.

'The streets are now awfully quiet and you're not trying to fight your
way past cheeky kids if you go out at nine o'clock,' says a thirty-three-year-
old woman, who admits the problem is keeping her own three children
occupied. 'It seems that, for my kids, there's nothing to do unless you
want to pay for it.' A positive aspect of the curfew is that her children will
always head home before the police round starts. In short, she knows
where they are. Though another part of the problem is that they are
mixing with children who have no fear of their parents, who recognise no
authority and who taunt adults to hit or discipline them, saying, 'You hit
me, and I'll get you jailed.'

While early figures showed crime among under-sixteens fell by a third
and complaints about youth behaviour were halved, the problem has to
some extent been cosmeticised. Children still have nothing to do. There
is, says another resident, no place where the children can develop social
skills, and the younger ones need a play area that is off-limits to older children. There are plans to adopt the Hamilton curfew experiment
throughout the country.

It could be argued that national identity can only come from an individual identity; and the extent to which individual identity is dependent
on role and function within society appears to be under continual review.
'The new approach being advocated by the Scottish Council Federation
is to focus on people's living conditions and to show the effect that unemployment, low income and poor housing can have on self-confidence,
self-esteem and mental health,' says a report published in November
1998. 'A lack of hope and optimism are as strong risk factors for heart disease as is smoking,' says one of the report's authors.[44]

44. *Observer*, 29 November 1998.

4

It's Goin Roon and Roon

'I'll sing a song of Glasgow town,
Where wealth and want abound;
Where the high seat of learning dwells
'Mid ignorance profound.
Oh, when will Glasgow make a rule
To do just what she ought –
Let starving bairns in every school
Be fed as well as taught!
And when will Glasgow city be
Fair Caledonia's pride,
And boast her clear unclouded skies,
And crystal-flowing Clyde?'

MARION BERNSTEIN, 'A Song of Glasgow Town'

Riverun

Most European cities with river locations use the water to enhance their buildings. A river seems to provide an architect with the perfect location. The idea certainly appealed to the Glaswegian town planners who built Carlton Place on the south side of the river, even though this splendid terrace, with Laurieston House in the centre, was no sooner built than it was hemmed in by commercial imperatives.

Westwards and across Jamaica Bridge on the other side of the river is the Clyde Port Authority headquarters. It's best seen at night, when street lamps on either side of the river and the city's new night architecture illuminate Laurieston House, Alexander Kirkland's suspension bridge, Jamaica Bridge, the old Custom House on Clyde Street, the railway bridges, and the former transit sheds and warehouses that run off the

Broomielaw. All were built with reflection in mind, even though the Clyde was then a working river.

A riverside setting gives a sense of theatre. It balances the buildings on its banks, acting both as an extension to a building and as a mirror of it. But Glasgow's recent riverside buildings – a cinema and restaurant complex, council flats, private houses, a casino – could have been sited anywhere; in fact they would be better situated away from the river, where the water only draws attention to their drab lack of imagination.

In *The Expedition of Humphry Clinker* (1771) Tobias Smollett wrote:

> The river Clyde runs by their doors, in the lower part of the town; and there are rivulets and springs above the cathedral, sufficient to fill a large reservoir with excellent water, which might be thence distributed to all the different parts of the city. It is of more consequence to consult the health of the inhabitants in this article than to employ so much attention in beautifying their town with new streets, squares and churches. Another defect, not easily remedied, is the shallowness of the river, which will not float vessels of any burden within ten or twelve miles of the city; so that the merchants are obliged to load and unload their ships at Greenock and Port Glasgow, situated about fourteen miles from the mouth of the firth, where it is about two miles broad.

Port Glasgow had been built when the town council bought 13 acres around Newark Castle in 1668, on the opposite bank of the Clyde, giving Scotland its first graving dock and new town development.

In 1769, under James Watt's supervision, John Goldborne began work on a series of jetties which made the river navigable as far as Carlton Place, taking boats to the old Glasgow Bridge at the foot of Stockwell Street. The first Glasgow Bridge connected the route from the Cathedral to the Clyde, with the village of Gorbals on the south side of the river, a wooden structure so important it was defended by William Wallace.

With a navigable river Glasgow became a port. The Act of Union spared Scotland the burden of the Navigation Acts, which maintained an English monopoly on colonial trade, stipulating that no goods could be imported or exported from the colonies on anything other than English-built or English-owned ships, and that certain products, predominantly tobacco, rum and sugar, could be shipped only to England, or to English colonies.

Glasgow merchants and other Scottish traders had previously con-ducted illegal transactions with America and the West Indies, and they were now in a prime position to take advantage of their new freedom. Using the northern route, which directed ships away from waters domi-nated by France or Spain, Glasgow's ships could complete two round trips across the Atlantic without being reprovisioned, and their insurance rates were lower as the route dispensed with the need for a pirate indemnity clause.

At a time when tobacco was said to cure deafness if blown in the ear, when doctors claimed it was good for the lungs, and its fumes were thought to purify the air, Glasgow's tobacco lords were a law unto themselves. They formed their own aristocracy, dressed in black-satin suits and scarlet cloaks, powdered wigs and shoes with jewelled buckles, and built the town's first pavement in front of the council chambers and coffee house. They began the city's love affair with America.

By 1771, while work on the Clyde continued, more than 46 million tons of tobacco had been imported, 3 million tons of which were for home consumption; the rest was exported, mainly to France. The sugar and rum trade was almost as extensive, and in less than a generation the increase and amount of individual wealth concentrated in what had been an out-of-the-way backwater was stupendous. Through links with the likes of Stirling, Edinburgh and Aberdeen, Glasgow merchants could export linen, serge and muslin to America. The most important trading connections were in the area around Chesapeake Bay, though the tobacco lords owned vast plantations in Virginia. The merchants used a 'store system' whereby Glaswegian employees traded with the planters and stored the goods till the ships arrived.

American trade disappeared with the War of Independence, though many merchants made a second fortune buying up what stock they could, storing it and later reselling at inflated prices. William Cunningham, who built what was regarded as Glasgow's most imposing mansion, was a leading exponent of this art. His mansion was completed in 1778, to be recased and enlarged fifty years later when it became the Royal Exchange. Corinthian pillars were added in 1880, when the building was used to house Glasgow's first telephone exchange. By this time any evidence of its origins was lost, though it had another lease of life as a library and was recently transformed into the Gallery of Modern Art. Cunningham's friend Patrick Colquhoun founded the world's second Chamber of Commerce and Manufacture in Glasgow in 1783. The first was in New York.

Glasgow's wealth was based upon its merchant legacy; and were it not for industry's influence and the changes it effected, Glasgow would probably be remembered as an ecclesiastical and academic centre, of neither political nor strategic significance. The town seems to have developed along two sites: a ford just below the Clyde's tidal reach which became the site of the old Glasgow Bridge, and a bosky glade about a mile uphill around the cathedral, where the body of the city's founder, St Kentigern, is buried. Nothing of his church survives, though Mungo, as he is popularly known, lives on through his miracles, which have been concentrated into an assortment of symbols collected as the city's coat of arms – a bird, a bell, a tree, a fish and a ring.

Neither Here nor There

Glasgow has never had an identity problem. Indeed, other parts of the country often seem swamped by its apparent brashness, its inability to know its place or to conform.

The Glasgow accent was especially frowned upon by Scots-language purists, who found themselves in a strange alliance with those who favoured a more genteel, English accent. To a generation of schoolteachers bent on improvement, the Glasgow accent was, without question, the language of the gutter. Some areas of the English-speaking world still find it impenetrable. Ken Loach's film *My Name is Joe* was shown at the Toronto Film Festival with subtitles. The way the Glasgow accent has permeated recent Scottish culture, thanks mainly to the influence of television, is considered especially galling. In the days before Billy Connolly made the voice acceptable, a Glasgow accent epitomised a lack of gentility.

Part of Connolly's genius was to accept no such pretension and to use the voice as a persistent strength. He made us laugh publicly at things which had previously been found amusing only in private, and he did so without resorting to racial or sexual stereotypes. Connolly learned his trade in folk-song clubs, from singers such as Alex Campbell and Matt McGinn, and he embodied, perhaps even personified, many of the folk-song movement's early attitudes. From the outset the Scottish folk-song revival was anti-establishment, and though its radical nature and approach were later emulsified, its early demeanour has never been lost.

Edinburgh trembled when Glasgow was accorded European City of Culture status. The city appeared to have come from nowhere to snatch what Edinburgh considered its own. And only when Edinburgh joined the Glasgow gravy train at the behest of the Scottish Tourist Board, who advertised and packaged both cities as tourist destinations across Europe and America, was the capital appeased. Edinburgh made a concerted bid to be City of Architecture in 1999, and when the title went to Glasgow, they settled for the new Parliament, both temporary and permanent, as well as the national museums.

A Ranting Killjoy

Glasgow's status as a market town was confirmed in 1491, when the bishops were allowed to operate a public weighing system, or tron, forty years after a university had been founded by papal decree, and the year before the cathedral was given the status of an archbishopric. In this it was in direct competition with St Andrews, and so it stayed, until the Reformation. John Knox, the most important figure in Scottish history, according to Edwin Muir, is not known to have visited, though his image now glowers over the cathedral from Glasgow's City of the Dead, where merchants paid to be buried in unconsecrated ground, away from the lime pits stuffed with plague bodies.

In 1998 a campaign was established 'to restore the historical standing of John Knox, the father of the Scottish Reformation, reviled by late twentieth-century man as a ranting killjoy . . . . He wanted a school in every parish, a college in every town and a university in every city. He also wanted regular, organised provision for the poor.'[1] Knox's emphasis on education, welfare and the poor law 'had been overlaid also by the sectarian dimension', and Knox's statue on the Necropolis hill 'was specifically positioned there because it overlooked the most desperately poor areas of Irish Catholic migration into Scotland'.[2]

Glasgow's break with its ecclesiastical past came when the cathedral hosted the 1638 General Assembly, which led to the banning of bishops and a defiance of royal authority. Following its ecclesiastical demise, the town reinvented itself as a trading and mercantile centre, in which role it continued until it was forced to reinvent itself again at the onset of the Industrial Revolution. The main trading partners were on the Continent, and goods were transported along the Clyde to the Forth and Clyde Canal, which followed the Roman route of the Antonine Wall, a route the railway builders later adapted.

A plaque on Glasgow Green marks the spot where James Watt was said to have got the idea of a separate condenser in 1765, while taking a stroll near the old wash house. By this time, the city's grid had started a simultaneous move north- and westwards. Within twenty years of Watt's idea, Glasgow's limits would extend as every available river, burn and stream acquired at least one mill whose adjacent fields were used for dyeing and bleaching.

The cotton mills used an unprecedented supply of labour; and the river's most significant import was people. Between 1780 and 1830 Glasgow's population rose to an estimated 200,000; impoverished Irish and Highland families arrived on every tide. Glasgow's surrounding villages were transformed. Many were absorbed in the city's expansion, and as the dredging and deepening work continued, large areas of river frontage were converted into docks.

Notices of Glasgow in Former Times

Immigration trebled the city's population between 1800 and 1830, though the housing stock remained static. Following further cholera and typhus epidemics in 1846 and 1848, the city boundaries were extended and the corporation began moving people out of the slums, culminating

1. *Observer*, 5 April 1998.
2. *Ibid.*

in the City Improvement Act of 1866. This was also the start of the railway expansion, and the combination of these two developments rendered further people homeless. 'Hordes of the criminal classes,' wrote the historian C. A. Oakley, 'sheltered in the dens and caverns of dwelling houses in the narrow lanes and dark closes, rendering the localities notorious in the annals of robbery and murder.'[3]

The City Improvement Act initiated in Glasgow the world's first slum-clearance programme. Among the areas cleared were the Old University buildings in High Street, along with the original Hunterian Museum, and the last of the half-timbered houses in the Saltmarket and Briggait. New stations built to accommodate the railways required the demolition of parts of Trongate, the Gallowgate, High Street and Saltmarket, where as many as a thousand people were living on a single acre.

'In every disgusting regard – overbuilding, with its attendant curtailment of ventilation and light, and overcrowding in the overbuilt buildings, with its attendant destruction of physical and moral life – Glasgow was pre-eminent. Because of its particular system of land sale and its lack of authority over the advantages to absentee landlords of "making down" or sub-dividing existing buildings, Glasgow appears to have distilled, concentrated and emphasised the ills of the Industrial Revolution as they were magnified in an urban setting,' says Anita Ventura Mozley, curator of photography at the Stanford University Museum of Art, in her introduction to the Dover edition of Thomas Annan's *Photographs of the Old Closes and Streets of Glasgow 1868–1877*.

The City Improvement Trust had commissioned Thomas Annan to record their work from 1868 onwards. Annan photographed the slum area round the High Street, Saltmarket, Trongate and Gallowgate, the alleys and back courts, the tenements and their inhabitants. 'The photographs were only supposed to show the old buildings which were to be destroyed. But Annan's photographs go beyond a simple statement of past history. Within them there is a broad sense of time and emotion – the desperate human past of the buildings is seen to enclose an optimistic future,' says Sara Stevenson.[4]

The pictures are composed in such a way as to make them aesthetically pleasing, particularly in the way objects are arranged and people positioned and the way light comes into the wynds and closes. This gives them an ambiguous quality, which removes the works from their historical context, leaving contemporary viewers both delighted by what they see and appalled by the conditions in which the pictures were taken. Given our preoccupation with realism and the place photography now occupies as a means of providing documentary evidence, we are inclined

3. C. A. Oakley, *The Second City*.
4. Sara Stevenson, *Light From the Dark Room*.

to accept Annan's pictures at face value. But his approach 'was not what we would call straight,' says Anita Ventura Mozley. 'He added clouds which brighten the skies over Glasgow's slums, and he whitened the wash on the line. He did this for pictorial effect, for nice balance.'[5]

Thirty years later, the former war artist William 'Crimea' Simpson painted a series of views of Glasgow based on sketches he had made more than fifty years previously, often featuring dens and caverns reformed by the City Improvement Act. Simpson would have been familiar with Annan's photographs, and, like Annan, he records the people as well as their surroundings. His intention was to preserve a record of the Glasgow he knew, covering transitions such as the construction of a new quay on the south side of the river, which later became Kingston Docks and is now a leisure complex, the construction of Barclay and Curle's shipyard, now the site of the Scottish Exhibition and Conference Centre, as well as the Gallowgate's picturesque and unique sixteenth-century wooden buildings. Most of the views are now unrecognisable, and areas like the Gorbals have been improved at least twice since Simpson's time, but his buildings are given proportion by the people on the street. The Trongate has fashionable ladies on the pavements, a policeman on the corner and a woman sheltering in a doorway, a child on each arm. Elsewhere, washing hangs from poles in the window, as Annan had recorded, women bleach their clothes on the grass by the river and sailboats and steamboats manoeuvre up and down the Clyde. People are in every picture, though the slum areas are anything but overcrowded and the folk are colourfully dressed.

Muirhead Bone was responsible for Scottish art's most fundamental shift, a move which has never been fully exploited. He brought art into the city, chronicling Glasgow and its working lives in a series of memorable and starkly dramatic etchings which acted as the precursor to literature's discovery of the subject by almost half a century. This was one of Glasgow's earliest shifts towards realism.

It is the scale of operations, the constructions that appeal to Bone. He is interested in the visual spectacle, yet, by choosing such a subject, he echoes Ruskin's dictum of every feat of engineering being inspired by man and celebrates the achievement. The figures are sometimes seen working, but they seldom retain the focus of Bone's attentions. They form part of the overall complexity, which is usually a scene of such grandeur that the figures intensify the scale of the operation.

His series *Glasgow, Fifty Drawings*, published in 1911, comprises an extraordinary portrait of the city and its people and the changes that affected both. The drawings are the antithesis of romanticism, showing a city often smothered in smoke, which appears like a haar from the sea,

5. Anita Ventura Mozley, Introduction, *Photographs of the Old Closes and Streets of Glasgow 1868–1877*.

where tradition in the form of buildings is demolished. There are few Glaswegians, though the energy of the city is intensified by their presence. They are a part of the whole, which is a mighty conglomerate, a self-perpetuating organism that, again, finds echoes in Patrick Geddes.

Bone became the century's first war artist; at war, again, the individual is lost in the overwhelming tide of technology. Towards the end of the war, he returned to Glasgow, where he produced a memorable series of lithographs, mostly drawn in the Clyde shipyards. He later went to America and served as a war artist in the Second World War.

By the end of the nineteenth century, Glasgow Corporation had not only inaugurated a massive slum-clearance programme and ensured the provision of a fresh water supply; they had also built an infectious-diseases hospital, set up a system for inspecting and controlling meat and milk production, established and maintained refuse-disposal and sewage plants, and provided baths and wash houses. Gas and electricity were taken into municipal control, and Glasgow had the country's first electric fire-alarm system; St Enoch's Station and the adjacent hotel were the first to be lit by electricity. Glasgow had the world's first municipal tram system, the busiest tramway crossing in the world, the world's first underground cable line and the country's first telephone exchange.

In a city which has had tenements and closes of one form or another since the sixteenth century, and where in certain districts a person's standing is measured by the colour of their sandstone building, whether the close entry is tiled, half-tiled or whitewashed, a sizeable number of citizens now live around municipally built lift shafts. In Glasgow's case, this was the result of an unstable housing market that virtually collapsed by the end of the First World War, when local government took over responsibility for working-class housing. They began with modest greenfield sites on what was then the edge of the city, quickly followed by larger developments in the likes of Carntyne, Mosspark and Knightswood, the biggest scheme in Scotland, providing shops, medical services, schools and a golf course.

In 1934, the year Muir was travelling on his *Scottish Journey*, when a quarter of Scots were dependent on poor relief, council-house subsidies, which had been withdrawn in 1931, were reinstated. 'Overcrowding was a peculiarly Scots phenomenon,' says Charles McKean in *The Scottish Thirties*. The worst overcrowding in England occurred in Sunderland with a rate of around 18 per cent: the least overcrowding in Scotland, in Edinburgh, was 17 per cent. The Clyde Valley towns had an average overcrowding rate of 40 per cent. National comparisons revealed an English rate of overcrowded homes of 3.8 per cent as compared with a Scottish rate six times worse.

These conditions underlay the ambitious housing programmes of the period. Mass housing formed the predominant construction, some 300,000 houses being built between 1919 and 1939, the scale of which created

immense problems of decentralisation and social isolation. The built
results were really only visible on the city outskirts as the new estates gulped
down cheap farming land. Little change was visible in the inner cities themselves, although the pressure on existing flats began to drop. The
preoccupation with solving homelessness, overcrowding and slums took
priority over the maintenance of existing stock, so that, by 1941, despite
those 300,000 new houses, the shortfall of decent homes was thought to
have *risen* to a new high of 500,000.[6]

Difficult To Define

Scottish romanticism dressed up and adopted a lost cause. It exaggerated
defeat and forced us to take pride in a picture of ourselves which was
essentially born in compensation for a loss of nationhood and identity.
We were offered a duality; and Glasgow epitomised that duality for Edwin
Muir. He thought Glasgow was the most important city in Scotland, 'since
it is an epitome of the virtues and vices of the industrial regions, which
comprise the majority of the population. A description of Scotland which
did not put Glasgow in the centre of the picture would not be a description of Scotland at all.'[7] Despite this positive assertion, his own
impressions were 'mostly, I am afraid, painful'. His happiest childhood
years were spent on the Orkney island of Wyre.

> I was born before the Industrial Revolution, and am now about two hun-
> dred years old. But I have skipped a hundred and fifty of them. I was really
> born in 1737, and till I was fourteen no time-accidents happened to me.
> Then in 1751 I set out from Orkney to Glasgow. When I arrived I found
> that it was not 1751 but 1901.[8]

The move to Glasgow precipitated the death of Muir's parents and
two of his brothers, one from tuberculosis and the other from a brain
tumour; on top of this his own health suffered. The shock of this 'time-
accident', as Andrew Noble points out, constantly evoked mythical
resonances of the Fall: 'It was not merely taste or aesthetic theory but the
very facts of his own experience which provoked in Muir such outright
opposition to the prevailing Scottish literary mores.'[9]

His own experience forced him to stare at the reality of Glasgow, to see
its materialism and the consequences of that materialism realistically.
Nowhere did he see commercial individualism, or those who allegedly

6. Charles McKean, *The Scottish Thirties.*
7. Edwin Muir, *Scottish Journey.*
8. Edwin Muir, *The Story and the Fable.*
9. Andrew Noble, Introduction, *Edwin Muir: Uncollected Scottish Criticism.*

benefited from this independent entrepreneurial spirit, living happily
with the traditional values of hearth and home, wife and bairns, or any of
the other sentiments of traditional society. We wanted it both ways and
the Caledonian Antisyzygy allowed us to have it both ways: Muir made us
stare into the face of a reality we longed to avoid.

The accounts of 1930s Glasgow are uniform in their findings. Muir sees
the slum-dwellers' lives as a lifelong imprisonment, a more dreadful pun-
ishment than death. His *Scottish Journey* section on the Glasgow slums
contains some of his most controlled, angriest writing, anger at the fools
who argue which slums are worse, at those who excuse or condemn the
people in them on social or religious grounds, at those who relate stories
of their awfulness, playing to an appetite which can never be sated:

> The appetite of moderately well-off and quite well-off people for these infa-
> mous morsels is one which has no connection with the sentiment of pity, but
> is likely to check rather than induce it, creating disgust in its stead. Disgust
> is the coldest of human emotions, colder than hatred because more self-
> centred. If one hates the slums one may do something about them; but if
> one is filled with disgust of them there is nothing but to turn away.
>
> Moreover, it is difficult to define a slum, and a more important fact is that
> the majority of the population of Glasgow live in some form of poverty
> caused by the working of the economic system. The insanitary slums are
> more picturesque, and more thrillingly horrible things can be related of
> them; but if one could conceive the total volume of colourless or bug-
> coloured poverty that exists in Glasgow, as in all other cities of its kind, one
> would be crushed by the knowledge. We manage to live with some comfort
> simply because we cannot conceive it. The life of the slums is infamous, but
> it is freer and more various than the life of the decent poor. A slum is a poor
> quarter in which the people no longer take the trouble to keep up appear-
> ances. Nothing in such places makes any attempt to keep up appearances.
> The houses have a rotten look, and send out a complicated bouquet of
> mingled stenches. All that respectable society conceals is openly displayed.
> Language has a flat and commonplace obscenity; knowledge, however vile,
> is frankly expressed; passions and hatreds let themselves go. All this happens
> within a sort of invisible cage, whose bars are as strong as iron. It is a life
> which through the course of generations has acquired a settled conven-
> tion; for children grow up in these places and are trained from their earliest
> years in the way of life which is suitable for them. The deepest hope of the
> decent poor is to bring up their children in a way that will give them the
> opportunity of a better life than their parents. What distinguishes the slum-
> dweller from the decent poor is that they have quite given up this hope, that
> they are quite static. They see no prospect for themselves or their descen-
> dants but the slums. This is because they are the final product of a system;
> there is nothing beyond them; and their existence has therefore a logic with

which there is no arguing. Yet this does not mean that these people are a special class outside the bounds of humanity, but merely that they are ordinary men and women in a hopeless position, who have been placed there by the operation of a process over which they have no control.

William Power's *My Scotland*, published in 1934, falls in with the convention of the times, mirrored in *Scottish Journey*, whereby a literary gent ventures north and offers his impressions for a readership to follow. There are things Power likes in 'Scotland's Genoa', such as the communal solidarity, Scotch comics, painters, and the city's surfeit of suitable subjects. Kelvingrove Park is a magnificent piece of urban scenery, he says, and Glasgow has become a literary centre.

> No longer do her literary lads o' pairts slip away to London as a matter of course. They are bound by cords of affection to their own city, where, also, the newspapers afford them a journalistic basis. They are strongly nation-conscious, and the increasing inter-relations of Glasgow and Edinburgh writers have helped to bring the two cities nearer each other for Scottish purposes.

But there is no doubting the city's blight.

> Glasgow is usually thought of as an ugly city. Its centre contains some handsome buildings, but they are too closely massed; the outlying tenement quarters are dull and dreary beyond description; the slum districts are ghastly; and everywhere there is evidence of the lack of aesthetic control. A city can scarcely be beautiful unless it wants to be beautiful. The visitor who is introduced to Glasgow by way of St Rollox, Parkhead or Polmadie gets an impression of unrelieved horribleness which he finds hard to remove.[10]

In a book he shared with Hugh MacDiarmid, also published in 1934, Lewis Grassic Gibbon considers the 150,000 people living five or six in a single room

> that is part of some great sloven of tenement – the tenement itself in a line or a grouping with hundreds of its fellows, its windows grimed with the unceasing wash and drift of coal-dust, its stairs narrow and befouled and steep, its evening breath like that which might issue from the mouth of a lung-diseased beast. The hundred and fifty thousand eat and sleep and copulate and conceive and crawl into childhood in those waste jungles of stench and disease and hopelessness .... They live on food of the quality of offal, ill-cooked, ill-eaten with speedily-diseased teeth for the tending of

10. William Power, *My Scotland*.

which they can afford no fees; they work – if they have work – in factories
or foundries or the roaring reek of the Docks toilsome and dreary and
unimaginative hours – hour on hour, day on day, frittering away the tissues
of their bodies and the spirit-stuff of their souls; they are workless – great
numbers of them – doomed to long days of staring vacuity, of shoelessness,
of shivering hidings in this and that mean runway when the landlords'
agents come, of mean and desperate beggings at Labour Exchanges and
Public Assistance Committees; their voices are the voices of men and
women robbed of manhood and womanhood.[11]

Here, as he suggests, he is emphasising a point made in his second novel,
The Thirteenth Disciple, published in 1931 under his own name of James
Leslie Mitchell. The novel contains unhappy accounts of both
Stonehaven and Glasgow, 'that strange, deplorable city which has neither
sweetness nor pride, the vomit of a cataleptic commercialism'.

What is seen as the archetypal Glaswegian novel is a product of the
times. *No Mean City* was published in 1935. It is said to have sold more
than a million copies throughout the world and has never been out of
print. Its author, Alexander MacArthur, who wrote the book in collaboration with a London journalist, H. Kingsley Long, died destitute on the
banks of the Clyde after drinking disinfectant. His book reinforced
Glasgow, and the Gorbals particularly, in popular memory as a city of
razor-slashers and alcoholics, a place of urban violence and squalor, a
place to be avoided at all costs.

Without Precedent and Impossible to Emulate

The work of Alexander Thomson, Glasgow's outstanding Victorian architect, was until recently either ignored, demolished or vandalised, but
enough remains not only to allow us to mourn what has been lost but also
to appreciate the originality and breadth of his achievements. These, in
Fiona Sinclair's judgement, 'far surpassed those of any of his immediate
contemporaries, so wholly original was his interpretation of Greek and
Egyptian forms – his style quite without precedent and impossible to
emulate successfully'.[12]

At least as important as any one of his buildings is the fact that
Thomson created a climate for good architecture. He trained and
encouraged a second generation of architects whose works transformed
the city. He also imbued Glasgow architecture with a confidence it has
never achieved since, the confidence to be independent, to ignore what
was happening elsewhere and to go its own way. He also maintained the

11. Lewis Grassic Gibbon, *Scottish Scene*.
12. Fiona Sinclair, *Scotstyle*.

pattern for architects to design the interiors of their buildings, typifying the marriage between austerity and sensibility, stone façades, elaborately fringed and decorated with highly coloured interiors, often employing skilled painters and stained-glass designers.

Charles Wilson, J. J. Burnet, James Sellars, William Leiper, Charles Rennie Mackintosh and James Salmon followed Thomson's example, not always by imitating the Greek and Egyptian styles he favoured. Their churches still crown street corners where lines of their tenements enhance the streets, their spires elevate the city rooftops, their offices and houses adorn city hills, though most of their buildings are no longer used for the function for which they were designed. Banks have become bars and restaurants, warehouses and offices have been converted into flats, and churches have been transformed into a theatre, a graduation hall for Strathclyde University or rehearsal accommodation for the Royal Scottish National Orchestra.

As far as the general public is concerned, Thomson's work seems to be respected rather than admired. The fact that he has a nickname gives him a familiarity his architectural geometry does not immediately suggest. This is partly because of the relative neglect from which his work has suffered. Until recently none of his interiors were accessible to the public and many of his buildings had been abandoned in a parlous state.

And despite international respect and the efforts of the Alexander Thomson Society, it seems Glasgow has fresh forces of destruction to contend with, or rather the return of something with which the city is now very familiar. An admired building is thought to be saved, but while its future is discussed, considered or even contested, it is left to rot further, often exposed to the elements.

> Alexander 'Greek' Thomson is responsible for many magnificent landmarks and his Egyptian Halls, built in 1871, were one of the architectural wonders of late Victorian Glasgow. In their monumental façades articulated with the interplay of light and shade on window and wall, Thomson realised the marriage of all the diverse influences on his style – Greek, Roman, Byzantine and Egyptian. Today they are Category A listed. For years, however, the upper storeys were left to rot by the owners of a first-floor Chinese restaurant. A recent compulsory purchase order from the City appeared to be the answer, with last March the due date for the start of restoration . . . . At the time of writing, however, the purchase order has been challenged by the owners.

The quotation comes from an article in *Scotland on Sunday*, published in May 1998; similar pieces were published in the *Herald* and *Private Eye*.

In *Scotstyle*, Fiona Sinclair describes Thomson's style as 'unmistakable . . . The Egyptian Halls in Glasgow could be by no other.' This assessment, published in 1984, concludes, 'The building . . . could do with a good scrub, lacking as it does the gaiety suggested by the wealth of beautiful ornament.' For Charles McKean, writing in *Central Glasgow: An Illustrated Architectural Guide*, it is 'the building in which Thomson gathered all his previous motifs into a single stupendous penultimate composition. Cast-iron framed, its façade is characteristic of Thomson's extraordinary originality and intellect.'

The Egyptian Halls seem to have been saved, though the scare showed the fragile status of some of the city's finest buildings.

Thomson's ability to fuse a wide variety of historical styles into a series of personal statements established him as a maverick at a time when Scottish architecture was presenting significant contributions to the identity debate, none more so than John Rochead's Wallace Monument, built in 1860. The evaluation 'He both suffered and enjoyed the role of an isolated genius', delivered in *The New Companion to Scottish Culture*, puts Thomson and his achievements beyond the mainstream of Scottish architecture. A frequent, rather more benign, evaluation of his work, made by Gavin Stamp, founder of the Alexander Thomson Society, in an assessment of Holmwood House is that he is one of 'the two great architects produced by Glasgow in the nineteenth century' – the other being Charles Rennie Mackintosh – and that his work 'arguably had more impact on Glasgow than any other architect'.[13]

Holmwood is now run by the National Trust for Scotland. It is the most elaborate of Thomson's Glasgow villas, containing an abundance of spectacularly fresh ideas, both inside and out, meticulous attention to detail, a lively sense of colour and a unique and profuse Classical ornamentation which reveals an individual, stimulating and precious architecture. According to Gavin Stamp, that the house 'still stands is in fact something of a miracle, as there was a grave risk of destruction when it ceased to be a school . . . and the grounds were ripe for development'. Holmwood is seen to complement the National Trust for Scotland's other 'architectural creation of great originality', Hill House in Helensburgh, designed by Charles Rennie Mackintosh, although, unlike Hill House, all Thomson's original furniture and furnishings have been lost.

Thomson designed three Glasgow churches. St Vincent Street Free Church still stands as a working building; like Glasgow School of Art and the City Chambers, it is used for the purpose for which it was built. Queen's Park United Presbyterian Church was bombed in 1943 and Caledonia Road UP Church was gutted by fire in October 1965, since when it has stood in majestic ruin.

The St Vincent Street Church was built in 1859, the year before

13. Gavin Stamp, *Heritage Scotland*, winter 1998.

Rochead's Wallace Monument, the climax of Scottish architecture's mid-nineteenth-century recovery of a vernacular voice. Rather than adding his voice to their pronouncements, Thomson returned to another, earlier, more decorative source which he used as a means of exploration and discovery as well as inspiration and invention. In so doing he set the standard for other identities, and towered over Glasgow architecture in the late nineteenth century as surely as David Hamilton had dominated the early part of the century.

Hamilton organised the reconstruction of Glasgow Green, transforming it into a civic park. He redesigned the Cunningham mansion as the Royal Exchange, enlarged Hamilton Palace, and designed the Falkirk Town Steeple and Port Glasgow's Town Buildings, as well as Glasgow's splendid Hutcheson's Hall, originally founded as a hospital in the seventeenth century for the relief of twelve old men and twelve boys, but rebuilt north of its original Trongate site in 1802 to realise what had become a commercial asset. He also designed the country's first monument to Horatio Nelson, the obelisk on Glasgow Green.

The genius of Charles Rennie Mackintosh could be said to overshadow the works and reputation of his close friend James Salmon, whose St Vincent Chambers, known as The Hatrack, is described by Charles McKean as 'One of the Glasgow Style's greatest achievements: ten floors of rippling red sandstone and glass within a single terrace house plot'.[14] In Charles McKean's opinion, Salmon 'came closest to synthesising the nationalist ideal with new technology, fusing the structure and the art of architecture into a homogenous whole'.

Similarly, Alexander Thomson overshadows his friend and contemporary, Charles Wilson, who also embraced a new technology. What is now the Great Eastern Hotel on Duke Street was designed by Wilson as a cotton-spinning mill in 1848, using cast iron and concrete. Wilson was trained by David Hamilton and used Hamilton to represent architecture in a series of relief panels depicting great men in various fields on the side of the Queen's Rooms in La Belle Place. Poesy is represented by Robert Burns, literature by Scott. The frieze, according to the authors of *A History of Scottish Architecture*, symbolised 'Glasgow's loyalty to the Union, to freemasonry and to political liberalism'.

Wilson was a prolific architect, known to respond best to commissions in his native city. His 'greatest work' – according to the authors of *A History of Scottish Architecture* – is

the Free Church College on Woodlands Hill. Like Playfair's Mound grouping in Edinburgh, Woodlands Hill was the scenic centrepiece of the new,

14. Charles McKean, *Central Glasgow: An Illustrated Architectural Guide.*

mid-century Glasgow, and the college was its crowning element. Its design also set out to broadcast the power and authority of the Free Church through a tall towered silhouette, but in an open, Glasgow fashion, seen not in a structured vista but as an asymmetrical cluster visible from all directions.

Cold White Erc-lamps Fizz like Gingerade

What became Glasgow's West End Park, now Kelvingrove Park, was a country estate for Patrick Colquhoun. It was the site of the 1888 Great Exhibition, which made enough of a profit to finance a competition in 1891 to design and build a new art gallery and museum; both were opened in time for the 1901 exhibition, forming the centrepiece of the 1911 exhibition, the profits from which were intended to provide a Chair of Scottish History and Literature at Glasgow University.

The commission to build a university on Gilmorehill was the biggest since the building of the Houses of Parliament. Sir George Gilbert Scott wanted to employ 'a style which I may call my own invention, having already introduced it at the Albert Institute in Dundee. It is simply a thirteenth or fourteenth century secular style with the addition of certain Scottish features peculiar to that country in the sixteenth century.'[15] Scott's appointment was greatly resented. Writing in *Enquiry*, Alexander Thomson objected to 'this invasion from the south'. The ventilated spire, which, like the Red Road flats, can been seen from the top of Ben Lomond and glimpsed from the heights of the Arrocher Alps, was added by Scott's son, John Oldrid Scott, because he considered the tower his father designed would be too heavy. He also added a spire to his father's other Glasgow building, St Mary's Cathedral on Great Western Road.

The relationship between the university and its surroundings is celebrated in 'West End Park Serenade', written by James Bridie when he was O. H. Mavor, a medical student at the university.

> It's long pest midnight, there's no one on the street,
> The consteble is sleeping at the corner of his beat;
> The cold white erc-lamps fizz like gingerade,
> And I'm beneath your window with this cherming serenade.
> Open your window, the night is beastly derk;
> The phentoms are dencing in the West End Perk.
> Open your window, your lover brave to see,
> I'm here all alone, and there's no one here but me.

15. Quoted by Frank Amiel Walker in *Perspectives of a Scottish City.*

The text needs to be sung in the accent of the area and is taken from the *Glasgow University Student Song Book*, published in August 1953, a collection which also contains 'The Ould Orange Flute', 'Kelly, The Boy from Killann', 'The Soldier's Song', 'The Darkies' Sunday School', 'Harry was a Bolshie', and 'Morphine Bill and Cocaine Sue'.

The 1911 Exhibition, which succeeded in 'reflecting the spirit of the age,' says Perilla Kinchin, was both a serious expression of nationalism and a lot of fun.

> The scenic contours of Kelvingrove Park lent themselves perfectly to a temporary fantasia of Scots Baronial architecture, executed in board and plaster. History this time took precedence over Industry and a building modelled on the Palace of Falkland housed a truly overwhelming collection of national treasures, designed to educate the populace, particularly the young, in their heritage.
>
> Not surprisingly, the public was more enthusiastic about the 'living history' which was prominent at this exhibition . . . a fake Auld Toon, evoking a romantic burghal past, complete with picturesque inhabitants and souvenir shops. There was also a Highland Clachan, a 'village' of typically primitive dwellings staffed by genuine Gaels, who could be observed spinning, bagpiping, and singing in their unintelligible tongue . . .
>
> With lovely weather, and 9,369,375 visitors, Glasgow's great Scottish exhibition was indisputably a success.[16]

Kelvingrove Park lies in a valley through which the River Kelvin glides, rising to Gilmorehill on one side of the river and to Woodlands Hill on the other. Woodlands Hill followed the beautifully named Blythswood Hill and Garnethill to become the third drumlin to be developed. The development extended the city westwards and coincided with the arrival of the first of the great plagues and the opening of the Necropolis, beside the cathedral, Glasgow's first private graveyard, built on secular ground and modelled on Père Lachaise. David Hamilton designed the Bridge of Sighs for the Necropolis, and some of Glasgow's greatest architects provided mausoleums for the city's merchant inhabitants.

Fiona Sinclair suggests the Park Circus development influenced John James Burnet's Charing Cross Mansions, a red-sandstone circular stretch of shops and a tenement, which survived the 1960s onslaught to have a motorway pass along the basement. The year after Charing Cross Mansions was built, J. J. Burnet and his partner John Campbell completed the Athenaeum theatre, which *A History of Scottish Architecture*

16. Perilla Kinchin, 'The Scottish Exhibition of 1911' in Carl MacDougall (ed.), *Glasgow's Glasgow: People Within a City.*

credits with introducing 'a new, vertical intensity to Glasgow street archi-tecture'. It was designed as an extension to what was the Athenaeum College, later the Royal Scottish Academy of Music, containing a the-atre, dining rooms, music rooms and a gymnasium, a lift and an elliptical staircase. Its influence was profound. According to *A History of Scottish Architecture*, 'This Baroque dynamism was to be of most influence in the exploitation, and enobling, of another, completely new building type: the multi-storey office block.'

As a centre of commercial impetus, for most of the nineteenth century, Glasgow was not only reckoned to be one of the great cities of Europe, but was also at the forefront of the social and economic transformation of soci-ety which was undermining the old political and religious interests. With Scottish industrial and commercial power flourishing in an international, imperial context, *A History of Scottish Architecture* is surely right in assuming 'anxieties about national identity were at an all-time low'. Architects, not surprisingly, maintained an affiliation to monumental Classicism, out-standingly in the case of Alexander Thomson. The same source credits Scotland in the later years of the century as being 'one of the richest countries in the world'. And with religion 'increasingly sidelined as a social force, the great competition between the two materialist philoso-phies of capitalism and socialism now began rising to a crescendo'.

Architecture divided itself into two main groupings. The Glasgow Classical tradition of Thomson and Wilson was being reinvigorated with elements drawn from the overseas Classical world of the Beaux-Arts, and especially from the country that, then as now, symbolised modernity: the United States. J. J. Burnet was the pre-eminent talent, while in the east a star was rising in the burgeoning second Scottish revival, led by Sir Rowand Anderson, which turned its back on urbanism.

Preserved at all Costs

Glasgow was the scene of architectural revelation in 1964, 'when the RIBA held its annual conference in the city, bringing architects from all over Britain, most for the first time, to a place renowned for its gang vio-lence and mass vandalism. They were astonished at what they found – not the slum-ridden, rat-infested place ripe for total obliteration that they had been led to expect, but on the contrary, a city which should be preserved at all costs.'[17]

The Victorian Group was formed after the RIBA conference. They organised a city-centre walk and invited the Lord Provost. Five hundred people turned out for the walk, which coincided with the height of the

17. Frank Worsdall, *The City That Disappeared.*

city's redevelopment. The Lord Provost reportedly asked if the local authority was expected to carry the financial burden of preserving all the city's Victorian buildings and made it plain he would not like Glasgow to be thought of solely as a Victorian city. The planning convener said the time would come when the city would have to consider putting up a plaque instead of retaining certain old buildings. And in 1972 the convener of the Highways Committee – 'a body responsible for unbelievable havoc in every quarter of the city' – said he did not want the new Glasgow to be a museum piece 'for the delectation and delight of visiting professors of architecture'.[18]

The Victorian Group became the New Glasgow Society, the earliest and most influential of the city's amenity groups. They were followed by others specialising in the conservation of smaller local areas. When the Charles Rennie Mackintosh Society was formed, the Scottish Civic Trust and the Scottish Georgian Society began to take an ever greater interest in what was going on in the city. Frank Worsdall writes that

> In recent years there has been a reaction against the policy of comprehensive redevelopment, and in an effort to preserve communities in areas of interesting character, Housing Associations with government backing have been set up to renovate the properties, bringing them up to an acceptable standard. One particular Association, in Woodside, has been so successful that its work has been given an award, and the organiser the Saint Mungo Prize.[19]

The irony of Glasgow enjoying the benefits of something their council may not actually have sought to destroy, but which they certainly did little to preserve, takes on a delicious satirical dimension that borders on buffoonery when the city's favoured son, Charles Rennie Mackintosh comes into the equation. It is not unreasonable to suggest that were it not for the formation and the persistence of the Charles Rennie Mackintosh Society, less of his work would have survived than is presently the case.

George Bruce's assessment in *The New Companion to Scottish Culture* is in keeping with Mackintosh's contemporary status: 'The most individual genius in Scottish architecture and the greatest architectural influence in Europe of his day.' Mackintosh is a composite in the list of tragic Scottish icons, a seminal figure whose art and life are difficult to categorise, an architect and designer who soars beyond these scant limitations.

He is the Scottish art world's Robert Burns in all but his personal life, which has avoided such rigorous scrutiny. Of course, there is a darker, mysterious side – hints of alcoholism and known depression; but, like Burns, his work has formed an identity matrix, giving him cult status. As

18. *Ibid.*
19. *Ibid.*

with Burns, our perception makes the life and work secondary, though public recognition has used the work to bolster perceptions of national identity, making Mackintosh, and what is thought of as his work, emblematic of imagined Scottish characteristics and traditions. As Richard Finlay has remarked about Burns, it is not so much how Mackintosh has shaped national identity, but how Scottish identity has shaped our view of him.

In the early stages of his career, commissions were few and successes brief. Disillusioned by a lack of recognition in Glasgow, he moved to Chelsea where he worked on a series of textile designs; and though his work was fêted on the Continent – he exhibited in Vienna, Munich, Dresden, Turin, Budapest and Moscow – it was condemned in his own country. The place where he had his greatest success, whose society he dignified by his presence, not only turned its back on him, but ignored him completely.

Today, Charles Rennie Mackintosh is internationally renowned for things he did not design. His patterns have been adapted to fit jewellery, mugs and textiles – now known, in Murray Grigor's memorable phrase, as Mockintosh. Like Burns once again, he relied on visionaries to recognise and promote his efforts.

There were two principal sources: Francis Newbery and Kate Cranston. Other, often unsung, sources of support are John Keppie, whose firm Mackintosh joined as a draughtsman in 1889, becoming a partner in 1904, and the publisher Walter Blackie, who not only used designs by Mackintosh and his friends in his publications, but also commissioned Mackintosh to design Hill House in Helensburgh.

Mackintosh was friendly with James Herbert MacNair, and the two of them married the Macdonald sisters, Margaret and Frances. This is largely how MacNair is remembered; his work, the ideas he exchanged with Mackintosh and the fusions of the group known as The Four have largely been dissipated or lost. Indifference caused MacNair to destroy most of his work, though Mackintosh hung on in Glasgow, when hindsight suggests he would have been better off elsewhere.

As with Burns, the ending is not happy and the image substantiates a questionable reality. The Mackintosh we remember is a darkly handsome young man, with a curled moustache, flamboyant bowed necktie and a loose-fitting shirt, romantically staring into the distance, square chin and stern jaw betrayed by a single curl at the centre of his brow, exactly in line with his nose, and a full mouth.

When Newbery prophesied, in his introduction to *The Glasgow School of Painting*, that an artistic movement based in the city 'may yet, perhaps, put Glasgow on the Clyde into the hands of the future historians of art, on much the same grounds as those on which Bruges, Venice and Amsterdam find themselves in the book of the life of the world', he was, as Roger Billcliffe suggests, both right and wrong, because as a relative newcomer to the city he had failed to realise that Glasgow as a city, and Glaswegians, whether as private individuals or civic dignitaries, were not yet ready as patrons of the arts to claim a place for Glasgow among the city-states listed in his prologue.

By the time Newbery's words were published, most of the Glasgow Boys had left the city, lured by the respect, acclaim and commissions that London (and even Edinburgh) was able and accustomed to confer on artists. The early criticisms of Mackintosh's work, which were later to grow in volume and vituperation and contribute to the acute depression which forced him to leave Glasgow in 1913, had already been voiced by 1897. After the public disquiet heard on completion of the first phase of the Glasgow School of Art in 1899 Newbery would have seen that history was about to repeat itself and that Mackintosh, too, would be forced to leave the city. Without Mackintosh, and the intellectual and creative force he represented, the Glasgow Style accelerated its artistic demise, following the path of fashion-led commercial diktat. When popular demand for works in the 'artistic' or 'quaint' style tailed off about 1914, the Glasgow Style died.[20]

Mackintosh, of course, did not work in a vacuum. The Glasgow Style was a synthesis of Scottish elements with a touch of Art Nouveau and the clear lines of the English Arts and Crafts movement. Co-ordinated interiors, a wide range of decorative arts often in a variety of media but all characterised by simple elongated motifs derived from plants and emaciated human forms, in mauves, greens and pinks, formed the hallmarks of a style.

'Numerous other designers, craftworkers, teachers and architects contributed to the upsurge of progressive artistic activity in Glasgow in the early years of this century. Many of them deserve more widespread recognition, such as George Walton, Talwin Morris, Jessie Newbery, Ernest Taylor, Jessie King, John Ednie, George Logan and Ann MacBeth,' says Juliet Kinchin.[21] What brought them together was contact with Glasgow School of Art and Francis Newbery, who championed Mackintosh and was influential in securing the commission for a new school of art, now recognised as one of the world's great buildings.

'Mackintosh's masterwork,' says Charles McKean in his architectural guide to the city, 'won in a limited local competition in which every competitor warned that the brief could not be realised for the money available. The project took shape in two separate stages, although where

20. Roger Billcliffe, 'How Many Swallows Make a Summer? Art and Design in Glasgow in 1900' in Wendy Kaplan (ed.), *Scotland Creates: 5000 Years of Art and Design*.
21. Juliet Kinchin, 'The Glasgow Style' in Carl MacDougall (ed.), *Glasgow's Glasgow: People Within a City*.

the tall studio windows gather the light along Renfrew Street, or the towering castle walls climb up the hill to the south, it scarcely appears so.'

Glasgow School of Art rises above Sauchiehall Street, around the
corner from Thomson's Grecian Chambers. It is a radical building, quite
revolutionary when compared with contemporary architecture, built in
two phases, with slices of money raised by Newbery and his students
through exhibitions and concerts, masques and plays. The first phase,
1897–99, took the building from the east wing to the entrance tower
above the doorway. The second phase was completed in 1907–09.

Fiona Sinclair is surely correct to caution against oversimplification.
'To categorise this building narrowly is to do it a sizeable injustice, since
there are a number of influences in evidence – all endowed with
Mackintosh's unique, slightly mystical, yet immensely practical touch.'[22]
It is a work to which one can return many times and find something
new; yet it is also a building whose first impressions remain, especially of
the library – two storeys of dark-stained balustrades, flashes of primary
colour, the grid of beams and pillars and their intricate crossings, the
reflective lights, wooden floors and desks. The large studio windows,
niches, inset windows, end windows, projecting bays and railings, the
continual use of natural light and contrasting stone, even the gently wel-
coming curved stone stairway leading to the front door and the
building's sole decorative sculpture above the door cannot prepare you
for the interior.

No architect embodies the twinning of opposites so clearly as Charles
Rennie Mackintosh. His design work is different from his architecture.
He believed his interiors should create an environment that ignored the
world outside. This obsession led to demands that his cats should be grey
because any other colour would be offensive to the shape and colour of
the fireside cushions he designed for them and even extended to stipulating the floral arrangements for Miss Cranston's tea-rooms.

'He set out to create a sensual world of elegance, simplicity and delight,
using new materials and forms in his furniture and creating a startling
contrast in his decorations between the world within and the elements
outside,' says Roger Billcliffe.[23] And just as Newbery's famed insistence
that quality should be cultivated and maintained gave the Glasgow Style its
freshness and appeal, but simultaneously ensured its products could only
be enjoyed by those who could afford them, so Mackintosh's designs,
especially those commissioned by Kate Cranston, were enjoyed by fashionable, middle-class Glasgow. 'Miss Cranston made the "artistic" tearoom
an object of international admiration,' says Perilla Kinchin. The tea-room,
she says, is one of Glasgow's great inventions. They 'flourished along with

22. Fiona Sinclair, *op. cit.*
23. Roger Billcliffe, *op. cit.*

the Temperance movement, catering for businessmen who could lunch lightly and fraternise in the all-male smoking rooms; and for women of leisure who now at last had a respectable meeting place in town'.[24]

Glasgow is not a modernist city. Nor have the previous generation's attempts to make Glasgow what they thought of as a modernist city succeeded. But their grandparents and great-grandparents made Glasgow a modernist city – arguably one of the world's finest – and what allowed them to do so was Glasgow's commercial position. 'One of the key elements in the architectural reaction against capitalist society and eclectic mainstream architecture was an urge towards artistic individualism – an urge that, in Scotland, stemmed ultimately from the romanticism of Robert Adam. This tendency took its most extreme form in the "Glasgow Style" pioneered by "The Four",' says *A History of Scottish Architecture.*

The central thrust of Glasgow Style was the development of the whole house rather than an individual room, and the relationship between one and the other; so that the divisions between Mackintosh the architect and Mackintosh the designer become increasingly blurred. 'It was his intense focus on architecture as an all-embracing art – an intensity backed, during the heyday of his career, by an indefatigable capacity for work – which set Mackintosh apart from the longer, but more diffuse careers of other turn-of-the-century "giants": Anderson, Burnet and Lorimer.'

Mackintosh's creation of a background of almost bland neutrality highlighted by areas of intense decoration or of decorative activity can best be seen in the architectural photo-fit of his former home at 78 Southpart Avenue, where he and Margaret Macdonald lived from 1906 to 1913. When the new wing of the Hunterian Gallery was opened in 1981, the principal interiors were reconstructed around the existing furniture and fittings, with the addition of the guest bedroom designed for Derngate in Nottingham and the exterior doorway halfway up the outside wall, a design feature not normally associated with Mackintosh. Similarly in Hill House, Helensburgh, or in the last of the four temperance temples he designed for Kate Cranston, the upstairs Room de Luxe in the Sauchiehall Street Willow Tea Rooms, where Mackintosh also designed the façade, the use of decorative friezes and light fittings and the way the furniture is placed are component parts of an overall creation. The Willow Tea Rooms are a partial resuscitation: the ground floor specialises in Mockintosh.

Mackintosh's quest for a national and individual identity, and to marry one with the other, not surprisingly resulted in a unity which is an expression and an extension of both, where one supports and informs the other. In common with writers such as Burns and Hogg, Scott and his

24. Perilla Kinchin, 'Tea Rooms' in Carl MacDougall (ed.), *Glasgow's Glasgow: People Within a City.*

near contemporary Robert Louis Stevenson, he has the ability to present a neutral, almost bland background, which then serves as a springboard into an area of almost frenetic activity. It is the stock-in-trade of the musician, the novelist and the painter, is especially evident in the works of Gavin Hamilton and David Wilkie, and can be found in the work of painters as diverse as Sir Joseph Noel Paton and William McTaggart. It is Mackintosh's central and continuing ability to use the past to inform the present, to use tradition as a springboard into modernism, to use traditional styles, structures, methods and effects in a new and decorative way and to continually marry oppositions, which places his work at the heart of national identity.

Mackintosh's insistence on getting his own way, his inability to compromise and the commitment he demanded from clients must have affected his reputation. His work on the Glasgow School of Art was fraught with argument, especially over the costs of the second phase. The first phase was over-budget and yet he still demanded specially made items.

There is an obvious, unquestionable truth in Roger Billcliffe's assertion that when he left in 1913,

> Glasgow and Mackintosh had had enough of each other. Like the Glasgow Boys before him he discovered that the city had not enough patrons to support men of his imagination. It was a double blow for Mackintosh, since he had refused to leave the city or Scotland when his reputation was high abroad. He had wanted to create a Scottish style, to develop centuries of tradition in his search for a new architecture for the twentieth century.[25]

His ambition then, seems concordant with that of Robert Burns, Walter Scott and David Wilkie; and, as Billcliffe also suggests, while the Glasgow Boys followed European fashion, 'Mackintosh and his friends led a movement that was to sweep across the Continent and spread to America'.

Not Life But Speech

'This century there have been at least two groups of poets who took notice of their environment,' writes Hamish Whyte in the introduction to his anthology of Glasgow poetry, *Mungo's Tongues*.

> First the Clyde Group of the 1940s whose aims were political, inspired by John MacLean and a commitment to Scottish Republicanism . . . . And the second, that group of Glasgow poets which emerged in the 1960s and 1970s, not a school, but individual poets with Glasgow connections which, with a

25. Billcliffe, *op. cit.*

distinctly non-parochial outlook, are revealed in their work: Edwin Morgan, Tom Leonard, Liz Lochhead, Stephen Mulrine, Alan Spence, Tom McGrath and others. With hindsight it can be seen that the time was ripe for a flowering of Glasgow writing. The city was going through physical change under the Comprehensive Development Plan, 'a dramatic swerve into the modern age' (Edwin Morgan). There were varying reactions: some, like Morgan, welcomed the marching multistorey flats and looping flyovers; others expressed themselves more traditionally and nostalgically.

In the finest of all Glasgow novels, Alasdair Gray's *Lanark*, the best-known passage is an exaggerated critique of itself: 'If a city hasn't been used by an artist not even the inhabitants live there imaginatively,' says Thaw. 'Imaginatively Glasgow exists as a music-hall song and a few bad novels.' In quoting this, Whyte also notes 'the development of a powerful body of Glasgow writing' over the past thirty years.

Central to these developments in poetry and fiction has been the voice. The Glasgow accent is an immediately recognisable badge of identity; and though writers have sought to extend their experiments beyond speech, or the ways in which speech is represented, the voice has nevertheless been central to the work. It has turned the concerns of both English- and Scots-language purists on their head by insisting language is defined by class as clearly as it is by country.

The movement is led by Tom Leonard, whose work is central to its understanding and development. From the mid-1960s, Leonard has consistently shown that a working-class form of expression is as suitable a vehicle for poetry and serious thought as any other. By firstly insisting there is neither good nor bad speech, Leonard's work gives the lie to the principle, however openly or tacitly stated, that literature and truth are reserved for those fluent in standard English. And for readers who expect their writers to sound, or even write, as though they had been properly brought up, his work can come as a surprise.

Writers have ignored the previous generation's obsession with standard Scots, concentrating on their own voices rather than adopting, or even adapting, a benchmark. Speech and its representation form a central, almost common unifying factor, and the models have been mostly American. Speech in Glaswegian prose is as natural as in the works of the previous generation's American writers. And though a twinning of opposites appears in certain narratives, particularly short stories, it rarely forms the basis of the narrative; and, rather than being set in a single location, the writers now freely move between urban and rural settings, often in the same piece. Nor are the treatments dour and one-sided. There are still writers who show the working class with the same capacity for dreaming that fired Edward Gaitens, George Friel and Archie Hind, who represent them seeking spiritual well-being as much as any material

improvement or obsession, or who show them living with the disillusion-
ment that can accompany improvement.

Muir suggests the attitude is obviously political; and this has fired the
following generation's approach to Glasgow speech, in all its poetic, fictional and dramatic forms. This has provided the springboard for the
majority of contemporary Scottish fiction, where class is taken for granted
and forms the basis of any subsequent search for identity. The voice is the
one medium open to a writer that does more than one thing simultaneously. And a generation of Glaswegian writers, now mostly middle-aged,
have understood this better than any Scottish writers since Stevenson,
whose position on the subject would appear to be concordant: 'As far as
[literature] imitates at all, it imitates not life but speech,' he wrote in *A
Humble Remonstrance, Memories and Portraits*, 'not the facts of human destiny, but the emphasis and the suppressions with which the human actor
tells of them.'

Now writers' groups across the country have encouraged people to
find a voice they did not know they possessed, which had often been
educated away or rendered inferior, a voice which simultaneously vali-
dated their experience and made its speakers visible. These experiences
are often treated in a romantic and sentimental fashion. In them we can
find poverty glamorised by nostalgia; hunger, exploitation, abuse and all
manner of indignities are often rendered harmless by a melancholic
warmth and behavioural excesses excused as part of the social mores of
the times. But the problem lies with writers whose experiences may well
carry the stamp of authenticity but who may not yet be able to face the
experience or its consequences, far less take the authenticity to a logical
conclusion, or even to draw conclusions from it.

'Hopelessly corrupt' is how one edition of the *Scottish National
Dictionary* described Glaswegian speech. Glasgow has a whole dictionary
devoted to its argot, as well as anthologies devoted to its writing. Perhaps
this has to do with the ways in which the city uses language rather than
the components of the speech. *The Patter* seeks to recognise the
Glaswegian way with words for what it is: a valid and vibrant regional
dialect, rather than a demeaned and impoverished form of Scots.

It would take a very fastidious linguistic expert to unpick the various
strands of Lowland and Highland Scots and Gaelic pronunciation, Irish
and even American influences that make up the Glasgow accent. But
recent developments in the city have rendered the exercise theoretical;
for what Glasgow's writers have done is not only to try to capture the
spoken word accurately, and in so doing to demonstrate a belief that the
way people speak is as valid a carrier of meaning as the words they use,
but also to give the narrator a voice similar to that used by his characters.

By using the Glasgow voice as a springboard into literature, Tom
Leonard and others have placed themselves in direct opposition to the

Scots linguistic purists. While the desire to preserve and restore the language is understandable, it surely must be amiss to encourage spoken
Scots and simultaneously to denigrate the natural forms in which it occurs.
There is no difference between teachers who tell a child to speak English
properly and those who do the same with Scots. It seems as though the
cart is being placed before the horse – that while committees decide on
spelling, proper and improper phrasing and usage, others decry those
writers who actually use, promulgate and expand the language.

Perhaps the problem is one of form. Almost every Glasgow writer has
been influenced not by Scottish literature particularly, though most are
acutely aware of our literary lifts and depressions. Inspiration has come
from across the Atlantic. Glasgow's American links continued after the
demise of the tobacco lords. Indeed, nineteenth-century Glasgow resembled an American, rather than a European, British or Scottish city, sharing
a similar dynamism and commercial intent. And the process was two-way:
Glasgow's philanthropic schemes were copied in America, as were its educational system and radicalism. Scotland's biggest export has been its
people and with them went the 'great Scottish Republic of the Mind'.

The Glasgow love affair with America is most obvious in cinema, where
the Glaswegian appetite for moving pictures is legendary within the
industry. None of the cinemas were gathered in river-bank complexes,
nor sited near an area needing an economic lift; although when Arthur
Hubner showed four short films in his Ice Skating Palace on Sauchiehall
Street on 26 May 1896, five months after the Lumière Brothers had given
the first public show in Paris and five weeks after its Edinburgh debut, it
was to revive an ailing business. By the end of November, Glasgow had its
first cinema, the 500-seat Colosseum in Jamaica Street, where the main
supplier of limelight and theatrical equipment to Glasgow's music halls,
Walter Wilson, converted part of his department store. The 1901
Exhibition showed landscape footage, lochs and mountains, viaducts and
bends shot from a wagon in front of a train on the West Highland Line.
An elephant coming out of its bath and walking towards the camera
made the audience scream.

The first purpose-built cinema was the Charing Cross Electric Theatre,
which opened in May 1910. From then on competition increased and
cinemas such as Pringle's Picture Palace in Calton and the George
Green's 1000-seater Whitevale Theatre in the Gallowgate were opened by
the first in a series of cinema entrepreneurs who have left their mark on
the city, its development and identity.

A. E. Pickard, who owned the Panopticon, the first stage to support the
young Stan Laurel, bought a Kilmarnock edition of Burns's poems for
£800 in 1928 and displayed it proudly in the foyer of one of his cinemas.
This was the sort of stunt for which he became famous. He was the first
man in Glasgow to own an aircraft and had eight limousines, one, he said,

for every day of the week and two for Sundays. George Urie Scott, who owned the Dennistoun Palais and the Pavilion Theatre, built most of Glasgow's major suburban picture houses and almost all the ABC cinemas, as well as a number of cinema buildings across the country, through his Cinema Construction Company. The ABC chain was founded by John Maxwell, a Glasgow solicitor who made the first British talking picture, directed by the young Alfred Hitchcock; Maxwell's company of filmmakers and distributors later grew into the Cannon empire.

They, along with men like George Singleton, who developed the Cosmo with Charles Oakley, and Alex Fruitin, who owned the Metropole theatre and sent its stars to entertain suburban cinema audiences between features, created such a climate that in 1939 Glasgow had 114 picture houses with a total capacity of 175,000 people – more cinema seats per head than any city in the world. There was even a range of architects who specialised in cinema design. According to the cinema historian Bruce Peter, Glaswegians went to the cinema

> on average 51 times a year, while the rest of Scotland went 35 times and the English a mere 21. For most Glaswegians there were at least two cinemas within ten minutes' walk of home. In some areas rival cinemas stood so close together that children queuing for matinées would be bribed with free sticks of rock by one manager and with free balloons by another.[26]

Today, fewer than forty cinemas survive, none in their original form. Only six still operate as cinemas.

Louis Armstrong, Sidney Bechet and George Lewis joined Count Basie, Ella Fitzgerald and Joe Williams, Stan Kenton, Woody Herman and Dizzy Gillespie, Frank Sinatra, Tony Bennett and Pete Seeger in their praise of Glasgow audiences. The other big American influence is in fashion. Up to and including the 1960s, when Tom McGrath founded and edited *International Times*, enhanced by his friendship with Allen Ginsberg and the other Beat poets, whatever fashion craze swept America was immediately adopted in Glasgow.

The most obvious and continuing American influence is found in the Glasgow singing style, wonderfully mimicked by Billy Connolly, who, incidentally, plays a guitar, a five-string banjo and an autoharp, all American instruments, or, as far as folk music is concerned, instruments which are played in an American style. Awful and embarrassing as it may be, Glasgow singers love to croon. And Glasgow pop groups mimic their American counterparts, at the very least adopting mid-Atlantic accents.

26. Bruce Peter, *100 Years of Glasgow's Amazing Cinemas.*

Glasgow Voices

The stylistic influences of writers from Hemingway to Hubert Selby Jr are
more obvious in recent Scottish writing than any native prose stylist,
though James Kelman's innovative marrying of narrative voice and nar-
ration can be traced back to Damon Runyon, who was inspired by
Mark Twain's use of this voice in *Tom Sawyer*, but more especially in
Huckleberry Finn. And despite the indigenous threads of Scott and
Stevenson, there is also the clear influence of fantasists such as Kurt
Vonnegut and Flann O'Brien to be found in the work of Alasdair Gray.
Another major Irish influence is Samuel Beckett, whose style and con-
cerns are evident in James Kelman's work.

Tom Leonard's debt to William Carlos Williams is clear, but the major
American influence on Glasgow's writers is found in Edwin Morgan's
inventive versatilities, inspired by the likes of space travel, computer and
concrete poetry, though Morgan, like the city's architects and folk, pop
and jazz musicians, uses the American dimension as a springboard into
discovering or enhancing the city itself. The city features, often as a character, in novels from the 1930s and later. The impact of these works,
whose tone is frequently gentle and understated, has been felt by a
number of writers. George Blake and James Barke have written novels
which strive to show the city as an entity, covering a variety of experience,
peopling the city with dreamers and artists, idealists who long for a fairer,
more equitable society where hope can flourish, not necessarily for them,
but for the coming generations. Though the drudgery of the workplace
or the relentless misery of poverty and unemployment are realistically
delivered, the working class here have a capacity for dreaming. Their
spirit strives to raise them above their circumstances, but events conspire
to constrain them. They are always driven under by forces inevitably
more powerful, and that domination is potent enough to shatter hope or
to render ambition and faith itself illusory.

Edward Gaitens was born in the Gorbals. His collection *Growing Up and
Other Stories* became the basis for a novel, *Dance of the Apprentices*. The story
The Sailing Ship shows Gaitens at his best, where the voice and the details
build up a relentless picture of unemployment in the 1930s.

Irish Catholicism runs through the novels of George Friel. And though
his characters do not belong to a violent city, or a place of such extremes
as Gaitens depicted, their districts, though populated by a respectable
working class, are sinking into squalor, their population sullen with
poverty and violence. Friel's territory is to the north of the city, often set
between the new housing schemes and industrial wastelands, offering a
sense of continuity in the suggestion that no matter how the city changes,
it will still fail its citizens because of the system that created it, which it in
turn perpetuates.

Gaitens and Friel are unjustly neglected. Eddy Macdonnel in Gaitens' *Dance of the Apprentices* is the precursor of Duncan Thaw in *Lanark* and of Mat Craig in Archie Hind's *The Dear Green Place*; and William McIlvanney, Gray and Kelman are foreshadowed not only in Gaitens' voice, but also in Friel's word play, his love of the surreal situation and awareness of the ways in which a novel communicates with its readers. More obviously, they share a common understanding; their shared sympathies resonate on every page. They are writing about the same people, the same city and similar experiences. Their work is not only a testimony to the Catholic and especially the Irish Catholic experience in Scotland, but, perhaps because of that, they also provide the setting that powered the realistic drive of the 1970s and 1980s. Both are sensitive, crafty and intelligent novelists whose works put recent developments in Glasgow writing into context and also explain some of its power and tradition.

The writer whose work has had the greatest effect on other Glasgow writers is, of course, Edwin Morgan, a poet who first saw the city as a place for celebration and who has continually sought to represent Glasgow in all its forms. Morgan's work is difficult to classify. He has worked in every poetic form and has an international reputation as a translator. A relentless modernist, he has consistently argued for modernity not because he felt it was essentially better, but because of its implications, that by definition modernism was all inclusive and accepted a multiplicity, that there was variety – not just in our national identity nor in how that identity is expressed, but because it accepted our past as well.

Tradition is not a word one readily associates with Morgan, surely because he sees tradition as a restriction, a network where preservation is a barrier to progress, something to retire behind, comfortable and safe. Yet he also regards tradition as a source of inspiration – 'The Five-Pointed Star', written for the bicentenary of Burns's birth, is a relatively recent example – and he can use it as a springboard into something radical and new, as in the reimaginings of work by other writers, or in the *Glasgow Sonnets*.

His work has a social and political dimension that is not always obvious. These elements are usually recognisable in his choice of subject, which implies a certain sympathy; though his explorations or investigations of any social or political subject are always done on the basis of an imaginative exploration, often adopting different voices or personae, imagining characters in strange and random situations, probing characters for aspects of humanity, breathing life into imaginary characters or placing real characters in imaginary situations. When he looks into history it is often from prehistory that his ideas spring, maybe even legend based around history, for instance, extending the legend that Pontius Pilate was born at Fortingall in Perthshire by showing him returning there in later life, or inventing a song Columba could have written; he lights upon something that can act as an imaginative springboard.

Within his work is a respect for tradition, as a liberating, rather than restricting, feature of national identity. And this, together with the range and accessibility of his work, has accounted for the spread of his influence, so that rather than leading a school of writers in or around Glasgow, far less throughout Scotland, as MacDiarmid actively sought to do, Morgan's positive approach has created a climate where writers are free to investigate and experiment, encouraging others to follow where he has led.

Morgan's influence has helped us to arrive at a position where Scottishness, and especially Scottish identity, is neither perceived nor defined in any narrow way, looking towards a series of ideas or symbols; far less has it offered us a hero. His work seems entirely suited to the spirit of the times, offering a sense of optimism and hope through experimentation and imaginative freedom. Writers now know who they are and where they come from, and they can pick aspects of the past to investigate or experiment without being trapped by language or approach.

This is a development that could scarcely have been imagined by the preceding generation, upon whom MacDiarmid's imperious pronouncements had an enervating effect. But the revolution, which Edwin Morgan and Tom Leonard may not have instigated but which they enabled and encouraged with continuously realistic and intellectually challenging contributions, was aided by the judicious use of a master stroke whose impact and influence had previously been almost entirely overlooked. Tom Leonard uses humour to emphasise indignation and contempt. The results can be hard and difficult, often emphasising an assertion, an attitude or an understanding; whereas Morgan's wit is gentler and is often more subtly used to expose pomposity and pretension, to lay open the more ridiculous aspects of humanity and, like Leonard, to achieve a seriousness which could not be reached in any other way.

The most audible evidence of our identity crisis is found in the ways in which we speak. Muir's observation that the majority of our writers come from working families bears no comparison to the ways in which our writers have expressed and continue to express themselves linguistically, which in turn reveals a basic contradiction. Indigenous speech does more than expose social origins; in Scotland it carries a judgement and a vulnerability which can be maintained to the point of shame. More than anyone, Leonard has improved the climate, simultaneously establishing a ground that is linguistically separate from emulsified middle-class speech and a language that was rooted in the past and allowed for little local and no urban variation. This has been the springboard for Leonard's humour, which is anything but pawky. The concept of impropriety in language carries a class-ridden and class-bound judgement; and by exposing himself to charges of impropriety and even relishing the associated implications, he has cleared the way for a multiplicity of working voices to create literature that reflects a variety of Scottish voices, rather than the monotonous ranges that once dominated our pages.

Leonard's style, and some of Morgan's styles, are so individual as to make them difficult for other writers to emulate. And the same is true of much of Liz Lochhead's work. Her reliance on accent and sound is as contingent as either Leonard's or Morgan's. Her work is fashioned for and almost entirely suited to her voice, is often driven by a rhythmic imperative that derives from her brilliance as a reader and performer, and it is this aspect, rather than her carefully crafted pieces, that often lies at the heart of her influence. Her work is freer and driven as much by a theatrical as by a poetic imperative, where the voice is taken for granted and the narrative is a necessary part of any linguistic, even poetic, consideration. Again, like Morgan, her purpose is to entertain, and like him she uses humour and a wonderfully inventive imagination which marries simile and metaphor with acute observation.

Lochhead has redressed the balance of a male-dominated poetry and in doing so has encouraged other women writers not only to do likewise, but to use their work as a springboard into other ways of seeing by looking from a woman's perspective, and to address issues that had previously been ignored because of their feminine mood. This need not necessarily include issues of domesticity, though that would certainly be one example; rather it is the creation of a space where women's voices can be heard in a way that is recognisable to other women, rather than being restricted or adjusted for male consumption.

To Catch the Throat and Break the Spine

Tommy Armstrong was a Durham collier. He was born in Shotley Bridge in 1857 and lived most of his life in the village of Tanfield. He is described as 'a small, sharp-faced, bow-legged miner with fourteen children and an indomitable thirst'. By he time he died in 1920, Armstrong was known throughout the north-east of England as the Pitman's Poet. Today he is remembered as a songwriter whose songs are still being sung, and variants are still being collected.

As a rule, Armstrong's songs were too localised both in text and in spirit to travel. They were often set to the strain of early music-hall tunes that lie close to folk song, or to familiar traditional melodies, mostly recognisable come-all-ye airs. He wrote songs of occasion, commemorative pieces, including strike ballads which are in effect tracts outlining the cause of the strike, negotiating positions, working conditions, and the effect the strike is having on the men and their families. His songs are usually located in a particular place, most obviously through the voice, but also through their subject, and are written for people who would not only know the place but would also know and be sympathetic to the conditions he was describing.

According to A. L. Lloyd, song-making proliferated among miners during the latter half of the nineteenth century, and Armstrong is one of a number who occupy a position in many ways similar to that of Matt McGinn in Glasgow:

> There's a fellow down the road that I avoid;
> He's one of them they call the unemployed.
> He says it's all because of me
> He can't get a job when I've got three;
> I've three nights and a Sunday double time.
> Three nights and a Sunday double time.
> I work all day and I work all night;
> To hell with you, Jack, I'm all right,
> I've three nights and a Sunday double time.

Again, the range of McGinn's work is impressive. One of his songs, 'A Magic Shadow Show', is the basis for an Edwin Morgan poem. Little of local, national or international importance escaped Adam McNaughtan or Matt McGinn.

Scottish literature's new realism is in many ways different from the old realistic stance of writers such as Edward Gaitens and George Friel, who share the ability of Tommy Armstrong, Matt McGinn and Adam McNaughtan to address an audience they already know about the political and social issues that affect them. Recent realism is literary realism. The writers do not really know their audience; in fact, it is likely that the audience who absorb the works of our contemporary realists are not those who know and understand the conditions being described in anything other than a second-hand way.

It isn't until the 1930s that we can see industrialisation and its effects take hold of the Scottish literary imagination. These works, in the main, resembled Tommy Armstrong's songs insofar as they were intended for consumption by people whose lives and working experiences were not dissimilar to those whose existences were portrayed in their pages. This is not to say that *The Shipbuilders* by George Blake was for the sole consumption of shipyard workers, or that *The Land of the Leal* or *A Scots Quair* were intended only for those from a rural background who came to the city in search of employment, but that they were works intended primarily for working-class consumption. Their message was unequivocally socialist and their intention was to evoke a sympathetic response from their audience.

That this is no longer the case is a significant shift, a shift of emphasis. The trend of writing for those whose experience can be reflected in the works has recently been replaced by writing for a more voyeuristic market, similar to that which consumed the works of George Eliot or Charles Dickens. It can no longer be assumed that contemporary realist literature is digested by those whose experience is similar to the lives it portrays. Writing that now describes aspects of the working-class experience may be written by those whose background and upbringing were working class but who are not necessarily still working class, a phenomenon which has been the subject of considerable discussion and analysis by those in that position. Nor are the readers generally working class, whatever that may be, though for these purposes a practical definition could be those whose experiences are being represented. A broader definition would be E. P. Thompson's, which, despite its obvious gender bias, is certainly handier than most: 'Class happens when some men, as a result of common experiences (inherited or shared) feel and articulate the identity of their interests as between themselves, and as against other men whose interests are different from (and usually opposed to) theirs.'[27]

Those people in the same position as contemporary fictional creations, or who have first-hand knowledge of the realities behind the fiction, may find their lives more accurately reflected in cinema, especially in films like *Ratcatcher*, *Orphans*, or even *Trainspotting*, or in what the press describe as the grittier television dramas. Though the miracle of a novel like *Trainspotting* is that it appears to have penetrated this market, an experience resolutely denied almost every other work of fiction, which makes it an anachronism rather than something it may be possible to emulate.

A Navigational Aid

As a city Glasgow was dependent on heavy industry. There was a brief respite following the First World War, when owners were anxious to replace the ships they had lost, but Glasgow did not recover from the Great Depression. When Cunard told John Brown they could no longer finance the contract for Order Number 534, the yard paid off 3000 men and a rusty hull hung over Clydebank for two years, a national symbol of the slump. The vessel was launched as the *Queen Mary* in 1936 and entered service in June the following year. By then, work had started flowing in again as Britain began to rearm against Hitler's Germany.

In 1938 Glasgow hosted its fourth exhibition in less than forty years. The Empire Exhibition boasted the best of contemporary design in a decade memorable for its innovations. The centrepiece was Tait's Tower, a splendid example of modernist architecture which exemplified the confidence of the city. The exhibition was a remarkably successful mix-

27. E. P. Thompson, *The Making of the English Working Class.*

ture of mythological and contemporary Scotland. Parts survive still: the Palace of Arts is still on its original location in the exhibition grounds at Bellahouston Park, beside a reworking of Charles Rennie Mackintosh's Art Lover's House, and the Palace of Engineering was rebuilt at Prestwick Airport. The Beresford Hotel, where my grandfather was the first head waiter, was built for the exhibition and is now Strathclyde University's Baird Hall of Residence. The exhibition layout and many of the buildings were designed by Thomas Tait, the most prominent Scottish architect of the interwar period, designer of St Andrew's House, the home of government in Scotland until the arrival of the new Parliament. Tait's Tower was properly known as the Empire Tower. It was 250 feet high and was built in just nine weeks, with a fully functioning restaurant and a viewing gallery at the top. By night the tower was lit and could be seen from 100 miles outside the city. It was demolished during the Second World War, as it was thought it might act as a navigational aid for German bombers.

A plan to rebuild the tower, to give Glasgow an identifiable landmark, like the Eiffel Tower or the Statue of Liberty, a structure with which the city could be immediately identified, seems to have been shelved on grounds of cost.

The Motor Car and the Aeroplane

Of all the cities broken in the Second World War, Warsaw was the only one deliberately levelled like a public-works project, for Hitler had decided that a flattened Warsaw would be rebuilt as an outpost to be peopled only by Germans, who would need a limited number of indigenous slave workers – the plan was to turn the district of Praga into a massive servants' quarters.

When the war was over, the people of Warsaw set about rebuilding their city, brick by brick. In Dresden, Leipzig and other major European cities similar acts of reconstruction took place. But Glasgow, a city of comparable size, whose city centre was relatively undamaged by the bombing, had the Bruce Plan (1945–46), produced in two stages by the city engineer, Robert Bruce.

Over a period of roughly fifty years, Bruce's scheme would tidy up the city. Every building, with the exception of the twelfth-century cathedral, would be swept away. In their place, a network of flyovers, expressways, roundabouts and railway terminals would take citizens to work in the city centre or home again to suburbia. The boundaries of the new Glasgow would be defined by main roads, turning the city centre into a network of straight streets, moving logically from one central point to another. Despite the carefully planned transportation network, Glasgow's principal means of transport would be the helicopter, 'a vehicle combining the properties of the motor car and the aeroplane'. Public transport would be provided by electric trains, which would run along an extended, revamped system including the central reservations of the new motorways.

Many Glaswegians lived in tenements near their work, but the population was distributed in an unusual way. The main employers were on the fringes of the city, while the majority of the population lived in or near the city centre. Noting that poor people were occupying expensive land, Bruce planned to demolish working-class houses and replace them with commercial developments, where the tenants would pay 'realistic rents'. Poor people would be moved from the centre to a ring of new high-density housing developments on the fringes of the city.

The Bruce Plan more or less coincided with the arrival of the Clyde Valley Regional Planning Report, which proposed the dispersal of Glasgow's 'overspill' population to new towns, such as East Kilbride, with a concurrent development of new industries. The overspill programme was not a success, and rather than lose its population and their income, Glasgow decided to proceed with building the new high-density housing developments Bruce had envisaged. Permission was given for Castlemilk and Drumchapel to be built. Easterhouse came soon after. Each of these places would accommodate a population the size of a town like Perth, but with neither pubs nor shops.

Bruce's ideas were seen as a radical approach to the needs of a new corporation. The council's dilemma was how to keep its population within the city boundaries, for Glasgow's problems were being seen in a wider context, and proposals to disperse the population and some of the newer industries to the burgeoning new towns such as East Kilbride were strongly supported. Nor did the clamour subside when it became apparent that any attempt to house the existing population within, or even outwith, the city margins, was all but hopeless. Bruce's scheme was not dismissed out of hand. With typical local-authority compromise, elements of the Plan survived and Glasgow altered accordingly.

The Imaginative Blending of Rural and Urban

In 1954 three sections of the central area were chosen for redevelopment. This new programme was to be bigger, better, faster and more comprehensive than anything attempted before. Politicians and journalists spoke of doing away with the slums completely. Everything would be demolished and rebuilt, including the roads, and the three pilot areas would eventually be expanded to twenty-nine.

The Gorbals-Hutchestown redevelopment was undertaken in stages between 1958 and 1973, the largest scheme of its type in the country. In Springburn the Red Road flats were built – the highest steel-framed buildings in Europe – and Anderson was flattened to build the main artery across the river, part of the country's biggest urban highway-redevelopment programme.

Architectural guidebooks urged visitors not to miss these new developments. The approaches to the Kingston Bridge, 'a vital link in the Inner Ring Road, an essential feature of Glasgow's current comprehensive transport plan', were called 'a good example of the imaginative blending of rural and urban'.[28] The bridge was opened in 1970; by 1999 it was collapsing. It carries the M8 Edinburgh–Greenock motorway across the Clyde on two parallel concrete structures, each bearing five lanes of traffic. During the 1980s it became a major traffic bottleneck at peak periods, when the volume of vehicles began to exceed capacity. It is said to be the busiest bridge in Europe and is maintained and supported at an unknown, some say incalculable, cost, undergoing a cyclical series of repairs during which lanes are frequently closed and traffic diverted through town. The irony of forcing lorries on to bridges built for the horse and cart while a bridge built for lorries is continually reinforced has not been lost on the travelling public.

The bridge itself is listed in none of the city guidebooks, yet it is part of every tourist itinerary, to and from the Burrell Collection, Hampden Park, Ibrox Park, the Citizens' Theatre and the Art Lover's House. Buses crossing in either direction raise a cheer when it's past, especially when the buses are filled with football supporters, and every taxi driver can tell a number of traveller's tales about bottlenecks or bodies mingled with the concrete.

Commuter traffic is set to increase, and this will obviously lead to further road congestion. Meanwhile, the argument about the completion of the southern link between the M8 and the M74 continues. Most European cities have closed down their motorways, and Edinburgh talks of banning cars from Princes Street, but Glasgow opened a new stretch of motorway in 1995 and is almost the only city in Britain to have a motorway through its centre.

The problem, it seems, is one of identity. In the week when the M74 row was reported, an economic initiative called 'The Glasgow Sphere of Influence' was launched. The central idea was that prominent individuals would take part in a number of 'sector focused' events throughout the city and attend an annual dinner. According to the *Scotsman*, it was 'an honest attempt to tap the common pride which exists among many who are originally from the city and channel it towards the greater good of the area'.[29] After comparing Glasgow with Dublin, Naples and Chicago, the writer concluded it didn't need this sort of image,

because it already has the right kind of substance and plenty of faith in its

28. A. M. Doak and Andrew Mclaren Young, *Glasgow at a Glance*.
29. *Scotsman*, 7 May 1998.

own reality . . . . Socially and culturally, though, it has failed to capitalise on earlier successes and now looks utterly limp. It is not a happening city any more. In the City Chambers, its elected members plot and squabble like ferrets in a sack. Its public services have the reek of decay and poverty about them. This loss of impetus could not have come at a more critical moment. Never – not even in the days when the shipyard cranes fell silent, or when the great locomotive workshops of Cowlairs sparked and clattered their last – has this great, vibrant city stood closer to the brink than it does now.[30]

And with the new Parliament in Edinburgh: 'The central belt of Scotland is starting to look like a side view of the sinking *Titanic*. In the east, at the stern end, is Edinburgh, its features high and proud against the skyline and still rising. At the other end is Glasgow, its decks slowly, but with increasing speed disappearing below the waves.' The answer, it seems, is a new image. 'Glasgow needs a new and co-ordinated city branding campaign.'[31]

It's the Capital of Culture; It's a Damned Disgrace

The Bruce Plan was born amid post-war optimism; it marked the start of another series of ambitious schemes aimed at resolving the problem of Glasgow's poor and overcrowded housing. Acres of Victorian tenements were demolished in the late 1950s under the Comprehensive Development Policy. The policy was heavily criticised by those who believed one of the world's great Victorian cities was being destroyed.

By the time work began on rebuilding the demolished tenements in the form of high-rise flats, Glasgow's economic base had shifted. Many shipyards and engineering works closed in the 1960s. Most of Springburn, for example, had been demolished to make way for a new development which would house those who worked at the railway-maintenance and engine-building works. Rebuilding work had scarcely started when the railway yards and workshops closed their gates.

But Glasgow's problems have also shifted. No longer is the district council anxious to keep the working population within the city, and few speak of slum clearance. They have adapted to the new political rhetoric and accepted the realities bequeathed by their predecessors, who produced the Clyde Valley Plan and then swathed the city in concrete. Some observers urged Glasgow to 'rediscover its past as a cultural and intellectual centre, challenging the philosophy that had ripped apart Britain's finest Victorian city'.[32] Out of this vision emerged a new Glasgow in the 1980s, 'proud of its past and its own distinct identity – summed up in

30. *Ibid.*
31. *Ibid.*
32. *Collins Encyclopaedia of Scotland.*

the upbeat slogan "Glasgow's Miles Better" . . . by rediscovering a past, Glasgow may have found a future'.[33]

Every promotion, every subsequent reinvention suggests there is something new in the city, an immediacy, a vibrancy, that the past is dead and Glasgow is marching towards a confident future. The suggestion is that Glasgow has preserved a past it now wants to share with others, a view Scotland's inaugural First Minister and Glasgow resident, the late Donald Dewar, endorsed: 'There can on occasion be a girn in the air, a downbeat, gloomy satisfaction in predicting a sad decline for the city, but it is not the mark of the place. Glasgow is a good place to live. It has no side, no ludicrous pretensions, but a cocky common sense and a willingness to offer a welcome to the world. It is a better place than Muir's divided and troubled city. It is a place where I want to live.'[34]

But Glasgow has an identity problem it cannot address, far less hope to solve while it seeks to emulate places whose assertions are better established. As Adam McNaughtan suggests, it was always more than a single-issue location:

> The Glasgow I belong to is a dear green place,
> It's the capital of culture; it's a damned disgrace.
> It's Kelvinside and Calton, pan loaf, plain breid,
> It's the Tron and the Tramway and the Sarry Heid.

'The Dear Green Place' was written in 1990 'to celebrate the many-sided nature of Europe's Capital of Culture'. The title refers to the spot where St Mungo is said to have founded the city and is also the supposed origin of the name of the place. *Glas chu* in Gaelic means, literally, the dear green place; the phrase has also been used as the title of a novel by Archie Hind. Since the mid-1960s McNaughtan has chronicled every stage of the city's development, beginning with 'They're Tearing Doon the Building Next To Oors' and 'Old Annie Brown' to 'Where is the Glasgow?' and 'Skyscraper Wean'.

The Reader's Digest Touring Guide to Britain claims that 'the famed arts galleries and museums of Glasgow have ensured that its cultural heritage now stands alongside Athens, Florence and Paris'. But other guides are more circumspect in their claims and more direct in their assessment of the city's past: 'For decades Glasgow was widely associated with hard drinking, pub brawling, massive unemployment and lawless, decaying housing estates such as Easterhouse and the Gorbals.'[35] This, it is claimed, is the predominant impression visitors bring to the city. Social

33. *Ibid.*
34. *Observer*, 18 April 1999.
35. *The Visitor's Guide to Scotland.*

problems have been endemic, due to the demise of the steel and ship-building industries which faltered during the Depression, began the slide in the 1950s and disappeared in the 1970s. 'These industries relied on tough, hard-working characters, plate-metal workers, welders and riveters who turned out the world's finest locomotives and ocean liners. Drinking was always the shipyard workers' favourite hobby and it must have been a terrible knock to their pride as well as their pay-packet to see these great enterprises go.'[36]

On the Edge

On the day Nick Danziger arrived in Glasgow the rotting body of a pen-sioner was found in his flat, eight months after he died. 'Neighbours hadn't seen the quiet eighty-two year old for months, but no one had reported him missing. Council officials only took an interest in Malkie when his rent fell into arrears and they moved in to evict him. When the police battered down his door the Christmas cards were still on the mantelpiece.'[37]

Danziger observed that Glasgow in 1990

> found new prestige as the cultural centre of Europe, but at first sight it is not a pleasant place, this sprawling metropolis with its grim twenty- and thirty-storey tenements and claustrophobic closes. For many Glaswegians it is not cheerful, or easy, or safe, or reasonable; it is, however, a passionate place, where both young and old, the hopeful and the disillusioned, find a life lived constantly on the edge. The city breathes with a vitality like no other city in Britain. In this Glasgow has much in common with New York.[38]

Danziger stayed in a housing scheme less than 2 miles from the city centre, in a place with neither boarding houses nor hotels, where strangers must be escorted, where ice-cream vans sell essentials at extor-tionate rates, where someone running is a sign of trouble, and where he was offered prescription drugs as soon as he arrived. The woman he lived with, a local activist who fought to establish a crèche, a drugs advice centre and a family flat for parents and young children, had her wedding ring stolen by her addict son. The successes achieved by women on the scheme also bred resentment, particularly among the men who were out of work. When the women managed to get funds to set up support groups, the men wanted a piece of the action – the job of running them.

The local pub has bricked-up windows; there have been thirty murders in five years; and drugs are a way of life:

36. *Ibid.*
37. Nick Danziger, *Danziger's Britain: A Journey to the Edge.*
38. *Ibid.*

Five people were stabbed to death the weekend I left Glasgow. The follow-ing week another person overdosed in the community I had visited. Christine sent me the clippings from the newspaper's memorial pages placed by the mother who had now lost a daughter in addition to a sister and a son

> 'In loving memory of daughter Christine, sister Julia, son Paddy:
>> As I wander to their graveside
>> Each flower I place with care
>> No one knows the heartache
>> When I turn and leave them there
>> My heart still aches with sadness
>> And secret tears still flow
>> For what it meant to lose you
>> No one will ever know
>> St Jude pray for them
> "If tears could build a stairway and memories a lane,
> I'd walk straight up to heaven and bring them back again."'[39]

The Top Three

Shettleston, in Glasgow's east end, was the former constituency of John Wheatley, architect of the 1924 Labour Government's Housing Act, 'designed to build houses at rents which workers could afford'. Shettleston is now the unhealthiest place in Britain, according to statistics from the Economic and Social Research Council's Health Inequalities Programme. When the statistics were translated into parliamentary con-stituencies, nine out of the country's ten healthiest constituencies were held by the Conservative Party, while the ten unhealthiest places were all Labour seats, seven of which were in Glasgow, including the top three – Shettleston, Springburn and Maryhill. 'Shettleston's death rate is twice the national average, with heart disease, cancer and strokes the major killers. Mental illness – in particular depression – is three times higher than in Britain as a whole,' says the report.

Glasgow's director of public health, Harry Burns, blames the culture of ill health on unemployment and poverty. 'When you take away work,' he says, 'you take away hope. That's why depression is so high. Without hope, people care less about themselves. Without work, there is also poverty. It is no wonder diet is so poor.' Political change, he says, will benefit Shettleston.

Glasgow is also the heart attack capital of the world. It has the world's worst diet, and is the home of deep-fried Mars bar with chips. More people smoke in Glasgow than in any other British city, it has the worst dental

39. *Ibid.*

records, the highest incidence of obesity, more teenage pregnancies than any other British city, and an unemployment record that hovers around 20 per cent of the population.

Things were so bad in the late 1980s that the city launched the Good-Hearted Glasgow Campaign, whose accompanying leaflet provided the previous statistics, setting out the problem precisely:

> The city's death rates from lung cancer and heart disease are among the highest in the world. And people living in Glasgow's most deprived areas are two-and-a-half times more likely to die before the age of 65 than people living in the most affluent areas .... Glasgow has the highest levels of social deprivation of any city in the UK. These are increasing, and becoming concentrated in areas of public sector housing ... levels of dampness, disrepair, overcrowding and lack of adequate heating are high, contributing significantly to ill-health ... theft, vandalism and crime increase stress and anxiety ... lead piping in water supply is still a hazard.

The campaign was mercilessly parodied by Adam McNaughtan, in songs such as 'Erchie Cathcairt' and 'Cholesterol', whose accompanying note states: 'Glasgow is recognised as the heart disease capital of the universe. Glasgow doesnae care.'

The Most Unsung of Them All

What is usually referred to as Glasgow's regeneration – the word renaissance has been used in some quarters – has been propagated by the tourism industry, by advertising the attractions rather than the place:

> From much of Glasgow ... you can see hills in the distance. Blocks of flats in the middle distance, granted, but real countryside beyond. Although this contributes to the windy feel, it also makes walking in Glasgow seem somehow more appropriate. There are also hills closer to hand, giving some streets a mini-San Francisco feel, which may discourage some. The city also has 70 public parks and gardens – more per capita than any other city in Europe.[40]

Only Glasgow's writers and artists seem capable of presenting the place with its contradictions intact. But occasionally, reality overtakes a plausibility fiction writers would have long since abandoned, when the place takes on a surreal quality and the consequences of a change in perception rather than substance leaves an impressive credibility gap: 'Last week in Glasgow, despite the warm weather, there was barely a drunk to be seen

40. *Independent on Sunday*, 30 August 1998.

on the streets,' *Scotland on Sunday* proclaimed in May 1998. 'The clearance is a result of the Prohibition of Consumption of Alcohol, operated by the police and city council for the past 18 months. Over that period around 10,000 people have been fined or warned about drinking on the city's streets. Between January and December last year, 4,884 drinkers were fined for swigging from beer cans or drinking wine and spirits in public view.' Alcohol is Glasgow's traditional drug of choice; and the wine referred to is more likely to be fortified rather than a pale Chablis or a cheeky little Beaujolais. The drunks may have been concealed from public view, but they're still around.

The first meeting of Alcoholics Anonymous in Scotland and the first in Britain outside London was held in Glasgow, which currently boasts more AA meetings than the rest of Scotland put together. AA was brought to Scotland by Sir Philip Dundas in 1948, and the early meetings were held in St Enoch's Hotel on a Tuesday night. In keeping with the spiritual foundations of Alcoholics Anonymous, Dundas remains a shadowy figure: 'Scotland has had a lot of unsung heroes in its history,' writes the editor of *Roundabout*, the magazine of Alcoholics Anonymous in Scotland, 'but the most unsung of them all is Sir Philip Dundas, the man who first brought Alcoholics Anonymous to Scotland.'

There are a number of anti-alcohol agencies in Glasgow, and while the city has not exactly been freed from a drug-dependency problem, it's reckoned that Glasgow's main social problem is still the drink. Yet, here as elsewhere, the bulk of the money granted to treatment centres and rehabilitation programmes is spent on drug addicts, obviously because of the possible implications for the crime statistics, though it is also reckoned that a more civilised drinking system – a greater number of pubs that open early or close late – has changed the city's drinking habits and is set to change them further. Campaigns against the alcohol problem seem to have a similar target market to the anti-smoking propaganda: girls as young as ten, and certainly those from twelve upwards. According to a report published in the *Guardian*, they are joined by divorced women, who are twice as likely to develop a drinking problem as their male counterparts, with loneliness the suggested alcohol-abuse trigger.

The Economic Importance of the Arts in Glasgow

The change in Glasgow's drinking habits was generated by the same motivation that led to the city being featured in a visitor's guide to Scotland. It's part of the reinvention process.

In 1982 the city was left with a run-down housing stock, rising unemployment, poor health and its major industries dead or dying. The council commissioned a report from John Myerscough of the Economic Policy Study Unit. He concluded that Glasgow had enormous assets. Its architecture was unique, it had the best municipal art collection in the country and an artistic life which was ready to be expanded. The problem was a lack of confidence and a lack of identity.

Just as the initial idea and impetus for the Edinburgh Festival came from outside the city, so Glasgow's regeneration is a story of intent. In 1983 the district council published a report which concluded that following the post-war demise of heavy industry, the city needed the sort of revitalisation that would boost both its economy and its morale. The city centre also required restoration; this, it was said, would simultaneously make the people more confident and turn the city into a pleasant place to stay. The retail sector needed the sort of expansion that would bring consumers into the city. Companies should be persuaded to locate their headquarters in Glasgow, and tourism had to be developed. The report suggested the initial regeneration should be concentrated on the city centre, eventually expanding to the outer areas.

Glasgow, the report said, had inherent cultural strengths, including the largest and best-resourced local-authority museums in the country, with collections more than twice the size of many other cities of comparable size and bigger than most of the national collections in London. Scottish Opera, Scottish Ballet and three major orchestras were based in Glasgow, which was also the home of the Citizens Theatre, the British theatre company that commanded most international respect.

Glasgow reinvented itself with Mr Happy and the slogan 'Glasgow's Miles Better'. The opening of the Burrell Collection in Pollok Park in 1985 designated Glasgow as a short-break destination and this was underlined by the Garden Festival in 1988. A report entitled *The Economic Importance of the Arts in Glasgow*, written by John Myerscough and published in 1988, declared that the city needed such regeneration every five or six years. It needed a focus, something to provide a fillip, to keep the gravy train rolling.

The Burrell Collection is still one of the city's main attractions. With more than eight thousand items covering over four thousand years of artistic activity, it started and in many ways maintains Glasgow's reinvention. The Garden Festival brought 4.8 million people and provided an opportunity to market the city's other cultural attractions, a move which was to prove valuable two years later.

Glasgow's year as European City of Culture for 1990 was a high-profile event, though it is rumoured that local councillors thought Edinburgh would win. Rather than concentrating events around a single day – Paris had Bastille Day in 1989 and Dublin had Bloomsday in 1991 – Glasgow went for a year-long festival which entailed more than three thousand separate events, some of which would have happened anyway, but others were deliberately imported to signal the city's intentions.

There was a total subsidy of more than £57 million from the two main local authorities, district and regional, at a time when the poll tax was inflicting its worst effects. The result was an 80 per cent visitor increase at a time when comparable venues were experiencing at least a 10 per cent decrease.

In the following eighteen months nine new venues opened, and developers seemed poised to undertake a number of refurbishment and rebuilding programmes, including a £13.5 million redevelopment of the area round City Hall, converting it into a performing-arts centre. The focus, it seemed, had shifted. Glasgow was looking at its infrastructure, considering its permanent assets, consolidating rather than expanding.

This was demonstrated by proposed residencies by the Leipzig Gewandhaus Orchestra, as well as the eighty-two actors and entire back-up company of the Maly Theatre of St Petersburg. Peter Brook brought every one of his new productions to Glasgow, where the Tramway had been created for his *Maharabata* in 1988, and The Wooster Group and the Tricia Brown Dance Company visited from New York. Rather than follow the lead of Edinburgh's Festival, where events were concentrated into three weeks, and so had little impact on the city's cultural expansion and development, Glasgow spread its events throughout the year and went for longer-term residencies and performances.

Especially and quite deliberately, a campaign of theatre-audience building was begun, putting popular companies into venues such as the Citizens and the Tron. This initially drew people into the theatre of their own volition, bringing them back to see main house companies and eventually moving towards the Tramway. Nowhere else saw this kind of complementary integration.

There is no doubt that these deliberate intentions came from the council, who employed Bob Palmer and Neil Wallace as cultural instigators, responsible for turning the city's thinking into reality, as well as providing some ideas of their own. They have now gone, and their positions have been amalgamated or left unfilled.

Cultured Out

Glasgow, it seems, not only needs further reinvention and restoration, but reinforcement as well. Excavation work caused the Virginia Galleries to drop by 10 inches. In October 1998 the *Herald* reported: 'The damage coincides with growing anger and dismay among public agencies and conservation bodies at the deteriorating state of property in the street. . . . Many of the buildings are listed and widely regarded as the city's finest examples of the era of the tobacco lords and cotton kings. However, almost 10 years have passed since the ambitious redevelopment plans were announced.' An accompanying article outlines these plans and states that 'only 50% of the project has been completed' and that 'the background is a tale of woe, even intrigue – of perceived inaction, of developers coming and going, and of squabbles over levels of public funding. Few emerge with credit.'

And less than a week later Glasgow's arts and cultural committee learned that there had been an 'alarming decline in the city's perform-ing arts, with theatre attendances dropping by nearly a quarter and concert-going down by nearly one fifth in a single year'. The fall affected theatres, museums and libraries. The report was included in a revised digest of cultural statistics produced by John Myerscough. It 'identifies that Glasgow's cultural organisations are substantially more important today than a decade ago, serving a market which has risen by 21%, with turnover up 61%, and jobs up by 13% over that period.' The figures cor-responded with the loss of £3 million in direct subsidy in the wake of local-government reorganisation, as well as a reduction in corporate sponsorship. This meant companies put on fewer and cheaper shows, which in turn affected audience figures. 'It also meant fewer festivals, fewer visits by touring theatre companies, and weaker cultural links with abroad.'[41]

The report confirmed what had been known and openly reported for more than a year, certainly since the collapse of Mayfest, whose last direc-tor was reported as saying, 'The city is cultured out. We are witnessing the end of a glorious 10 years.' And in the week the city's jazz festival folded, he blamed the Internet, among other things, for tempting audiences away from the performing arts.

> The city has used culture, cappuccino and Calvin Klein to cast off the yoke of slum tenements and smokestacks. But behind the Versace shades, Clydeside's artistic revolutionaries are thinking the unthinkable, saying out loud what people have only dared whisper. The anxiety has been grow-ing all year as audiences have slumped at the city's biggest venues and a financial crisis has forced renowned galleries to shed staff and close . . .
>
> Local government reorganisation two years ago, in which the giant Strathclyde Regional Council was abolished, has destroyed Glasgow's rev-enue base. Deep cuts have been made in local budgets . . . the Scottish Office has cut its £818 million grant by £27 million. The budget for Glasgow's museums and galleries alone has been cut by 20 per cent. About 2000 council jobs have been lost.[42]

While the city failed to alter the terms of Sir William Burrell's will, a move which would allow them to loan works overseas, 'councillors and marketing executives who have used culture to combat recession and

41. *Herald,* 19 October 1998.
42. *Observer,* 5 October 1997.

industrial decline deny the Glasgow dream is played out. But they concede there is a "mood of change".'[43]

Govan Is a Constituency Changed

All this brings the city's endemic problems back into focus. The fringe
housing schemes are scarcely the paradises Bruce imagined, and the loss
of traditional industries has muddied the city's identity. Govan, for example, 'is a constituency changed beyond all recognition since the days
when it was a noisy shipyard seat, crammed with immigrants bossed by
working-class, Tory-voting Orangemen, all building great ships which
underpinned Britain's Empire,' according to a profile in the *Herald*.

> For a while the yards, with their Protestantism imported from Ulster, mainly
> by Harland and Wolff, were the making of Govan. But the Irish legacy
> proved to be a curse. Govan gained a name for sectarianism when, in fact,
> it had been no more guilty of intolerance than most of the rest of Scotland.
> Bigotry is said to have departed with the jobs. Today's Govan suffers from
> another bad reputation, that of the defeated inner-city slumland filled with
> an expanding underclass. Govan's most celebrated fictional character is the
> feral Rab C. Nesbitt who, if he walked down Govan Road today, might
> stand a chance of being lynched for shaming the place. On the other hand
> he might just find himself among some kindred spirits.

According to the Scottish Office area-deprivation index, Possilpark is
the most deprived community in Scotland. Unemployment is at more
than 18 per cent, four in five tenants receive housing benefit, and 68 per
cent of pupils qualify for free school meals. Further out, in the Balmore
Road in Milton, just inside the city boundary, one in three adults are
unemployed and half the children live in one-parent families. 'There is
extreme poor health, high levels of crime and vandalism, and a high suicide rate. Drug addicts skulk around dilapidated high-rises, their
movements closely tracked by weary police and worried parents.'
Another report revealed that 75 per cent of the youngsters surveyed
living there had tried drugs before their sixteenth birthday, 'by which
time two-thirds have been in trouble with the police, the courts, or the
children's panel'.[44]

The relentlessness of statistics can emulsify their impact. What would
seem to be the concentrated weight of the city's social problems could
undermine the continuing difficulties of those who live in these conditions and the work being done in a number of areas to help relieve the

43. *Ibid.*
44. *Herald*, 3 March 1998.

difficulties. The figures also tend to marginalise the council's problems.

Plans to mingle private and local-authority housing, in areas like Keppoch, which borders Possilpark, and in housing schemes like Castlemilk, Garthamlock and Drumchapel, are being developed. And part of the new rhetoric is a series of private housing developments whose properties are built from kits in a style that could be adapted for anywhere, with names that are more suited to an English seaside resort than a Glasgow housing scheme: Hunter's Grange, The Steadings. These places have no identity; their existence is the antithesis of identity. They present an image.

With the last of the traditional Gorbals tenements gone, the area that had become a byword for violent squalor in the 1930s, where the 1960s high-rise flats were known as Dampies and that now, according to a report in the *Herald*, is 'acknowledged within Europe as leading the field in urban regeneration' has its own heritage trail. *The Gorbals Heritage Trail Guide*, published in 1988, tells us Gorbals was a seventeenth-century burgh, laid out as a fashionable suburb and later swallowed by city expansion. It was the nearest Glasgow came to having a ghetto, with several distinct ethnic groups settling in the area. By the 1930s it had dozens of cinemas, more than 130 pubs, over 1000 shops and a population of more than 90,000. Today's population is nearer 9000.

In the first phase of the redevelopment private money was put up only because of the public-sector investment. But before the project reached the halfway stage, the position was reversed. The plan includes business and shopping centres, office and student accommodation, small industrial units and a public park. Three quarters of the houses are for sale; the others will be rented.

'If ever there was a case of a prophet being "not without honour, save in his own country", then this is it,' the *Herald* said of the new development. 'Planning experts may come from around the world to find out for themselves about the Crown Street Project, the latest being from Boston . . . but Scots remain largely ignorant of the prestige the initiative has won for the city internationally.'[45]

However, already there is criticism that such 'an architectural triumph' has ignored other needs. 'There are those who believe that the whole Gorbals project has been bricks and mortar led,' says the *Herald*,

> . . . just another symptom of the way that people's needs have come second to urban gloss. While money has been pumped into the creation of high quality housing, high quality social support is rapidly diminishing. Now denied the status of Area of Priority Treatment, Gorbals seems to some to have become a sham community. The splendid Disneyland High Street

45. *Ibid.*

pretends a make-believe prosperity, masking the traditional problems the Gorbals has always known.[46]

While this and other newer housing developments across the city reverse Glasgow's traditional immigration pattern, whereby people came to the city looking for a new life, there now remains a divide between those who lived through the regeneration process of the 1960s and those who have been attracted by the subsequent regeneration. Extreme poverty is reported on one street, juxtaposed in the next with the comparative wealth of those who can afford a new house:

> The facilities offered by an organisation such as the Gorbals Umbrella Group, which co-ordinates community projects, or the youth drop-in centre, or the unemployed workers centre, are of little interest to the Dinkies (Double Income, No Kids couple) who have bought a pied-à-terre in Glasgow's City of Architecture centrepiece. Dinkies go across the river for their shopping and entertainment: Marks and Spencer and the Early Learning Centre have more appeal than the decaying Queen Elizabeth Square shops and the Unemployed Workers Centre toy library, which lends out the latest playthings at 10p a week.[47]

A 3 Per Cent Chance

And such conditions bring miseries in their wake. A recent report titled 'Social Inequalities in Coronary Heart Disease' recommended children should be given free fruit and vegetables at school. It found that a third of children were living in poor households. The effects begin at birth; children with a low birth weight go on to have a higher risk of heart disease. 'The poorer areas of Glasgow simply do not have access to fresh food. They do not have cars to drive to the supermarket so they cannot buy cheap fruit and vegetables.'[48]

Almost one third of all Glasgow households are headed by a lone parent, according to an unnamed report quoted in the *Herald*, and 43 per cent of pupils receive free school meals, while 58 per cent receive clothing or footwear grants. According to Unicef, the percentage of low-weight births in Castlemilk can be as high as 14 per cent – twice the UK average.[49] In Easterhouse more than 80 per cent of children qualify for school-clothing grants. 'Deaths in the first year in Easterhouse have been around 46 per 1000, compared with only 10 per 1000 in nearby affluent

---

46. *Herald*, 20 April 1998.
47. *Ibid.*
48. Quoted in the *Herald*, 29 October 1998.
49. Quoted in the *Herald*, 4 February 1998.

suburbs,' says Bob Holman, a visiting professor at Glasgow University's
Department of Social Policy, who lives in Easterhouse.

> Children in Easterhouse are also twice as likely as children elsewhere to be
> involved in serious road accidents. This is despite the fact that only one in five
> households has the use of a car, compared with four out of five elsewhere.
> The explanation is that many people live in blocks of flats without gardens,
> so children play in the streets that drivers from outside Easterhouse use as a
> short cut. Long term poverty hurts in other ways, too. The poor do less well
> at school. Research compiled by the Glasgow Health Board shows that chil-
> dren coming from an advantaged area have a 70 per cent chance of attaining
> three or more Highers [the Scottish equivalent of A-levels]. Those from a dis-
> advantaged home and area have only a 3 per cent chance.[50]

In 1980 Sir Douglas Black, in a report commissioned by the first
Thatcher Government, found wide differences in death rates between
the rich and poor and recommended measures costing £2 billion to
address them. The report was dismissed by the then Secretary of State for
Social Services, Patrick Jenkin.

Another inquiry, chaired by Sir Donald Acheson, the former government chief medical officer, recommended free fruit in schools, nicotine
patches on prescription, and a variety of improvements in housing,
employment and education. The report said

> Britain is now the most unequal country in the world after the US in terms
> of the gap between rich and poor, which is wider than at any time since the
> Second World War. While the rich have got richer over the past 20 years,
> the numbers on Income Support have more than doubled from 4 million
> in 1979 to 9.6 million in 1996. A quarter of all children under 11 lives in
> families on Income Support.

'Poverty breeds debt,' writes Bob Holman. 'Banks and building societies
are rarely interested in poor areas.'[51] Yet poor people need credit, not for
mortgages or cars, but for fridges, fires, clothes and food. And changes in
government policy have made matters worse. Before 1988 social-security
claimants were entitled to grants to replace worn-out domestic essentials.
The Conservative Government abolished most grants and installed dis-
cretionary Social Fund loans; the repayments are deducted from weekly
Giro cheques. Thus a family may have £30 a week taken from an income
that is itself supposed to be a minimum. This loan system, on its own,
increased the number of poor debtors by more than a million.

50. *Independent*, 17 October 1998.
51. *Ibid.*

New Labour, which had condemned the Conservative changes while in opposition, decided to uphold them. Applicants whose requests for an official loan were refused might turn to legal, high-interest lenders, where the advertised interest rate is an already high 29.9 per cent – but the small print entails obligations that raises them to 55 per cent. Others turn to illegal loan sharks who may charge 50 per cent or more interest *per week*, which is enforced by a threat of violence. According to Holman, a young man who had stolen his wallet later 'showed me his knee, beaten in by a baseball bat. He had borrowed to buy goods for his kids and could not keep up the repayments. He stole from me in order to avoid another beating.'

Strategies That Are Failing

On January 3 1998 Britain's youngest-ever drugs-related death was recorded. Thirteen-year-old Allan Harper was found in the early hours of the first Saturday of the year and one of the coldest nights of the winter in a close in Startpoint Street, not far from his home in Bellrock Street, Cranhill. His shoulder had been partly gnawed by three bull terriers belonging to his mother's boyfriend.

Mothers Against Drugs (MAD) was formed by women who remember a community which 'used to have two secondary schools with swimming pools and facilities which could be used by the community at night . . . . With the school closures, the buildings were just shut down and we begged to keep the swimming pool and games hall – to run it ourselves as a community facility – but they just demolished it.'[52] Drugs, they say, 'have become so much a part of life everywhere, there is no escape from them'. According to a report on the Cranhill community, published ten months after Allan Harper's death,

> school children as young as 10 act as drug couriers for the dealers here who peddle heroin, Ecstasy and cannabis. The youngsters – in their school uniforms, Adidas trainers or Tommy Hilfiger sweatshirts – are already on their way to becoming addicts themselves. According to one local, there are two 15-year-old Cranhill girls, both heroin addicts, who sell their bodies for sex in the red-light district of Anderston. The teenage boyfriend of one of the girls is her pimp. In Cranhill, it is easier to get drugs than it is to get a packet of cigarettes from the ice-cream van. It is easier to get a £10 bag of heroin than a fresh pint of milk from the local shops; the shops run out of milk, but the dealers never run out of heroin.[53]

The article speaks of illegal squats and hash houses: 'Knives, guns, heroin

52. *Herald*, 23 June 1998.
53. *Herald*, 14 November 1999.

and cannabis are stashed here amongst the baleful wasteland, where junkies "chase the dragon". Kicked-in doors are a testimony to both raids and fights between rival drug dealers.'

MAD is reported to be 'attempting to become a national movement'. Central to their strategy is a belief 'that current anti-drugs measures have failed and that any new initiative must be developed, managed and maintained by local people with intimate knowledge of the issues'. They also want 'a Cranhill-wide letting initiative that would give locals complete autonomy over the selection of council tenants' as well as a programme 'based on US-style drug courts where . . . there is a choice between a prison sentence or a rehabilitation programme'. The MAD spokeswoman, Gaille McCann, a Glasgow councillor, says, 'If the experts listen to us maybe something could be done. There are too many grey suits that sit behind desks and adopt strategies that are failing. The Government needs to go to the communities who are suffering from drug problems. That's where the answers are.'

Since the group was formed the women 'have been receiving threats from drug dealers in the form of quiet intimidation. Veiled threats, being accosted in the street and verbal intimidation is commonplace now. Drug dealers walk into public meetings and sit there eyeball to eyeball with the mums.' One woman said,

> We are not stupid around here. We know nothing's being done. You only need one spoonful of soup to know the whole bowl stinks . . . . It is the communities that are on [the] receiving end of the drugs crisis, yet we are expected to watch our children disintegrate before our eyes, while the so-called drug experts attend more meetings and produce more and more reports. The evidence is here. The West Street Crisis Centre for addicts in Glasgow has only 12 beds to cover the whole of Strathclyde. We need 1200 beds and rehabilitation centres in every town in Scotland. If not, we will lose a whole generation. Our kids are being murdered.[54]

A month before the Cranhill piece was published, a Scottish Office report showed that the poor are more prone to mental illness and to major cancers other than breast cancer, as well as heart disease and strokes.

> Their tendency to be less likely than affluent people to get a coronary bypass or angioplasty may be due to their overall ill health rendering them unfit for the procedures – or it might be that more affluent people made better use of the NHS . . . . The report, which overturns 20 years of denial by the Conservative Government that ill health and poverty are linked, is

54. *Ibid.*

expected to reinforce government policy aimed at reducing smoking, poor housing and unemployment.[55]

'Scotland has one of the highest rates of tobacco-related deaths in the world, with women on low incomes most likely to take up smoking and least likely to give up the habit,' the *Herald* reports, adding that lung cancer kills more women in Scotland each year than breast cancer. A majority of the smokers surveyed said they believed they would benefit from nicotine-replacement therapy, providing it was available on prescription.[56]

Six months previously, the National Statistics Office's General Survey for 1996 showed that while smoking had declined dramatically, the decline had levelled off. 'We are down to the hardcore now, but that hardcore is still recruiting. The highest proportion of smokers is found amongst those in their early twenties, and the number of women smokers is rising slightly. Contrary to the myths, the employed are more likely to smoke than the unemployed.'[57]

Earlier in the year the Scottish Needs Assessment Programme proposed that smoking be banned in public places, including pubs, where research revealed non-smoking staff face higher risks from passive smoking than non-smokers in other occupations.

In December 1997 it was reported that the NHS in Scotland 'spends £100m a year to treat respiratory diseases such as asthma, bronchitis and pneumonia'. Every night 'more than 1000 individuals will sleep in cardboard boxes over warm air grills in darkened city lanes, or in basements with the garbage of multi-storey flats, at the back doors of supermarkets, on riverbank benches, or under motorway flyovers just yards from the traffic'. This figure excludes more than 41,000 families 'who have had to apply to local authorities in Scotland for emergency housing. They may not have been sleeping on the streets when they made their application, but they would have been equally desperate: the mother fleeing with her children from domestic violence; the family evicted because of mortgage arrears.'[58]

Family break-up is often the route to the streets. 'Often the public think these young people's plight is self-inflicted, but the public don't have a clear view,' says a city worker with the homeless. And less than a year later, 'as the Government orders a new deal for the 51,000 children in care in England', a further aspect of homelessness was revealed – 'the alarmingly high number of young people who run away' from local-authority care.

And Britain has the world's highest rate of unmarried teenage mothers.

55. Quoted in the *Herald*, 14 October 1998.
56. *Herald*, 4 February 1999.
57. *Independent on Sunday*, 30 August 1998.
58. *Herald*, 19 December 1997.

'The first worldwide survey of young women's sexual activity showed that 87% of the 41,700 children of 15 to 19 year old girls in the UK were born outside marriage, compared to 62% in America and just 10% in Japan,' says the *Herald* report. 'The figure was also higher than the rate in the Third World, according to the survey of 53 countries, including six from the developed world . . . . The Scottish Health Statistics for 1997 showed that pregnancies among girls aged 13 to 15 rose by 10% to 916, the highest number for a decade.'[59]

Two months later a study revealed that young women agreed to having unprotected sex because condoms spoiled it for men. One twenty year old, quoted in the *Observer*, explained: '"People just won't use them because they hate them. It spoils the whole effect of it. It's like chewing toffee with the wrapper on."'[60]

Another study of the sex lives of teenage girls reports that 'the taboos about premarital sex have been broken but the traditional idea that sex is a "man's pleasure and a woman's duty" is alive and well.' Young women spoke of having unprotected sex, 'of not using condoms, even when they were to hand; of making no protest at rape; of accepting violence; of coming under pressure to have unwanted vaginal penetrative intercourse rather than non-penetrative sex'.[61]

A survey conducted by the magazine *Prima* 'captured a very clear snapshot of attitudes to family life in Britain today – a strong vote of confidence goes to family life and the importance of marriage,' according to public health minister Tessa Jowell.[62] Almost 90 per cent felt the demands of balancing a career and home were tougher than ever before, and 68 per cent said single mothers should be encouraged to work. Seventy-eight per cent described marriage as 'vital for stable family life' and more than half thought divorce should be more difficult. Eighty per cent thought tax breaks were the best motive for getting married and staying married. 'In an interview to launch the survey, Mr Blair said families were under a lot more stress than they used to be.'

What School Did You Go To?

As Glasgow moves towards a pavement café culture – a move inspired by the same relentless logic that gave us flat-roofed buildings – remnants of the older city stubbornly cling to their own ways. The Kings Café in Elmbank Street has blue and bronze ashtrays on every table. The blue ashtrays advertise Capstan, the bronze ashtrays advertise Capstan Full Strength.

59. *Scotland on Sunday*, 8 February 1998.
60. *Observer*, 26 April 1998.
61. *Ibid.*
62. Quoted in the *Herald*, 4 February 1999.

The café takes its name from the theatre on the corner of Elmbank Street and Bath Street. It is still possible to get a roll with Lorne sausage and brown sauce in any one of a number of establishments similar to the Kings, whose fashions are immutable. Perhaps they are a throwback to the days when Glasgow's buildings were black, when it rained all the time, when there was plenty work and a pub on every corner. Certainly they brought a sense of the exotic to a very practical city. Some names betray their origin – Lido, Val d'Oro, Tivoli – though rumour has it that most of the Italians came here by mistake, having assumed, as did the Irish before them and the Eastern Europeans afterwards, that this was a stopping-off point for America in general and New York in particular. Given the size of the Tuscan hill town Barga, an extraordinary number of its families became Glasgow Italians; and there are supposedly some who actually thought they'd arrived in New York when they reached Glasgow.

Though successive Regional Trends surveys show Scotland has a lower population of ethnic minorities than any of Britain's regions, Glasgow's identity has always been based on its immigrant population. There are few native Glaswegians who cannot trace their origins beyond the city boundaries. Highlanders have been coming since the sixteenth century, the Irish since the seventeenth, and though they initially followed the trade routes here, the Irish famine and Highland Clearances brought thousands to Glasgow, moves which coincided with the city's industrial expansion. At the height of the Irish famine in 1845, 8000 Irish immigrants were reportedly coming to Glasgow every week, though many used the city as the first stage in their flight to America. One of the lasting legacies of the Highland and Irish immigration has been the religious divisions exemplified in Rangers and Celtic football clubs. For many, that sense of identity is stronger than any other. This is the city where the question 'What school did you go to?' is more than just a social inquiry.

'The Old Firm phenomenon shows that Northern Ireland most certainly does not have a total monopoly of the sectarian religious tension to be found in these islands. It also demonstrates that one corner of Britain exists where large numbers of people both understand and identify with the rival nationalist causes which are at the root of the warfare in Ulster' is how Tom Gallagher explains the curiosity which underpinned his study *Glasgow: The Uneasy Peace*, undertaken in the early 1980s.

For the average Glaswegian today, Gallagher's findings are as remote as they are disturbing. Sectarian violence is no longer a prominent feature of city life. Perhaps these passions have been emulsified by drugs, though when an incident flares up, as in the case of a sixteen-year-old supporter stabbed to death because he was wearing a Celtic strip, it seems shocking because of its relative rarity. Though Gallagher's conclusions are of their time, he warns of incipient violence which could erupt at any time, of simmering resentment, and, given the scope of his investigation, he is strongest on the background to the acrimony and the reasons for its development, being especially acute on the interests it serves. He argues that because the Scots were unsure of their own identity, the Irish were seen as a complicating force who not only did not fit, but also exported their prejudices along with their population. 'The blight of unemployment and its corrosive influence on a previously strong sense of community means that in the 1980s many young Glaswegians are prepared to rally behind rival Irish causes in a bid to give some meaning and importance to their cramped lives.'

On the same subject, Joseph M. Bradley asserts that 'Football is a crucial element of religious identity in Scotland, and national, cultural, social and political expressions become more explicit in the Scottish football arena. As a flexible vehicle, football in Scotland allows for the reinforcement of various ideological associations.' Anti-Catholic feeling, he believes, runs deep, though to call such a feeling, or the conduct that stems from it, sectarian is to shroud the character of the Irish immigrant experience and identity. 'Identity,' he says, 'is a much more useful concept than sectarianism for our understanding of religious cleavage and cultures in Scottish society.'[63]

Bradley remarks that

> An observer may also hear derogatory references from many Celtic fans aimed towards the British Royal Family, as well as the Masonic and Orange Institutions in Scotland. In the aftermath of the 1988 Scottish Cup Final in which Celtic played Dundee United, a game which was witnessed by the Prime Minister Margaret Thatcher, a national newspaper reported that 'Celtic supporters waved tricolour flags and sang choruses of Irish rebel songs and there were chants of anti-British slogans from sections of the crowd.'[64]

He offers some surprising statistics about the national allegiances of some Celtic supporters, yet curiously manages to misquote the Billy Boys, a song which he tells us is sung by 'clubs from all over Scotland'. It 'and other songs (which are seen as supporting the union of Great Britain and Northern Ireland and condemning the Pope, the Catholic faith and the IRA), are sometimes sung which state support for the loyalist paramilitary tradition in Northern Ireland.'[65]

These suggestions appear to be in concordance with Tom Gallagher's: that because Scottish identity is at best a fragile and ultimately elusive distinction that is not experienced by all sections of the community, some find their identity in another country's causes or subsume the very vestiges of their identity on the football field.

63. Joseph M. Bradley, *Ethnic and Religious Identity in Modern Scotland*.
64. *Ibid.*
65. *Ibid.*

The Latest Information Available From the Most Reliable Sources

Glasgow has the oldest city mission in the country. The crucial aspects of their work appear to be their consistency and lack of an overt social or religious message. Their clients trust them because they believe they are there to help.

On a Friday night from 8 p.m. a collection of rags and leaking shoes stand in the doorways around Wellington Street and Cadogan Street, the area where prostitutes are confined, a business centre during the day and a looking-for-business centre at night, Glasgow's contribution to the Caledonian Antisyzygy.

Glasgow prostitutes have not had the same effect on Scottish literature as their Edinburgh counterparts. From Allan Ramsay's *Lucky Spence's Last Advice*, or those who populated Robert Ferguson's masterpiece, *Auld Reekie*, to the hures o' Reekie celebrated by Sydney Goodsir Smith in *Under the Eildon Tree* or Register Rachel and Nae-Neb Nellie who caught Robert Garioch's eye, they have been both a muse and a fundamental part of the capital's life. Most of Edinburgh's prostitutes have been removed into massage parlours, yet the city protests at plans for a prostitutes' drop-in centre.

Some Glasgow prostitutes make an evening pilgrimage to Edinburgh, where prices are double those in Glasgow and there are more 'clients'. The wealth gap between Glasgow and Edinburgh is widening, according to research carried out by a team from Glasgow and Heriot-Watt Universities. In the first systematic assessment of economic and social conditions in the two cities, they found that in Edinburgh gross domestic product was a third higher than in Glasgow. A table of contrasts show that since 1971 the number of Edinburgh jobs has risen by 13 per cent, while the number of Glasgow jobs fell by 21 per cent; that more new enterprises have started than have failed in Edinburgh, while the reverse is true in Glasgow; that Edinburgh's rate of recorded unemployment is 5 per cent, while Glasgow's is 11 per cent, converting to an estimated real rate of 13 per cent and 30 per cent respectively; that household incomes are 7 per cent above the Scottish average in Edinburgh, but are 4 per cent below in Glasgow; that car ownership is 60 per cent higher in Edinburgh than in Glasgow; and derelict property comprises 9 per cent of Glasgow but 1 per cent of Edinburgh. As well as dramatic differences in such areas as poverty, social exclusion and ill health, the report also showed that Glasgow produces 34 per cent of Scotland's GDP as opposed to Edinburgh's 18 per cent.[66]

According to the *Herald*, 'The reaction from Glasgow's movers and shakers was to ridicule the report, claiming it was simply a restatement of historical data.'[67] Two days later, under the headline 'To take Glasgow's

66. Quoted in the *Herald*, 24 November 1999.
67. *Ibid.*

problems seriously', they published a letter from the researchers expressing disappointment at the way their report had been misrepresented.
'The report is not out of date, as some have tried to suggest,' it says. 'It
uses the latest information available from the most reliable sources.'[68]

Particular Problems Glasgow is Facing

The *Herald* announced in March 1998 that a reported £25 million had
been allocated to give the city 'a millennium flourish': 'The proposals
could create up to 450 jobs in the retail and construction sectors. It is
hoped the facelift will maintain Glasgow's reputation as the second most
important retail centre in the UK.' The Glasgow Regeneration Alliance
(GRA) would produce 'a strategic plan for the city'. And council leader
Frank McAveety said the policies of the new Labour Government were a
welcome change to the previous Conservative Government, which was
accused of bias against Glasgow. 'He said the GRA could help tackle the
"scourge" of poverty and unemployment and take the city forward.'

A month later the Conservatives were blamed for Glasgow's residents
being forced to pay 'the highest local taxes in Scotland for the second
year running'. Councillors were being forced to implement £32 million
of service cuts and lose 850 jobs, but 'The prospect of Glasgow becoming
the temporary home for the new Scottish Parliament was trumpeted . . .
as a catalyst that could lead Glasgow out of its worst financial crisis yet'.[69]

Meanwhile, in just over six months, Glasgow's total outstanding housing debt was reckoned at £1,097,123,925, or £10,368 per house. In
October 1998 the *Herald* reported that the national housing agency
Scottish Homes and the Convention of Scottish Local Authorities published a paper on the issues surrounding what was reported as being 'the
Government's key housing policy' New Housing Partnerships, which
encourages councils to transfer their housing stock to outside agencies,
'but the major stumbling block is that the market value of Scotland's
600,000 council houses is £2000m, while the outstanding debt on the
properties is £4000m'.[70]

And within six months the Accounts Commission reported that Glasgow
Council had rent arrears of 15 per cent and had collected the lowest proportion of council tax – 75 per cent. The *Herald* report said, 'A spokesman
for Glasgow City Council, Scotland's largest local authority, said: 'The league
tables don't give the full picture. There are particular problems Glasgow is
facing that are not analysed in the simple performance indicators.'[71]

68. *Herald*, 26 November 1999.
69. *Herald*, 6 March 1998.
70. *Herald*, 16 October 1998.
71. *Herald*, 5 February 1999.

5

The True and Unforgettable Voice

'Beautiful Monikie! with your trees and shrubberies green,
And your beautiful walks, most charming to be seen:
'Tis a beautiful place for pleasure-seekers to resort,
Because there they can have innocent sport,
By taking a leisure walk all round about,
And see the anglers fishing in the pond for trout.
Besides, there's lovely white swans swimming on the pond,
And Panmure Monument can be seen a little distance beyond;
And the scenery all round is enchanting I declare,
While sweet-scented fragrance fills the air.'

WILLIAM McGONAGALL, 'Beautiful Monikie'

That Blasted Region

Carfin Grotto is on the edge of Strathclyde Park. In 1935 Muir
described its foundation as 'an astonishing story' and saw the place itself
as 'the only palpable assertion of humanity that I came across in the
midst of that blasted region. . . . The abstruse ugliness of this black iron
and coal region is such a true reflection of the actual processes which
have gone on in it during the last hundred years that the landscape has
acquired a real formal and symbolical significance which one cannot
find in the slatternly chaos of Glasgow.'[1]

Carfin, he thought, was a haven, a sanctuary, created in imitation of the
Grotto at Lourdes by a group of pilgrims who, in the summer of 1920, in
vacant ground opposite the church, built a shrine dedicated to St
Thérèse of Lisieux, who called herself the Little Flower of Jesus. More

1. Edwin Muir, *Scottish Journey*.

than three hundred people helped build the shrine and in the summer
of 1923 a quarter of a million people visited it in three months, with
queues six or eight deep waiting to drink from the well. By then Carfin
had been hailed as the Scottish Lourdes; miracles had been reported.
The resulting increase in the number of pilgrims made it necessary for
the grotto to be enlarged and an extended grotto was opened on Easter
Monday 1924.

> Here in one of the most hideous stretches of country-side, in an industrial
> region festering with poverty and unemployment, a flourishing shrine has
> grown up in a few years, one of the causes of whose popularity is that it pro-
> duces miraculous cures of quite ordinary ailments. Many of these ailments,
> moreover . . . are directly produced by the working of the Industrial System
> in the middle of which this shrine stands. On the other hand, it has risen
> without the help of that system, and by means which are foreign to it; for
> the Grotto is the result of voluntary labour, the labour of poor men.[2]

Muir's reiteration of his surprise suggests he found something more than
sanctuary, that he was moved by the place in a way that had little to do
with the miracles and more to do with the place's 'power of communi-
cating peace which is extraordinarily rare in the modern world'.

He would scarcely recognise the region today. Its physical appearance,
which he hated, has been altered as pressures beyond Lanarkshire forced
the disappearance first of the fruit and tomato glasshouses along the
road and rail links from England into the heavily industrialised north,
and then of the county's industrialisation itself – the mines and steel-
works have also gone. Today it stands off the M8, with reliquaries, shrines,
a glass pavilion, a chapel and the ghost of Ravenscraig in the background.
There is a Pilgrimage Centre and a tea-room.

Stoneypath and Little Sparta

Stoneypath at Dunsyre, on the fringe of the Pentland Hills, is on a road
similar to those Muir admired around Pinwherry, beyond Barrhill, where
he 'slid down between ordinary fields'. It is the home of Scotland's international artist and poet, printmaker and polymath, Ian Hamilton Finlay.
He and his wife settled here in 1969 and set up the Wild Hawthorn Press,
producing prints, booklets and cards that combine words, ideas and
images with a beautiful simplicity.

These, along with the works often done in collaboration with other
artists who effectively realise his ideas, have given Finlay an international
reputation, enhanced by the creative landscaping of his garden at

2. *Ibid.*

Stoneypath, which contains many objects in stone, glass and wood. Stoneypath was renamed Little Sparta, in opposition to the Athenian grandeur of Edinburgh, during a battle with the Scottish Arts Council and Strathclyde Regional Council over grants and rates exemption.

Ian Hamilton Finlay is unique. He occupies a position like no other writer or artist, initially working in one discipline, then moving towards another, and now occupying a position within the two, so that assessments of his work appear in surveys of both art and literature; he could just as easily be considered in architectural analyses, since his garden is, most obviously, a spatial creation, filled with words and phrases beautifully sculpted in stone or wood. Most famously, 'Bring Back The Birch' is carved on a headstone in Times Roman lettering; the stone is in front of a small birch tree. Or there's the sculpture, '*Et in Arcadia Ego* – after Nicholas Poussin', in which the mausoleum in Poussin's original depiction of the pervasiveness of death is replaced by a tank. Often, Classical order is invaded by modern symbols that offer a variety of meanings or interpretations pertaining to our contemporary situation.

Finlay refuses to allow his poetry or art to become decorative, nor are his explorations solely technical. Rather, he offers conceptual visions that not only assert an intellectual primacy, but have also provided Scottish modernism with a focus, reviving its impetus to provide genuinely productive insights.

The writer he is most often compared to is Edwin Morgan. Both occupy a position outwith the mainstream of Scottish literature, though Morgan goes with the flow more readily than Finlay. Though both share many literary interests, they also redress an imbalance. By celebrating a city, Morgan goes against Scottish literature's traditional involvements and concerns; by his continual awareness not only of words but also their meaning and importance, Ian Hamilton Finlay has created a different literary image within which the look of the word or phrase, its position on the page and its surroundings are more important than the sound. Both men are far removed from the influence and legacy of MacDiarmid. Their initial unity as devisers of concrete verse came from a shared desire to create shape as well as form and meaning from poetry and to use poetry as a spare means of imparting images as well as ideas. But there were obvious differences. Morgan's concrete verse was more playful, often relying on witty shapes and word games, while Finlay showed a more classical, almost understated approach, using colours and phrases printed in elegant typefaces, so that, again, the phrase becomes an image.

At Little Sparta Finlay has created a garden temple in the Classical tradition, using materials such as glass, stone and wood to give substance to both his poetry and art. He gives classical imagery a contemporary relevance by mingling nautical and military motifs with classical allusions. His poems and constructions share a simple and beautiful integrity, often highlighted in a phrase which cannot be repeated or re-formed in any other way without losing something of its original beauty and simplicity. The way words are used to form a picture, often delicately lettered against a rich background, suggests a lightness of touch; it also displays a love and respect for the land and the sea, as well as the ways in which people earn their living, which places him closer to the mainstream, traditional Scottish concerns than would at first appear to be the case.

Finlay's early work coincided with a time when painters were following Joan Eardley's and John Bellany's investigations into a common ancestral heritage that placed community at the centre of the work, suggesting it held a similar position in Scottish life. These works, often conceived on an epic scale, expressed an unofficial, submerged history that is perhaps to be found in the novels and stories of Neil Gunn or Lewis Grassic Gibbon, emerging also in the subjects of song or folk tale, though it is more usually lost in local anecdote. They were also expressions of a working life where the work is seen as a communal activity, placed at the centre of a bleak community, as in John Bellany's *Kinlochbervie*.

Scottish art's involvement with the sea, most directly evidenced in Sir William MacTaggart's paintings, is equally obvious in the work of Joan Eardley, who gave Scottish landscape painting a new energy and direction. Ian Hamilton Finlay shares this fascination with fishing boats and the sea, and thereby also touches aspects of Scotland's national identity. 'The shadows of Scotland's history and people are retraced in a mixture of elegy, wonder and irony,' writes Tom Normand, not of Finlay alone, but of a movement that he almost certainly stimulated. 'The strongest contemporary works are inspired by the memories of an authentic national consciousness and seek out modes of expression which make these relevant to the modern experience. In this way art has been created which is neither parochial nor retreatist but fully explores the interval between nationhood and international community.'[3]

The writer who most resembles Ian Hamilton Finlay is Alasdair Gray, who designs and illustrates his own work, making his books immediately recognisable and individual. He was well known as a painter and muralist, a leading figure in Glasgow's figurative school, before *Lanark* was published. Again, there is a sense of playfulness. Gray famously provides a misleading list of plagiarisms in *Lanark*, whose opening is guarded by a sturdy Hobbesean figure, representing the State and made up of its population, holding the Sword of Force and the Sceptre of Persuasion. He rules Scotland, from the Dounreay nuclear power station and the North Sea oil rigs to the Faslane nuclear base and the Hunterston nuclear power station, with the Grangemouth oil refinery, Edinburgh, Glasgow,

3. Tom Normand, 'Scottish Modernism and Scottish Identity' in Wendy Kaplan (ed.), *Scotland Creates: 5000 Years of Art and Design.*

Stirling, the Wallace Monument, the Forth and Tay Bridges in between. The author's father stares at his son from a peak in Arran and a paddle steamer moves towards Dunoon pier.

Gray's texts and illustrations are often similarly integrated. He likes to play with typography, often to provide a dislocation of narrative and text, diverting the reader with marginalia or a series of textual dead ends, or maintaining the narrative texts within texts. The endpapers to his first collection of stories, properly titled *Unlikely Stories Mostly*, show a map of central Scotland and a list of Scottish writers. The same collection includes a short story featuring Sir Thomas Urquhart, the Royalist who was imprisoned by Cromwell and is said to have died of laughter when he heard of the Restoration of Charles II. In Gray's endpapers Sir Thomas Urquhart is shown sailing away.

Gray obviously shares Urquhart's enjoyment of language, and though it is difficult to find any single continuing influence, such is the breadth and idiosyncrasy of his reading, he often resembles Kurt Vonnegut's invention and social and political directness, especially in the ways he moves narrative backwards and forwards in time and offers disseminations and critiques on the ways in which power is gathered, shaped, maintained and controlled. He is particularly and similarly scathing on the breadth and totality of commercial interests and how what is usually termed progress in society has inevitably meant a loss of excellence, goodness and merit, harking back to a time when values he considers important were maintained, and on the ways in which the quest for a better society has been subverted by commercial pressures.

Which gives his work an important moral force. The political dimension is especially potent when allied with a realism that will not let him look away from the consequences of our folly. This is where he most resembles Vonnegut, in the way he allows what would in lesser hands be termed science-fiction or fantasy techniques both to underline and transcend the layers of demotic prose that accompany Gray's vision of urban realities.

His playfulness has often masked his textual seriousness and content, just as the gift for absurdity he shares with Flann O'Brien, especially in declaiming national and political irrationalities, tends to draw attention to his humour, providing a diversion from Gray's sense of history, his social conscience and a dislocating tendency towards surrealist imagery and irony. But it is these very qualities that lie at the heart of his writing and vision, which include not only a marrying of arts through his diversity and techniques, but also the ways in which he deconstructs his own position as thinker and author to question the position of any central narrator, while simultaneously decrying abuses of authority over the working-class cultures with which he strongly identifies.

Rights of Way

The journey from Carfin left Muir discontented. Not until he reached Stirling, 'with its bright, solid, stylish country town air', does he realise that he had been feeling as if he 'had been wandering in a strange world' and was now back again in the Scotland he knew. At Perth he stopped only to buy strawberries, then 'pushed on to a remote part of Angus where I wished to see a married couple, old friends of mine, who were running a farm there'. They told him of great changes in Scottish country life during the previous twenty or thirty years. Farmers were becoming more urbanised, losing the traditional, country way of looking at things.

However, Angus is a part of Scotland that appears, at least, to have remained unchanged for centuries. Scotland is covered with hill tracks, used by stalkers and drovers, as well as a number of old roads whose origins can only be guessed – Roman roads, medieval roads, drove roads, kirk roads, coffin roads and military roads. Most are rights of way, crossing wild and desolate places where eagles, wild cats, ptarmigan, even capercaillie, can be seen. Nowhere is this secret network more evident or necessary than in the Angus glens, where a series of interlocking tracks and trails take one from the fruit-laden Carse of Gowrie to the heart of the Grampian Hills.

The Mounth roads are a series of right-of-way passes covering an area of more than 50 miles. A list of eleven Mounth roads was prepared by Sir James Balfour of Denmilne in the early seventeenth century, and the earliest written mention of them was in 1384. They define a landscape whose romance was beautifully evoked by the Grampian-based writer Nan Shepherd:

> Light in Scotland has a quality I have not met elsewhere. It is luminous without being fierce, penetrating to immense distances with an effortless intensity. So on a clear day one looks without any sense of strain from Morven in Caithness to the Lammermuirs, and out past Ben Nevis to Morar. At midsummer, I have had to be persuaded I was not seeing even further than that. I could have sworn I saw a shape, distinct and blue, very clear and small, further off than any hill the chart recorded. The chart was against me, my companions were against me, I never saw it again. On a day like that, height goes to one's head. Perhaps it was the lost Atlantis focused for a moment out of time.[4]

Muir's farming friends in Angus were echoing the contemporary mood. The 1930s saw Scotland make a leap into modernity, which was reflected in the architecture of the times. Rearmament programmes

4. Nan Shepherd, *The Living Mountain.*

created employment, which, together with an increase in service industries, encouraged chain stores to move north and gave rise to extensive
new developments across the country, ranging from industrial estates
such as Hillington, outside Glasgow, to a wave of pavilions, dance halls,
cinemas and pubs, as well as the building of private houses and bungalows. These buildings were not only physically new; they used new
materials and presented Scotland with an optimism it had scarcely
known, a mood reflected in the brilliantly white or coloured imagery
that is central to 1930s architecture. The buildings that survive from that
time, and there are many spread across the country, still reflect something of that optimism, if only in their positioning: the Beresford Hotel
in Sauchiehall Street, opened for the 1938 Empire Exhibition, is placed
at a position absolutely central to the development of the Glasgow grid,
at the top of a street, a striking building which can be seen all the way up
Elmbank Street; a similar position is held by the former Stirling's Library
at one end of Ingram Street with the old University at the other and
spectacular buildings like the Ramshorn Kirk and Hutcheson's Hospital
on Ingram Street at the top of the tributaries.

The Coming of Colour

The architecture of the 1930s reflected the mood of the country, and the
climate of optimism is equally obvious in painting and literature. The
1930s saw the rise of the so-called Scottish Colourists, J. D. Fergusson,
Leslie Hunter, Samuel Peploe and Francis Cadell, a group who did not all
work or even congregate in the same place at the same time, like the
Glasgow Boys, but who comprised a group in terms of their stylistic similarities – mainly a predilection for bright and vibrant colours. Largely
ignored or castigated in their lifetimes, they had a seminal influence on
the development of Scottish art in the twentieth century, especially bright-
ening, extending and freeing Scottish artists' relationship with landscape.

Peploe and Fergusson worked for long periods in France. Fergusson
was a Francophile who eventually settled in Paris in 1907; Peploe also
moved to France after his marriage in 1910. They immersed themselves
in contemporary French life, and though they were clearly respectful of
the work of their predecessors in Scotland, the French influence was pivotal. Cadell had trained in Paris. He visited Venice in 1910 and painted a
series that rivalled the boldness and intensity of Peploe and Fergusson,
who returned to Scotland at the outbreak of the First World War.

Though now better known for his still-life paintings and interior studies, usually of elegant women in Edinburgh drawing rooms, Cadell
joined Peploe on painting trips to Iona throughout the 1920s and 1930s.
They painted many versions of the view across to Mull, of sand, rocks and
sea, and these paintings are in direct contrast to Fergusson's geometric

studies under the influence of Cézanne and the Cubists, or his explorations using rhythm and dance. But the vibrancy of the colour, the
strong combinations and the subtle use of light influenced a generation
of painters and became the hallmark of the Colourists' style.

Leslie Hunter was more of a loner, a self-taught artist whose observations and reading reinforced his fascination with light. Most of his work
is a response to Loch Lomond, where the combination of houseboats,
trees and water seemed endlessly fascinating, though he also painted in
Fife, where the red pantiled roofs and vivid green landscape exuded a
similar freshness for Hunter as the shores of Iona had for Peploe and
Cadell. Hunter's technique was slower to evolve than that of the other
three, but though initially less daring, he eventually achieved an intensity
and clarity concordant with the works of his colleagues.

During the interwar years Peploe and Cadell painted in France, while
Fergusson explored his fascinations with Celtic mythology and design,
dance and rhythm. Apart from the vivid intensity of colour they introduced to Scottish painting, the group also explored new ways of looking
at landscape, drawing on an older, stronger, somewhat darker tradition.
By using traditional culture in an open, non-restrictive way, they not only
encouraged and embraced experimentation, but also placed traditional
culture within the scope and terms of an international contemporary
context. This tendency is, of course, reflected in the literature of the
time, especially in the works of Hugh MacDiarmid, but it was the later
generation who gave such an idea its impetus and allowed the implications to be digested and expanded.

Meanwhile, Back at the Palette

While the Colourists were absorbing the influence of Matisse and the
Fauvists, becoming associated with the birth of modernism, another
group of Scottish painters, principally those who exhibited as the
Edinburgh Group, were maintaining the romantic symbolist tradition.
The group comprised a number of painters, including Dorothy
Johnstone, Cecile Walton, Eric Robertson and Mary Newbery, most of
whom were students at the new Edinburgh College of Art, which opened
in 1909. A focal point for their meetings was the studio of John Duncan,
a leading figure in the turn-of-the-century Celtic revival who was heavily
involved in Patrick Geddes's *Evergreen*.

And while Duncan was exploring Celtic myths, the artist's relationship
with the land was being pursued by D. Y. Cameron, whose etchings of
Scottish towns such as Perth and Berwick show an architectural understanding and sympathy which later transferred to his landscape paintings.
Here the elements of the landscape are layered in a way that expunges
romanticism, reflecting trends that Charles Rennie Mackintosh in Port

Vendres and, later, William Crozier in his sparse view of Edinburgh from Salisbury Crags would explore and extend.

That artists as diverse as Muirhead Bone, Cameron and Duncan simultaneously coexisted, producing their highly individual interpretations of Scottish life, landscape and history, demonstrates the fluidity, range and diversity of Scottish art in the early part of the twentieth century; it also indicates the melting pot in which other painters existed. In many ways Scottish painting reflected the investigations that were being made in other areas of artistic endeavour, but it is here that the range and diversity, the struggle to find a linking, communal thread, are most obvious.

The Scottish leap into modernism is also apparent in the later pictures of James Cowie, which experiment with the other world where dream and reality mingle. In 1936 he moved to Arbroath, along the road from Monikie, a village at the centre of an area scattered with Iron Age forts, sculptured stones, earth houses and chambers – the mysterious evidence of earlier settlements. The road from Monikie to Arbroath gives an expansive view of the sea. The town lies barely 20 miles from the Mearns, which four years earlier had featured in Lewis Grassic Gibbon's *Sunset Song*. Cowie's painting *Falling Leaves*, in which he explores a girl's passage into adolescence, has been directly compared with the novel for introspective intensity.

Which Likes To Ponder

The musicologist John Purser has written that Scotland's great

> variety of linguistic and cultural backgrounds is reflected in our music and can still be clearly related to the geography of the country. One can travel north and west from the Central Belt where classical music flourishes alongside a powerful urban and rural tradition of song and dance, to the Highlands with a Gaelic tradition stretching back at least 1500 years. During that journey you would move from medieval cathedrals and abbeys with cathedral choirs and polyphonic music, through the more sober hymns and psalms of the regular church of Scotland, to the far west where many churches are smaller than a barn and where there are no organs, no choirs, but a style of singing possibly as old as Christianity. Or you could start southwards from the Northern Isles with their Norwegian-influenced fiddle playing to the Borders and their ballads in Scots, or up the east coast from Fife to Nairn through county after county rich in ballads and dance music. Yet over the entire country you would almost always know from the music that you were in Scotland.[5]

5. John Purser, *Scotland's Music*.

The same is true of other Scottish arts, and it is nowhere more obvious than in the ways Scottish artists have related to the landscape, our immersion in the countryside, in rural aspects and concerns. In his beautifully evocative essay 'The Land', published in 1934 in *Scottish Scene*, the book he shared with Hugh MacDiarmid, Lewis Grassic Gibbon writes that the rural life is not for modern man or woman. Shrinking from geographical impropriety 'as my Kailyard literary forerunners shrank from description of the bridal bed', he asserts that the farm life 'belongs to a different, and alien generation'.

> *That* is The Land out there, under the sleet, churned and pelted there in the dark, the long rigs upturning their clayey faces to the spear-onset of the sleet. That is The Land, a dim vision this night of laggard fences and long stretching rigs. And the voice of it – the true and unforgettable voice – you can hear even [on] such a night as this as the dark comes down, the immemorial plaint of the peewit, flying lost. *That* is The Land – though not quite all. Those folk in the byre whose lantern light is a glimmer through the sleet as they muck and bed and tend the kye, and milk the milk into tin pails, in curling froth – they are The Land in as great a measure.

From the time of Robert Burns, and largely through his influence, the countryside was seen as the guardian and protector of what was worth preserving in the Scottish way of life, a position which is not difficult to understand given the horror with which industrialisation was greeted. The sweep of English and French literature from Dickens, Zola and the like, charted the course of the Industrial Revolution, giving us a national collective consciousness upon which our ideas of that revolution, if not Victorian society itself, are largely based. Such a movement bypassed Scotland. As far as our writers were concerned, nothing much was happening in the place that has since been called the cradle of the Industrial Revolution. This phenomenon has never been properly addressed, and perhaps there is no explanation as to why such momentous changes were steadfastly and uniformly ignored by all but the Kailyard writers, for whom the city was an offstage hell. Apart from folk songs, where industrial horrors in both Scotland and England were faithfully recorded, there is little to reflect the transformation the country was experiencing, as they were experiencing it. Robert Burns may have compared the Carron Iron Works to hell, and Scott may have regretted the mass of humanity being concentrated into the towns, but neither expressed these concerns in their main body of work. And, apart from Thomas Annan's photographs, which portray the people whose labour fuelled the Industrial Revolution, there is barely any visual evidence, although William Simpson made some watercolour sketches of Glasgow that record something of the city's industrial transformation: factory buildings and workshops, which have only recently been considered worthy of architectural recognition.

John Galt approaches the subject in *A Rich Man*, his portrait of a Glasgow merchant, written, we may suppose, around the time the city was changing; but Galt died in 1839 and spent the last five years of his life in Greenock, where he could not have failed to notice the increase in Glasgow's dimensions and maybe even its boundaries, the deepening of the river, the surfeit of population and transportation. Thomas Carlyle moved to London in 1834; Hugh Millar opposed Chartism and the formation of trade unions from his outpost in Sutherland; there is little in Stevenson to reflect the urban despair and scientific materialism sweeping the country at the time he was writing. Such was Stevenson's influence and stature that capitalism and industrialisation were well into decline before Scottish writers approached the phenomena and their effects. And here they were not alone. Painters also preferred rural landscapes; even the Glasgow Boys avoided the city.

A probable answer to why Scottish literature opted for the Kailyard model – deathbed conversions and pawky wisdom delivered in idealised settings where everybody knew their place – lies in the fact that immediacy is not always the preferred approach in Scottish literature. We do not have a tradition of writing that involves the here and now. Until recently it was a position few Scottish writers adopted and even then it was from a single aspect, class or position. Ours is a literature that likes to ponder. We need time to weigh things up, to consider. The historical novel and the psychological novel were invented here. A Scot gave detective fiction its greatest, most memorable character.

When Scots became part of Britain, they clearly began to consider the nature of the self, and these considerations have appeared in all their philosophical and imaginative writings, most obviously in the works of Tobias Smollett and David Hume. *Dr Jekyll and Mr Hyde* was written by a Scot best remembered for his adventure stories; and long before Freud directed us to look inward, Scots were implying similar motivation for human behaviour. Dickensian sweeps are not our style. We deal mainly in character and incident; this is what makes our stories so memorable. We appear content to let the grand events carry on without us; we dive in rather than jump out. In our literature the oral tradition, especially the aspects dealing with folklore, are never far away. Ours is a literature of hindsight, a literature of that which is not always obvious and does not always deal with the obvious. We have a talent for imaginative discourse; realism arrived late north of the border.

There were, of course, lonely voices, most notably James Thomson's allegorical poem 'The City of Dreadful Night', as well as the Glasgow poets Alexander Smith and James Macfarlan. Apart from the novels of Patrick MacGill, contemporary social and political commentary can be

found in voices such as Marion Bernstein and many other poets in
Radical Renfrew, a collection whose stature has grown since it was published in 1990. Tom Leonard's aim was 'to be part of that process by
which anyone can use the public library to reclaim and reconstruct their
own past'. Compiled from the archives of Paisley Central Library while he
was writer in residence there, Tom Leonard's anthology brought to
public attention poets whose work was uncollected or had lain unread on
library shelves while *Whistle-Binkie* and the *Poetic Gems* of William
McGonagall were presented as the best we could produce. But if *Radical
Renfrew* shows anything it is to confirm what folk song has shown, that
writers were always prepared to tackle the social and political issues of
their day. And that it took a committed writer, working on his own, to
reveal this, partly explains the problem. It also shows our difficulties are
neither new nor unique.

> The belief is widespread that poetry is not about the expression of opinion,
> not about 'politics', not about employment, not about what people actually
> do with their time between waking up and falling asleep each day; not
> about what they hear, not about how much the food costs. It is not in the
> voice of ordinary discourse, contains nothing anyone anywhere could find
> offensive, above all contains nothing that will interfere with the lawful
> exercise of an English teacher going about his or her duty in a classroom.[6]

Tom Leonard brings us to the heart of the matter; for if identity is to
become a recognisable part of our national life, it will have to be educated into our consciousness and into the consciousness of successive
generations, as surely as it has been educated out. And Leonard argues
that the shrinking of literature into 'Teachable Literature' has a powerful
instigator and ally. He complains that a look at the annual volumes of
Modern Scottish Poetry (1878–93) gives the impression that Scots poetry
consists largely of a male nostalgic hymn to hearth, established religion,
domestic gems of women, and fellow boys-at-heart men. This restriction
in content has much to do with the fact that Scots words and usages were
barred from the diction of the classroom by teachers representing 'the
diction of governance'. Moreover, changes in the language were seen as
the result of an immigration substantially Irish Catholic as well as
Highland Gaelic.

> There was a certain amount of looking back on what was seen as the once-
> dominant language of a single-religion people . . . . That tradition of Scots
> poetry hostile to the status quo and to clergymen of any denomination;

6. Tom Leonard, *Radical Renfrew*.

that Protestant tradition of Scots poetry expressing conflict and difference of opinion within the church itself – all this was dropped in favour of a shy alliance of writers 'allowed' to keep their language going within the establishment as it was allowed to exist in Scotland. The angry became the pawky. It was anger at the end of a string.[7]

What we find is not so much a twinning of opposites as a domination of one opposing faction over another. That while painters and architects, and later composers, were looking into our social and historical past to create a national statement, the one medium that could have given that statement expression and the means of expression, as well as extending its imaginative and social influence, was not just thirled to the forces of reaction – it was working hand-in-glove with them to isolate any impact the movement would have. It is not too fanciful to assume it was thus ensured that the strands of these activities remained separated. The imaginative glue that language would have provided was missing.

The power of *Radical Renfrew* provides hope that others will follow where Leonard has led, not only in delving into their free public libraries – 'The place where a democratic freedom of encounter with Literature has occurred' – but to give themselves the right to do so.

Once you accept that the model of Literature is based on universal equality of human existence, past and present, then you can travel in Literature, as a writer or as a reader, wherever you like. And it is not a 'broad-based subject' – 'Open Literature' or 'Social Studies' – with a new caste charged to grade the responses of those who approach 'it', that I'm talking about; for it is that very system of grading and exams which turns the living dialogue between reader and writer into a thing, a commodity to be offered in return for a bill of exchange, i.e. the certificate or 'mark'. But no caste has the right to possess, or even to imagine it has the right to possess, bills of exchange on the dialogue between one human being and another. And such a dialogue is all that Literature is.[8]

Rites of Passage

Although there was 'no renaissance in Scottish music in the 1930s'[9], Francis George Scott's settings of poems by his former pupil, Christopher Murray Grieve, better known as Hugh MacDiarmid, were something of a high point. 'Milkwort and Bog-Cotton' is described as 'a masterpiece which makes this astonishing lyric an even more deeply moving and

7. *Ibid.*
8. *Ibid.*
9. John Purser, *op. cit.*

understanding statement of love for the whole creation . . . one of the greatest songs of any age'.[10]

The 1930s were MacDiarmid's decade, when the achievements of the early lyrics and *A Drunk Man Looks at the Thistle* (1926) were consolidated with a harder, more exploratory and certainly a more political poetry. Directly political poems accompanied a more personal poetry, as well as satirical verse and extended contemplations. Such is the force and dynamic of this poetry that it overshadows the work of other writers of this period which deserves wider recognition. Edward Gaitens, for instance, who followed Muirhead Bone into the city and began to publish stories which not only introduced an urban setting but did so with a lyric intensity, in a celebration of life and working-class dignity that is still reverberating through Scottish writing today, deliberately moving Scottish literature from the rural setting it had occupied for more than 150 years.

The 1930s were also a time of uncertainty, when, in Muir's opinion, the mood of optimism made identity questionable, and the uncertainty gave rise to a need for assertion. This led to the need to devise ways of ensuring Scottish identity would become re-established. Many institutions that are now seen to foster national identity, such as the Saltire Society and the Scottish National Party, and projects such as the *Scottish National Dictionary*, who still issue requests for Scots words and phrases, were initiated at around this time, when writers were consciously searching for ways of asserting and investigating their national identity.

Novelists such as Eric Linklater and Naomi Mitchison, and playwrights such as James Bridie and Robert MacLellan, raised the issue in a variety of ways. Linklater and Mitchison adopted the Byronic position of depicting a variety and range of humanity, Mitchison's case often in a historic setting, with tolerance and candour. Bridie's more traditional approach is seen in *Mr Bolfry*, where the eponymous hero is the devil disguised as a minister, whereas Robert MacLellan wrote plays in Scots, often with a historical theme. MacLellan's *Linmill Stories*, written for radio between 1960 and 1965, compare with the stories of Lewis Grassic Gibbon as examples of the century's finest Scots prose.

The Linmill stories are written entirely for the voice, in a vigorous Scots which MacLellan surely heard as a boy working in the fruit farm his grandparents kept on the banks of the Clyde near Lanark. They give an accurate picture of rural Scots life at the end of the nineteenth century, recorded through the eyes of a young boy whose recall is anything but rosy, but their characters, like the Glasgow Boys' rural paintings, are also imbued with a dignity one feels can only come from their life and work. Even in stories dealing with the exploitation of mentally handicapped men and women, a practice which still continues in parts of the country, providing

10. *Ibid.*

cheap and biddable, reliable labour for the farmer and money for the local authority, 'the daft men' are never undermined and are given the same rights and quiet dignity as others in the stories.

These stories are driven by their language. While incidents and characters may fade, what remains always is the power of the voice. They also provide a model of unsentimental recall, giving a sense not only of character and language, place, and farm work and practice, but also of geography, setting them entirely in a particular time.

The National Drama

Peculiar to Scotland and dealing with Scottish subjects, the National Drama was *the* nineteenth-century dramatic genre, centred on the works of Scott. It is said to have brought many Scots into the theatre for the first time, but this can hardly be true, for theatrical devices have played a part in Scots lives since medieval times. Sir David Lyndsay's *Ane Satyre of the Thrie Estatis*, first performed in Cupar in 1552, could scarcely have arrived from nowhere, and, so far as we know, the performance took place in the Scottish court, a natural centre for entertainment, where theatre was maintained until the move south.

Apart from the standards of court entertainment, such as masques and tournaments, there were religious observations and the ordinary folk revels, which would obviously include plays, usually performed at festivals such as May Day and New Year, when men dressed as women and women as men, when black-faced devils ran through the kirk as the world turned upside down on the Festival of Fools. Kirkyards often provided a natural setting for plays, being flat and central, and we know there were a stream of active performers, apart from the minstrels and players who were attached to the court, such as the dancers, singers, story-tellers and jugglers who used kirkyards as the setting for their performances.

The Reformed Church seem to have spent a disproportionate amount of time banning such performances, ostensibly because of their Popish leanings, and eventually the General Assembly passed a series of acts clamping down on popular theatrical performances, which, along with the removal of the Scottish court was seen as the force behind the loss of theatre from Scotland.

The eighteenth century saw theatres established in Glasgow and Edinburgh and with them the arrival of two plays which bring us on to definite and recognisable territory. The first, Allan Ramsay's *The Gentle Shepherd*, is more like a ballad opera from the John Gay mould, with its songs and music and pastoral charm. It has an appealing, slightly subversive, if implausible, plot, in which shepherds turn out to be aristocrats, but its main strength is a vigorous use of Scots, a device Ramsay unfortunately did not maintain throughout the text. This is completely missing from the other major contemporary work, John Home's *Douglas*, although its first performance brought the oft-quoted response from a member of the audience, 'Whaur's yer Wullie Shakespeare noo?'

The theme of *Douglas* is certainly Scottish, but the language and what we can recognise of the style are anything but. There are dull passages of flashbacks which do little either to inform or advance the plot. A fairly recent revival during the Edinburgh Festival put the play into its historical context, suggesting that it only makes sense in the atmosphere of revived Scottish interest, real or imagined, that followed James Macpherson's *Ossian*.

Edinburgh dominated eighteenth-century theatre, but touring companies did missionary work throughout the country, and the rise of literacy brought chapbooks and broadsheets which also helped the spread of popular theatre. They also helped spread *The Gentle Shepherd*, which remained in the repertory of theatre companies well into the nineteenth century.

Victorian Scotland saw the rise of the geggies, and a pattern of theatre building was established to cater for the new urban working class. The geggies were travelling companies which included singers, actors, jugglers and musicians, and these in turn gave rise to the music halls and variety theatres. This was the most significant development in nineteenth-century Scottish theatre, for with them came the rise of the pantomime, which, according to the theatre historian Alasdair Cameron, has provided the basis for one of the most interesting features of contemporary Scottish theatre, having allowed 'working-class playwrights in the twentieth century to develop a unique and distinctive style, unencumbered by any notion of the well-made play which was to be such a burden for James Bridie in his attempts to please the West End'.[11]

The twentieth century has seen a revival in Scottish theatre, which, as with Scottish poetry, could lead the unwary to assume it had always existed. In fact, as with poetry, Scotland has virtually had to reinvent its mainstream theatre, having relied on amateur companies to keep it alive between the wars. In the 1920s it was the amateur Scottish National Players who became, despite staunch work by the Glasgow Repertory Company, a virtual national theatre company, touring the whole country, working in the fledgling BBC, and aiding the development of the newly formed Scottish Community Drama Association.

This created something of a fertile climate for new writing, though the Scottish National Players rejected the Fife miner Joe Corrie's play *In Time o Strife* in favour of a work by Neil Gunn, which intensified Highland

11. Alasdair Cameron, 'Theatre in Scotland: 1214 to the Present' in Paul H. Scott (ed.), *Scotland: A Concise Cultural History*.

mythologies. This censorship of what was considered political drama was later underlined by the choice of radio plays fixated on the historical, rural aspects of Scotland, leaving the harder-edged writing, the overtly political and contemporary issues, to companies and individuals formed around the trade union and labour movements.

Companies such as the Curtain Theatre in Glasgow introduced the plays of Robert MacLellan, and their formation allowed Duncan Macrae and Lennox Milne to become the first Scottish professional actors living and working in Scotland for more than a century. They established a pattern whereby the lines and distinctions between straight and variety theatres were blurred, with actors moving seamlessly between the two.

In 1943 James Bridie founded the Citizens' Theatre in Glasgow, and a few years later he inaugurated what is now the Royal Scottish Academy of Music and Drama. The Citizens' was the first Scottish theatre to receive a government subsidy, and was rivalled by Glasgow Unity, which was made up of a number of left-wing amateur companies. Between them they encouraged writers like Ena Lamont Stewart, Alexander Reid and Robert McLeish, who created a body of new work that has come to be seen as the beginnings of contemporary Scottish theatre.

With the exception of John McGrath, who wrote for his own company, no other Scottish playwright has been able to establish as substantial a body of work as Bridie, who wrote more than fifty plays. He was also an influential promoter of new talent, not always for the theatre, and seems to have conducted a continuous battle with MacDiarmid, whom he described as 'one of the glories of Scotland' – as a poet. As a pamphleteer, however, he believed 'Hugh MacDiarmid is just plain daft. A colleague of his and mine once said that printer's ink was poison to him. I am afraid that this was true.'[12] In a survey entitled 'Scottish Literature, 1920–1967' for the *Burns Chronicle*, however, MacDiarmid seems to have had a change of heart: 'So far as drama in Scotland is concerned,' he wrote, 'the greatest figure remains the late Dr Osborne Mavor (James Bridie).'

The way Bridie disseminates ideas and argument, the playful manner in which his characters establish their identities, especially their thrawnness, and his delight in contrasting oppositions, especially in his heroes, vindicate MacDiarmid's judgement; but we are left with a question as to why his impact and influence on later Scottish writers was not more persuasive.

Glasgow playwrights such as Tom McGrath, Marcella Evaristi and Liz Lochhead were distinguished in other writing disciplines before turning to theatre, and brought similarly imaginative qualities to their stage writing. Bill Bryden, Hector MacMillan and Tom Gallacher are also West of Scotland writers, whose influence on Scottish theatre has been

12. See Alan Riach, Angus Calder and Glen Murray (eds), *The Rauchle Tongue*.

as important as any, excepting the founding of the Traverse Theatre in Edinburgh and the work of John McGrath's 7:84 touring group, which introduced Scottish history and its implications to a generation of Highlanders. And Donald Campbell, Roddy MacMillan, John Byrne, Iain Heggie and Tony Roper have all provided plays in recognisable settings, which challenge established perceptions and are written with a degree of linguistic realism.

The work of these writers is staged in the main by small-scale touring companies who take the plays to small- and medium-scale theatres across the country. They exist alongside main house companies in Perth, Dundee, St Andrews – all founded in the late 1930s – Pitlochry, Glasgow and Edinburgh.

And Fink's Die Sprachstamme des Erdkreises, sooth

Arguably, in retrospect, the dominant Scottish voice of the period covered by *Modern Scottish Poetry* (1878–93) is that of a man who sought to write in the Queen's English and who failed so spectacularly that his lumping, elephantine verse turned him into a clown. To what extent are William McGonagall's pretensions and his desire to please, to be something other than a Dundee weaver, significant factors in the way he is regarded? That he failed so ludicrously and spectacularly does in some way make him a metaphor for and a warning to, however placidly or minimally stated, all who would follow his route, would try to rise above their station. It is the antithesis of dialogue, designed to keep us in our place.

Which is not to make any claims for McGonagall's *Poetic Gems*. No one could seriously suggest we should not laugh at McGonagall – an impossibility given the relentlessness of his failure – but it seems reasonable to question what we are laughing at, and to suggest the laughter takes us beyond the work whose 'inimitable combination of bathos, perversity, irrelevance, wayward rhymes and confused scansion have earned [McGonagall] the title of "the world's worst poet", a hard-won and wholly deserved accolade quite compatible with the affection in which he is held and the frequency with which he is quoted'.[13] Other disciplines have their McGonagalls; they are ignored. No doubt about it, Hamish Henderson is right: there are those who are laughing at poetry while laughing at William McGonagall.

There is of course a sense in which we find ourselves mirrored in McGonagall: he becomes a metaphor for us all, endlessly trudging towards Balmoral, just as his contemporaries, consciously or unconsciously, sought similar approbation from our improvers south of the

13. Hamish Henderson, *Alias MacAlias.*

Border. McGonagall, seeking royal approval, parading himself as Macbeth, appearing in a circus, being laughed at by his workmates, continually aspiring to be taken seriously, haunts us and our desire to accept improvement. The more he tried the further he strode from acceptance.

> And yet how many more have written worse.
> Why such hatred for your bad verse
> when every day we see our literature
> weakened by loss of passion, loss of power?
>
> Why should you suffer the anonymous
> theses and poor parodies of those
> whose competence is just as small as yours -
> when they unlike you don't even love verse!
>
> Except that they see mirrored in you their own
> impenetrable dullness.

Iain Crichton Smith's question and answer contains the germ of a theory, that McGonagall is us and we are him, that he reminds us of ourselves, is too close and is therefore best forgotten or at least despised. Especially melancholy is the notion of the two McGonagalls inhabiting the one body: the buffoon with his eye on the main chance and the miserable versifier who thought he might become Poet Laureate, the worker with ideas above his station, whose failure urges us never to try.

MacDiarmid may have been right in saying that the point is not that McGonagall was a bad poet, but that he simply wasn't a poet at all. But, as Hamish Henderson has pointed out, the man he called the Langholm Byspale was not above his own lapses in poetic judgement:

> Infernal fantasies contrived to hide
> The simple unacceptable truth!
> – Read Hommel's History of Babylonia,
> And Fink's Die Sprachstamme des Erdkreises, sooth.
> The Atlantis Fable is but a colossal exaggeration
> Of the natural catastrophe of 1031BC
> Which broke in upon Cornwall – fantastically embellished
> To hide the simple report of the Scilly Isles tragedy.

The poem '6000 Years of Gaelic Grandeur Unearthed' deserves to be recycled in full, together with an explanation. It's one thing to write such dross; many of us have done it. But why did MacDiarmid publish it, and then suggest he had done so for our sakes?

Henderson says MacDiarmid wrote some of the best poetry Scotland has seen and also some of the worst. Could it be that his devotion to him-self and his use of a variety of causes and positions to put himself in the limelight forced him to accept McGonagall's role, the role of the writer as hero?

The MacDiarmid poem quoted is not the only example. It was used because it shows all McGonagall's art of repetition, nonsense, extending the line to get a rhyme and especially of passing information off as poetry, which gives rise to the notion that his poetic and journalistic talents merged, or that one was subsumed by the other. McGonagall, too, was not so much a bad poet as an enthusiastic journalist. Nothing escapes his attention, every detail is recorded:

> Then as for Leith Fort, it was erected in 1779, which is really grand,
> And which is now the artillery headquarters in Bonnie Scotland;
> And as for the Docks, they are magnificent to see,
> They comprise five docks, two piers, 1,141 yards long respectively.

McGonagall, says Henderson, is the poetic master of the art of the belly flop; and though he bowed the knee to no one but Shakespeare, rather than being seen as an art poet he can be more readily classified as a come-all-ye style of broadside balladeer. But Henderson reckons the dif-ference between McGonagall and scores of folk poets, or would-be art poets, is that he had something unique:

> a gift so extraordinary and so personal to himself that he remains one of the few virtually unparodiable poets. Completely devoid of the lyrical knack which would have set his productions on the road to becoming folk-songs, he had the compensating ability – or compulsion – to use *nothing but* the hobbling and broken-backed rhythms and verbiage of pedestrian folk-poetry, and to use these so consistently from end to end of poem after poem that in effect he created a new style. This style was formed out of the debris and detritus of folk-song – out of all the things which song composed in 'the idiom of the people' sheds in the process of becoming folk-song.[14]

McGonagall's work, he says, 'was a sort of frowsy doss-house in which every wooden phrase, every gormless anti-climax was sure to find a bed'. Such entities do not survive the scrutiny of the folk process, which means they are not only sung, but are also well enough liked to be retained and passed on, a process so mysterious that we can scarcely understand any-thing about it other than its influence and importance. Of course, the very factors that have been accused of threatening folk song are now said to aid the process of transference: television, radio, recordings, newspapers,

14. *Ibid.*

industrialisation, transport and so forth certainly popularise certain types of songs, which in turn are retained and circulated, but these pieces survive in something other than the folk process. When the early song collectors began recording, the songs they gathered were often written and the music annotated in order to be published, a form in which they, like the ballad and the songs of Robert Burns, were circulated without music, thereby acting as a deterrent rather than an influence to their being spread.

And Henderson is surely correct when he claims that to the extraordinary collective known as the Scottish bourgeoisie, a poet, and not simply a versifier of the McGonagall school, was someone to be treated with amused contempt, mingled with hostility. Ridicule and apathy can be added to the list, along with scorn and, at best, indifference.

Norman MacCaig took great delight in telling how he once showed a collection of his poems to an acquaintance, who examined each one carefully before returning the book with his finger on a particular poem: 'That's the worst,' he said.

A Star Gings Glaidly Ower the Hill

The clarity and intensity of MacDiarmid's early poetry was unlike anything in Scottish writing before or since; it was neither an act of discovery nor a reinvention, more a rediscovery of Scots, a rediscovery of language combined with daring imagery which often seems to withhold meaning, or to release a variety of meanings simultaneously. That such a language, whose condition was seen to be reduced to the parochial, could be used to convey modernist ideas was the most daring experiment of all.

MacDiarmid's intention was to overthrow the staid complacency into which Scots writing had sunk in the nineteenth century. Towards this end, while living and working as a journalist in Montrose, he castigated the provincial and simultaneously sought to recover the Scottish psyche from the moribund condition in which it had languished since the Union of 1707.

That he succeeded is obvious; though the extent of his achievement is not always obvious, either in its range or its complexity. As well as trying to be a poet, he was also trying to forge the Scottish nation. And in his own poetry, as well as the poetry of those he inspired, the quest for a national identity and the search to give it a meaningful philosophical basis are both obvious and distinctive. Though it has become fashionable in certain quarters to use the extremes of his personality against him and to condemn all his work because of some of his more outlandish and ill-conceived notions, he remains the dominant figure of twentieth-century Scotland. In old age he lost his sparring partners. His intention to shake Scotland out of its complacency and a lifetime spent in perpetual opposition disintegrated into a continual battle for self-aggrandisement.

It is no exaggeration to suggest we are now enjoying the fruits of his conquests, and if our national identity is as secure as it appears to be, so that we can in many areas not only take it for granted, but also use it as a springboard into other investigations, it is largely MacDiarmid's doing.

The twentieth century has seen a great, unprecedented flowering of Scottish poetry, of such a quality and power that it is easy to imagine it has always been there, that contemporary writers are working in what is an unbroken tradition, which, of course, is not the case. The generations since MacDiarmid have produced sufficient poets of quality, with others in the pipeline, to allow us to suggest it has become a permanent feature of Scottish literary life. There was a remarkable first flowering in Scots, but examples are now equally evident in Gaelic and English. Lewis Spence, Marion Angus and Violet Jacob were contemporaries of MacDiarmid's, while William Soutar and Helen Cruickshank came slightly later, but these initial Scots protagonists were from Angus or Perthshire. To them, the Scots Renaissance must have come as an enormous relief, as though it gave their voice a credibility. One can almost feel them relaxing into the discovery of something that had always been there.

Nan Shepherd's evocation of the Grampians, quoted earlier, could equally have been written by any one of the three prominent women poets. Helen Cruickshank described the poem 'Shy Geordie' as her 'dripping roast', anthologised so often that in the end she refused permission for republication. It had, she said, been repeatedly broadcast, recorded for the gramophone and television, and set to music by Dr Buxton Orr.

> Up the Noran water
> In by Inglismaddy,
> Annie's got a bairnie
> That hasna got a daddy.
> Some say it's Tammas's,
> An' some say it's Chay's;
> An naebody expected it
> Wi Annie's quiet ways.

When she wrote the poem, she hadn't even been up the Noran Water. 'The origin of the poem is my own affair,' she added pertly. She was a suffragette, who on the death of her father was forced to 'say goodbye to my hopes of being able to wed my penniless artist' and 'bid farewell to my free and easy bohemian life'. She nursed her elderly mother for forty years. Cruickshank was a friend of both Lewis Grassic Gibbon and William Soutar, and she writes well of them in her autobiography.

The place of William Soutar (1898–1943) in the Scottish Renaissance has been both misunderstood and undervalued. He is a deeply complex writer, whose work could be dissected by both philosophers and literary scholars. For the last fourteen years of his life he was confined in bed in a single room, his only view the sky and the small hills beyond his father's garden:

> Lift up yer een and greet nae mair
> The black trees on the brae are still
> And saftly in the mirkled air
> A star gings glaidly ower the hill.

Soutar was concerned with the problem of identity, especially in his shorter lyrics. He was also greatly concerned with language, contributing a number of Perthshire words and phrases to the *Scottish National Dictionary* and writing a number of what he called 'Bairnrhymes', poems designed to familiarise children with the Scots language. Like his other work, they have their darker side, yet the force of the language and the rhythm of the voice is obvious, especially to musicians from Benjamin Britten to James Macmillan, who set some Soutar pieces to music. Others, such as Francis George Scott and Ronald Stevenson, as well as a number of folk singers, have found his work a continual source of inspiration.

It is also common to find references in his poems to his childhood, and though the images are often tinged with melancholy, there is neither rancour nor regret, but rather a celebration of himself as he was:

> I lang for the day whan I'll be a loon
> And naebody tae daur me;
> Wi' a fare-ye-weel to this auld, grey toun;
> And the weys o the world afore me.

In his introduction to the *Collected Poems*, after praising Soutar in the most general terms, MacDiarmid considered 'the lack of longer poems in Soutar's work, the extent to which he devoted himself to extremely short poems, and to trifling oddments like his riddles and epigrams, was a consequence of his bedridden state'. It is strange that 'The Auld Tree', a poem on identity some 350 lines long, though dedicated to MacDiarmid, was omitted from the 1947 edition of Soutar's *Collected Poems*, which MacDiarmid edited. There has been some speculation as to why this should be, including the suggestion that MacDiarmid sought to reduce Soutar's achievements to aggrandise himself. MacDiarmid also omitted 'The Tryst' from Soutar's *Collected Poems*, though he included it in his *Golden Treasury of Scottish Poetry*, published in 1943.

Soutar is one of the finest diarists Scotland has produced. His diaries often betray their inspiration, W. N. P. Barbellion's *The Journal of a Disappointed Man*, which Soutar bought in April 1930, when he knew he would spend the rest of his life as an invalid; yet they and the series of journals, dream books and common day books are a wonderfully rich and stimulating legacy, especially in recording his swings between personal philosophy and the Lawrentian principle of the righteousness of life, pacifism and Scottish nationalism. Soutar kept a note of everything, including the letters he received and when they were answered; not surprisingly, he kept a note of the poems he worked on, though strangely he seems to have hoarded few worksheets, unless the poems came to him in a piece, the initial idea being the most important.

William Soutar's best-known poem, 'The Tryst', gives every impression of having been written by an able-bodied man. The fact that Soutar was not able-bodied gives the poem an added piquancy.

> O luely, luely cam she in
> And luely she lay doun:
> I kent her by her caller lips
> And her breists sae sma' and roun'

He could, of course, have been coming to terms with his illness; but the theme of a ghostly visitor reconnecting with a former lover is known to folklorists across the world, defined by Child as The Grey Cock or Lover's Ghost theme, a ballad where the girl is visited by the ghost of her dead lover. Soutar's achievement is to cut through the details, making the lyric both personal and universal, using the first line as an echo of loss in the final verse.

Born in the second half of the nineteenth century, Violet Jacob's poems are in the lyric tradition, which she infuses with a vigorous Scots. In her work the folk influence is evident, both in the language and subject matter. Hers is a poetry of place, concerned with the people and their lives, with childhood, courtship and marriage, the small observances of country existence, Hogmanay and ploughing matches, as well as a celebration of the places and the people who inhabited them, their innocence, pride and follies. Throughout it all, the strongest voice is the voice of place:

> Comin' oot frae Kirrie, when autumn gowd an' siller
>   At the hindmaist o' September-month has grips o' tree an' shaw,
> The mune hung, deaved wi' sunset, no' a spunk o' pride intill her,
>   Nae better nor a bogle, till the licht was awa';
> An' the haughs below the Grampians, i' the evenin' they were lyin'
>   Like a lang-socht Land o' promise that the cauld mist couldnae smoor;
> An' tho' ye didna see it, ye could hear the river cryin'
>   If ye stood a while to listen on the road to Kirriemuir.

Gowrie and Catterline

Scottish writers are not alone in their fascination with the soil. From David Runciman's use of the Perthshire Hills and Scone Palace as a background to his painting of Milton's *L'Allegro*, to the work of James Mackintosh Patrick, landscape has dominated Scottish art, where it has been used, as in literature, to reflect conflict and inner turmoil. In the hands of a painter like William Johnstone or Joan Eardley it is a very powerful weapon.

James Mackintosh Patrick is the contemporary painter whose relationship with the landscape around his Dundee home is probably the least ambiguous of all Scottish painters. He obviously loved the Angus small roads and byways, and delighted in the features of which landscape is composed as much as the landscape itself. He painted bridges, trees, houses and fields, with barely any sky, and was interested in representing the landscape at work; he has consequently been compared to Breughel for the ways in which he shows aspects of country life. His was a cultivated landscape, often viewed from an elevated position.

For many, Mackintosh Patrick's is the dominant view of contemporary Scottish landscape, as important to our time as Horatio McCulloch's bare hills and peaks were to the previous century, as Kirkcudbright was to the Glasgow Boys, as Fife and Loch Lomond were to the Colourists. These landscapes have a common denominator, apart from the theme of place. There are few people. Scotland is still a landscape of the mind.

Mackintosh Patrick was a less adventurous, less innovative painter than those mentioned above, and this may be the reason for his extraordinary popularity. His pictures question nothing, not even our view of ourselves. He presents an unchallenging, fairly placid view of the world. His pictures could easily be of parts of rural England or Ireland; they are far removed from the dramatic representations of mountain, loch, sea and sky that have been exported as the dominant image of Scotland. He painted what he knew: the farmland roads of the Carse of Gowrie and the areas around Dundee. They are honest, unchallenging pictures which present a cosy view of rural Scotland to city dwellers. It is a timeless landscape, a dream image, something both comfortable and familiar, a Scotland we knew must exist, not because of what it represented, but because of what we imagined it represented. Nature is here, serene and tamed. We see lambs in the field rather than the lambing, snow on the hills rather than blocked roads, and there is scarcely a rain cloud anywhere.

Joan Eardley, on the other hand, found landscape anything but tame. Her later work is suffused with an elemental force and passion. In Glasgow she developed a technique of using thick, dense oils to evoke images of tenement life through the drab hopelessness of the children whose suffering she portrayed sympathetically and without sentimentality. These paintings retain a vitality and energy even though the children's clothes and appearance are echoed in their background, a technique which became especially telling when she addressed the environment directly, reflecting the chalked and graffiti coloured walls, giving the children a richness and warmth that belie their surroundings.

In the early 1950s she moved to Catterline on the Aberdeenshire coast, where her work reflected a similar energetic vitality, at times more intense, drawing its richness and force from the seascapes and land around her, making her paintings by representing the forces of nature that had shaped the village and its inhabitants. It is a violent identification with nature; and although she never painted those who work the shores directly, the slabs of colour and abstract intensity reflect the efforts of those forced to labour in these timeless, unyielding elements and the dangerous nature of their everyday lives in a way that is entirely suited to the Scottish landscape and psyche.

The Simple Outpourings of Illiterates and Backward Peasants

The golden age of Scottish culture, which included the lifespans of Burns and Scott as well as the duration of the Enlightenment, was followed by a period of industrialisation and empire building, when the Kirk held sway and songbooks exhibited sanitised versions of their originals, mawk-ish portrayals of couthy sentimentality or stirring songs of braggadocio patriotic fervour for export to the colonies or for city consumption, intra-venously fed through the music hall.

Then, in the early years of the twentieth century, the Aberdeenshire dominie Gavin Greig and the Rev. James Duncan slowly and dedicatedly amassed one of the world's largest song collections. So thorough and varied was their work that subsequent collectors have headed for the same north-eastern corner. The great folk-song collections were made in Angus and the Mearns. Strathmore lies in the lee of the Grampians, sheltered on the other side by the Sidlaws. It is the great fruit-growing district of Scotland. Here berry-pickers came in mid-July, spending a week or two camped near Blairgowrie. Strawberries and raspberries still grow in Strathmore and along the Carse of Gowrie, but the fields have been turned into pick-your-own centres and the Dundee jam factories, which bought the fruit, have closed.

Glasgow and Dundee sent contingents to the berry fields, holiday-makers mostly, but the tone was set and the music provided by the travellers, members of the semi-nomadic Scots tinsmith clans, the Stewarts and the MacPhees. 'They, in chief, are the carriers, dispensers, performers and glorifiers of one of the most voluminous oral cultures in Europe, and the all-star cast of the world's most successful unofficial folk festival.'[15] When the Traditional Music and Song Association organised their first festival in 1966, it was held in Blairgowrie, where huge informal get-togethers with singers and musicians had been held in and around the berry fields at the height of summer. Hamish Henderson has described song collecting there as being 'like holding a tin can under the Niagara Falls'.

Since then, folk-song clubs and other festivals have spread across the country. Their arrival has been accompanied by a healthy song-making resurgence. These songs are often political, but they are also social, satiric and celebratory, maintaining the Scottish tradition of mingling high art with the more demotic informalities, producing a number of poet-songsters such as Ewan MacColl, Hamish Henderson, Maurice Blythman, Adam McNaughtan, Brian McNeill, Michael Marra, Dougie MacLean and Matt McGinn.

'Each resurgence of the creative spirit in Scotland since 1707 has been associated with renewed interest in popular culture, and with something of a folk revival,' says Tom Crawford. 'Each has felt the need to tap the popular tradition, which is, perhaps, the most abidingly *national* part of our culture.'[16]

Just as the role of the first-person narrator is the most obvious feature of Scottish stories, so the influence of folk song has been a constant feature of Scottish poetry, from Burns to the present day. This was clear to Goethe, who attributed Burns's greatness to the fact that he was born into the carrying stream of the folk tradition. The folk influence appears to be a corollary of both voice and place, as well as the means whereby the language was preserved and enriched. When writers such as Soutar, the Angus or Mearns writers, and perhaps even MacDiarmid himself in his earlier lyrics, have direct and continuing contact with the people who are part of the land, then something more than their speech rhythms and cadences is transmitted; the voice and the culture of the place is absorbed as well. And when that culture, like the writer, comes from the working people, then the influence is obvious.

And yet, in a talk on folk song given in 1968, MacDiarmid claimed that 'the great treasury of Gaelic song . . . is almost wholly art song'. We were the only European country not to have a school of national composers, having a succession of kirk organists instead, he declared, and folk song was too minor a manifestation to do any real harm. Folk singers had a hatred of high art and a basic anti-intellectualism. Nor were the ballads folk songs.

There are some passages of magnificent poetry in a few of the ballads – passages which soar out of the worthless context on to a different plane

15. *Ibid.*
16. Quoted in Hamish Henderson, *op. cit.*

altogether. But these invaluable passages are few and far between, and I do not think any authority on the subject today would try to claim that these passages were folk-productions, made communally or collectively rather than like all the rest of the world's great poetry the work of exceptionally gifted individual poets head and shoulders above most of their fellows.[17]

And in the correspondence columns of the *Scotsman* four years earlier, he had famously described folk song as 'the simple outpourings of illiterates and backward peasants'.[18] Such statements coming from anyone else would have been written off as tripe.

But in an essay on Francis George Scott published in the *Scottish Educational Journal* in September 1925 he wrote, 'We hear a great deal about the Scots being a musical people . . . . If [this] has any reality it would make it all the more inexplicable . . . that a people possessed of a folk song that has probably no equal in the world . . . should have become so completely disorientated and precluded from the natural exploitation of it.'

As a polemicist, MacDiarmid urged us to find our heritage; when we found it, he castigated us for ignoring the role of those such as himself. The New Testament teaches that truth can best be expressed in paradox, while Marxism fashions diametric opposites as regularly as Scottish fiction. And the American ballad scholar Bernard Bronson is of an opinion with which MacDiarmid would surely have concurred in both stages of his life:

> Eighteenth-century Scotland, there is no doubt at all, was a nation of ballad singers and ballad lovers. How much earlier had it been so, no one knows; but it is a fact that what we today know as British balladry at its best is a mass of texts taken down by interested persons from living Scottish tradition in the latter half of the eighteenth century, or learned then and transmitted to print or manuscript early in the following century.[19]

The Bonnie Briar Bush

Along the A926, heading eastwards from Blairgowrie, at the foot of the Angus glens lies Kirriemuir, birthplace of J. M. Barrie, founder of the Kailyard school. William Nicholson painted Barrie stranded, alone against a bland background, his shadow the only relief. Dressed in black, with a white shirt and come-to-Jesus collar, the most obvious feature is his stature.

Scottish identity has always had a very clear, well-established local

17. Quoted in Alan Riach, Angus Calder and Glen Murray (eds), *op. cit.*
18. Quoted in Hamish Henderson, *op. cit.*
19. Bernard H. Bronson, *The Traditional Tunes of the Child Ballads With Their Texts.*

dimension. The local, even the parochial, has been the springboard of every attempt to establish or define a national consciousness, from the Kailyard to the Scottish Renaissance, whose sweep and emphasis was away from the provincial and whose aims were international. The ways in which Scots writers, in common with writers the world over, have used locality as the basis of discovery and invention would suggest that the Kailyard movement was scarcely part of Scottish literary life at all. Which is not to deny its impact, especially when the ghost sporadically returns to haunt us, and over the years some of the genre's more familiar aspects have reappeared with monotonous regularity. But, however difficult the strain is to analyse, it must be seen as an anachronism when the bulk of Scottish literature is assessed.

Locality has provided Scottish fiction with a clear foundation, giving it an identity, a rhythm and a voice it would otherwise lack. The works of Lewis Grassic Gibbon, Robert MacLellan, Jessie Kesson and Neil Gunn reverberate not only with the accents and mannerisms of a place, but also with its geography, as do the works of contemporary writers as diverse as Alan Spence and Irvine Welsh, James Kelman, Janice Galloway, Duncan McLean, Gordon Legge and William McIlvanney. Poets from Robert Burns to Don Paterson, Kathleen Jamie and W. N. Herbert have shown a similar tendency. Not only is it difficult to imagine the work of these writers being set in another country, even in another part of the British Isles, it is just as difficult to imagine it being set in another part of Scotland. And as Scottish writing has spread across the country, moving from a rural to an urban setting, from the suburbs to the schemes, the Kailyard and its influence may appear to have diminished, but the roots are still in place and flourishing. 'Its popularity,' Ian Campbell suggests, 'has been too universal, and too long-lasting, to ignore.'[20]

The hallmark of Kailyard writing was a lack of equilibrium; there were no symmetrical attributes to either the characters or their situations. Scott, Dickens, and a host of other writers used purple prose and littered their work with sentimental passages, but it was always done within the context of the story, and when it did appear it was balanced by another part of the narrative. This the Kailyarders failed to accomplish. Changes of heart, especially just before death, were as frequent as family reunions, sudden conversions and the discovery of a relevant biblical passage that gave a character's actions a context. Kailyard life was monotonous, black and white. There were no grey areas; everyone knew their place, and there were no balancing virtues.

The Kailyard's origins can be traced to Henry Mackenzie, author of *The Man of Feeling* (1771), and the philosophies which propelled the

---

20. Ian Campbell, 'Kailyard' in David Daiches (ed.), *The New Companion to Scottish Culture*.

Scottish Enlightenment. Stevenson's sense of romance, his symbolic fantasy and nostalgic rusticism have also been seen as the source. The Kailyard movement ran almost consecutively with the end of Stevenson's life. He was exiled, having published *Dr Jekyll and Mr Hyde* in 1886 and *The Master of Ballantrae* in 1889, the same year that Barrie published *A Window in Thrums*. Kailyarders Crockett and Maclaren were in full flight as Stevenson was dying, indeed *Beside the Bonnie Briar Bush* was published in the year of his death. Stevenson's exile, the rise of industrialism and the climate created by the Kailyard writers refocused and marginalised his influence, resulting in romantic adventure novels from the likes of John Buchan and Neil Munro rather than the harder, more realistic approach Stevenson had developed through a stronger emphasis on characterisation; this would be rediscovered and extended within a decade of his death by George Douglas Brown and James MacDougall Hay.

It appears to be possible to find traces of the Kailyard throughout Scottish literature, though given what was happening throughout the country during its development, the cause of its origin and popularity would appear to be social. Kailyard novels are set in a preindustrial utopia, populated by hard-working, solid and reliable individuals whose wisdom carries the stamp of undeniable truth. Given the upheaval and shift of the population across the country, as well as from Ireland and the Highlands, it is not difficult to see why the prodigal's return and deathbed conversions were so common, why religion was upheld and virtue rewarded. And the fact that Scots words and idioms were not sufficient to discourage English or American readers, among whom the works were popular, suggests the Kailyarders did little more than respond to the social mood of the times.

Another reason why the Kailyard movement can scarcely be seen as a constant part of Scottish literary life is that from James Hogg to Irvine Welsh, through the novels of Sir Walter Scott and Iain Banks, Naomi Mitchison, Alasdair Gray and Muriel Spark, Scottish literature has excelled in unreliable narrators, men and women who generally use the first person singular to give their inventions an intimacy entirely suited to the undertone of irony they wish to explore. And though this can also be found in the writing's structure, it is the ways in which events and situations, people, places and things, conspire, the ways in which the odds seem stacked from the outset, that keep the reader in place. These writers rarely withhold information; rather they tell all, allowing events to speak for themselves. The opposition lines of demarcation are well drawn and the narrator struggles on against a variety of destructions until a resolution, though not always with an accompanying explanation, is provided.

Kidnapped is the archetypal example, an adventure story with attitude wherein the underlying subtleties found in David Balfour's priggishness and Alan Breck Stewart's romantic spirit can be explored or renounced without detraction. Stevenson spawned a succession of similar stories, like Neil Munro's *The New Road*, in which the Scottish landscape becomes the backdrop for adventure, and the hero's strength and guile are pitted as much against the natural surroundings and his own will and character as any enemies or dangers he may face.

John Buchan's 'shockers' fall into a similar category, and though they lack the psychological depth and insight of his predecessors, the certainties of Calvinism are never far away. Here we seem to be seeing as strong an influence of the Kailyard as we find in A. J. Cronin's *Tannochbrae*. Evil and savagery lie below the surface, and heroes such as Richard Hannay are forced to fight for what they know to be right while maintaining a middle course that exposes the dangers of fanaticism. Hard work and determination sit beside a strong sense of place, and the certainty of not only knowing right from wrong, but also of doing the right thing.

Viewed from the perspective of the unreliable narrator, however, Buchan's works take on a new perspective. In many ways his life and career are comparable with Scott's, and he must have been aware of the role writers such as Burns and Scott played in establishing Scottish identity, as well as the role being played by MacDiarmid in his own time. Buchan is a fascinating and complex writer whose work can be easily dismissed, but upon investigation a succession of puzzles, patterns and complexities is revealed, layered and contained within each other. Despite the extravagant successes of his career – over a hundred books, a novel a year for fourteen years, Governor-General of Canada – his internal oppositions remain, as surely as an ersatz mythology which encourages us to look beyond ourselves, to our historical and geographic position to explain what may well be inexplicable internal contradictions.

Christopher Harvie suggests that in his later novels Buchan communicates a critique of his own career and the causes he served; this brings him even closer to another writer who enjoyed almost unparalleled success in all but his private life, the creator of Peter Pan and Knight of the Kailyard, Sir James Matthew Barrie.

By the time of his death, Barrie was an isolated and lonely figure. Scottish writing had left him behind. Yet towards the end of his life he produced one work, a novella, *Farewell Miss Julie Logan*, which, although on its own is insufficient evidence upon which to base an entire reassessment of Barrie's life and work, should nevertheless trigger a re-evaluation, especially regarding the way he saw his own position.

Even in his earlier work, one often has the impression that Barrie sees through himself. An occasional ray of self-awareness shafts through his clouds of sentimentality. In *Farewell Miss Julie Logan*, published in 1932, it is as though the Kailyard never existed. The novella works on many fronts, as a state-of-the-nation novel, a psychological study, an autobiographical fragment, and a ghost story set in a remote glen. It is an uncluttered work: Rev. Adam Yestreen begins his diary while the glen is locked in snow; no one can get in or out. In a first-person narrative of surprising and immediate intimacy, Barrie quickly engages the reader's confidence, in places almost whispering his intimacies, so that authenticity is never in doubt. The fact that we trust the narrator is crucial. Barrie is separating himself from the position of the omnipotent author he adopted so often in the Kailyard. He wants us to believe him and uses the most effective means of establishing poise and secrecy open to a writer. That done, he can take us anywhere, tell us anything and we will believe him. In this context it is a risky device: the slightest variation in emotional authenticity and integrity would be immediately obvious. The device alone establishes Barrie's credentials.

Barrie teases the reader with his eponymous heroine, eventually admitting more than halfway through the story, 'I do not know how many times I have sat down to write about her, and then taken to wandering the study floor instead. My mind goes back in search of every crumb of her, and I am thinking I could pick her up better on my fiddle than in written words.' This equation, identifying Julie Logan in Yestreen's mind and therefore in the mind of the reader not only with music, but with Scottish traditional music, is a stroke of considerable mastery and subtlety. There exists, as Barrie surely knew, a tradition of naming tunes after women, especially slow airs, often slightly melancholy pieces, rising, graceful tunes that even musicians often find it difficult to recall after hearing them; Niel Gow's 'Lament for the Death of His Second Wife' is a perfect example.

Later, at the end of Chapter Seven, Yestreen imagines Julie Logan as his wife, sitting in the minister's pew, wondering if the seat would be too low for her: 'and such is my condition that, if I had brought nails and a hammer with me, I would have raised it there and then'. This depth of feeling is the very antithesis of the Kailyard, wherein national characteristics are stabilised in a rural past, the old concerns of voice and place – and therefore emotional honesty – simplified in the midst of great industrial, social and intellectual fervour; and where the stoicism so often attributed to the English was adopted as Scotland's own, suggesting it was a British, rather than Scots or English, characteristic.

Only and Alone for Freedom

Along the road from Kirriemuir is Arbroath, Fairport of Scott's *The Antiquary*, a sea port famed for smokies – haddock smoked over a hardwood-chip fire. Their smell pervades the town. The red sandstone used to build the abbey encircles the place, from the Auchmithie Cliffs, past St Vigean's church and houses. This is a coast where a promontory is called Red Head and where Red Castle replaced William the Lion's red fort. Arbroath Abbey was founded in 1178 by King William the Lion. Samuel Johnson thought the ruin afforded 'ample testimony of its ancient magnificence'.

This was where the Stone of Scone was left by those who removed it from Westminster Abbey in 1951. It was here on 3 April 1320 that Robert Bruce signed a declaration of national identity. The Declaration of Arbroath asserted the right of Scots to their own kingdom. It followed the Wars of Independence, a time when Scottish culture and identity were entwined as never before. It is a request to Pope John XXII to acknowledge the independence of the Scots. It opens with an extraordinary discourse on the origins of the Scots, a discourse which prefaces current theories on Celtic migration and stresses our protection by St Andrew, St Peter's brother.

The declaration also makes clear that the monarch is bound by reciprocal ties, just as the commonweal obliges the people to respect and obey the monarch acting within the law and obliges the monarch to respect and act within the law and to defend the people's rights as his or her own. Failure by the subjects is treason. Failure by the king ensures abdication. It summarises Edward I's tyranny and praises Robert the Bruce, 'who has brought salvation to his people through the safeguarding of our liberties.' But should even Bruce yield Scotland or the Scots to the English, he would be thrown out and another king would be chosen to defend national freedom. The most quoted passage in the declaration says, 'For so long as a hundred of us remain alive, we will yield in no least way to English domination. For we fight, not for glory, not for riches nor for honour, but only and alone for freedom, which no good man surrenders but with his life.'

The Utmost Part of the World

St Andrew's bones were said to have been brought back from Patras by St Rule in the fourth century. Andrew had been crucified on a saltire and his relics preserved. In a vision St Rule was told to flee with the relics to a region 'situated in the utmost part of the world'. A storm washed him ashore at St Andrews where he built his cathedral, later destroyed in the Reformation, a scene gloriously depicted by John Galt in *Ringhan Gilhaize*. Other versions combine similar elements, as in the story of the saltire's formation at Athelstaneford. The cathedral's importance as a religious and administrative centre is said to have rivalled Iona and Whithorn. The town makes its way towards the ruin on the edge of the sea.

St Andrews University is the oldest in Scotland, founded early in the fifteenth century, and this was where Robert Adamson had his first studio. Adamson and the Edinburgh painter David Octavius Hill broadened Edinburgh's horizons when they produced their astonishing series of more than three thousand photographs, mostly portraits. Hill and Adamson worked together from 1843 to 1847. The bulk of their work is portraiture, seeking to classify the country in terms of images. They were the first to imbue photography with a social significance. This extraordinary experimental and creative period both paved the way for and in many ways inspired other Scottish photographers, such as James Valentine in Dundee, George Washington Wilson in Aberdeen and Thomas Annan in Glasgow, a tradition which continues with Joseph McKenzie, Oscar Marzaroli and Colin Baxter today. Adamson had produced photographs in his St Andrews studio using Fox Talbot's Calotype method. He and Hill came together in 1843, when Hill was working on a painting of the dissenting ministers who had broken from the Church of Scotland to form the Free Church of Scotland. The photographs were used as an aid to Hill's painting.

Golf has been played on the St Andrews links probably since the twelfth century. Football was a source of domestic disorder. In 1424, James I decreed 'that na man play at the fute ball'. In 1454 his son, James II, decreed that 'the fute ball and golfe be utterly cryed downe and not to be used'. In both cases, the intention was to encourage archery, which was considered more relevant to national interests. This and other bans seem to have helped the game prosper. Mary, Queen of Scots was criticised for playing golf a few days after the murder of Darnley.

Golf seems to have been a Scottish invention. Though the word appears to be of Dutch derivation, the Low Country game seems to have many similarities with croquet. Emigrant Scots took the game to America; and for many golf carries the essence of national identity. It appeals to and is played by all levels of society and is still relatively cheap to play in a country which has more than four hundred courses; many of them, especially the seaside links courses, provide extraordinary settings.

Again, landscape would appear to be a key player. The Royal and Ancient Club of St Andrews continues to organise the Open Championship, held in Scotland every second year, though the first Open Championship was played at Prestwick, when the prize, a belt of red leather and silver, was won outright by Tom Morris, whose father Old Tom Morris had won it four times. His son kept the trophy by winning it in successive years. The tournament was suspended while a new trophy was produced. It is still in use today and was first played for in 1872, when it was won by Young Tom Morris.

The Warld Is Ill-Divided

In Dundee the jute mills have been converted into flats and jam production has been reduced, though journalism survives in the offices of D. C. Thomson and Co., publishers of the *Sunday Post*, the *Dandy* and the

Beano. In the aftermath of the General Strike, David Cooper Thomson forced his employees to sign a document that surrendered their right to trade union membership. It is still in force.

Port Glasgow and Greenock comfortably stink and rot on the Clyde estuary, wrote Muir, 'two of the dirtiest and ugliest towns in Scotland, with a natural position second only to Dundee, which is the dirtiest and ugliest of all'.[21] George Blake saw it as

> An East Coast town with a West Coast temperament . . . a place without any distinguishing marks save its somewhat strange political history during recent years and certain other associations that do not, however, seem to have grown naturally out of its essence. It is something to have returned to Parliament within twenty years or so both Mr Winston Churchill and a Prohibitionist so austere as Mr Edwin Scrimgeour.[22]

The last jute fibre came ashore in October 1998. It 'shaped the city of Dundee and forged one of the nation's grittiest working-class communities,' said the *Herald*'s report. At the turn of the twentieth century 50,000 Dundonians were employed in jute processing. When jute was at its zenith, Broughty Ferry was said to be the richest square mile in the world because of the number of millionaire inhabitants. And as the last jute ship docked, Dundee was reported to be the third most profitable place in Britain. As well as inflicting a comprehensive gubbing on the more financially favoured in Scotland, Dundee also comfortably outperforms London, according to a study by Experian, a global information company: 'It surveyed profit margins based on sales figures of 200,000 businesses in 285 towns and cities. Dundee came third, showing an average of 18.75%, just a whisker behind Warrington and the overall winner, Worthing in West Sussex.'[23]

Dundee also boasts one of the best fish-supper shops in Scotland and two of the best bakers. 'Few cities have such a single good viewpoint,' says *Scotland the Best!*, referring to 'the panoramic perspective of the city on the estuary of the silvery Tay. Best to walk from town. The one-way system is a nightmare.'

The former Verdant Works is now a heritage centre, which outlines the jute workers' conditions, and the restored RRS *Discovery*, which took Scott and his crew to the Antarctic, is permanently berthed at Discovery Point. Whale oil was used to soften the jute fibre before it was spun, and the *Discovery* was based on earlier whaler designs. The *Balena* and the *Terra Nova* were renowned Dundee-built whalers. Local pride in a hard

21. Edwin Muir, *op. cit.*
22. George Blake, *The Heart of Scotland*.
23. *Herald*, 1 September 1998.

industrial past and the identity it established is reflected in *Songs and Ballads of Dundee*, more than seventy songs collected by Nigel Gatherer. This was where Hamish Henderson first recorded songs from 'the redoubtable Davie Stewart' and where Mary Brooksbank's 'Jute Mill Song' has become a local anthem:

> Oh dear me, the warld is ill-divided,
> Them that wark the hardest are aye wi' least provided.

Dundonians are well used to the likes of Muir's assessment, or, worse still, of finding that condescension follows praise. Blake feels Dundee is 'neither quite one thing nor the other', which seems in keeping with its West Coast temperament. Fionn Mac Colla's judgement is harsher: 'the completest monument in the entire continent of human folly, avarice and selfishness; a perfect object-lesson in what results from the divorce of economic life from ethics'. Written in 1935, his final Old Testament-style prediction was premature: 'that which brought Dundee into existence as an industrial city is no longer able to maintain it even at the level of its one-time sordid and poverty-bound prosperity. Dundee is a great industrial derelict.'

Dundee followed Glasgow into the redevelopment boom of the 1960s and, like Glasgow, has cosmeticised or demolished its obvious excesses. Dundee has also taken the artistic road to economic prosperity. Dundee Rep now hosts the country's only full-time theatre company, comprising fourteen actors, and hosts jazz and guitar festivals. Nearby, on the Nethergate, Dundee Contemporary Arts is a sympathetically converted warehouse space which houses cinemas, galleries, a shop, a print studio and the Jute Café Bar.

Dundee provides spiritual sustenance to Michael Marra, whose songs celebrate Queens Park FC, owners of Hampden Park and the first football team to pass the ball to each other, changing the game forever, and the wonderful 'Hermless', a subtle and deceptive, non-militaristic national-anthem submission. He celebrated the bicentenary of Ullapool with a piece about wife abuse:

> Then down by the post office
> Enter a sailor
> Fresh from the queue for the coffee he smiles
> And they laugh by the job club
> And he throws down his coat,
> And palm trees are swaying
> And gulls they are singing
> And Moira is smiling with stars in her eyes
> Under the Ullapool sky.

The fourth-biggest city in Scotland, Dundee's relationship with the surrounding countryside, and the migratory habits of its citizens (who moved easily between one and the other), has preserved the distinctive local accent. This accent has found its way into the poetry and novels of John Burnside, Don Paterson, W. N. Herbert and Andrew Murray Scott, and has placed Dundonians at the core of research by folklorists and Scots-language devotees.

And just outside, on the slopes of the Sidlaw Hills, is St Marnock's Church at Fowlis Easter, which dates from 1453 and contains medieval painted panels of the Crucifixion. James IV visited Fowlis Easter and St Andrews in 1497. Along the road is Dunsinane, said to be Macbeth's rampart – local pronunciation, Dunsinnan, rather ruins Shakespeare's rhythmic structure – and further along the B953 lies Birnam.

'The collegiate church has a double importance in Scotland's cultural history,' says Michael Lynch.

> It was the vehicle of a new, much wider kind of religious patronage, involving the laity from the Crown down to the newly incorporated urban craft guilds who had been given their own altars in the expanded great burgh churches; and it was the venue for a wider range of artistic patronage, involving architecture, decoration, music and music schools, and various kinds of devotional literature, including missals, psalters and books of hours. Nobles, lairds and the larger burghs had already joined the royal Court and the ecclesiastical establishment as patrons of the arts.[24]

As far as we can tell, the great Scottish abbeys and cathedrals combined exterior and interior statements lavishly, a Babylonish trait which caused their destruction during the Reformation. The Crucifixion panels at Fowlis Easter and the fragmented interior paintings at the Innerpeffray Church, by the River Earn, and an extraordinary private library, as well as a number of painted ceilings across the country not only reflect the change in patronage from Church to monarchy, the spread of wealth and rise of literacy, but give a lie to the standard interpretation of our national Reformers.

'The evidence for both public and private uses of painting is such that it is quite clear that Scotland, far from being kept in joyless (and unpainted) gloom by a dominant caste of black-browed Presbyterians, was actually rather a jazzy place,' says Duncan Macmillan. 'Not only the number of painted ceilings that survive, but also the range of dwellings in which these, or traces of them are found, is such that we have to conclude

---

24. Michael Lynch, 'Scottish Culture in its Historical Perspective' in Paul H. Scott, *Scotland: A Concise Cultural History*.

that painted decoration of considerable elaboration was the norm even in relatively modest houses.'[25]

Between the Rivers Dee and Don

'Bleakness, not meanness or jollity, is the keynote to the Aberdonian character, not so much lack of the graces or graciousness of existence as lack of colour in either of these,' wrote Lewis Grassic Gibbon. 'And this is almost inevitable for anyone passing his nights and days in The Silver City. It is comparable to passing one's existence in a refrigerator. Aberdeen is built largely and incredibly, of one of the most enduring and indestructible and appalling building materials in use on our planet – grey granite.'[26]

An Aberdonian is someone born between the Rivers Dee and Don, which, coincidentally, is where the local maternity hospital is situated. When Gibbon wrote this piece, the feeling was that Aberdeen had barely changed for centuries, isolated by the sea, the Cairngorms, the Grampians and the Mounth hills to the south. This gave the city a cosmopolitan feel: its position forced it to trade with Europe, the Low Countries and Scandinavia. These factors are said to account for the number of words of obvious European derivation in the local dialect, which supposedly arrived in return for the fish and woollens Aberdeen exported. Granite from Rubislaw quarry lines London streets and the docks of Rio de Janeiro, as well as Queen Victoria's mausoleum. And the city is proud of the people it attracted before they were known elsewhere, such as the American comedy juggler W. C. Fields, who appeared at the Tivoli, reputedly alongside Scott Skinner, or the young Charlie Chaplin, who performed at the Palace for three weeks as part of Fred Karno's troupe. And Harry Houdini was strait-jacketed, wrapped in a sack and padlocked, then lowered into Aberdeen's Albert Dock to attract audiences to the Palace.

Of all the places where local identity was secure, many felt Aberdeen, with its distinctive speech and locally based industries, dependent on the land and sea, was the most singular in Scotland, the place where the nine-year-old Byron, whom it is difficult to imagine with an Aberdeen accent, was beaten by a devout Calvinist nurse, who, in the words of his mother's financial adviser, 'brought all sorts of Company from the very lowest Description to his apartments'.

Oil changed Aberdeen. The city expanded and the skyline shifted. Glass and concrete structures sit beside the granite kirks; the local banks

25. Duncan Macmillan, *Scottish Art 1460–1990*.
26. Lewis Grassic Gibbon, *Scottish Scene*.

and building societies, the local shops of which Aberdeen was justly proud, have been replaced by smart new designer stores, restaurants, national branches or offices with no distinctive local character. But Aberdeen and the surrounding countryside have been stubbornly resilient to other changes; a local Doric Festival, designed to maintain their distinctive linguistic traditions, runs for three weeks every year, and other local festivals are held annually in the likes of Banchory, Keith, Lossiemouth and Aberdeen itself.

It's a far cry from *Bothy Nichts*, a locally produced television programme where amateur singers, musicians and comics, dressed up as ploughmen, re-enacted a sanitised version of what was supposed to be home-made entertainment, singing local songs with local farm characters such as the bailie and the kitchy deem coming in to augment the activities. These plays were scripted by and starred local people, and the programme was very popular; but it was killed off, it is felt, by oil. It was thought to be a bit too parochial for the Texans, who found it unintelligible.

Diminutives abound in the local accent. 'Hundreds of mothers through-out Aberdeenshire and Banffshire,' wrote J. M. Bulloch in *The Delight of The Doric Diminutive*, an essay in a collection called *The Scottish Tongue*, 'every night put their "little wee bit lookikies" and "little wee bit lassikies" to their "bedies", while the infant of the household, described as the "little wee eenickie", that is a "teeny weeny eenie" – lies in its "cradlie".' Diminutives are our only emotional outlets, says Mary Symon in the same anthology. We have practically no endearments.

Aberdeen's local radio station Northsound broadcasts to the rigs, to the men working offshore in the middle of the North Sea. They work out-side in all weathers, twelve hours on and twelve hours off, fourteen days at a time. They are familiar with 60-foot waves, and stormy nights when the anchors break and rigs drift around the sea.

The conditions under which the riggers work were highlighted during the Piper Alpha inquiry. Aberdonians are said to remember where they were and what they were doing when they heard of the disaster that Wednesday night. It appears to have caused a change in the way the oilmen see themselves. Prior to Piper Alpha they put up with the condi-tions without complaint. The macho attitude has gone now; oilmen are more mindful of their own and others' safety.

Oil touches everything. Everyone, it seems, knows someone who works in oil. It is bigger than the fishing trade, which was thought to be peren-nial. The city has progressed through a series of sea-associated trades, from shipbuilding to fishing and now to oil. And even in the mid-1980s, when there were 10,000 lay-offs, when the price for oil per barrel dropped, almost halved, it was pointed out that no other industry in Scotland could survive such a reduction.

Fishing still survives, but on the periphery, in the fish factories where the catches are processed. Gibbon mentions Friday night in Aberdeen – the fact that everyone congregates on Union Street when the shops close. Now everything is open later and the town has grown. Small villages such as Cove, a holiday destination until the 1980s, are now part of Aberdeen. The old villages have been absorbed or bypassed by the huge dual carriageways.

Prosperity has made the cost of living higher and, unless they work in oil, few locals can afford to buy a house. Like Edinburgh, Aberdeen has a property market that has remained confident and buoyant. Like Edinburgh, but unlike Glasgow and Dundee, Aberdeen escaped major redevelopment.

Surrounded by the farms and smallholdings that nurtured the bothy ballads, Aberdeen is still a provincial city. Writers from here or here-abouts have been dominated by the land. From William Alexander's *Johnny Gibb of Gushetneuk*, through Ian Macpherson's *Shepherd's Calendar* and Lewis Grassic Gibbon to Duncan McLean's *Blackden*, the myth of the land has permeated the writing of the north-east. Nan Shepherd has written about a woman escaping the illusions and prejudices of those around her, struggling to free herself from a narrow background, a theme specifically taken up by her protégée, Jessie Kesson. Kesson's emancipation is more literal, more realistic. It is from the oppression of poverty and the prejudices of the working class, particularly the ways in which these prejudices and classifications affect women, objectifying and curtailing them simultaneously, denying even the possibility of escape.

Ploughing, Drilling, Seed-Time, Harvest

James Leslie Mitchell was born in 1901 and died in 1935. Writing as Lewis Grassic Gibbon, he was the most influential Scottish novelist of the twentieth century. He used the familiars of voice and place to establish an archetypal statement of identity while living in Welwyn Garden City, setting his finest work in a landscape which has been refashioned by man and maintained by man, whose red clay soil is reflected in the sections of *Sunset Song*: Ploughing, Drilling, Seed-Time, Harvest. And though the voice and personality of Chris Guthrie lies at the heart of *A Scots Quair*, it is in the first part of the trilogy, *Sunset Song*, which deals with her upbring-ing and young womanhood, where she is most strongly felt. It is a novel whose stature seems to increase, especially in the way Gibbon analyses the division in Chris Guthrie, the two Chrisses:

> You hated the land and the coarse speak of the folk and learning was brave
> and fine and the next you'd waken with the peewits crying across the hills,
> deep and deep, crying in the heart of you with the smell of the earth in
> your face, almost you'd cry for that, the beauty of it and the sweetness of
> the Scottish land and skies.

The novel is structured almost as a retrospective diary which returns to the present at the end of each chapter. The voice is intimate, driven, Tom Crawford asserts, by a device quite rare in fiction, which Gibbon may even have invented: the self-referring you, which dramatises Chris's thoughts and thought processes, while a generic you, equivalent to everybody, strengthens the impression of commonality and intimacy by addressing the reader directly. Even at the most intimate, quiet moments, Chris's experiences are shared, emphasising the main theme of this and the other two books: that nothing endures but change. Duncairn, the town in *Grey Granite*, the final novel in the trilogy, is clearly modelled on Aberdeen, with aspects of Dundee and Glasgow. The novel offers no deliverance, again centring on the divided self.

Mitchell obviously carried Scotland around in his head, and, like a ball in the air, the places he knew are always changing, always the same. He was driven by an enormous creative energy, producing seven books in the last two years of his life, all written straight on to the typewriter with few revisions. His other works as Lewis Grassic Gibbon also manage to retain the rhythm and vitality of the voice, joining *A Scots Quair* in under-lining the spirit of place and establishing an identity which served not only the Mearns but all of Scotland, and whose influence is more domi-nant today than any other Scots writer of his time. The five stories he set in the Mearns use the same idiom as *Sunset Song*, and match the accom-plishment. *Smeddum*, *Clay* and *Sim* introduce characters and situations which are explored in the trilogy, but here their mood and humour and the power of the writing is initially involved with, then sustained by, Gibbon's strain of poetic realism, which marries poetry to work and land in a way that finds a parallel only in folk song. Again, the narrative style, the way he insinuates the voice, both colloquial and lyrical, and through the voice describes the place and work, thus conveying the entirety of a life experience to the reader – all this could be achieved in no other way.

The trilogy remains his finest achievement, its style modelled on the rhythms and patterns of a Scot from the Howe of the Mearns speaking English. This emphatically places the narrative in a way no previous writer achieved, using the voice of a community to drive the text, coercing it into mainstream Scottish literature.

The writer who most resembles Gibbon is the man credited with lead-ing the movement of voice and place away from the Highland glens and shorelines. James Kelman's writing is like Gibbon's in the ways in which his characters marry autobiographical voice with narrative discourse, bridging the gap created by the likes of Walter Scott, whose characters spoke Scots while he used English to tell us what they were doing. Kelman also uses the voice and the intimacy of first-person narration to insinuate an entire experience.

As in Tom Leonard's work, the linguistic power relationship is at the heart of James Kelman's work, and by refusing to move outwith the ex-periential sphere of his creations he resists the role of omnipotent author to the extent that he offers no privileged insights, nor does he even adopt a narrative voice which is different from that of his characters, often directly reflecting their thought processes. This has given his work a dimension that appeals to younger writers such as Janice Galloway, Irvine Welsh, Duncan McLean and Gordon Legge. Like Gibbon, he can do what earlier realists could rarely do: he can write about the world his characters inhabit, the world of urban decay and low-paid work, the world of unemployment and imitation Crombies, without the slightest trace of condescension.

All Its Airs and Graces

Further up the coast is Fraserburgh, a herring port with 'the highest rate of heroin addiction in Britain. But these aren't stereotypical addicts. Here, the junkies are well-to-do housewives and trawlermen with money to burn.'[27]

There are 325 known addicts among the town's population of 14,000. An article in the *Independent Magazine* describes one of them: 'A young mum, her hair tied back in a neat chignon, gold buttons sparkling on her tailored red jacket, is lifting her child out of the back of a shiny blue Range Rover' by a neat garden and curtains, a ranch-style bungalow with shopping at the door. She needs a fix after an exhausting day with the children. Children as young as ten turn up to Guides with £20 notes to pay their 25-pence admission fee, and the local GP believes parents are too busy earning money. 'They neglect family activities,' he says. 'You never see families walking out together.'

No one understands the reason for the problem. 'Young fishermen come ashore with £700 in their hands and only two days to spend it.' The local GP wants to see an all-weather running track, greater involvement from community organisations like the church, the conversion of the old police station into a drop-in centre. These things, it is felt, will make a difference. 'For all its airs and graces, Fraserburgh has the definite feel of being at the end of the world.'[28]

27. *Independent Magazine*, undated.
28. *Ibid.*

6

Essential Silence Chills and Blesses

'You told me once how your younger brother died.
It was by drowning. In the tar-black sea
he sang a psalm to bring his rescuers near.
That did not save him though. One cannot hide,
you would have said, from destiny. So here
there are two meanings working side by side.'

IAIN CRICHTON SMITH, 'You told me once'

Against all Highland Characteristics

It is possible to cross Drumossie Moor, following the run of the last pitched battle fought on British soil, to imagine the driech rainy day, viewing what no soldier could have seen on 16 April 1746: the respective commanders' positions, with flags aloft. The location of the Hanoverian and Highland troops are marked, viewing stances show the run of the battle and the Well of the Dead, and the mass clan graves are as gloomy as ever.

Driving on the A9 to Inverness, Edwin Muir passed a sign for Culloden at the start of the B9006, he says, 'but remembering my lack of instinct for battlefields I held straight on'. *Scotland the Best!* advises, 'If you go in spring you see how wet and miserable the Moor can be,' adding, 'No matter how many other folk are there wandering down the lines, a visit to this most infamous of battlefields can still leave a pain in the heart.'

The site is owned by the National Trust for Scotland, and, like most of their properties, Culloden has a shop, an information centre, a tea-room, a museum and an interpretative exhibition. By promising 'to promote the preservation of this heritage of fine buildings, beautiful landscape and historic places, and to encourage public enjoyment of them', the

National Trust for Scotland has become a major Scottish landowner, especially in the Highlands, where Glencoe, Ben Lawers, Beinn Eighe, Killiecrankie and Inverpolly are among a number of sites entrusted to their care. Their commercial arm is well developed. They produce a range of Scottish products, from woollens to music, shortbread to walking sticks, often selecting items they feel would be suitable for a particular location in order to convey a certain individuality among their range of history books, posters and the like.

The image of Charles Edward Louis Philip Casimir Stewart dominates the Culloden shop, just as images of betrayal dominate the Glencoe site, wildlife and nature trails feature heavily in Ben Lawers and Killiecrankie. The Young Chevalier is spread across a range of products. Like the images of Napoleon sold on the site of Waterloo, it is impossible to tell that he lost. George, Duke of Cumberland, victor of Culloden, known in Scotland as Butcher Cumberland, is nowhere to be seen. In most of the images, Bonnie Prince Charlie is young again, bedecked in Royal Stewart tartan and setting the tone and style for future royal visitors such as George IV. Asking whose interests this image serves yields an answer as pedestrian as questioning the mythology that surrounds his time in Scotland.

On 5 July 1745, disguised as a divinity student, Charles Stewart boarded the *Du Teillay* at Nantes and, against his father's wishes, began an eighteen-day journey to Scotland. A skirmish in the English Channel on the fifth day forced the prince's boat to carry on alone. He landed in Eriskay, at a place now called Prince Charlie's Bay, uncelebrated and unmarked, where nothing much appears to have changed from then till now.

Nearly four weeks later the red-and-white silken standard of the House of Stewart was raised on another National Trust for Scotland site in the vale of Glenfinnan at the head of Loch Shiel. A month later Charles's troops commanded Edinburgh. Prestonpans and the march to Derby followed; then the retreat. On Boxing Day Charles led his ragged army into Glasgow. He brought in the New Year and left on 3 January having recruited 'ane drunken shoemaker'. Nowhere, he said, had he found so few friends.

Somewhere along the way he was joined by Dougal Graham, whose rhyming doggerel 'History of the Rebellion' appeared five months after Culloden. 'John Highlandman's Remarks Upon the City of Glasgow' was probably Graham's most popular broadside. The stance is of an urban sophisticate poking fun at the language and naïvety of the Highlanders, who began their exodus to the city in the wake of the 1745 rebellion.

Glasgow's main casualty was Clementina Walkinshaw. She became the prince's mistress, followed him to France and bore his only child. He is said to have publicly horsewhipped her on the streets of Bruges and then abandoned her in Paris, where she survived the French Revolution. Surprisingly, the last years of her life were the hardest. Her state was so desperate that a plea for assistance was made to the British Government on her behalf. It was refused. She died in 1802 of what appears to have been malnutrition, outliving both the prince and his daughter.

The overwhelming feeling at Culloden is not of the man, but of the prince, a leader in waiting, a hero. It is the Bonnie Prince Charlie of legend, our king across the water, rather than the pathetic and broken reality.

Mythology ties Bonnie Prince Charlie to Flora Macdonald and his escape from Benbecula over the sea to Skye, disguised as her Irish maid Betty Burke. Flora was subsequently arrested and for a time imprisoned in the Tower of London, eventually being released under the 1747 Act of Indemnity. She was visited at her home at Sleat by Boswell and Johnson, who found her 'a woman of middle stature, soft features, gentle manners and elegant presence'. A 10-foot-high Celtic cross marks her grave on the Uig–Staffin road. The original memorial was chipped away by souvenir hunters.

The prince's survival and escape is the stuff of legend. For five months he avoided capture by the Hanoverian forces, despite there being a price of £30,000 on his head – a sum said to be equivalent to £2 million today. Though he has been blamed for leading the clansmen to destruction at Culloden and abandoning them when the battle was lost, nothing explains his extraordinary appeal, nor why, with such a high price on his head, he was never betrayed.

In 1774, with their former way of life all but gone, Flora Macdonald and her husband, Allan, emigrated to Darien in North Carolina, a community formed by survivors of another disaster and where many Gaels had settled. At first all was well; such a romantic couple were bound to be stars in society's firmament. With the first rumblings of the War of Independence, a regiment of Highlanders was raised to defend the Crown and Allan Macdonald, an avowed Jacobite, became an officer. Again, they picked the wrong side. When the British forces were defeated at Moore's Creek, Allan Macdonald was jailed and Flora was exiled to Nova Scotia, eventually returning to Scotland to live in South Uist until Allan's release. He finally returned to Scotland penniless, at a time when, if anything, circumstances were worse than when they had left.

When news of the Culloden victory reached London, George Frederick Handel inserted 'See The Conquering Hero Comes' into the opera *Judas Maccabeus*. The wounded at Drumossie Moor were killed where they lay. And after the battle more than three thousand men, women and children were imprisoned and shipped south, where 120 were executed and more than a thousand banished and transported. Some were freed, but hundreds died in captivity of their wounds, or hunger or disease. Meanwhile, Cumberland was earning the sobriquet 'Butcher' by implementing a brutally repressive regime throughout the Highlands.

'A drive was made against all Highland characteristics,' writes Agnes Mure Mackenzie. 'Till 1782, the use of the kilt, the tartan, or the pipes by anyone who was not in government service involved transportation, while Gaelic was suppressed by all possible means.'[1]

'Chatter about "the clans" being defeated at Culloden ignores the fact that there were only some 5000 men in the Jacobite army that day when the population of the Highlands must have been about a quarter of a million,' writes Gordon Donaldson. 'It was not a military defeat that transformed Highland society.'[2] The Highlands, he says, have been erroneously identified with Jacobitism.

'After the Reformation the Highlands became one of the few parts of the kingdom where the Catholic Church survived, although this only partly explains the support given by the clans to the Jacobite rebellions,' say Ian Donnachie and George Hewitt.

> Thereafter, the population was seriously reduced by the effects of the Clearances, not to mention the extensive recruiting of Highland regiments in these years. Towards the end of the nineteenth century, at least until the passing of the Crofters Act (1886), the grievances of the crofting community were a major issue creating bitter hostility towards certain landowners. Today it is a region with a declining population, dominated in some parts by the doctrines of the Free Church and mainly dependent on tourism for a livelihood.[3]

Wae's Me For Prince Charlie

Marx dissected the Highland Clearances and John Ruskin recorded the results: 'Now a Highland scene is, beyond dispute, pleasant enough in its own way; but, looked close at, has its shadows,' he says, going on to describe low, clear autumn sunshine on scarlet ash berries and golden birch leaves, a ewe carcass drowned in the flood

> nearly bare to the bone, its white ribs protruding through the skin, raventorn; and the rags of wool still flickering from the branches that first stayed it as the stream swept it down . . . . Lower down the stream, I can just see over a knoll, the green and damp turf roofs of four or five hovels, built at the edge of a morass, which is trodden by the cattle into a black Slough of Despond at their doors, traversed by a few ill-set stepping stones, with here and there a flat slab on the tops, where they have sunk out of sight, and at the turn of the brook I see a man fishing, with a boy and a dog – a

1. Agnes Mure Mackenzie, *The Kingdom of Scotland.*
2. Gordon Donaldson, *Scotland: The Shaping of a Nation.*
3. Ian Donnachie and George Hewitt, *A Companion to Scottish History.*

picturesque and pretty enough group certainly, if they had not been there all day starving. I know them, and I know the dog's ribs also, which are nearly as bare as the dead ewe's; and the child's wasted shoulders, cutting his old tartan jacket through, so sharp are they.[4]

Muir blamed Scott and Queen Victoria for the final conversion of the Highlands.

> Scott sent the tourist wandering over the Highland hills, and Queen Victoria built Balmoral . . . . The Highlanders' numbers have been thinned, their mode of life degraded, by a series of objective calamities. They have kept through all these changes their courtesy, their dignity, and one might almost say their freedom, for that seems to exist independent of any service, however menial, which they made render. But these qualities are bought at the expense of the disdainful resignation which a proud people feels in acknowledging defeat, a resignation so profound that it can treat its conqueror with magnaminity, while keeping him at a distance. Whether that is a good quality or a bad one I do not know, but it is in any case an extraordinary one.[5]

To which must be added the thrill of romance. 'It is now generally accepted as fact,' writes Ivor Brown,

> that within ten years of Culloden's disaster Charles visited London under the name of Mr Brown and walked into the card-party at Lady Primrose's house in Essex Street, Strand. He also called upon Dr King, the principal of St Mary Hall, at Oxford. King said he spoke fluent French, Italian, and English, the last with a foreign accent. He could have added Gaelic . . .
>
> But in Scotland the legend grew. Long after Culloden the songsters were taking boat and sail to live and die with Charlie, over whose defeat the national Muse began to utter a continual pibroch. It is as easy as it is common to call the Scots incurable sentimentalists, but there was more in the building of a Bonnie Prince Charlie myth than an emotional debauch.

Brown goes on to suggest that the Prince began to stand, in his absence and after his death, for 'something that Scotland subconsciously knew it had lost, the National Being'.[6]

In 1842, when Queen Victoria was staying at Taymouth Castle, John Wilson, a Scotch singer, submitted a proposed list of songs for royal assent. She amended the list, asking him to sing 'Wae's Me For Prince

4. John Ruskin, *Modern Painters, Volume 5*.
5. Edwin Muir, *Scottish Journey*.
6. Ivor Brown, *Summer in Scotland*.

Charlie', her favourite song. This was the first indication that Jacobite sentiments, as well as Jacobite sentimentality, were welcomed at court. The
song is the work of a Glasgow writer, William Glen, who was born in
1789, the year after Charles's death. Though not a Jacobite sympathiser,
Glen saw the opening for another piece of lachrymose mythology and
wrote one of the most enduringly popular Jacobite songs, in which a
common Highlander mourns his lost leader and, by inference, all that
went with him.

> On hills that are by right his ain, he walks a lonely stranger.
> On ilka hand he pressed by want, on ilka side by danger.
> Yestreen I met him in a glen. My hert it bursted fairly,
> For sadly changed indeed was he, O wae's me for Prince Charlie.

Jacobite songs, or, perhaps more properly, songs which express Jacobite
sentiments, organically link the loss of Charlie with the loss of independence and even nationhood. Song did for Bonnie Prince Charlie
what *Braveheart* has done for William Wallace. Songs like 'Rise! Rise! Wha
Widna Fecht for Charlie' can still bring an SNP rally to its feet, and 'Will
Ye No Come Back Again' is sung as a song of parting.

To understand the mythological power of song we need only look to
Ireland, where traditional music has always asserted a sense of national
identity and in turn has been reinterpreted to become an immediately
recognisable emblem of nationality and place. In Ireland, as elsewhere,
traditional musicians have always met together to play, but what we now
recognise as an Irish traditional music group was virtually invented by
Sean O'Riarda.[7] Nor, as elsewhere, are what we generally think of as Irish
traditional songs necessarily native. In volume seven of the Greig–Duncan
folk-song collection, song number 1480 is called 'The Wild Rover':

> I've been a wild rover this mony a year,
> And spent all my money on brandy and beer,
> But I'll quit all my roving, lay money in store,
> And never shall play the wild rover no more.
> Nay! no! never! never no more.
> I never shall play the wild rover no more.

This is the second of six versions collected in Aberdeenshire at the turn
of the last century. The editors trace its publication to London roughly
thirty years previously. The song reappeared in recordings by the Clancy
Brothers and Tommy Makem in the 1960s.

The role of traditional music is no less diverse or profound in Scotland,

7. See Ciaran Carson, *Last Night's Fun.*

where the songs of Robert Burns especially occupy a central and pivotal place, but writers such as Hogg, Scott, Ferguson, Ramsay and Tannahill have contributed to a common fund. 'Native music,' says John Purser, 'was being cultivated alongside the native landscape.'

Yet across the world the military-tinged swell of the pipe band with its rasping kettle-drum accompaniment is immediately recognised as the music of Scotland; an accordion-led Scottish country-dance band occupies a similar domestic role.

Short, Stout-built, Honest

In her idiosyncratic *Memoirs of a Highland Lady*, Elizabeth Grant remembers staying at the inn at Inver when Niel Gow was called to play for her. The music 'had so over-excited me the night before that my father had had to take me a little walk by the riverside in the moonlight before I was rational enough to be left to sleep,' she confesses. Gow's music seems to have had a similar effect on many young women. He often had to play for twelve hours at a stretch, and on one occasion when the ladies would not stop dancing, though supper had been announced, he berated them: 'Gang down to your suppers, ye daft limmers, and dinna haud me reelin' here, as if hunger and drouth were unkent in the land – a body can get naething dune for you.'

Robert Burns, who also could rustle a tune from a fiddle, met Gow and his wife at Inver on 31 August 1787, during his Highland tour, describing him as 'a short, stout-built, honest Highland figure, with his greyish hair shed on his honest social brow – an interesting face, marking strong sense, kind open heartedness mixed with mistrusting simplicity'. He commemorated the visit in a short poem, reproduced on a plaque outside Gow's cottage, a verse which somehow seems unfinished, especially given the poet's description and the pair's obvious liking for each other, as though both rhythm and subject expect something less minimalist:

> Nae fabled wizard's wand I trow
> Had e'er the magic art o' Gow
> When in a wave he draws his bow
> Across his wondrous fiddle.

Gow not only made a living from music but also, in Purser's words,

raised the status of [the] professional musician, which in those days was not very high. Even for a Haydn, a Mozart or a Beethoven, living by music was both financially and socially hazardous and they were working in one of the wealthiest environments in the world. For a man like Gow to hold his own

amongst the aristocracy on whom he depended took, as Burns no doubt
knew also, a good deal of moral courage.[8]

Not only was the role of the professional musician low; his craft was filled
with indelicate suggestion. Fiddling has always had a double entendre in
Scotland, and in certain company the mere inference of pipes and
whistling was considered so unspeakable as to be denounced from the
pulpit. Only harps were played in heaven and these were not instruments
necessarily native to Scotland, though they were an instrument favoured
by Ossian.

At a time when Highland culture and society were being destroyed and
its music dragooned into military service, writers were actively gathering
and preserving folk music in the Lowlands, and in the area now known as
Highland Perthshire Niel Gow was not only blazing a trail through freelance musicianship, but was doing so with music whose style and
composition was intrinsically Scots. In defining, maintaining and enhancing a recognisable native Scottish culture, Gow's role can only be
compared to Robert Burns, James Hogg and Walter Scott. As surely as
they and other writers used native Scottish language, history and character and based their works upon native themes which they enriched and
expanded, so Gow developed, enriched and expanded the Scottish traditional fiddle repertoire.

To consider him a simple country musician who composed merry
tunes is not only to do him a disservice, but to misunderstand the Scottish
musical tradition. Like any musician, Gow obviously composed tunes that
would display his skills and provide a vehicle for personal expression; but
there is also the other obvious fact that Gow was working within a tradition – that, like Burns, he was preserving as well as expanding. He was by
no means the only Scots composer of the time, nor the only one to have
contributed to the preservation of traditional music. A near neighbour,
Red Rob MacIntosh from Tullymet, was one of a number of fiddlers
whose music flourished in the days after the Kirk tried to stop dancing; it
is still being played today, having been adapted for a variety of instruments, the Scottish small pipes and clarsach being the obvious but not
the only examples. Nor were they the only musicians this small area has
produced. For example, Inver is also the birthplace and home of Charles
Mackintosh, who was also a composer and fiddle-player, as well as a nat-
uralist whose expertise was admired by Beatrix Potter, who met Charlie
during many summer holidays spent with her family at Dalguise. She
reputedly used him as the model for Mr McGregor.

Though Niel Gow is the better known, his sons, Nathaniel, who started
life as a Scottish state trumpeter, William, Andrew and John, are still

8. John Purser, *Scotland's Music.*

revered as composers, publishers and fiddlers in a tradition where music's function was chiefly to accompany dancers in reels, strathspeys, jigs and hornpipes. Elizabeth Grant, travelling home to Rothiemurcus after Gow's death, called him

> the last of our bards – no one again will ever play the Scotch music as he did. His sons in the quick measure were perhaps his equals, they gave force and spirit and fine execution to strathspeys and reels, but they never gave the slow, the tender airs with the real feeling for beauty their father had. Nor can anyone now hope to revive a style passing away. A few true fingers linger amongst us, but this generation will see the last of them.[9]

As with many other pronouncements of the death of a tradition, Mrs Grant was wrong, though her opinion of Gow's musicianship is well substantiated. And Nathaniel Gow's slow fiddle air, 'Miss Hamilton of Pencaitland', which also uses the bagpipe scale, shows all his father's delicacy. He also wrote 'Caller Herrin'' and 'The Fairy Reel'.

Slow airs still seem to show Niel Gow at his most personal and intimate. While his dance music was written for the community, it is difficult to imagine the 'Lament for the Death of his Second Wife' being written for anyone other than himself and his family, to express a loss he could scarcely articulate in any other way. Similarly, the jaunty diversity of his 'Farewell To Whisky' not only lifts the air above melancholy, but seems imbued with memory. The piece was written when whisky distilling was forbidden. The strathspey 'Whisky Welcome Back Again' was composed when the ban was lifted.

Gow played at society dances and local ceilidhs, his brother providing a bass accompaniment on the cello. And his music took him beyond the Inver Inn. He was a frequent guest at Blair Castle, where what was reputedly his fiddle is now kept, and even played for London society balls and functions. This practical aspect of Scottish music is something that has continued to the present day. Sir Jimmy Shand also played for dancers, and many Scottish traditional musicians, such as James Scott Skinner from Banchory, known as the Strathspey King, were also dancing masters.

Gow has no biographer, so the details of his life are scarce. We know he was patronised by three Dukes of Atholl and painted by Henry Raeburn, who treated Gow in the same way as his grander subjects. Gow has a contented, well-fed look about him. The portrait mirrors Burns's description almost exactly, except for the grey hair. The 'unabated vigour of the man' is obvious. He is seated, legs astride, in tartan trews, holding his fiddle. His face is clear, open and intelligent, with clear eyes and a sensuous mouth. The face is the most animated aspect of this ostensibly

9. Elizabeth Grant, *Memoirs of a Highland Lady*.

simple and dignified painting. It is easy to believe Gow berated the 'daft limmers' as reported and also to accept his supposed lack of conventional sophistication, exemplified in his disdain for written music.

In a Wave he Draws his Bow

Duncan Macmillan suggests that Raeburn's portrait of Niel Gow links the painter's art with Gow's music, 'and so he identifies with folk music the aesthetic character of his own approach to perception'.[10] It is an approach adopted by many writers and painters, both in their choice of subject and in its execution. Perhaps it is most obvious in David Wilkie's paintings, such as *Pitlessie Fair* and *The Blind Fiddler*. The first, painted when Wilkie was a young man, clearly echoes Burns's poem 'The Holy Fair' and carries the suggestion of the satirical impudence of Robert Fergusson's 'Hallow Fair', taking the ordinary landscape and events of Wilkie's own village as its subject. *The Blind Fiddler*, says Macmillan, 'has stepped directly out of the background of *Pitlessie Fair*'.

The identification with rural life and pleasure, the movement towards what was seen as honest and dignified simplicity, and the link between the work of writers and painters, especially the ways in which they shared themes, is analysed by Duncan Macmillan. He stresses the influence that the poetry of Robert Fergusson and Burns had on David Wilkie, and the ways in which Wilkie is 'comparing a harmonious society held together by human relationships, to one that is governed by the abstract values of law and profit' in a painting like *Distraining For Rent*. Closer still is the relationship between David Wilkie and his contemporary John Galt, whose novel *The Annals of the Parish* (1821) was turned down by the Edinburgh publisher Archibald Constable as being too Scottish and therefore too parochial. Constable changed his mind, but contemporary critics found Galt's themes and concerns too local to have any national significance, his characters too vulgar for the refined and gentrified – the emerging genteel Scots reader.

Which seems to encapsulate Galt's point entirely: his first-person voice took him to the heart of his subject, allowing us to observe both the public and the private character, something that was especially significant in matters of personal security and public persona. Galt's masterly use of changing internal registers mirrored his characters' continually shifting response to local conditions, something to which the autobiographical feel he sought to exploit was especially suited. His craft was to use parochial concerns as a springboard into national issues, to identify the empathetic character of his own approach to understanding, and by so doing to show that ordinary people were capable of sophisticated

10. Duncan Macmillan, *Scottish Art 1460–1990*.

reasoning. And he clearly hoped to demonstrate that the moral implications of what was being done by those in a position of power were as
significant and ultimately as ruinous to them and the community at
large as the social changes that were being effected. He sought to show
that great and grand schemes have a local dimension, and that their
effects on individuals and communities can point towards a greater
national malaise and potential tragedy.

When, in *The Annals of the Parish*, the venture to establish a new cotton
mill – symbolising parvenu fortunes and economic progress – collapses,
the village is left in a state of confusion and despair. A creeping sense of
alienation affects the whole community; what was seen as a boon, a
source of mutual harmony and prosperity, soon becomes the cause of
personal and communal ruin. The sense of community and something of
the spirit of the place are established when the narrator, Mr Balwhidder,
describes a penny wedding, so called because the celebration was a sort of
open house, to which everyone was invited and expected to make a contribution to the happy couple's future. A penny was as much as most folk
could afford, though there were also 'siller' weddings.

Galt's description matches Wilkie's picture. Writer and painter not
only share a similarity of subject, character and community, but, more
importantly, they share an atmosphere and a spirit of conviviality which
involves the whole community – where, after a drop of punch, the elderly
residents show the youngsters a step or two.

Wilkie depicts his subjects in a meticulous detail that underlines his
message. He uses a rather literary technique, insofar as his subject is
immediately obvious, though the details which comprise the picture, the
places where the story and character reside, are highlighted. The surroundings and the generational sweep, from the young girls on the left of
the picture to the matronly ladies on the right, the costumes and earthen
floor, are clearly depicted. The details are highlighted by his use of light,
which is especially telling since there is no obvious source. The light
comes from the artist's position in the audience, away from the painting.

This technique is repeated in *Distraining For Rent*, which has a dull
window centre right at the back of the picture. Again, it seems as though
the light is coming from the artist, whom we assume to have taken the
position of the kitchen range, so the light comes from the fire. The warm
red and yellow tones underscore this appearance, which gives a sense of
contrasting incongruity to the grimness of the subject. At first it is difficult to marry the sympathetic tones to the appearances of the subjects.

In *The Penny Wedding* Wilkie adds depth to his perspective through the
scenes at the back of the picture where wedding guests are seated at
tables, which draw one into the dark interior. The sweep of the picture,
from the musicians, the bride, groom and bridesmaid on the left, past the
table and dancers to the older guests on the right, gives a generational

message in keeping with the times; yet the wonder is that one can almost select the focus by concentrating on a particular group.

In *Distraining For Rent* the approach is more conventional. Fifteen characters are covered in a single sweep, from what could be friends or serving girls on the left of the picture, to the anxious, worried onlookers, perhaps representing the villagers, at the back by the door. These onlookers are perfectly balanced with the bailiff and his men, with the washstand and bowl. The impoverished couple have been beaten into submission. The pale wife with a child by her side and a baby on her lap looks as if she has just fainted, while her husband has their middle son beside him, a child no more than three or four who holds the rim of his father's jacket. His father sits at the table, his head supported by his left arm. The parents are too distraught to care even for their children; while behind the father what we assume to be his neighbours, friends or relations argue with the bailiff, dressed in long coat and three-cornered hat, anticipating Dickens's Mr Bumble by more than twenty years. His henchmen, clerk and porter, are behind him, and from the bed the picture fades to darkness. The spinning wheel, empty crib and bedding, well to the fore of the picture, now take on a significance beyond their immediate symbolism: the couple will be cursed, as the Bible predicts, to succeeding generations.

While painters had been using narrative techniques for centuries, Wilkie's detailed technique seeks to do more than depict. In *The Penny Wedding* he tries to encompass a newly married couple's hopes and expectations, while simultaneously locating their place in their community. And in *Distraining For Rent* he attempts to delineate a family's experience, presumably through no fault of their own, where a communal aspect is equally obvious, where the personal tragedy, as well as the motivating forces behind it, are there for all to see. This broad narrative technique would appear to be inspired by the novelists and story-tellers of the time, and both owe their moral authority to the philosophical mores of the period.

In Proportion to its Extent

Time and again, poets like Allan Ramsay, Robert Fergusson and Robert Burns, novelists like James Hogg, John Galt and Walter Scott return to identity and place, using the voice as the means of placing the narrator in both simultaneously, and by implication inviting the reader to enter the world the writer is anxious to preserve, expose and explore. Wilkie seeks to do no less as a painter. Often these writers appear to present little more than the evidence, yet their sweep and scope is so all-encompassing that they seem to have included most of Scottish life and character. But subsequent events they could scarcely have foreseen – such as the rising

it seems, are the starting points from which his works are built, and his purpose is as strong as Galt's. His sense of place is clear. It may not be immediately obvious that the paintings are set in Scotland, though the artist's name and the picture's titles do give sufficient, immediate clues, but the very settings and subjects of *Pitlessie Fair*, *The Blind Fiddler*, *Distraining For Rent* and *The Penny Wedding* themselves provide a location which brings the voice along with it. These people, we know, speak the language of Burns and Galt. 'These two paintings are a high point in his career,' says Duncan Macmillan, referring to *Distraining For Rent* and *The Penny Wedding*, 'but they are also a central point in the history of Scottish art. Somehow in them so many of the different streams of Enlightenment thought converge. Fed by this convergence, Wilkie stands alongside Burns and Scott.'

Vigorous and Earthy Pleasures

Wilkie studied at the Trustees' Academy in Edinburgh, which was opened in 1760 to provide instruction for pupils already in, or who were interested in following, a domestic trade. The original intention was to provide an industrial training school rather than an art academy, and though the third master, Alexander Runciman, appears to have challenged the emphasis, it was his successor, David Allan, who established a balance between the two approaches.

In David Allan's *Highland Wedding at Blair Atholl* (1780), also known as *The Highland Dance*, Niel Gow and his brother play for the guests. It is a rather stately affair, though the piper taking a dram behind the musicians on the left, the girl adjusting her garter, a piper's arm on her shoulder, the soldier and his lass on the right, the girl peeking from behind the foliage and the rather animated appearance of the male dancers in the centre of the picture suggest it is unlikely to remain so. The fiddlers hold their instruments informally, as did Niel Gow; and the dancers wear hard shoes, which obviously have a percussive effect.

Allan's later watercolour, *The Penny Wedding*, is an altogether livelier affair, extending the documentary interest of the earlier work. The fiddlers are more animated, the guests hungrier, and the dancers certainly more graceful, caught in an idyllic pose, as though they were experiencing the joy of life itself, extending the warmth and simple pleasure of pastoral existence. The view is such that children peer down from the rafters like approving guardian angels and figures descend from above by ladder to join the merriment. The only dissent is represented by two dogs in the corner growling over a bone.

In a pen-and-ink wash, dated some time between 1785 and 1795, Allan again used the theme of dance to try to encapsulate Highland society. Again, he shows a panoramic sweep. The man dancing with his back to us, his kilt revealing a fine and sturdy leg, is the only figure whose pose is the same. The positions of the couple in the centre are reversed, though their dance is no less stately. The musicians are to the right. A pair of pipers sit above the crowd, while a cellist tunes up behind them and the fiddler accepts a generous dram, poured by an unseen hand.

In all these works Allan seems to be simultaneously depicting and attempting to preserve a vision of an unspoiled rurality, which owes much of its intellectual underlay to the Ossianic vision of James Macpherson, but which is also upheld in the works of Robert Fergusson and, most especially, Robert Burns. It is a vision that places rural life and peasantry at the centre of the natural order, at the centre of human well-being and harmony, suggesting not only that they are the core of the nation's fabric, but also that whatever it means to be Scots, whatever parts of our national heritage are worth preserving, are to be found here, among these people, rather than among the urban residents with their relentless pursuit of wealth. In this sense, Wilkie was Allan's heir.

Burns collaborated with Allan from 1792 onwards, when Allan was commissioned by George Thomson to illustrate Burns's songs in a collection that included settings by Beethoven and Haydn. And from the surviving letters it is clear Burns felt that Allan's work complemented the songs entirely. Burns and Allan died in the same year, 1796. At the time of his death, Allan was working on illustrations for Burns's volume of *Scottish Songs*.

It is not too fanciful to suggest that Allan's and Wilkie's *Penny Wedding* paintings owe their style, subject and presentation to a curious piece by Jacob de Wet, *Highland Wedding*, which Sir John Clerk of Penicuik records as being part of his collection, crediting 1724 as when the work was painted. It is, says Duncan Macmillan, 'a rumbustious picture which introduces a new element into Scottish painting, the depiction of the vigorous and earthy pleasures of ordinary people'. Macmillan suggests, not unreasonably, that Allan Ramsay's additional verses to 'Christ's Kirk on the Green', the original of which is attributed to King James I, were inspired by de Wet's *The Highland Wedding*. Ramsay and Sir John Clerk were close friends, and as well as Fergusson and Burns, Allan and Wilkie also fell under his spell.

The Scottish Highlander Joined the American Indian

Tourists have been coming to Scotland since there were roads to take the coaches, not that they were ever up to much, if Sarah Murray's accounts are to be believed. From the middle of the eighteenth century, travellers came to see Europe's Noble Savage in his natural setting.

The circumstances affecting Scotland at that time were neither local nor particular. The central tenet of the Enlightenment was being challenged across Europe. The ideal – that by exercising his rational powers man might steadily improve the human condition – did not match the reality of increasing industrialisation and urbanisation. But, as is often the case, having believed in the cause and argued for it, despite the evidence of population on the move, polluted rivers and smoky skies, no one would say the ideal was wrong – it was just that events had not caught up with the ideal; so rather than call this belief wholly into question, an unstated compromise was reached, making those areas where man appeared to be living in his natural state appear all the more precious. If the apogee of human achievement was industrialisation, then reason had failed, having created a mockery of human improvement. Salvation would have to come from a different quarter; and Rousseau's advocacy of a return to the natural condition of our ancestors, that of an open and benign emotionalism, led philosophers back to nature.

And thus began the search for the Noble Savage, for those people whose condition most closely resembled that of our ancestors. 'The fate of the Jacobite Rebellion seemed to exemplify the sacrifice of an ancient and noble culture on the altar of the destructive forces of rationalist civilisation,' suggests Kenneth Simpson. So the Scottish Highlander joined the American Indian as prime contenders for the title, solving, at a stroke, the Scots problem of identity. 'The mantle of open emotionalism and natural benevolence fell upon the Scot and he seized it eagerly: here was an identity which gave him pre-eminence on the European stage; and at the same time Scotland's right to cultural partnership in the Union must surely be legitimised,' says Kenneth Simpson.[11] And right on cue arrived the Noble Savage as poet, Robert Burns, to be fêted by the Edinburgh *literati*, to read Henry Mackenzie's *The Man of Feeling* to Edinburgh ladies. They wept together. Then, as now, it was felt that to be openly emotional showed one to be a Noble Savage. It was a reaction against rational restraint. Reason, after all, had failed to deliver human improvement, and therefore man must restore contact with his original feelings.

It may seem rather odd, as Kenneth Simpson suggests, that Burns's persona in 'To a Mountain Daisy' should use such tender endearments to a flower whose stem he had severed with a plough; but in the context of the return to nature and the values of sensibility, such an attitude becomes understandable. In playing the part of the 'Heav'n-taught ploughman', Burns had to pretend to be divinely inspired. As a recent and eager, thoroughly Lowland recruit to establishing Scottish rather than Highland pre-eminence in the values of Noble Savagery, Burns's call for a spark of nature's fire reduced a widely read, intelligent and sophisticated writer to a peasant poet, a definition which has bedevilled and confused his reputation ever since, bringing forth in his wake a host of

11. Kenneth Simpson, *The Protean Scot.*

'hedgerow poets', as they were called in Ireland. If Burns could be a poet and a ploughman, then stand forth the butcher poets, the trades-man poets whose influence MacDiarmid deprecated. Nor was Burns the only one to manipulate, or be manipulated by, Noble Savagery. The very phrase carries a notion of separation, a sense of the remote. It is a con-junction of two disparate ideas, to which we may even aspire, suggesting something, a condition or a state in the broadest terms, that has been irremediably lost; another Eden.

Even now there is something remote about the Highlands of Scotland. They too are separated by their very name, which glows with inaccessi-bility. They are defined by their position on the edge of our geography, locked in an obscurity that places them at the knuckle end of Europe. The image shimmers in our imagination: snow-capped peaks where wild animals roam, rolling mists and ruined castles, lochs where monsters have been seen since the days of Columba. We picture a driech, rainy landscape with vegetation as bland as the steppe, where even the insects don't like us, especially when we wander around on foot. It is a place sep-arated by language, custom, and a past which underlines its remoteness.

Civilised Europeans did not necessarily see their Noble Savage per-sonified in the Highlands, but they did consider what they saw there the closest extant approximation to him. And this attitude hardened the existing division in Scottish attitudes. When Boswell and Johnson returned from the Highlands, their safety and arrival was celebrated in Edinburgh, causing Johnson to comment, 'I am really ashamed of the congratulations which we receive. We are addressed as if we had made a voyage to Nova Zembia, and suffered five persecutions in Japan.'

The Highlands provided European Romanticism with the perfect land-scape. It was a place of fantasy for Goethe, Napoleon, Mendelssohn, Coleridge, Keats and the Wordsworths, a place that was rendered remote to its very inhabitants, a landscape upon which anything could be written.

In the Bardic Oral Tradition

James Macpherson was a boy living in Inverness when the Jacobite stan-dard was raised at Glenfinnan. He knew some Gaelic and, as Rory Watson has remarked, 'had contact with the oral tradition, as well as considerable sympathy for Highland culture'.[12]

As a handsome tutor and teacher in his mid-twenties, he surrendered himself to fame. His reputation had been made in 1760 when he pub-lished *Fragments of Ancient Poetry Collected in the Highlands of Scotland and Translated from the Gaelic or Erse Language*, which were supposed to be love poems and battle verses from the Ossianic tales of the third century,

12. Roderick Watson, *The Literature of Scotland.*

handed down in the oral tradition, or copied and now translated by Macpherson. These fragments were followed by *Fingal, Temora* and the *Works of Ossian.* 'There is probably no Scottish literary event in our history that created so great a stir at home and abroad,' wrote D. S. Thomson.[13] Burns, Scott and Byron were devotees, and Napoleon is said to have carried a copy everywhere. Sheridan thought Ossian 'excelled Homer in the Sublime and Virgil in the Pathetic', fixing it 'as a standard of feeling . . . a thermometer by which they could judge of the warmth of everybody's heart'. More importantly, Ossian joined the Noble Savage 'as a key figure in the evolution of Romanticism from Goethe to the Gothic novel'.[14]

Macpherson claimed he was preserving the traditions of the Highlands, that Highlanders were refugees from the Flood. Samuel Johnson famously claimed the poems were fraudulent; David Hume suggested Macpherson should produce the originals and, after Macpherson's death, Henry Mackenzie was appointed convener of a committee of the Highland Society of Scotland established to investigate and authenticate the Ossian poems. They concluded that while poems existed which could be termed Ossianic, Macpherson had added passages of his own.

To some, the Ossian controversy 'is striking proof of the fact that literary works neither exist outside national identities and traditions nor arise in isolation from the spirit and intellectual climate of their day'.[15] To Kenneth Simpson, 'The fate of Scottish culture is inseparable from Scotland's experience of Romanticism, an experience that was quite singular among the countries of Europe'.[16] He adds that when the first stirrings of Romanticism were felt, Scotland was no longer an independent nation, 'and as a people she was already preoccupied with an image of herself that was rooted in a distant and largely unreal past'.

Macpherson's influence reached well beyond literature. Remnants of the cult survive in sites such as Ossian's Hall at the Hermitage, and a number of Ossian Stones. In 1772 Alexander Runciman painted the Hall of Ossian for Sir John Clerk's son, Sir James, who had sent Runciman and his brother John to Italy to study painting, on the understanding that when the brothers returned they would decorate Sir John's new home, Penicuik House. John Runciman died in Naples in 1768.

'The Hall of Ossian was a room thirty-six feet by twenty-four feet with a coved ceiling,' writes Duncan Macmillan.

> The central part of the ceiling was an oval in which Ossian was seen singing to an audience on the sea-shore. The four corners of the rectangle of the

13. D. S. Thomson, 'Macpherson and Ossian' in David Daiches (ed.), *The New Companion to Scottish Culture.*
14. Roderick Watson, *op. cit.*
15. *Collins Encyclopaedia of Scotland.*
16. Kenneth Simpson, *op. cit.*

ceiling left by the oval were filled with four river gods, the rivers of
Scotland; the Tay, the Spey, the Tweed and the Clyde, gigantic
Michelangelesque figures, but each set in a landscape of appropriate character. In the cove, that is the curved surface between the flat of the wall and
the flat of the ceiling, there were twelve compositions, mostly, but not all,
illustrating the poetry of Ossian. The exceptions were scenes from 'the era
of Ossian' as James Macpherson described it in an introductory essay to his
publication of the poems.[17]

Runciman later painted his friend Robert Fergusson as *The Prodigal Son*,
while Fergusson celebrated the Ossian paintings in 'On First Seeing a
Collection of Pictures by Mr Runciman' and, as Duncan Macmillan spec-
ulates, probably imitated them in his 'Ode on the Rivers of Scotland'.

'The Ossian controversy . . . transformed the idea of ancient Scotland
from a land of inaccessible savages ill-disposed to civilisation, to a nation
of Dark Age poetic heroes, with a primitive culture haunting heather-clad
fastnesses. Travellers ventured north to emote at frightful waterfalls; and
suitably ghastly grottoes, moss houses, hermitages, ancient springs, vista
fillers and dovecotes were erected to satisfy the yearning,' says Charles
McKean.[18]

And while none were better than Sir Walter Scott at pitting the two
Scotlands against each other – as in *Rob Roy*, when he refers to his
eponymous hero as a kind of Robin Hood who conducted his brigandry
40 miles from the city of Glasgow in the Augustan age of Queen Anne –
Malcolm Chapman clearly delineates the lasting effects: 'Since the
eighteenth century . . . the Scottish people have increasingly looked to
the Highlands to provide a location for an autonomy to which they could
lodge their own political, literary, and historical aspirations. They have
thereby been allowed to reap all the benefits of the Union, while at the
same time retaining a location for all the virtues of sturdy independence.'[19]

Like a Fiery Cross

A landscape devoid of people has become one of many symbols for the
country, while the history, language and culture of that region have come
to symbolise the nation as a whole. A recent Gaelic education television
programme was called *Speaking Our Language*, despite the fact that four
fifths of Scots live in the Central Lowlands, where Scots and English are

17. Duncan Macmillan, *op. cit.*
18. Charles McKean, 'The Scottishness of Scottish Architecture' in Paul H. Scott,
    Scotland: A Concise Cultural History.
19. Malcolm Chapman, *The Gaelic Vision in Scottish Culture.*

traditionally spoken. The programme ignored a common Gaelic complaint that the language is being emulsified, that local variations have been taken over by Lewis Gaelic.

Gaelic currently has minority-language status, which means television viewers can watch a soap opera, cookery programmes, DIY programmes and the like in Gaelic. Despite the £14 million subsidy, continuing census figures show a decline. Per head of population, more is spent on Gaelic education than on education for English speakers in Scotland. Gaelic schools and playgroups flourish across the country, but more than half the Gaelic speakers in Scotland live outwith the Gaelic area. The problem seems to be that to young people, life appears elsewhere: American and Australian soap operas and pop music sung in mid-Atlantic accents are considered trendier, and peer-group pressure to speak English is more powerful than any number of initiatives to encourage native speakers. Yet the rock group Runrig use the language as a means of establishing their identity, in much the same way as The Proclaimers use the accents of Fife – to separate them from the pop-group norm. And despite their enormous popularity, the linguistic barrier remains.

The Highlanders' language, culture and society traditionally separated them from the rest of Scotland. It is possible that the outward appearances of Highland life and society were similar to those of the rest of the country, but nowhere else did kinship and family form the basis of a social and political structure, nor was any other part of the country so remote as to afford the likes of Johnson and Boswell the approbation and admiration of their London society friends when they risked life and limb venturing north, to see unknown sights and experience what could be found nowhere else on the British Isles.

The Highlands is still a darkly beautiful area whose concerns seem to separate it from the rest of the country as surely as it is separated by its geology – it is said that the oldest rocks in Europe are to be found there. The National Parks debate is central here, even though the hills are scarred with ski runs, and whenever a new Munro is claimed, or a new peak is added to an existing Munro, within weeks the hillside is blemished by a new pathway to the summit. These same hills are 800 million years old. While the debate centres on preservation, in some areas land management appears to be motivated by a desire to return to a wilderness state. Intervention was required recently to preserve Victorian lodge houses on the Cairngorm estate which had been scheduled for demolition. Walkers trudge along the abandoned railway tracks, stalkers' paths, and the roads built by Generals Wade and Caulfeild to ease troop movements, and the Skye Bridge has the highest tolls in Europe. As always, it is the locals rather than the tourists who are leading the protests.

Across the country, village communities are dying because facilities such as the local shop or the village hall are not being used. New residents stay in at nights and prefer to drive to the nearest supermarket for their shopping. Other changes are more pernicious. Incomers are often active in forming a community council to establish speed limits and street lighting, things whose absence often attracted them to the village in the first place. Or cottages have become holiday homes.

Living in Highland Perthshire, with his home and studio located in the school he once attended, and watching the changes that have taken place in his community, these issues are very pertinent to the songwriter Dougie MacLean. For him national identity is both personal and local. It is a question of belonging.

His concerts sell out wherever he goes, and though he has written music for film and theatre, songs are his trademark. Well-crafted and lyrical, often with deceptively complex guitar accompaniments, they cover a range of subjects from exile and longing to the treatment of the Australian Aborigines. A Dougie MacLean song is immediately recognisable. As with most Scottish songwriters, he saves his strongest passions for the issues nearest home. MacLean can carry a strong, direct and political message, and though his targets are seldom obvious, the meaning is always clear. When he mourns a loss, it is the loss of a tradition, the continuing rebirth succeeding generations bring to a place, something the Highlands have irremediably lost. He takes us behind the anger to make a point that is political, nationalist, protesting and caring, a volatile combination:

> Let me tell you about the land that you play on,
> Your gain is our ultimate loss.
> Let me tell you about the soil you decay on
> And hold it up to you like a fiery cross.

The tourists and part-time residents are using the Highlands in much the same way as the aristocracy from Queen Victoria's arrival at Balmoral onwards have always used the Highlands: as a place where one can relieve the strains of city living. Although the Highlander fights for the protection of his way of life and language in the face of such barbarity, the language and mores of the white settlers have come to dominate the argument. And it's easy to see why. As in most things, John Ruskin put the case with his usual combination of enthusiasm and insight: 'There is no country in which the roots of memory are so entwined with the beauty of nature instead of the pride of men; no other in which the song of Auld Lang Syne could have been written.'[20]

The return of the Jacobite army from Derby is supposedly commemorated in the internationally famous song 'Loch Lomond', which, like

20. John Ruskin, *Praeterita*.

most of the popular Jacobite songs, can be sung in Scots or English. 'Scarcely anybody knows how to sing it,' says John Purser.

> It has heaped upon its head more appalling and ignorant performances than any song has a right to bear. Its subject-matter is one of bitter and ironic tragedy. The Jacobite soldier awaiting execution claims he will reach Scotland before his companion as his spirit will get there first by the low road. This is usually rendered by singers and arrangers with an inane chirpiness more suited to selling washing-up liquid.[21]

'In many countries Scotland is known as a land of romance,' wrote Edwin Muir in *The Scots and Their Country*, published in 1946. 'There is a genuine romantic strain in the Scottish character, and especially among the peasantry. Scotland is a country where history turns very easily into legend.'

'Leave the bleak regions . . . for the cattle to breed in, and let men remove to situations where they can exert themselves and thrive. The traveller who looks only at the outside of things might easily assent to this reasoning,' Robert Southey wrote of the Highlands, adding,

> I have never – not even in Galacia – seen any human habitations so bad as the Highland *black-houses* . . . The worst of the black houses are *bothies* – made of very large turfs, from 4 to 6 feet long, fastened with wooden pins to a rude wooden frame. The Irish cabin, I suppose, must be such a heap of peat with or without stones . . . . But these men-sties are not inhabited, as in Ireland, by a race of ignorant and ferocious barbarians, who can never be civilised till they are regenerated – till their very nature is changed. Here you have a quiet, thoughtful, contented, religious people, susceptible of improvement, and willing to be improved. To transplant these people from their native mountain glens to the sea coast, and require them to become some cultivators, others fishermen, occupations to which they have never been accustomed – to expect a sudden and total change of habits in the existing generation . . . to expel them by process of law from their black houses, and if they demur in obeying the ejectment, to oust them by setting fire to these combustible tenements – this surely is as little defensible on the score of policy as of morals.[22]

Time has vindicated Southey's judgement in every aspect, except his opinion of the Irish. Nor was he alone in condemning the policy as

---

21. John Purser, *op. cit.*
22. Robert Southey, *Journal of a Tour in Scotland.*

shortsighted, cruel and, ultimately, stupid. Condemning what he calls 'this epidemick desire of wandering', Dr Samuel Johnson urges an end to emigration:

> In more fruitful countries, the removal of one only makes room for the suc-
> cession of another: but in the Hebrides, the loss of an inhabitant leaves a
> lasting vacuity; for nobody born in any other parts of the world will choose
> this country for his residence, and an Island once depopulated will remain
> a desert, as long as the present facility of travel gives every one, who is dis-
> contented and unsettled, the choice of his abode.[23]

Visiting Skye in 1773, Johnson and Boswell saw many instances of Clearance and the simultaneous militarisation that was in progress. Between 1740 and 1815 fifty infantry battalions were raised, mainly in the Highlands, as well as fencible and militia regiments. Francis Thompson suggests that, having seen their clan chiefs turned into landlords, and being at the mercy of their agents, facing eviction, emigration or starvation, Highlanders turned to the Free Kirk, which was formed after the Disruption in 1843.

Prior to 1886 and the arrival of the Crofters' Holdings Act, no statutory legislation was applicable to the crofting situation in Scotland. Even the term crofting emerged slowly, deriving, it is thought, from the Gaelic, though another source gives the word an Anglo-Saxon origin, 'certainly not Gaelic'. It first appeared in Highland records in the nineteenth cen-tury and quickly acquired its specialised connotation.

The crofts came with the Clearances. A system of smallholding that is especially associated with the Highlands and Islands, it has never been able to sustain the families who manage the crofts, far less the Highland population as a whole, and while the Reform Act of 1976 made it easier for crofters to buy their crofts, many have been amalgamated to form viable units, since crofts are often incapable of providing even a subsis-tence living. This leaves the crofter to do what his ancestors have done: to supplement his income from other sources. Kelp-gathering and fishing used to be most popular; now it is bed and breakfast and fish farms.

Essential Silence Chills and Blesses

Many who settled in the Highlands of Scotland may have arrived with the global village, but most come to retire or to carry on their businesses, usu-ally in tourism, hotels, guesthouses, restaurants and the like. Emma Wood came from Norfolk to escape Thatcherism, arriving in Sutherland in 1989.

---

23. Samuel Johnson, *Journey to the Western Isles of Scotland.*

I had to admit my wonderful life wasn't really working out. I would never have enough of the views from my steading or tire of the company of the folk who were my neighbours, incomers and natives alike. But unlike many of the English in that part of Sutherland, I had not gone there to retire. All the casual work available in the area like tree-planting, deer stalking and farm work wasn't quite compatible with looking after a toddler and I'd failed to find anybody interested in making mutual childcare arrangements. So it appeared I was not properly qualified to make a living in Sutherland and I had begun to realise that living in the empty, remote Highlands did not nowadays entail the same sort of frugal subsistence that had, perforce, been practised there by earlier generations. I was irrevocably tied to the demands of the modern cash economy. For one thing, I needed a reliable car which would not grind to a halt on a lonely road (few roads in Sutherland are anything else) or fail to start when I had to fetch vital supplies. Heating can be quite expensive 300 feet above sea-level and only 1200 miles (less than the distance to Paris) from the Arctic Ocean. I wasn't trying to survive in a desert but there was definitely less margin of error than in more convenient, less spectacular places. Yet it was not just pride which stopped me from considering going back to England for good. I was hooked: I had revelled in the Highlands where, as Robert Louis Stevenson wrote, 'essential silence chills and blesses'.[24]

A move a few miles south to Easter Ross initially diminished her sense of isolation and put her into contact with other women, who weren't all that interested in how she came north to improve her quality of life. They were, she says, more concerned about how far away their men would have to go to earn a living. But their attitude gave rise to a newer feeling: 'It was in Easter Ross that I understood a little of what it must be like to be judged and found wanting according to the relatively accidental factor of birthplace or skin colour.'

Wood made her own survey, which revealed similar attitudes. One woman who moved north in the 1960s encountered a 'fiercely anti-English, anti-outsider atmosphere' in school: 'Enough,' she said, 'to stay with you forever.' Married to a Highlander and part of the community, she nevertheless had seen changes brought by the arrival of two other non-indigenous groups. Firstly, what she called the Hi-Jimmies, the Glaswegians who came north looking for work. These have, she claimed, radically changed the identity of the Highlands. She was harsher on the second group: the English White Settlers, the ones she called the quality-of-life brigade, those who come north after making money selling their homes in the south. 'Oh,' writes Emma Wood, 'for punctuation marks to

24. Emma Wood, *Notes From the North.*

denote dismissive contempt in [the] voice of a speaker.' Wood suggests that English incomers' feelings of insecurity can be blamed on their failure to get involved in local affairs, something far more common than the stereotypical incomer who tactlessly tries to take over everything or the dour implacable natives who resist southern innovation.

Another informant told her that, apart from her Englishness, she could think of no reason why she should have been shunned by her neighbours for the five years since she, her husband and their family arrived from an English city. Her husband's job had brought him north; they felt they could take advantage of a strong rural community and all it implied. 'I've never felt lonely like I've felt lonely up here,' she said.

The common feeling is that incomers become aware of what it must be like to be black in a predominantly white area, though others have found integration easier because of their work. Emma Wood still lives in the Highlands, where she makes a living teaching English. 'Some of my closest moments with real (i.e. born and bred here) Highlanders are with the youngsters to whom I give English lessons to help them prepare for the Scottish Examination Board exams,' she says.

The economic costs of Highland life are reflected in the price of petrol: Scottish motorists are paying far more than the average UK motorist to run their cars. The Scottish Office Central Research Unit reported that for something like thirty communities, the garage is their only local shop, though shopkeepers suggest the shops subsidise the petrol.

The oil companies seem to hold the key to the mystery of why rural motorists are charged a premium rate. Figures obtained by the *Herald* at the beginning of 1999 showed that in 1994 'a network of 40 of Esso's most remote sites in the Highlands and Islands was making £1 million a year profit'.[25] And in November 1998 research by the Scottish Office found that many of the most remote sites are also the most profitable, though reliable reasons could not be established 'because of the low level of response to financial questions'.[26]

Tourism, we are told, is worth £2700 million a year to the Scottish economy. 'It has genuine, indigenous growth potential for itself, and is highly influential in performance and perception mode for every other potential inward investment. At last count it employed more than 177,000 people . . . and accounted for 14% of the entire Highland economy.'[27]

25. *Herald*, 31 March 1999.
26. *Ibid.*
27. *Herald*, 27 March 1999.

Images of Tragic Grandeur

William McTaggart was a Highlander. His landscapes are unique: immediately recognisable, with a highly developed and refined sense of colour and tone. His desire to paint exactly what he saw, to represent the landscape of the west coast of Scotland in all its moods, has brought comparisons with the Impressionists. Like them, he valued truth over beauty and the truth of light and colour were of paramount importance.

He painted outdoors, initially in the summer, making oil and water-colour sketches which he would work into larger canvases in his Edinburgh studio over the winter. By the late 1870s, spring and early summer found him working in Carnoustie, on the Angus coast, moving to Machrihanish, near Campbeltown, where he was born, to paint until October. In 1889 he settled in Broomieknowe, Midlothian, where he painted landscapes, returning to the sea in summer.

His work has an immediacy of light and context, and his canvases have the feeling of being painted out of doors, on the spot. The paint is applied quickly and McTaggart seems to have worked the whole canvas simultaneously. This is especially obvious in his treatment of the Scottish weather, which is something of a recurring, if not a central, theme. He painted isolated shorelines and deserted beaches, where a few children play. Most of his landscapes contain people.

Though his subject is Scotland, from farmlands and snowscapes to storms and the gentle lapping of a single wave, McTaggart's move to the east coast of Scotland seemed to intensify his love of the west, and he not only sought to represent the landscape, but also its history. Implicit in his paintings of storms is the effect on a sea-faring community; and he carries this sense of community into prehistory, with the coming of Columba, a scene of idyllic charm and contentment. But he was also aware of the circumstances that forced a people to abandon their way of life, turning them into fishermen. *The Sailing of the Immigrant Ship* is in direct contrast to Tom Faed's treatment of the same subject. McTaggart shows the ship on the horizon, in full sail. Light is breaking from beneath a dark cloud and there is the hint of a rainbow. The foreground carries the suggestion of figures on the shore, barely sketched, as though they are in the act of disappearing: a woman alone, with a baby in her arms, a howling dog in the centre and empty boats by the shoreline that almost mingle with the sea.

'What is extraordinary about this group of pictures,' says Duncan Macmillan, 'is the way that they tackle themes that were topical, moving and of deep personal significance to the artist himself, yet they ignore completely the Victorian conventions of narrative and instead develop McTaggart's own landscape of subjective mood . . . to the point where it can realise by almost abstract means a series of images of tragic grandeur.'[28]

Nothing There That Looks Like Scotland

Where is history's place for Arthur Freed, producer of *Brigadoon*, who came here looking for locations in which to shoot his film and later recalled, 'I went to Scotland and found nothing there that looks like Scotland.'

Neil Paterson, Crieff's best-known film resident in the days before Ewan McGregor, won an Oscar for *Room at the Top*; in Scotland he is better remembered as author of *The China Run* and *Scotch Settlement*, which he memorably adapted as *The Kidnappers*, starring Duncan Macrae. The film was remade in 1990 as *The Little Kidnappers*, starring Charlton Heston, who, in keeping with most of the cast, affects an unrecognisable accent.

The novels of Walter Scott and Robert Louis Stevenson, John Buchan, Compton Mackenzie, Alistair Maclean and A. J. Cronin have done their bit for Scottish moving-image culture, and offerings such as *Geordie* or *The Bridal Path* could also be relied upon to reinforce stereotypical imagery. From *The Prime of Miss Jean Brodie* or Vera-Ellen in *Happy Go Lovely*, set in Edinburgh, Bertrand Tavernier's *Deathwatch* in Glasgow, Brigitte Bardot in *Two Weeks in September*, filmed at Dirleton, Kirk Douglas on the Ballachulish Ferry in *Catch Me a Spy*, or Bette Davis as *Madame Sin* on Mull, Scotland has provided an atmospheric setting similar to that given by Robert Garioch, Edinburgh's poet laureate, who was the pianist at the Lyric Cinema in Nicolson Square. But it's not our only contribution.

Donald Crisp not only claimed he gave Chaplin his first film break, he also appeared with Buster Keaton, played General Grant in *Birth of a Nation*, appeared with Charles Laughton in *Mutiny on the Bounty*, won an Oscar as Best Supporting Actor in John Ford's *How Green Was My Valley*, and cornered the market in J. M. Barrie adaptations by appearing in both *The Little Minister* and *What Every Woman Knows*. Crisp also appeared in *The Bonnie Briar Bush* and in both versions of *Greyfriars Bobby*, the first provocatively titled *Challenge to Lassie*, in which the Skye terrier becomes a collie.

Eric Campbell, born in Dunoon, joined Fred Karno's Circus. This took him to America, where, in the two years before his death, he became the perfect villain for Charlie Chaplin, memorably appearing in *Easy Street*. Campbell's funeral oration was delivered by his friend Stan Laurel. Hopalong Cassidy's faithful partner, Andy Clyde, was born in Blairgowrie and raised in Helensburgh, birthplace of Jack Buchanan and Deborah Kerr. Clyde appeared with Crisp in *The Little Minister*, and his father, John Clyde, was Hollywood's first Rob Roy.

28. Duncan Macmillan, *op. cit.*

The antidote to *Geordie* or *The Bridal Path* could well be *Whisky Galore!* In *Scotland The Movie* David Bruce suggests that Alexander Mackendrick and Compton Mackenzie provided a cultural dimension which gave the narrative a credible context. He also points to the collaborative nature of the production:

> The billeting of the eighty outsiders in bed-and-breakfast accommodation around the island meant that the accent and rhythms of Barra speech and the patterns of Barra life were absorbed automatically by the cast. There was a great deal more of the real Barra, Eriskay and South Uist in the fictional Great and Little Todday than would have been the case with more usual filmmaking practices.

Alexander Mackendrick was born in Boston to a Glasgow family. At the age of six he came to Scotland, attended Hillhead High School and Glasgow School of Art, and joined Ealing Studios as a writer in 1946 after the end of the Second World War. Five of his nine films were made for Ealing. Mackendrick made *The Maggie*, to his own script, on Islay.

David Bruce has suggested that Michael Powell and Emeric Pressburger's *I Know Where I'm Going*, which was shot on Mull, offers a greater sense of place than any incoming film, with the possible exception of the Mackendrick films. Powell included an obligatory ceilidh sequence, complete with choir and choirmaster, but there is also a lovely series of visual gags, such as a phone box near a waterfall which makes conversation impossible. 'The tale of a stranger subverted by myth and purified by ordeal is certainly not unusual in cinema but it is rarely presented with such redeeming wit,' says Bruce. Powell's attachment to Scottish islands had been established in *The Spy in Black*, which he filmed in Orkney, and *The Edge of the World*, his early film about the St Kilda evacuation.

Laurel and Hardy in *Bonnie Scotland*, Robert Donat on the Forth Bridge in *The 39 Steps*, Lillian Gish as *Annie Laurie* – none are as memorable as Orson Welles playing a Highland Laird in *Trouble in the Glen*. It is the perfect non-believer's antidote to *Citizen Kane* reverence, even better than the sherry adverts. 'There are some occasions when even the most determined effort to suspend disbelief is of no avail,' says David Bruce. 'Faced with the sight of Orson Welles as a Perthshire Laird resplendent in kilt, even the most dedicated audience was liable to collapse in laughter.'

But it appeared in the mid-1950s, a time when light Scottish subjects, featuring delightfully cunning natives and spectacularly lonely scenery, were in vogue. David Niven, bedecked in tartan, had followed Ivor Novello in playing *Bonnie Prince Charlie*. The music for the 1948 extravaganza was by Iain Whyte, founder and conductor of the BBC Scottish Symphony Orchestra, and Peter Watkins' *Culloden* had yet to appear. Based on John Prebble's account of the battle, Watkins' film used a succession of revolutionary techniques, such as interviewing protagonists and editing, thus placing the viewer in the thrust of the action. It remains a powerful and telling statement, although it has in many ways been overshadowed by *The War Game*, which Watkins made three years later; the BBC, who commissioned the film, refused to show it, causing him to abandon television film-making altogether.

Bill Douglas was 'one of the indisputably great film-makers Scotland has produced'. Few would argue with David Bruce's assessment. Douglas made three short films, *My Childhood*, *My Ain Folk* and *My Way Home*, of such harsh clarity and realism that he was entirely shunned by mainstream commercial film-production concerns. His was a personal cinema; Jamie's story is his own. When *My Childhood* was first shown in 1972, it was unlike anything Scottish cinema or literature was producing. Douglas used a very literary technique, one which cinema has yet to embrace fully. Cinema has still to find a way to adopt fully Douglas's unrelenting poetic vision. His honesty and integrity make uncomfortable viewing. He will not let us look away.

Douglas predated what is now known as urban realism with a hard and uncompromising picture of his own childhood poverty and a vision of Scotland that is as far removed from the type of film being made in this country in the early 1970s as it is possible to be. He never shrinks away, holding shots and retaining silences until they are almost unbearable, allowing ideas and subtext to be absorbed before moving on, and, by making it clear that Jamie's family are an unexceptional part of the community, he draws disturbing pictures. He never tries for sympathy or nostalgia, nor does he cheat. He is true to himself and his own vision in a way that is uncommon for any artist, but is so rare as to be almost without parallel in cinema. His influence and importance can only grow.

Scotland's cinematic contribution seems likely to increase, with government pronouncements about establishing an industry and using native talent coming more regularly than ever before. Bill Forsyth, Billy Connolly, Robert Carlyle, Ewan McGregor, Bill Paterson, Brian Cox and Sean Connery are the most obvious names from an impressive list of those who have contributed to world cinema; though with Scottish film-makers following literature's current preoccupation with the city, Highland life is where it has always been – a backdrop to the rest of society, forever a bit-part player where landscape is the star. The irony is that we cannot even have our own landscape in films such as *The Highlander*, *Rob Roy* and *Braveheart*. If films such as *Orphans* or *Ratcatcher* have shown the way to a new Scottish cinema, it is on a trail blazed by Bill Douglas. And proof of a Scottish film industry will come when the Highlanders and their landscape are represented in a way they would recognise, in the same manner as their poets have shown them for a generation.

Not on Calvary

My eye is not on Calvary
nor on Bethlehem the Blessed,
but on a foul-smelling backland in Glasgow,
where life rots as it grows;
and on a room in Edinburgh,
a room of poverty and pain,
where the diseased infant
writhes and wallows till death.

Gaelic poetry was transformed by 'Calvary', written when Sorley Maclean
(Somhairle MacGill-Eain) was a student in Edinburgh in the 1930s. And
the last fifty years or so have seen an almost unprecedented rise in Gaelic
writing, remarkable given that a survey carried out in 1991 concluded
there were approximately 65,000 Gaelic speakers in Scotland. A recent
assessment gave rise to the blunt statement: 'By the second half of the
20th century almost no one spoke only Gaelic.'

Outside influences on contemporary Gaelic poetry were evident from
the first, especially in Maclean; he had met and like almost everyone else
had come under the influence of MacDiarmid. The publication of *Dian di
Eimhir agus Dain Eile* in 1943 is generally regarded as a milestone in modern
Gaelic poetry. It cemented Maclean's reputation. Though his poetic output
was never prolific, the extraordinary tension of the love lyrics, evident even
in the author's translations, his musical and opaque images and metaphysical conclusions were unknown in Gaelic poetry. The passion and
commitment of the love poems, especially the haunting images of desola-
tion, have lifted Maclean's influence beyond the Gaelteachd.

As with MacDiarmid, a number of poets followed Maclean's example,
not always writing in Gaelic alone. A near contemporary, George
Campbell Hay (Deorsa MacIan Deorsa), son of the author of *Gillespie*, was
a self-taught Gaelic speaker, who also wrote in Scots and English. Derek
Thomson (Ruaridh MacThomais) is a critic and a scholar as well as being
the founding editor of the enormously influential Gaelic quarterly *Gairm*.
His poetry often subtly delineates a continuing problem for Native Gaels.
Thomson's engagement with his Lewis boyhood carries the implicit
recognition that the island is no longer an environment in which he can
reasonably work, and therefore he can barely live there:

I never noticed the coffins,
though they were sitting all around me;
I did not recognise the English braid,
the Lowland varnish being applied to the wood,
I did not read the words on the brass.

Donald MacAulay (Domhnall MacAmhlaigh) is another Lewis scholar-poet, whose poetry also bears the influence of Pound. He presents a wonderful twist on the island's grim religious observances, simultaneously deploring the narrowness of religion and seeing psalm-singing and prayer as 'my people's access to poetry'.

Iain Crichton Smith (Iain Mac a'Ghobhainn) died in November 1998. He is remarkable in that as he got older, his range of subjects widened and he seemed to be finding a truly expressive poetic voice to which he was entirely suited. Life had prepared him, and he moved from autobiography into a world of imagination where his hold on reality is bound by love.

> Listen, I have flown through darkness towards joy,
> I have put the mossy stones away from me,
> and the thorns, the thistles, the brambles,
> I have swum upward like a fish
> through the black wet earth, the ancient roots
> which insanely fight with each other
> in a grave which creates a treasure house
> of light upward-springing leaves.

He came from Bayble, the same Lewis village as Derick Thomson, and was also from a Free Church background. He was one of the finest Scottish writers of the century, occupying a position many Scottish writers have taken, from Burns and Scott to MacDiarmid and Maclean, where he is comparable with no other. The quantity of his output masked its extraordinary quality. His poetry in English alone is comparable with W. H. Auden and Robert Lowell, yet he also wrote novels, stories, plays and criticism in both Gaelic and English and was amazed and appalled by the prolixity of Scott:

> Walking the room together in this merciless
> galaxy of manuscripts and notes
> I am exhausted by such energy.

Iain Crichton Smith was capable of finding as much source material from a tin can on the beach as in a galaxy of stars, often turning to familiar literary sources for inspiration, especially Shakespeare. But his constant, almost cyclical return is to the places where he lived and to the people, to the ordinary circumstances of the wind, the rain and a woman coming home from the shops. It would be possible to construct a picture of contemporary Highland village life from details in the poetry of Iain Crichton Smith.

Many poems have an autobiographical feel; and though there are autobiographical sequences – *Lewis 1928–1945, Aberdeen University 1945–1949, National Service 1950–1952, Clydebank and Dumbarton*

1952–1955, Oban 1955–1982 and *Taynuilt 1982* – these poems not only detail the poet's individual circumstances, they also carry an indication of what he was thinking. Iain Crichton Smith's intellectual life often seems more important than reality itself. His work often reduces places and his experience down to a series of images which he seems incapable of understanding, invariably twinning opposites, which he treats with opposing emotions of love and hate.

He does not sit well with his contemporaries. There is a feeling with the post-MacDiarmid poets – Norman MacCaig, George Mackay Brown, Edwin Morgan – that their work is in many ways a reaction to MacDiarmid, that MacCaig concentrated on subjects MacDiarmid seldom tackled, Edinburgh and the countryside, subjects MacDiarmid would have found, or would have affected to find, trivial. Like MacDiarmid, Edwin Morgan avoids introspection by reaching into space, and Mackay Brown is more like MacCaig, an observant poet of place, who celebrates the Orkneys and their mythology as surely as he wishes to preserve a way of life he found threatened by modernity. All their work is crafted; all their work can be intellectually and often sensually stimulating. The feeling is that they became poets by force of will. Morgan and MacCaig, for example, never lost their academic backgrounds. With Crichton Smith, the feeling is that he did not care for his work, that once it was written it was forgotten, that he wrote because he could do little else, that his reading informed his poetry and that he had plumbed depths few others could know, which gave him an enormous freedom, a freedom of personal expression.

Like Edwin Morgan, Iain Crichton Smith has brought us to the position where Scottishness, and especially Scottish identity, is not defined in any narrow way, looking towards a series of ideas or symbols. Writers now know who they are and where they come from and can pick aspects of the past to investigate or experiment without being trapped by language. Morgan's experiments and investigations and Crichton Smith's ability to use a small-town mentality as a source of humour and comic invention have brought us to a place which is anything but obvious.

The novella *Murdo* contains the essential Iain. Murdo stares at the white mountain, trying to write. He writes to Dante, asking where his work was first published, tries to order *War and Peace* by Hughie Macleod from the library and leaves his father-in-law a stone in his last will and testament. The humour and compassion, the wonderful sense of isolation he generates in a few sentences and, especially, the feeling of a free mind on the verge of collapse, confined by the narrowness and restrictions of living in a small Scottish town, raise the story and its miraculous inventions beyond Highland life. The Highland life Murdo knows and the romantic life that Sorley Maclean says 'has been predicated on the Gael and his poetry' are entirely separate. Murdo struggles as much against his background and the day-to-day circumstances of his existence, the people in the village and what they think of him, as against his self. Indeed, it could be said that the absence of romanticism in Murdo's life and his recognition of this need is the cause of his woes. This is one of Crichton Smith's most delicious ironies.

Sorley Maclean has this to say about Gaelic romanticism:

> The special brand of romanticism attributed to the Gael and his poetry is a romanticism of the escapist, other-worldly type, a cloudy mysticism, the type suggested by the famous phrase 'Celtic Twilight'. This Celtic Twilight never bore any earthly relation to anything in Gaelic life or literature. It was merely one of the latest births of the English literary bourgeoisie, and its births to Gaelic eyes are exceedingly strange.

Gaelic poetry, he says, contains more than a common amount of realism, something that he reckons will come as a shock to those with Celtic pretensions.

> Of course, with the kind of people who call Mrs Kennedy-Fraser's travesties of Gaelic songs 'faithful reproductions of the spirit of the original', I have no dispute. They are harmless as long as ignorance and crassness are considered failings in criticism of poetry. They have had their hour in the drawing-rooms of Edinburgh and London; they have soothed the ears of old ladies of the Anglo-Saxon bourgeoisie: they have spoken after dinner, hiding with a halo the bracken that grew with the Clearances . . .[29]

And Maclean's testimony can be echoed throughout the whole of Scottish life and letters. There can be no dispute with those who wish to preserve what they know, those for whom a cosmeticised Scotland is better than the real thing, especially when the real thing is frustratingly difficult and the romanticised Scotland is far more palpable, far more easily digested, remembered and understood than the cruel and often vindictive reality and the guilt that caused the birth of our romance with ourselves and the ways in which we have emulsified our past.

Scotland has no problem with individual identity, yet, as Moray McLaren said, 'The one thing that unites the Scots is the fact they are not English.'[30] National identity is a problem because of a series of symbols that have come to represent ourselves and our nationality, and, added to the symbols, a panoply of mythological heroes stretching across all our history and permeating every aspect of our life and culture. We have begun to deconstruct the symbols, to demystify the process, to unlearn and rebuild, to do what others in a similar position have done: to

29. Sorley Maclean, *As An Fhearainn: From the Land.*
30. Moray McLaren, *The Scots.*

strip away the symbolism and build upon those things that are indigenous and relatively untarnished by political positions, often implicit, which are not in our interests. It may seem something of an impossibility to undo the workings of more than three hundred years, but the entire process may not need to be undone. As Sorley Maclean suggested with regard to Marjory Kennedy-Fraser's *Songs of the Hebrides*, there will always be a warm reception for such cosily facile mirages, as well as those who earn their living from their promotion.

Their Own Ideas and Variations

Kilts have become almost *de rigueur* at national sporting events, and it is common to see them worn at a number of social occasions, as well as the obvious weddings and family celebrations. They are generally worn, with many varieties of shirts, socks and shoes, at ceilidh dances across the country. And the enormous popularity of ceilidh dances is another recent phenomenon.

In Glasgow and Edinburgh queues form outside the venues where regular dances are held. They never start on time, and when they do start the first dance is a Gay Gordons, usually introduced as 'a couple dance', followed by a Dashing White Sergeant, which is introduced as comprising 'sets of three, two men and a woman or two women and a man'. From then until the interval there will usually be the dances Edwin Muir thought extinct: a St Bernard's Waltz, a Military Two-Step, a Highland Schottische, a Pride of Erin Waltz, a Strip the Willow and a Canadian Barn Dance. And the second half will be similarly ordered, with maybe an Eightsome Reel, a Britannia Two-Step and a Virginia Reel thrown in. For many, ceilidhs represent a sort of Scottish aerobics, a pleasant form of exercise to music; and though the term 'ceilidh dance' is something of a misnomer – a proper ceilidh would include all forms of entertainment – the term has come to describe a style of Scottish dancing that used to be popularly known as country dancing.

At first, the differences between the first object of the Royal Scottish Country Dance Society – 'to practise and preserve Country Dances as danced in Scotland' – and the aims of Bob Blair, who pleads for dances to be added to the ceilidh dance repertoire, would appear minimal. But there is a considerable gulf between those who are taught the Dashing White Sergeant, for which callers encourage participants by saying, 'If you can count up to four you can do this dance,' and those who share Jean Milligan's motivation. Milligan, a principal teacher from 1923, has had the most influence upon the dancing style adopted by the Royal Scottish Country Dance Society, and from the mid-1950s was 'left alone to guide the Society through a period of great expansion, especially overseas'. In 1924 she wrote:

As with any other possession which is gradually being forgotten and sinking into decay, these dances are losing their fineness and beauty, and are becoming influenced by other less admirable types of dancing. It is the especial object therefore, of all who are endeavouring to revive these Scottish National Dances, to bring them back in their most beautiful and refined form, and to preserve in them those national traits which were their outstanding characteristics when they were danced originally.

The RSCDS manual lays stress on 'the learning and understanding of basic technique'. And replying to a charge of overstylisation by the Society, Miss Milligan wrote to the *Scotsman* that neither the Society nor its teachers wished to make these dances rigid and formal, but 'free expression, virility and enjoyment in the social performance of Scottish dances . . . can only be safely permitted if they are accompanied by a sound basic knowledge of technique and formation'. It is interesting to compare the RSCDS dancing style to that adhered to by those who were taught away from the mainstream of Scottish education. Toffs, it would seem, still dance in an older way. The style of dances performed at country-house parties has been unaffected by a sound basic knowledge of technique and formation.

Billy Forsyth, writing 'as a dancer, adjudicator and as Chairman for some years of the Scottish Official Board of Highland Dancing,' tells us,

> Highland dancing is the solo step dancing of Scotland . . . their origins lie in dances of battle, dances of victory and descriptive dances of places, people and events of bygone times. The characteristics of Highland dancing are . . . zest and vitality linked to intricate footwork, descriptive arm movements, first-class deportment and a demonstration of strength with agility.

Competition, he claims, is not only inevitable; it improves the level of achievement. However, as a young man competing in Highland games across the country, he was

> exposed to many different ideas on how Highland Dancing was meant to be performed, but had to alter my style of dancing to meet the expected standards of the different areas . . . . In almost every area there were certain steps and movements which were the recognised competition ones for that district . . . [and] most of the steps and movements which appeared in competition were accepted by all dancers, but some well-known exponents had introduced their own ideas and variations which were adopted only by their own students and admirers.
>
> I could not understand why I should have to amend my performance to suit all those ideas and local requirements if I was to gain prizes . . .

Now, he adds later,

all around the world dancers are judged on the same technical basis, to the same standards and within the same competition structure, thus allowing dancers to compete on equal terms over regional and international boundaries. This would not have been possible without the Scottish Official Board of Highland Dancing, now celebrating over forty years of successful administration of all aspects of Highland dancing, from agreement on basic technique, discipline, dress and deportment, to the competition structure and organisation.[31]

Alex McGuire belongs to the Scottish Official Highland Dancing Association, formed in Edinburgh in 1947 by Bobby Cuthbertson, whose younger brother Willie was Billy Forsyth's teacher.

It was inevitable that because of distance, a sense of parochialism and at the same time, poor means of communication, various dance styles, technique, steps and movements developed which were peculiar to particular regions of Scotland. This, of course, added to the beauty and richness of the dance style and gave the exponent of the art an opportunity to excel in whatever suited him best and also gave the dancer the freedom and opportunity to formulate and to choose which were regarded as the most 'difficult' and 'intricate' of steps.

This tradition is in danger of being lost, he says, because of standardisation – 'or is it regimentation?' Rather than help the adjudicators, it hinders them because it is ultimately boring to adjudicate sameness. The SOHDA are resurrecting the movements, steps and histories of the dances which have been standardised to a point where 'dancing seems to have been turned into a puppet show'. The outlook and approach are so limited that we are in danger of losing a wealth of culture and folklore because dancers and teachers are being told to toe the line. 'Today's dancer has been stifled by stupid, insensitive ideology which doesn't allow him to express himself in his own personal way' – and so he appears brainwashed into performing certain steps from a restricted repertoire. McGuire concludes: 'I watch the performances of today's dancers and what do I see – mechanical performances, replicating each other – too scared to deviate from the data-chips that have been fed into them over the years – and that is I'm afraid exactly what today's dancers have turned into – robots who can't think for themselves.'[32]

Standardisation has been the blight of Scottish culture, whether it be from drumming individual pipers into competition bands, folk songs that have been adapted for the drawing room, high-rise pre-cast concrete

31. *Scotland's Dances*, published by the Scottish Arts Council.
32. *Scotland's Dances*, *op. cit.*

buildings, writing-club short-article competitions or elocution lessons. All in the name of sophistication, which David Wilkie believed corrupted taste.

A quasi-classical aspect has been imposed upon our culture, presented as the optimum to which we must aspire; so our country dancers do hornpipes, jigs, strathspeys and reels in ballet-dancing pumps rather than the hard shoes that make it a percussive activity; Scotch singers do not sing through their nose; and musicians adopt classical styles and poses. The variety has been removed. Standardisation means there is a wrong way of doing things.

There have been persistent attempts to impose standardisation on every aspect of Scottish culture, gradually harnessing, taming, containing and sanitising the traditions by redefining what it means to be Scottish, by making it more acceptable, presumably, to the middle classes, whose quest for Anglification has always been coupled with a sentimental regard for what they were changing, probably because it reminded them of their own backgrounds. Of themselves, the improvements are nothing, as harmless as Marjory Kennedy-Fraser's adaptation of Gaelic song. But in some cases they appear to have overtaken every other variation. When the refiners are presented as the sole custodians of a single and variable tradition, we are in danger of seeing the performing troupes of native regional singers and dancers so beloved of Stalin.

Sorley Maclean is right. With those who consider this an acceptable entertainment, there is no dispute. But it is possible to dispute their right to tell others how our culture should be interpreted. Their judgements have to be questioned, especially when they demean alternative ways of doing the same activity, when often they have transformed their art into a separate activity, rather than an extension of the same, and certainly not into anything better; they have made it into something different. Their position recalls the assertion that high birth is synonymous with good, strong character, when history tells us exactly the opposite.

Does a classically trained violinist offer a better interpretation of a Niel Gow slow air because he can play the Kreutzer Sonata? Can someone trained to leap in *Giselle* show how the *sean truibhas* should be danced, or a singer who can move a concert audience to exaltation give a good rendition of 'The Twa Recruitin Sergeants'? It's possible, but unlikely. Would you want to learn scuba diving from someone who won an Olympic gold medal for the breast stroke and knows what scuba diving is but may not think much of those who do it?

Scotland is in danger of losing the very sources from which these replicas sprang, or we are liable to accept further bastardisations. Because Scottish culture with the passion removed has been deemed acceptable for Scottish audiences, we have now learned to do it to ourselves; we remove the passion in the same way that there is a general element of

reduction in every culture, especially those with tourists to entertain.
Writing about the ballad, Edwin Muir said,

> There are hundreds of them, and they contain the greatest poetry that
> Scotland has produced. We do not know now who made them, or how they
> were made, for it took generations to cast them into the shape in which we
> now know them. They bring us back again to the Scottish people and its
> part in the making of Scotland; for it was the people who created these
> magnificent poems. The greatest poetry of most countries has been written
> by the educated middle and upper classes; the greatest poetry of Scotland
> has come from the people.[33]

This position is not only in direct contrast with MacDiarmid's judgement; it carries the implicit assumption that what is worthy, valuable or
even interesting in our culture will always be preserved and is worthy of
preservation for its own sake, that we will recognise it as easily as we
recognise authenticity and will automatically preserve it.

That assumption can no longer be justified; indeed it is because that
assumption was made that the standardisers could complete their labours
of equivalence. It is no more the case than the assertion that the ballads
are poetry – that is the most widely accepted piece of standardisation.
Our tradition-bearers learned them as songs.

And what kind of person could describe these songs as 'the simple
outpourings of illiterates and backward peasants'? It is a remark that has
more in common with tight evangelistic sects who proclaim themselves
right against all oppositions and who narrow experience down to their
own particular. It is a remark that says more about our search for ourselves and our quest to find a leader who could achieve on our behalf
what we could not achieve for ourselves. The amazing thing is not that
such a remark went virtually without opposition, but that it was one of
many pronouncements whose sole intention was personal aggrandisement.
Anyone making such a statement now would find themselves facing a
wider literary condemnation than the lone voice of Hamish Henderson.
And for that we have to thank the climate created by the man whose
debilitating ego could not allow him to enjoy the fruits of his own creation: MacDiarmid.

> Events got him in a corner
> And gave him a bad time of it –
> Poverty, people, ill-health
> Battered at him from all sides.

33. Andrew Noble (ed.), *Edwin Muir: Uncollected Scottish Criticism.*

So far from being silenced,
He wrote more poems than ever
And all of them different –
Just as a stoned crow
Invents ways of flying
It had never thought of before.
No wonder now he sometimes
Suddenly lurches, stalls, twirls sideways,
Before continuing his effortless level flight
So high over the heads of people
Their stones can't reach him.

Norman MacCaig, 'A Writer'

The Dead Have Been Seen Alive

Pipe music, says Hamish Moore, should be freer than the music with which we have become familiar. The bagpipes we know, indeed the pipe band, were adopted by the military, who used pipe music for marching and stirring up patriotic fervour. Properly, the smallpipes, or cauld wind pipes, are from an older tradition and are still played for the small set dances in the kitchen, now being studied by Moore and his wife Maggie, and being actively imported from Cape Breton, Canada. There the Gaelic singing, playing and dancing have been passed on through the generations from the times of the Highland Clearances, giving us an indication of the richness and diversity of the Gaelic tradition.

They are still in Hallaig
MacLeans and MacLeods,
all who were there in the time of Mac Gille Chaluim:
the dead have been seen alive.

Sorley Maclean's evocation of voice and place could apply equally to the inhabitants of Cape Breton as to the woods of Hallaig, where the Scottish fiddle, dance and piping traditions are being kept alive without the quasi-classical aspects imposed in the name of acceptable respectability.

A recent Celtic Connections brochure carried an advertisement for Sabal Mor Ostig, the Gaelic College in Skye. It shows a fiddle player holding her instrument in a classical position, arm, fingers and bow, a simple casual mistake, but important; it shows again, says Hamish Moore, the need to reclaim our culture.

Many aspects of our traditional culture have only survived on the edge of society, in places like Shetland and the Hebrides, or even in the Borders, that escaped the standardising process; as did the travellers, those so far removed from society they scarcely occupy the fringes.

Travellers don't sing 'Mhari's Wedding', dancers don't line up in straight lines to dance in Cape Breton, or dress in a kilt to play the fiddle in Shetland; but when they do perform it hits you like a bullet. Hamish Moore's assertion that we know the real thing when presented with it is surely correct, and is never more apposite than in the case of those who took their culture with them from the West Highlands when they were cleared, and have preserved ever since the old ways of playing and dancing. We know this because there are recordings of pipers made in South Uist in the 1950s and 1960s, men whose styles are indistinguishable from the traditional dance pipers in Cape Breton. Hamish Moore asserts: 'There existed in Scotland one of the richest and most exciting music and dance cultures in the world.'[34] Which is not incompatible with his belief that it doesn't take long to break a tradition, but once it's broken it can take generations to repair. The process has started.

The Scottish dance-band scene boasts a vast wealth of musical talent, though their music is mostly led by a piano accordion with a second accordion imposing the heavy chordal accompaniment, a formula from which there is little deviation. If a fiddle joins the band, it is rarely heard. Jim Johnstone seems to detect a change: 'When I was young we were playing for our own age group – and that's starting to happen again – young bands are playing for young dancers.' And with that comes a change of line-up: fiddles, for example, are taking a more dominant position, often leading the band or playing along with the accordion rather than as a subsidiary instrument, or, in one case, by dominating the line-up, as in one band which consists of three fiddles with guitar accompaniment. Others have a fiddle, flute and accordion line-up. 'Every player has their own individual style,' says Maggie Moore, 'as does every dancer, and it is the subtlety and personal expression which comes out in the music and dance which gives it variety and interest.'

Towards the end of the eighteenth century at least 30,000 Gaelic-speaking Highlanders were settled in Cape Breton Island in eastern Nova Scotia. The concentration of Highland names to be found there is astonishing, and Stanford Reid's assertion that 'parts of eastern Nova Scotia, particularly Cape Breton Island, became as Gaelic in speech and outlook as the Highlands themselves' suggests that emigration has resulted in the survival of an old culture. The communities of settlers remained intact and relatively isolated. Travel inside Cape Breton was restricted until the 1940s because of rough roads and a lack of transport, and a lack of electricity meant people were not exposed to radios or gramophones and therefore had to make their own entertainment. Their forebears had brought with them the music and dances that were popular in the Highlands and Islands of Scotland. Cross-referencing between Scottish

34. Hamish Moore, Introduction and Notes to *Dannsa' Air An Drochaid*.

and Cape Breton sources reveals remarkable similarities. In trying to restore some of these dances in Scotland, Maggie Moore has found some families, famous for retaining singing, piping or dancing skills – often families descended from the nineteenth century's peripatetic dance teachers – who have had these steps and dances passed down through the generations here as well as in Cape Breton.

At the beginning of the nineteenth century Scotland seems to have had a dance heritage common to the Gaels who stayed in Scotland and those who emigrated. Social changes here, especially in the context in which these dances were performed – in village halls instead of kitchens – as well as the influences of English and European styles, have given us a varied dance tradition. In Cape Breton, by contrast, geographic isolation and social stability led to a narrower seam of dancing, though the introduction of community halls in the early twentieth century changed the pre-eminence of some dances for social occasions.

And though the tunes are often the same as those played in Scotland, the style in which the music is played has remained constant. Step dancing has very defined rhythms and tempi. The reason these rhythms and tempi have not changed is that the music has remained inextricably linked to the dance, making the steps a rhythmic anchor to the music, while in Scotland the music became divorced from the dance. Step dancing died out, and so the music associated with dance shot off into different rhythms and tempi, especially under the influences of the military, the piping competitions and quasi-classical fiddle-playing, as well as the common influences from Europe and beyond. In Cape Breton, as well as in parts of Newfoundland, the music is still played as it has been taught through the generations.

That inveterate observer and recorder of curiosities far from home, B. Faujais St Fond, heard a Highland bagpipe competition in 1784.

> After having listened to eight pipers in succession, I began to suspect that the first part was connected with a warlike march and military evolutions: the second with a sanguinary battle, which the musician sought to depict by the noise and rapidity of his playing and by his loud cries. He seemed then to be convulsed; his pantomimical gestures resembled those of a man engaged in combat; his arms, his hands, his head, his legs were all in motion; the sounds of his instrument were all called forth and confounded together at the same moment. This fine disorder seemed keenly to interest every one. The piper then passed, without transition, to a kind of andante; his convulsions suddenly ceased; the sounds of his instrument were plaintive, languishing, as if lamenting the slain who were being carried off from the field of battle. This was the part which drew tears from the eyes of the beautiful Scottish ladies. But the whole was so uncouth and extraordinary; the impression which this wild music made upon me contrasted so strongly

with that which it made upon the inhabitants of the country, that I am convinced we should look upon this strange composition not as essentially belonging to music, but to history.[35]

Which is what has happened. In reclaiming our losses, we may decide we like things as they are, that we prefer our symbols. If that happens, they will at last have a significance. Even the bunches of lucky white heather will have meaning.

Our shift has been a shift of perspective. Realism today is the realism of identification, which gives a voice to the inarticulate. The difference here is that our artists are working within a long and established historical and cultural tradition that has never ventured far from the mainstream but whose continuing shift in perspective has reinvigorated the mainstream at regular intervals. We need to push the boat out further, to restore these rhythms and tempi so that the music is once again inextricably linked to the dance, making the dance a rhythmic anchor to the music, allowing for the subtlety and personal expression to come through.

And the good news is that as we arrive at a position where Scottishness, and especially Scottish identity, is neither perceived nor defined in any narrow way, we are no longer looking towards a series of ideas or symbols, far less searching for a hero, this kind of work is entirely suited to the spirit of the times, offering a sense of optimism and hope through experimentation and imaginative freedom that shows no sign of diminishing.

When the Treaty of Union was signed in 1707, Lord Chancellor Seafield said, 'There is the end of an auld sang.'

> Let our three voiced country
> Sing in a new world
> Joining the other rivers without dogma,
> But with friendliness to all around her.
> Let her new river shine on a day
> That is fresh and glittering and contemporary:
> Let it be true to itself and to its origins
> Inventive, original, philosophical,
> Its institutions mirror its beauty;
> Then without shame we can esteem ourselves.
>
> Iain Crichton Smith, 'The Beginning of a New Song'

That such a poem could even be written, never mind used to open the new Parliament, is the most hopeful sign of all.

35. B. Faujais St Fond, *Travels in England and Scotland.*

Random Bibliography

This is most of them; though there will be some I've forgotten, entirely because of my ramshackle ways of working, which involve me reading a book, or looking something up, then neither recording nor remembering what I've found nor where I've found it. You'd think I'd've learned by now. It has caused no end of trouble in the past. There are obviously newspapers, journals, magazines and pamphlets which have contributed to this work, and I've tried to keep a record of them, but that is usually because they were easier to retain or photocopy. The trouble is that I wasn't always aware I was reading for this book, which is an explanation rather than an excuse.

And while I am at it, I would like to thank the folk who loaned books, magazines, journals and pamphlets for extended periods, often, I am sure, believing they were gone forever. I cannot possibly express my thanks any more than I can offer a list of those who suggested books, gave or posted me extracts of books or bought books for me. The stuff on loan should now have been returned. If not, please contact me.

Aitken, W. R. (ed.), *Poems of William Soutar: A New Selection*, Scottish Academic Press, Edinburgh, 1998.

Anderson, W. E. K. (ed.), *The Journal of Sir Walter Scott*, Canongate, Edinburgh, 1998.

Annan, Thomas, *Photographs of the Old Closes and Streets of Glasgow 1868–1877* Dover, New York, 1977; published in the UK by Constable.

Batsford, Harry and Fry, Charles, *The Face of Scotland*, Batsford, London, 1933.

Bennett, Margaret, *Scottish Customs from the Cradle to the Grave*, Polygon, Edinburgh, 1992.

Billcliffe, Roger, *The Scottish Colourists*, John Murray, London, 1989.

Bold, Alan, *MacDiarmid*, John Murray, London, 1988.

Bradley, Joseph M., *Ethnic and Religious Identity in Modern Scotland: Culture, Political and Football*, Avebury, Aldershot, 1995.

Brown, Catherine, *A Year in a Scots Kitchen*, Neil Wilson, Glasgow, 1996.

Brown, George Mackay, *Selected Poems*, John Murray, London, 1996.

Bruce, David, *Scotland the Movie*, Polygon, Edinburgh, 1996.

Bruce, George, and Rennie, Frank (eds), *The Land Out There: A Scottish Land Anthology*, Aberdeen University Press, Aberdeen, 1991.

Brown, Ivor, *Summer in Scotland*, Collins, London, 1952.

Burton, Anthony, *The Caledonian Canal*, Aurum Press, London, 1998.

Burkhauser, Jude (ed.), *Glasgow Girls: Women in Art and Design 1880–1920*, Canongate, Edinburgh, 1990.

Calder, Angus, *Revolving Culture: Notes From the Scottish Republic*, Tauris, London, 1994.
—— and Donelly, William, *Selected Poems of Robert Burns*, Penguin, London, 1991.
Carson, Ciaran, *Last Night's Fun*, Pimlico, London, 1996.
Carswell, Catherine and Donald (eds), *The Scots Weekend and Caledonian Vade-Mecum for Host, Guest and Wayfarer*, Routledge, London, 1936.
Clancy, Thomas Owen (ed.), *The Triumph Tree: Scotland's Earliest Poetry 550–1350*, Canongate, London, 1998.
Collins, Mal, Harket, Dave and White, Geoff, *Big Red Songbook*, Pluto, London, 1988.
Cowan, Edward J. (ed.), *The People's Past: Scottish Folk, Scottish History*, Polygon, Edinburgh, 1980.
Cramb, Auslan, *Who Owns Scotland Now? The Use and Abuse of Private Land*, Mainstream, Edinburgh, 1996.

Daiches, David (ed.), *The New Companion to Scottish Culture*, Polygon, Edinburgh, 1993.
Danziger, Nick, *Danziger's Britain: A Journey to the Edge*, Flamingo, London, 1997.
Donaldson, Gordon, *Scotland: The Shaping of a Nation*, David St John Thomas, Nairn, 1993.
Douglas, Sheila (ed.), *The King o the Black Art*, Aberdeen University Press, Aberdeen, 1987.
Donnachie, Ian and Hewitt, George, *A Companion to Scottish History*, Batsford, London, 1989.
Drabble, Margaret, *The Oxford Companion to English Literature*, Oxford University Press, Oxford, 1985.
Dunn, Douglas (ed.), *Scotland, An Anthology*, HarperCollins, London, 1991.
—— (ed.), *The Faber Book of Twentieth Century Scottish Poetry*, Faber, London, 1992.

Emmerson, George S., *Scotland Through Her Country Dances*, Johnson, London, 1967.

Ferguson, William, *The Identity of the Scottish Nation: A Historic Quest*, Edinburgh University Press, Edinburgh, 1998.
Finlay, Ian, *Scotland*, Oxford University Press, Oxford, 1945.
Flett, J. P. and T. M., *Traditional Dancing in Scotland*, Routledge & Kegan Paul, London, 1984.
Francis, David (for the Scottish Arts Council), *Traditional Music in Scotland: Education, Information, Advocacy*, Scottish Arts Council, Edinburgh, 1999.
Friel, George, *A Glasgow Trilogy: The Boy Who Wanted Peace; Geace; Miss Partridge, Mr Alfred MA*, Canongate Classics, Edinburgh, 1999.

Gaitens, Edward, *Dance of the Apprentices*, MacLellan, Glasgow, 1949.
Gallagher, Tom, *Glasgow: The Uneasy Peace*, Manchester University Press, Manchester, 1987.
Gibbon, Lewis Grassic [James Leslie Mitchell], *A Scots Quair*, Jarrolds, London, 1946.
Gibbon, Lewis Grassic and MacDiarmid, Hugh, *Scottish Scene*, Jarrolds, London, 1934.
Glancey, Jonathan, *Twentieth Century Architecture: The Structures That Shaped the Century*, Carlton, 1998.
Glendinning, Miles, MacInnes, Ranald and MacKechnie, Aonghus, *A History of Scottish Architecture*, Edinburgh University Press, Edinburgh, 1996.
Gray, Alastair McIntosh, *A History of Scotland. Book 5: Modern Times*, Oxford University Press, Oxford, 1989.

Halsby, Julian, *Scottish Watercolours 1740–1940*, Batsford, London, 1986.
Hamilton, William of Gilbertfield, *Blind Harry's Wallace*, Luath Press, Edinburgh, 1998.
Harris, Paul and Halsby, Julian, *The Dictionary of Scottish Painters 1600 to the Present*, Canongate, 1998.
Harvie, Christopher, *Travelling Scott*, Argyll, 1999.
Henderson, Hamish, *Alias MacAlias: Writings on Songs, Folk and Literature*, Polygon, Edinburgh, 1992.

Industrial Revolution, the concomitant desecration of landscape and life – suggest that they present less than the whole story.

Few writers present a complete picture of the society they inhabit. Burns and Scott, as well as other writers of the period, such as Hogg and Galt and maybe even Ramsay and Fergusson before them, were writing from personal experience. Yet they were not writing in a vacuum, and the fact that they romanticised their historical and rural past, and sought to preserve values and a certain way of life, suggests that they were aware of what was happening throughout the country. Both Burns and Scott travelled across Scotland; they could see the changes for themselves.

In 1788, when William Symington travelled across Dalswinton Loch, Dumfriesshire, in a boat powered by an atmospheric twin-hulled engine, the first recorded paddle steamship's maiden voyage was watched by Robert Burns and Alexander Nasmyth, who may even have taken a trip in the boat. And though Burns missed the significance of this trip, he could not have missed the significance of events taking place in the Highlands, especially given his familiarity with Jacobite song and the fact that he also saw the loss of the Jacobite cause as a blow for national identity and even independence. And what Burns did see of the burgeoning Industrial Revolution he despised.

Nor was Scott blinded by change. 'The state of society now leads so much to great accumulations of humanity that we cannot wonder if it ferment and reek like a dunghill,' he wrote in his journal on Tuesday 19 February 1828.

> Nature intended that population should be diffused over the soil in proportion to its extent. We have accumulated in huge cities and smothering manufactures the numbers which should be spread over the face of a country, and what wonder that they should be corrupted? We have turn[e]d healthful and pleasant brooks into morasses and pestiferous lakes; what wonder the soil should be unhealthy?

Wilkie presents a view of a society he wishes to preserve, but he indicates what will happen to that society if its incipient morality is not heeded, and if the threatening changes, obvious to anyone seeing the pictures when they were painted in 1815 and 1818, are not contained or even reversed. *Distraining For Rent* was viewed by the aristocracy as an attack on their rights, a fact which tells as much as anyone need know about the attitude of the aristocracy towards their subjects, especially since the picture presented a scene which was to be re-enacted throughout Scotland for many years, affecting many generations. As with the Clearances in the Highlands, the landowners sought to keep that side of their activities from public view, and could stand no criticism of their actions.

Wilkie's work is more than simply narrative or figurative. These aspects,

Herdman, John, *Poets, Pubs, Polls and Pillar Boxes: Memoirs of an Era in Scottish Politics and Letters*, Akros, Kirkcaldy, 1999.
Hobsbaum, Eric and Ranger, Terence (eds.), *The Invention of Tradition*, Cambridge University Press, Cambridge, 1983.
Hunter, James, *A Dance Called America: The Scottish Highlands, the United States and Canada*, Mainstream, Edinburgh, 1994.

Irvine, Peter, *Scotland the Best!*, HarperCollins, London, 1998.

Jennings, Humphrey (ed.), *Pandaemonium: The Coming of the Machine as Seen by Contemporary Observers*, André Deutsch, London, 1985.
Jacob, Violet, *Songs of Angus*, John Murray, London, 1923.
——, *The Scottish Poems of Violet Jacob*, Oliver & Boyd, Edinburgh, 1945.

Kaplan, Wendy (ed.), *Scotland Creates: 5000 Years of Art and Design*, Weidenfeld & Nicolson, London, 1990.
Keay, John and Julia (eds), *Collins Encyclopaedia of Scotland*, HarperCollins, London, 1994.
Kydd, Robbie and Nora (eds), *Growing Up in Scotland*, Polygon, Edinburgh, 1998.

Lindsay, Maurice (ed.), *Scotland: An Anthology*, Robert Hale, London, 1974.
——, *The Discovery of Scotland*, Robert Hale, London, 1964.
Linklater, Magnus and Denniston, Robin (eds), *Anatomy of Scotland: How Scotland Works*, Chambers, London, 1992.
Leneman, Leah and Mitchison, Rosalind, *Sin in the City: Sexuality and Social Control in Urban Scotland, 1660–1780*, Scottish Cultural Press, Edinburgh, 1998.
Leonard, Tom (ed.), *Radical Renfrew: Poetry from the French Revolution to the First World War*, Polygon, Edinburgh, 1990.
Lloyd, A. L., *Folk Song in England*, Lawrence & Wishart, London, 1967.
Lockhart, G. W., *Highland Balls and Village Halls*, Luath Press, Edinburgh, 1997.
Lyle, Emily (ed.), *Scottish Ballads*, Canongate, Edinburgh, 1994.

MacCaig, Norman, *Selected Poems*, Chatto & Windus, London, 1985.
McCallum, Neil, *A Small Country*, James Thin, Edinburgh, 1983.
MacDiarmid, Hugh [Christopher Murray Grieve], *Complete Poems 1920–1976*, edited by Michael Grieve and W. R. Aitken, Martin Brian and O'Keefe, London, 1978.
——, *The Letters of Hugh MacDiarmid*, edited by Alan Bold, Hamish Hamilton, London, 1984.
——, *The Rauchle Tongue: Hitherto Uncollected Prose, Volume III*, edited by Angus Calder, Glen Murray and Alan Riach, Carcanet, Manchester, 1998.
MacDonald, Colin, *Highland Journey*, The Moray Press, Edinburgh and London, 1943.
MacDonald, Murdo, *Scottish Art*, Thames & Hudson, London, 2000.
MacDougall, Carl (ed.), *The Devil and the Giro: The Scottish Short Story*, Canongate, Edinburgh, 1989.
——, *Glasgow's Glasgow: People Within a City*, The Words and the Stones, Glasgow, 1990.
—— and Gifford, Douglas (eds), *Into a Room: Selected Poems of William Soutar*, Argyll, 2000.
McGillivray, Allister (ed.), *A Cape Breton Ceilidh*, Sea-Cape Music, Nova Scotia, 1988.
McKean, Charles, *Edinburgh, Portrait of a City*, Century, London, 1991.
——, *Stirling and the Trossachs: The Illustrated Architectural Guide*, RIAS/Scottish Academic Press, Edinburgh, 1994.
——, *The Scottish Thirties: An Architectural Guide*, Scottish Academic Press, Edinburgh, 1987.
——, Walker, David and Walker, Frank, *Central Glasgow: An Illustrated Architectural Guide*, RIAS/Mainstream, Edinburgh, 1989.

Mackenzie, Agnes Mure, *A Historical Survey of Scottish Literature to 1714*, Maclehose, London, 1993.

——, *The Kingdom of Scotland*, Chambers, London and Edinburgh, 1940.

Mackie, Alexander, *Readings in Modern Scots*, Chambers, London and Edinburgh, 1913.

MacLaine, Allan H. (ed.), *The Christis Kirk Tradition: Scots Poems of Folk Festivity*, ASLS, Glasgow, 1996.

McLaren, Moray, *The Scots*, Penguin, London, 1951.

——, *If Freedom Fail*, Secker & Warburg, London, 1964.

Maclean, Sorley, *As An Fhearainn: From the Land*, Mainstream, Edinburgh, 1986.

——, *Collected Poems: From Wood to Ridge*, Carcanet, Manchester, 1989.

Macmillan, Duncan, *Scottish Art 1460–1990*, Mainstream, Edinburgh, 1990.

Magnusson, Magnus and White, Graham (eds), *The Nature of Scotland: Landscape, Wildlife and People*, Canongate, Edinburgh, 1991.

Maine, G. F., *A Book of Scotland*, Collins, London, 1956.

Marr, Andrew, *The Battle for Scotland*, Penguin, London, 1992.

Martine, Roderick, *Homelands of the Scots: A Guide to Territories and Locations of Historical Interest Connected With the Clans and Major Families of Scotland*, Spurbooks, 1981.

Mitchison, Rosalind and Leneman, Leah, *Girls in Trouble, Sexuality and Social Control in Rural Scotland, 1660–1780*, Scottish Cultural Press, Edinburgh, 1998.

Montgomerie, Norah and William (eds), *Scottish Nursery Rhymes*, The Hogarth Press, London, 1946.

——, *The Well at the World's End*, Bodley Head, London, 1975.

Morgan, Edwin, *Nothing Not Giving Messages*, Polygon, Edinburgh, 1990.

——, *New Selected Poems*, Carcanet, Manchester, 2000.

Morrison, Allan, *Whaur's Yer Wullie Shakespeare Noo? Scotland's Millennium Souvenir*, Neil Wilson, Glasgow, 1998.

Morton, H. V., *In Search of Scotland*, Methuen, London, 1929.

Muir, Edwin, *Scottish Journey*, Mainstream, Edinburgh 1979; first published by Heinemann, 1935.

Muir, Edwin, *Scott and Scotland*, Routledge, London, 1936.

Munro, Ailie, *The Folk Music Revival in Scotland*, Kahn & Averill, London, 1984.

Noble, Andrew (ed.), *Edwin Muir: Uncollected Scottish Criticism*, Vision, London, 1982.

Nuttgens, Patrick (ed.), *Mackintosh and His Contemporaries in Europe and America*, John Murray, London, 1988.

Oakley, Charles, *The Last Tram*, The Corporation of the City of Glasgow, 1962.

Oliver, Cordelia, *Joan Eardley, RSA*, Mainstream, Edinburgh, 1988.

Osborne, Brian D. and Armstrong, Ronald, *Scottish Dates*, Birlinn, Edinburgh, 1996.

Peter, Bruce, *100 Years of Glasgow's Amazing Cinemas*, Polygon, Edinburgh, 1996.

Peter, Bruce, *Scotland's Splendid Theatres*, Polygon, Edinburgh, 1999.

Philip, Neil, *The Penguin Book of Scottish Folktales*, Penguin, London, 1995.

Power, William, *Literature and Oatmeal: What Literature has Meant to Scotland*, Routledge, London, 1935.

Power, William, *My Scotland*, The Porpoise Press, Edinburgh, 1934.

Purser, John, *Scotland's Music*, Mainstream/BBC Scotland, Edinburgh, 1993.

Robb, William, *A Book of Scots*, Grant Educational, undated.

Roberts, John L., *The Highland Geology Trail*, Luath Press, Edinburgh, 1998.

Robertson, Edna, *Glasgow's Doctor, James Burn Russell 1837–1904*, Tuckwell Press, East Linton, 1998.

Ross, David R., *On the Trail of William Wallace,* Luath Press, Edinburgh, 1999.
Roy, G. Ross (ed.), *Studies in Scottish Literature Volume XXX,* University of South Carolina, 1998.
Ruskin, John, *Selected Writings: Chosen and Annotated by Kenneth Clark,* Penguin, London, 1991.

Scarlett, James D., *Scotland's Clans and Tartans,* Lutterworth, Guildford, 1975.
Scott, Alexander (ed.), *William Soutar: Diaries of a Dying Man,* Canongate, Edinburgh, 1991.
Scott, Alistair, *Native Stranger,* Warner, London, 1995.
Scott, Paul H. (ed.), *Scotland: A Concise Cultural History,* Mainstream, Edinburgh, 1993.
Scott, P. C. and Davis, A. C. (eds), *The Age of MacDiarmid: Hugh MacDiarmid and his Influence on Contemporary Scotland,* Mainstream, Edinburgh, 1980.
Scottish Arts Council, *Scotland's Dances: A Review of the 1994 Conference on the Diversity of the Scottish Tradition of Dance,* SAC, Edinburgh, 1994.
Shuldham-Shaw, Patrick and Lyle, Emily, *The Greig–Duncan Folk Song Collection,* 8 volumes, Aberdeen University Press, Aberdeen, 1981.
Simpson, Kenneth, *The Protean Scot: The Crisis of Identity in Eighteenth Century Scottish Literature,* Aberdeen University Press, Aberdeen, 1988.
Simpson, Kenneth (ed.), *Love and Liberty: Robert Burns, a Bicentennial Celebration,* Tuckwell Press, East Linton, 1997.
Simpson, William, *Glasgow in the 1840s: Watercolours by William Simpson, 1823–1899,* Glasgow Museums, 1998.
Sinclair, Fiona, *Scotstyle: 150 Years of Scottish Architecture,* RIAS/Scottish Academic Press, Edinburgh, 1984.
Smith, Alexander, *A Summer in Skye,* Alexander Strahan, London, 1865.
Smith, Bill, *D. Y. Cameron: The Visions of the Hills,* Atelier, Edinburgh, 1992.
Smith, G. Gregory, *Scottish Literature,* Macmillan, London, 1919.
Smith, Iain Crichton, *Collected Poems,* Carcanet, Manchester, 1992.
Smith, Sheenah, *Horatio McCulloch 1805–1867,* Glasgow Museums and Art Galleries, Glasgow, 1988.
Stamp, Gavin and McKinstry, Sam (eds), *'Greek' Thomson,* Edinburgh University Press, Edinburgh, 1994.
Stevenson, Neil, *Architecture,* Dorling Kindersley, London, 1997.
Stott, Louis, *The Ring of Words: Literary Landmarks in Stirling and Clackmannanshire,* Creag Darach Publications, Aberfoyle, 1993.

Thompson, Francis, *Crofting Years,* Luath Press, Edinburgh, 1997.
Thomson, Duncan, *Raeburn: The Art of Sir Henry Raeburn, 1756–1823,* Scottish National Portrait Gallery, Edinburgh, 1997.
Turnbull, Michael T. R. B., *Scotland The Facts: Everything You Ever Wanted to Know About Scotland,* Neil Wilson, Glasgow, 1998.

Watson, Ian, *Song and Democratic Culture in Britain,* Croom Helm, London, 1983.
Watson, Roderick, *The Literature of Scotland,* Macmillan, Basingstoke, 1984.
West, T. W., *Discovering Scottish Architecture,* Shire Publications, Princes Risborough, 1985.
White, Colin, *The Enchanted World of Jessie M. King,* Canongate, Edinburgh, 1989.
Whyte, David, *Visitor's Guide: Scotland,* MPC Hunter, 1995.
Wood, Emma, *Notes From the North: Incorporating a Brief History of the Scots and the English,* Luath Press, Edinburgh, 1998.
Wood, H. Harvey, *Scottish Literature,* Longmans, Green, & Co., London, 1952.
Worsdall, Frank, *The City That Disappeared: Glasgow's Demolished Architecture,* The Molendinar Press, Glasgow, 1981.